POLAR PILOT

The Carl Ben Eielson Story

Carl Ben Eielson

POLAR PILOT

The Carl Ben Eielson Story

by

DOROTHY G. PAGE

Conceived and Researched by
Violet Bjerke

Edited by
Ada M. and Hiram M. Drache

INTERSTATE PUBLISHERS, INC.
Danville, Illinois

Dedicated to

MRS. VIOLET BJERKE

for her tireless efforts, dating back to the 1960s, in gathering material, tracking down early Alaskans for interview, and aiding Dorothy Page, who wrote the original manuscript. Without her devoted labors and financial assistance, this book would not have been possible.

ABOUT THE BOOK

This is the story of one of America's unsung heroes in the field of aviation—Carl Ben Eielson. Eielson grew up in an upper–middle-class family in Hatton, North Dakota, and was endowed with sufficient talent to make a comfortable living in any career he desired. Since early in life he dreamed of nothing but flying.

After being trained as a military pilot in World War I, he spent two years as a barnstormer in the upper Midwest. In the fall of 1922 he went to Alaska to teach school and at once saw the need for aerial transportation in that massive, uncharted land of isolated settlements. In 1923 he flew the first airmail flight in interior Alaska, which made him an instant hero to all Alaskans, who were accustomed to waiting for months between mail deliveries. In 1924 he flew the first airmail flight under government contract between Fairbanks, Nenana, and McGrath.

His fame as a pioneer bush pilot enabled him to win the pilot's position with Sir Hubert Wilkins, and the two thrilled the world with their flight from Barrow to Spitzbergen and later with their flights in the Antarctic.

In 1929, at age 32, Eielson met death while on a flight over the frozen wastes of Siberia. A 100-day, three-nation search kept his name before the public in 1929–30, but his exploits and contributions have all but been forgotten.

Ada M. and Hiram M. Drache

ABOUT THE COVER

Philip Thompson, professor of art at Augsburg College, has captured the setting of the story. Carl Ben Eielson, in his World War I Jenny, is taking off on his historic first airmail flight from Fairbanks to McGrath, Alaska. The dog team, which brought the mail to the plane, depicts the traditional method of travel in the North. In the background is Mt. McKinley, which served as a beacon to early pilots. Ben, in his flier's helmet and fur-lined parka, smiles at the view.

Foreword

When the Russian AN-26 landed in Fairbanks in March 1991 with the remains of the Eielson Hamilton NC10002, many things went through my mind. After lying on the Siberian tundra for over 60 years, the plane arrived back home to Fairbanks and brought full circle a major event in Alaska aviation history.

In January 1929 the brand new Hamilton was brought to Alaska by my father, Noel Wien. It was the most modern and the first all metal airplane to come to the Territory. Dad flew the Hamilton 450 hours and with it made the first flight between North America and Siberia in March 1929. He took food and mail to a stranded ship, the *Elisif*, and brought out a valuable load of furs.

It was in the same airplane the next winter that Carl Ben Eielson lost his life while flying to the *Nanuk*, a sister ship locked in the ice at North Cape, Siberia. The *Nanuk* was stranded in almost the same spot the *Elisif* had been the year before.

The search for Eielson and his mechanic/copilot, Earl Borland, during the winter of 1930 was an epic story. Pilots from Russia, Canada, and the United States participated in the largest air search that had ever been conducted. The heroic efforts of Joe Crosson and Harold Gillam in open-cockpit airplanes in the Siberian Arctic never cease to amaze me, especially when one realizes Harold Gillam had learned to fly the summer before and had had only one cross-country flight on his own.

This tragic accident ended the life of the father of Alaska aviation and a world-renowned Arctic pilot. Eielson was one of those rare visionaries who had a dream of building an airline in Alaska when the airplane was still an infant, unreliable machine. His eight airmail flights from Fairbanks to McGrath the winter of 1924 ended the era of the dog team as the main mode of winter transportation in the Territory. Things were never the same. Not much was known anywhere about cold-weather flying with skis. Eielson led the way for those who followed, including my father, Noel Wien, and Joe Crosson, Harold Gillam, Russell Merrill, and many more.

I remember as a small boy when Sir Hubert Wilkins was in our home telling how he and Ben walked off the Arctic ice after being forced down north of Barrow. That was heralded as a master survival and navigational feat. They were the first to fly over the Arctic ice pack.

The team of Wilkins and Eielson pioneered aerial exploration of both the Arctic and the Antarctic, which included the famous polar flight from Barrow to Spitzbergen in 1928.

My father said in the book *Pioneer Bush Pilot*[1]: "I met Ben Eielson in Anchorage in June of 1924 when I was going in and he was going out. He was about 27, a slim, fine-looking Scandinavian fellow from North Dakota who really believed in Alaska flying—the need for it. He was soft spoken and intelligent and he was nice to me. 'You'll like it up here,' he told me, and 'you'll do well.'"

Although some license was obviously taken by the author, Dorothy Page, in the conversational aspect of the story, I believe she was able to portray accurately the events and the essence of the man. It's a story that needed to be told in its entirety, and I thoroughly enjoyed reading the manuscript. I became even more impressed with the life of Carl Ben Eielson.

RICHARD A. WIEN

---

[1]Ira Harkey, *Pioneer Bush Pilot: The Story of Noel Wien.* Seattle: University of Washington Press, 1974.

Preface

Any biography written in collaboration with others is a ticklish venture. The facts of Ben's life filled my head for five years. Many pages were written; many interviews with old-time Alaskans held. At the end of the research, much of Ben's life I knew by fact. But the big question was, had I read between the lines with enough perception to know the man? What was Carl Ben Eielson like? He had to speak to the readers. While the conversation in the book is written in fictional style, it is hoped that it has an authentic ring, for it is based on factual research.

I found that Colonel Carl Ben Eielson was a man well worth writing about. In his heart, he had a dream. He loved to fly, but more than anything else, he wanted to bring about acceptance of the airplane as the principal means of transportation to and in Alaska.

It wasn't that Ben Eielson was the most proficient pilot of his day. It wasn't that he could and did fly when others would not. It was that he had the vision to see aviation's bright future in Alaska. There's no doubt that aviation would have developed and prospered in Alaska had there been no Carl Ben Eielson, but its coming would have been delayed several years.

While flying a war surplus Jenny in 1923—the lone pilot in the skies over Fairbanks, Alaska—Ben dreamed of pressurized planes, great airports, communication facilities, the establishment of large air force bases in Alaska because of its strategic importance, and flights across the top of the world to Europe and to Asia. In a matter-of-fact manner, he made the almost impossible dream of airmail service come true in Alaska as early as 1923-24.

Even after Ben became world famous because of his flights with Sir Hubert Wilkins, he remained the same modest man. Regarding polar flights, General H. H. Arnold, noted American authority on aviation, wrote:

> The Arctic flight which catches the fancy more surely than any others, . . . is the flight of Carl Ben Eielson, carrying Sir Hubert Wilkins from Point Barrow, Alaska, over the top of the world to Spitzbergen, Norway, in April 1928. . . . Two details give this expedition first place for sheer nerve and phenomenal daring. In the first place, a landing was made in the Arctic wastes en route and considerable time was spent in scientific observation and discovery. . . . [Second,] this trip was made in a lone plane with

a single pilot and without outside support or aid. There was no radio contact. . . . These two bold adventurers simply climbed into a plane and, without weather reports, set out across a trackless waste, picked a likely landing spot on the ice, and landed; then, when their work was done, took off in the same matter-of-fact style as from a landing terminal at home. What unprecedented cock-sure courage! What cold nerve! . . .

Many informed men believe Carl Ben Eielson to have been the best Arctic flier of our time. His loss, in a crash in . . . Siberia, was a severe one to those who believe that the airplane is the only means of opening the locked portals of the last unexplored regions, the Arctic and Antarctic. Men like Eielson cannot be replaced.

So often people who achieve are forgotten. It will be most gratifying if this book serves to impress upon its readers that Alaska did indeed have men of such stature that they "matched her mountains."

Carl Ben Eielson did not live long in years, but he lived a wide, full, and useful life and was willing to risk his own to save others. Just what happened to cause the crash on November 9, 1929, in Siberia, when Ben and Earl Borland lost their lives, will forever remain one of the many mysterious secrets of the Arctic.

It is hoped that this book will serve to impress upon Alaskans and others an indelible memory of the one for whom the Eielson Air Force Base, near Fairbanks, is named.

Also, they should visit Mt. McKinley National Park; they can view a lesser peak—Mt. Eielson—located near mighty Mt. McKinley, highest on the North American continent. Mt. Eielson is plainly visible from the favorite viewing spot at Eielson Visitors' Center. Under bright blue skies on a July day in 1961, the Eielson Visitors' Center at Mt. McKinley National Park was dedicated, 32 years after Ben's death.

The location of the visitors' center is at Camp Eielson, so named because Carl Ben Eielson made the first airplane landing near there on June 17, 1924, at 11:15 P.M.

During the years of researching and writing this book, I came to know Ben well. Listening to his brother Oliver talk, I came to know him even better. Taped interviews with Ben's sister Elma and letters from her on special topics were a big help, too. Talking with old-timers in Alaska who remembered him added much to my store of knowledge.

The man I pictured (if he were to return to fly over Alaska again) would not be amazed at the changes. Where there was only wilderness, towns and air bases have sprung up. Where only muskrats swam, roads wind through the bush country.

Yes, Ben had a rough time with his flying, but Alaska still challenges today's aviators. Ben never had radio facilities, reliable weather reports, or landing strips in the remotest parts of the country.

Ben wouldn't be astounded at the changes in Fairbanks, his "home town," or at the fact that regular airmail service is the rule in Alaska today and not the exception. Ben predicted aviation would open up Alaska and it would become a progressive state. He was correct. It has.

DOROTHY G. PAGE

Acknowledgements

I express my deep appreciation to the Eielson family and to Erling Rolfsrud, author of *Brother to the Eagle*, who gave permission for parts of his book to be used. Oliver Eielson said that Mr. Rolfsrud's was the most factually correct book written about Ben.

Special thanks to Vi Bjerke, who traveled many thousands of miles to collect authentic information on Colonel Carl Ben Eielson. Bundled against the cold, Vi spent many hours sorting yellowed newspaper clippings and photographs in the Eielson home. Vi's first trip to Hatton was in 1968–69 to collect material for the Carl Ben Eielson section of the Transportation Museum in Anchorage, Alaska, and material for a biography. On one of her trips, Vi purchased a scrapbook of clippings that a 14-year-old boy, Oscar Jemtrud, of Mayville, North Dakota, had collected on Ben's activities and on the aerial search for him. When she returned to Anchorage, Vi obtained data saved by Earl Borland's sister. Earl Borland, Jr., gave permission for their use.

I made every effort to trace ownership of material contained herein and regret any error unconsciously made.

Time and space do not permit listing all who assisted with collecting information for this book, but special mention should go to Norma Hoyt, of Anchorage, and Carrie McLain, of Nome, now deceased, who lived in Nome during the Eielson search. Also, special thanks to Karen Lee, who read and edited the first draft; to Mary Lawsine, base librarian at Eielson Air Force Base; and, last but by no means least, to my husband, Vondolee S. Page, who had to add an extra room to our home to accommodate the Eielson material.

DOROTHY G. PAGE

EDITORIAL COMMENT

The original manuscript, as written by the late Dorothy G. Page and submitted to us by Vi Bjerke, was 980 typed pages plus 100 pages of introduction, documentation, and appendices. After lengthy discussion with Mrs. Bjerke and correspondence with Mrs. Page's husband, Vondolee, we are satisfied that every effort was made to be as factual as possible.

Mrs. Page constructed conversation as accurately as anyone could and used what she called "fictional style" to liven the story. She did her job well. Specific dates and events were checked wherever possible, and her information was always correct.

Unfortunately, this extremely interesting story of Carl Ben Eielson contains no citations. However, Mrs. Page did prepare a bibliography of the sources that she and Vi Bjerke used. Many newspaper clippings were undated and without the name of the paper. The interviewees were not listed, so no trace could be made of them. At the end of her bibliography she wrote, "Space prohibits listing all articles, letters, and personal interviews with Alaskans."

Again, we are confident the information is accurate and in no way should the omission of citations detract from the validity of the story. Read, enjoy, and feel comfortable with the facts.

ADA M. DRACHE   HIRAM M. DRACHE
Historian-in-Residence
Concordia College

Contents

POLAR PILOT

The Carl Ben Eielson Story

1

Ben's Home and Family

CARL BEN EIELSON'S FATHER, Ole, was a pioneer settler, merchant, and banker in Hatton, the trading center for a farming area in the Goose River Valley, one of North Dakota's most fertile spots. Ben's drive, ambition, courage, dedication to duty, and perhaps even his restlessness, were largely ingrained family traits. As a youngster, his father, Ole, had been restless too. Ole didn't mind the hard physical work on his father's Wisconsin farm, and the monotonous routine of farm work was not to blame for this attitude. Perhaps his father's hesitancy to try new farming methods was more responsible.

Ole realized that if farming methods were to change, the changes would come with the opening of new farming areas. The north central part of the United States was relatively unsettled then, and Ole decided that those who got in at the beginning could try new ideas.

Born of Norwegian immigrant parents at Coon Valley, Wisconsin, March 17, 1863, Ole was only 13 years old when he made plans to leave Wisconsin and the subsistence farming he'd grown to dislike. His father hoped that Ole would change his mind and grow to love the family farm and take it over some day. Ole explained that the security of remaining at home and inheriting the farm did not appeal to him. He wanted to search for his fortune elsewhere.

Mature beyond his 13 years, and physically strong because of the demanding work he had done on the farm, Ole had no trouble finding work. His first job was with a railroad construction crew. In spite of his age, he did his work with such care and enthusiasm that he made a good name for himself. From the time he got his first job, he never was unemployed. He was gradually given added responsi-

3

bilities and accepted them gladly. He became very efficient in organizing new and unskilled workers. He was put in charge of men much older than he and handled his new position with diplomacy.

Until 1883, Ole labored on railroad grades, moving about the country a great deal. He came in contact with people in all walks of life and learned to adjust to his new life style in the various construction camps where he lived. He always put part of his wages into savings. He studied at night, reading books and learning all he could on many subjects. He offered to help the accountants free of charge if they would show him how to keep books.

At first Ole enjoyed the constant travel and the changing scenes. Although his life was exciting, he respected those farmers who had settled down to domesticate the wilderness and decided that it was time to look for a permanent place to live. Working for the railroad was not the same as being his own boss and owning a home and land. He learned that some of the other men thought the same. They had heard much about the virgin and fertile soil of the Dakota prairies and the golden opportunities in the Red River Valley. It never crossed Ole's mind that he should go back to Wisconsin. He already had decided that, just as his father had carried the family banner from Norway to America, he should take it farther west. In the spring of 1883 he wrote his family that he planned to quit his job on the railroad and head for the Dakota Territory.

Not long after the letter was mailed, Ole told his construction crew friends goodbye, took his savings, and started for the Red River Valley. Once there, he liked what he saw.

Ole eventually found his way to Hatton, a small frontier town founded in 1882. When Ole arrived, Hatton had only one store, operated by Hegge and Nelson. There he obtained his first employment as a clerk.

Somehow, Ole just couldn't picture himself farming. He was still not 21 years old and could not get a homestead, so he decided to keep working in the store and save his wages. He also worked at odd jobs for extra money. His employers immediately noticed that he was ambitious, used to hard work, and a definite asset to the store. He appeared eager to please the customers, going out of his way to help.

After he received a raise, Ole decided to stay in Hatton and grow up with the town. He saw many possibilities for additional businesses. He enjoyed the marketplace more than the farm, and when the right time came, he planned to establish his own business.

In just a few years the town had grown large enough to support two stores, and Ole knew the time had come to open his own. Although he started out in a small way, he was soon the proprietor of what was then considered a first-class general store. Ambitious, dependable, and with a pleasing personality, he found his patronage steadily increasing. He built a small house near the store and began to buy furniture.

Ole found that he liked everything about the store business, from ordering the merchandise to keeping the rooms clean and neat. When he closed each evening, he went over his accounts and carefully wrote up new orders. Except for attending Sunday morning worship services and going to church socials, he spent the rest of his time working. On the days his supplies came in on the train, he worked far into the night. His friends often teased him about being the most eligible bachelor in town, but he didn't seem to mind.

However, Ole's life changed on the day Olava Baalson came to Hatton from Brooten, Minnesota, to visit relatives. While shopping in the Eielson store on the day of her arrival, Olava was introduced to Ole. For the first time since he'd opened his store, Ole forgot about the after-hours work he had planned to do. Somewhat flustered, he bravely asked the attractive visitor if he could come to call that evening.

Soon "Hatton's most eligible bachelor" and the charming and attractive young lady from Brooten began a courtship that culminated in their marriage on May 30, 1892, in the Big Grove Church, at Brooten. Olava was the daughter of Ellen and Kari Baalson, natives of Hallingdal, Norway. They had come to America in 1861, settling first at Spring Grove, Minnesota, and later near Sauk Centre. Olava was born on January 21, 1871, in a humble log house, which the Baalsons had built while clearing their land.

The Hatton folks were pleased when Ole announced his plans to marry. They knew that this meant he would stay and make Hatton his permanent home.

Following the marriage, Ole worked even harder in the store and added several new lines of merchandise. Olava was an excellent housekeeper and cook, and her neighbors always found the cozy

Eielson home sparking clean and attractive. Over the years nine children were born to the couple. Elma was the first child, followed by Edwin, Carl Benjamin, Adeline, Oliver, Arthur, twins named Helen and Hannah, and another daughter, Hannah, who was named after the twin, Hannah, who died in infancy.

Elma, the oldest daughter, married one of Hatton's leading merchants, Elmer Osking, and had two children. Following her mother's death in 1911, Elma took over as "mother" for the younger children. Edwin, the oldest boy, died while Ben was serving in the U.S. Air Service during World War I.

Oliver, who was five years younger, to the day, than Ben, distinguished himself in the field of finance. Arthur, Ben's younger brother, became an engineer and worked for the Western Electric Company in New York City. Adeline became a school teacher and later Mrs. William Impett, of St. Catharines, Ontario. Her scrapbook of Ben's career in aviation was very helpful in putting together the story of the Eielson family. Helen, the twin who lived, became a registered nurse and later Mrs. Ed Sheehy. Hannah, the youngest sister, also became a school teacher.

While the five older children were still very young, Ole moved his family into the largest and most impressive home in Hatton. The three-story, gabled gray-and-white house, purchased from the Nelson family, stood on six spacious lots, shaded by large elm trees. There were six large bedrooms on the second floor, running water, a large white bathtub, and lights that turned off and on with a switch. The electric lights intrigued Elma, but Ben was more impressed with the windmill. Ben's mother was overjoyed. She picked fine new furniture to fill the rooms, including a grand piano.

The Eielsons emphasized education and admonished their children to think for themselves. Many years later, when Ben turned to flying, it's probable that Ole was a little disturbed. He remembered how Ben had listened carefully to the stirring tales of Viking explorations. In later years, students of aviation history pointed out that Ben's temperament and climatic inheritance fitted him well for his successful career in flying. They compared him favorably with that gallant old Norseman, Roald Amundsen, who topped the long list of Scandinavians gaining fame in Arctic and Antarctic explorations. Ben was reserved, but his enthusiasm allowed him to come to the fore and take his place in the limelight. He was modest but never unsure of himself. In any new endeavor, his patience was endless, and his sense of humor always sharp.

Ben's mother wielded a strong influence on her children's lives. Her determination not to quell their spirit of adventure took most of the Eielson children far from Hatton as they sought success in a variety of careers and pursuits. There's no doubt her attitude helped to give Ben the courage to dare something startlingly new when he pioneered aviation. Along with his brothers and sisters, he had all the opportunities assured an intelligent child in a well-ordered American family.

The Eielson children's school studies were fully complemented by strict home and religious training. Olava Eielson was very active in church work. In addition, she was a real mother—an untiring companion, confidante, and guide to her children. Ole and Olava Eielson also had a wide circle of interesting business, professional, and political friends. Olava was always happy when Ole asked her opinion on business or civic matters and appeared to value her judgment.

As the town of Hatton flourished, Ole became its leading citizen. He was the town's banker and, for 12 years, its mayor. In 1905 Ole helped organize the Farmers and Merchants Bank of Hatton. He served on the board of directors of the bank from the time it was organized until 1931.

In addition to his local civic and political activities, Ole also served as the Republican chairman of Traill County for many years. During his days as county chairman, Ole was approached by several Republican officials and asked to run for elective office at the state and national levels. He always turned down such offers because he did not want to spend more time away from his growing family.

However, Ole was very proud to think that a man of his limited formal education was even considered for such positions. The first time the invitation was extended to him, the Eielsons held a family conference. Ole explained that, although he felt it would be a challenge and an honor to serve his country at higher levels, he was turning the offer down, with regret. He added that he hoped some day one of his sons would seek a career in public service. Later, when Ben's brilliance in debate tipped the scales in favor of law courses instead of commerce, Ole actually thought for a time that Ben might be the one to become a statesman.

At an early age Ben showed an interest in flying, and it was soon obvious that he would not easily forget about it. He constantly asked questions about kites, balloons, and flying machines. Ole had always encouraged the children to ask questions about many things. He was usually very patient in answering their many inquiries. Yet, because of Ben's repetitious questions about flying, this was one subject on which Ole's patience wore thin. "I'll just have to be a little easier on the boy," he told himself, hoping Ben would find another interest.

Although normally mischievous, the Eielson children were unusually well behaved. Ole and Olava considered themselves fortunate to have such lively but obedient children. They took the children to church with them on Sundays, even though most of the sermons were in Norwegian. They did not permit many things to take precedence over church attendance.

In later years, when his father cautioned him about "risking his neck in an untried machine in a distant land," Ben replied, "Perhaps the reason I'm doing it is that you always told us to be mindful of the needs of others." Ben then explained that the people truly needed the airplane for transportation.

Ole promptly changed the subject, for he had learned, as Ben grew older, that it was increasingly difficult to keep him from talking about flying. While Ben was still in elementary school, Ole was able to divert his young son's attention by saying, "Ben, it's better to concentrate on your lessons now. When you're in high school and college we can spend more time talking about aviation. There will be more reliable information available then, too."

When he was a youngster, Ben's attention could be turned away from flying only by a good adventure story about ships or overland treks through the Arctic and the Antarctic wilderness by explorers. He also took a peculiar interest in the weather. He had one scrapbook in which he carefully pasted accounts of unusual storms, tornadoes, heavy snowfalls, floods, earthquakes, droughts, and any prolonged heat waves.

Ben enjoyed being at the depot when the trains arrived and spent so much time there that one day the depot agent jokingly asked him, "Are you planning to be a railroad engineer when you grow up, Ben?"

Shaking his head, Ben replied, "Oh, no, sir. I'm planning to be a pilot and fly an airplane, but don't tell my father I said that. He doesn't like to have me talk so foolish."

The depot agent, somewhat taken back by Ben's startling disclosure, said, "If I were you, Ben, I'd stick to cars and trains. Nothing wrong with being a railroad engineer."

Shortly before school started in the fall of 1908, Ben and four of his best friends, including Garvin Olson, got permission to go on a week's camping trip to Lake Tobiason. Their elaborate plans called for traveling to the site with a team of horses pulling a hayrack decked out to resemble a covered wagon. The boys planned to camp in tents, cook their meals over a campfire, and go duck hunting and fishing.

One boy's father promised the use of the hayrack and a team of black horses. The other parents promised to supply food and camping equipment for the big trip. Ben was given permission to choose most of the group's "grubstake" and survival gear from the shelves of the Eielson store. He methodically picked out the staples needed for the outing: bacon, beans, flour, lard, raisins, salt, chocolate, hardtack, cheese, baking powder, eggs, oatmeal, sardines, matches, sugar, and feed for the horses. His father was pleased with the good selection. Another boy was to bring some ham, potatoes, and corn.

After reaching Lake Tobiason, the boys had many exciting times as they fished, hunted, and took turns cooking their meals over the campfire. Ben, the most self-reliant of the group, acted as leader. The boys were especially proud when they caught enough fish for several days and cooked them. At night, the boys almost hated to put out their evening campfire and retire. So, while sitting around the campfire, Ben told them exciting adventure stories. One night Ben fabricated an interesting story about two men who flew to the moon, landed, and explored its surface.

"That's crazy," Garv said. "You can tell better stories than that."

"What's the matter?" Ben asked. "Don't you believe men will fly to the moon some day? I do!"

On their way home, as they left Lake Tobiason, one of the boys said, "I wish we didn't have to go to school next week. I like summer vacation best of all."

"Not me," Ben said. "I'm looking forward to school. There are so many things to learn. Vacation's nice, but if we ever want to amount to anything, we have to get an education. My dad says that's very important."

After Ben arrived home, one after the other the children told Ben the news of the past week. When they had all finished talking, Ben said, "I didn't realize how much I missed everyone until tonight. I guess half the fun of any trip is coming back home."

"Ben will be ready for school," his mother said. "I think he's even a little happy that school's starting so soon."

2

Ben's Flying Machine

BEN FOUND LITTLE that bothered him in school, for the work came easily to him. Bursting with energy, he usually completed his work before the other students were finished. His teachers constantly sought new ways to keep him occupied. His grades were good. On report card days, he always looked forward to seeing his mother's face light up when she checked his card.

In the summer of 1908, Ben's twin sisters, Helen and Hannah, were born. This time, Ben's mother didn't regain her usual vigor as fast as she normally did. Elma tried extra hard to help her mother do the housework and care for the twins.

Ole worried constantly about his wife and finally ordered her to get more rest. He sent to Norway for a new hired girl, Guri, to replace the one who had been with the family a long time and who then left to get married. When she first arrived, Guri couldn't speak English. In the process of teaching her English, the older Eielson children improved their Norwegian.

In 1908 Ben had his first real disagreement with his father over aviation, a subject that was to become a bone of contention between them for many years. It was a custom in the Eielson home for Ole to read selected news articles aloud to the family. In this way he kept the older children informed about the world beyond Hatton. One September evening, about midway down the second page he noticed a short article about the Wright brothers. Suddenly Ole cleared his throat, and with a loud snort said, "Huh! Those crazy Wright brothers are going to kill themselves in that silly contraption if they keep on with their experiments! If the good Lord meant for men to fly, He'd have arranged to have babies come into the world with little wings built on some place."

The children laughed at their father's joke. Ben was the only one who didn't laugh. Instead, he pressed closer to his father's shoulder and pleaded, "Please read the article about flying, Dad."

Ole looked at Ben in surprise but began reading the short paragraphs aloud. They told of the series of experimental flights made by Orville Wright at Fort Myers, Virginia, in a plane ordered from the Wright brothers for use in the United States Army. Following several successful flights, Thomas Selfridge, an aerial pioneer who was a passenger in the plane piloted by Orville Wright, was killed when the plane crashed. Orville also was injured.

His eyes shining with excitement, Ben said, "Gee, Dad, that's great! You know, that plane made several flights before it crashed. Why, it must have been at least 400 feet up in the air, maybe more."

Ole said, "Mark my words, if the Wright brothers keep on with such foolish experiments, they will both be killed!"

"Someone has to be the first to fly," Ben said quietly. Then he asked, "What about Wilbur Wright? He took a plane to France. Does it tell anything about Wilbur?"

"I think this flying business is just a fad," Ole stated. "Many other people feel the same way I do. Some people even think the Wright brothers are crazy!"

"Well, sir, I'd like to fly. I mean I don't think the Wright brothers are crazy."

Ben noted his father's expression and stopped speaking. Prior to his rash comment about flying, Ben had never dared to disagree with his father. Ben squirmed in embarrassment, wishing he had never opened his mouth, then added, "Well, I've just been thinking about the Wright brothers. Maybe they are right. Just because lots of people think they're crazy doesn't mean they are. I mean . . ."

Ole turned quickly toward Ben, intending to lecture him on proper manners. Then he noticed how nervous his son was. He realized how much courage it had taken for Ben to speak out in defense of the Wright brothers. He was actually a little proud of his son.

Ole said quickly, "Well, Son, we'll talk about the Wright brothers again soon. We really don't have to decide the issue of their sanity tonight."

Feeling a little ashamed of his boldness, Ben sat down uneasily on the edge of his chair. He knew only too well that his father was displeased with him. More than anything else, Ben hated that. He knew exactly why his father was displeased, too. His father valued a man's life above flying.

Ben went out to the windmill. Climbing to the level of the platform, he sat in the growing darkness staring at the lighted windows of the house. He knew his father had every right to be angry with him. Chin in hand, Ben contemplated the events of the evening, thinking, "I've got to tell Dad I'm sorry the man was killed, first thing. After that, maybe I can get him to change his mind about flying. Dad is very progressive. He was one of the first in Hatton to buy a car."

Suddenly, Ben felt relieved. He was certain that his father would change his mind about flying. He just knew it. "Why," Ben told himself, "flying machines are just like cars; they're here to stay."

Ben climbed down from the windmill, rushed indoors, and went upstairs. As he passed his father's door, he stopped and said, "I'm sorry that man got killed in the plane crash, Dad. After this, I'll listen more carefully when you're reading to us."

"Off to bed," Ole said. "We'll compare our ideas on flying machines more carefully, too."

That night Ben talked in his sleep about flying. He always talked in his sleep if something bothered him or if he had a difficult problem he couldn't seem to solve.

The next morning Edwin teased him, saying, "Boy, you sure talked a lot last night. You kept me awake for hours, talking about flying!"

Ben buried remarks of the Wright brothers for some time when his father was near. Instead, he busied himself with school and made the honor roll for the first semester.

Before the winter of 1908–09 was over, baby Hannah became very ill and failed to recover. She had been with the family only a short time, but her death brought sadness. Ben tried to cheer up his mother by writing a funny play about searching for gold in Alaska. He recruited Elma and Oliver and his friends to act in the play and was very pleased that his mother enjoyed it. He told his father, "She hasn't laughed that hard since before we lost our baby sister."

Near the end of the school year, word reached Hatton that the Prairie Chautauqua was coming to town. The traveling group of musicians, speakers, and entertainers, sent out on a circuit tour from Chautauqua, New York, had been to Grand Forks and the other bigger towns in North Dakota before, but this was the first time Hatton was included in the tour.

Ben and his friend, Garvin Olson, were very excited about the event. For Ben, the biggest miracle of all was that a man would lecture on the Wright brothers flying machine! In addition to the lecture, the Wright Flyer would be on display.

Ben wanted to go to the Chautauqua. The admission was 25 cents to get inside the tents, one of which held the flying machine. Ben arrived at the store early and hoped that his father was in a good mood.

Ben asked if he could have 25 cents to see the flying machine when the Prairie Chautauqua arrived in town. He continued, "I hope that's all right with you, Dad. I really want to hear the aviation lecture and see the Wright Flyer."

Ole frowned slightly and said, "Son, there's a good musical program scheduled, and I'd hoped you'd be interested in that instead. Why do you want to spend your money looking at a flying machine?"

Before Ben could answer, the phone rang. Ole took the receiver from the hook, listened intently, and dashed off to find Oscar Tryten, a local farmer whose house was on fire and who was in town.

After the fire, Ole returned to the store. Ben hurried to finish his work and then went with Garvin to see what had happened to the Tryten house. The boys pedaled their bikes as fast as they could and soon arrived at the site of the farm home only to find that all that was left were the smoking, charred remnants.

"Just what Dad said would happen," Ben commented. "He's been telling the city council that Hatton needs a new fire truck. He's tried to convince them of that for a long time."

The boys stood watching the salvage operation for a moment. One of the farmers in the crowd of men milling around the site of the burned home approached the boys and said, "There's really nothing you young ones can do here now."

But as the boys turned to leave, he added, "If you're looking for work and want to earn some money, I'll need mustard pickers later on. But first you must get permission from your fathers. They both know me. Tell them Emil is looking for two good mustard pickers."

Garv turned to Ben and asked, "Will your father let you have time off from the store? I sure want to work, Ben."

"Well, Dad always tells us that there's plenty of work to do at the store, but he also wants us to learn how to work for other people," Ben said. "I think it will be fine with him."

Ben was right. His father thought it would be good experience for him to work for someone else for wages.

When the mustard was ready for picking, Ben and Garv rode their bikes to Emil's farm, leaving home at daybreak. Although there was no one to supervise them after Emil showed them what to do, both boys worked diligently all day, and each earned 50 cents.

On the morning of the Prairie Chautauqua, Ben was up before anyone else. He raced to the field at the edge of town where the men were busy setting up big tents. Off to one side he saw two men working to assemble what looked as though it might be the flying machine. He stood watching them silently until he could no longer contain his curiosity, and then he asked, "If you fly the machine, may I go up with you?"

"Oh, this flying machine won't fly," one of the men said. "It's just a model. Orville and Wilbur Wright couldn't afford to show their real flying machine. Someone might copy it."

Ben tried to cover his disappointment. His first glimpse of a flying machine and it was one that couldn't fly. He hurried home and found the family at the table waiting for him. Ole looked up as Ben entered and asked, "Where have you been, Son? You've kept the family waiting."

"I went to see the big tents they're putting up for the Chautauqua," Ben replied.

Adeline, bursting with excitement, asked, "Did you see the sleeping lady? I want to go and see the sleeping lady."

After hearing Adeline's request to see the sleeping lady, Ben felt a little braver and stated boldly, "I want to see the flying machine. I was there this morning before they had it put together, Dad, and you don't have to worry—it's not even going to get off the ground. It's just a model." Almost as an afterthought, he added, "I can use 25 cents of my mustard money and pay my own way."

Ole sighed in resignation and replied, "Since you earned your money by hard work, you can spend it any way you wish, Son. If you want to waste it looking at a model flying machine that won't even fly, I guess that's up to you."

Later in the day, after receiving their father's permission, Oliver and Ben found themselves standing up front by the ropes that separated the crowd from the flying machine. Ben listened intently to a man in striped trousers and a long-tailed black coat lecture on the history and the wonders of the flying machine. He told about men who flew kites and dreamed of riding them through the air, and about gliders. He went on to tell how the Wright brothers had experimented for years before they had a heavier-than-air craft that could take men up into the air and transport them from one point to another.

The lecturer next explained the various parts of the model flying machine, which looked like a huge box kite with a tail sticking out behind. There were two long wings made of wood and covered with cloth.

Ben studied the model flyer and mentally noted the shape of the body, the wings, and the tail. He decided that perhaps he could build a model flyer himself if he could get the design down on paper as soon as he got home. He thought to himself, "Tomorrow I'm going to start building the Eielson Model Flyer. Dad should have lots of empty wooden crates, and Mom will give me some cloth for the wings. Dad will have to show me how to get started, then I'll be able to finish it."

That evening, Ben's mother asked, "Well, Son, do you think you learned something today? Was the flying machine worth seeing?"

"Oh, yes," Ben replied. "I studied the way it was built, and I'm going to build one of my own."

After the boys left the room, Ole said, "I'm afraid we haven't heard the last about flying machines from Ben. That boy has never been so impressed with anything before. He's obsessed with the flying machine. We must see he doesn't neglect other things."

His father was right. After Ben's visit to the Chautauqua, he read everything he could find about flying. He searched the papers to see if the Wright brothers were doing something new.

In one corner of the back yard Ben's collection of building materials grew daily. He was about ready to begin construction work on his flying machine. Ben had asked his mother to give him some cloth for the wings. He also asked her to save all the old magazines, and he searched them carefully for any stories on balloons or flying.

With many arguments about where to start, Ben and his friends finally started to work on the body of the model flyer. It wasn't long before the skeleton of a flying machine began to take form. Shaping the wood for the wings proved to be the most difficult.

"Well," Ben said one day, "we can't do much more until we find some wheels. We should have had them to begin with. Also, we have to make a new propeller. That first one we made isn't balanced."

After the model flyer was completed, Ben spent his spare time sitting on the windmill platform. He tied his kite to the platform and sat for hours, fascinated by the sight of the kite soaring in one direction and then another.

Ben said to his brothers, "I guess it will be a long time before I get a real flying machine. You know Dad said that after we finish high school, we have to go to college. It's a good thing I like school, because I'm going to be in school for a very long time."

The balance of the summer passed happily for the Eielson children. The family had an unusually large number of fishing trips, family picnics, visits from relatives, and Sunday afternoon outings. Yet, as in the summer before, when it came time for school to start, none of the children was happier than Ben.

3

School Days

THE YEAR BEN FINISHED the eighth grade, 1910, brought news that there would be a new baby in the family. The children rejoiced when another sister was born. She was named Hannah, after Helen's twin, who had not lived.

Following Hannah's birth, Ben's mother experienced another difficult recovery and was required to have complete bed rest. The children tried to brighten her days by visiting her briefly each morning before school and when they came home in the afternoon.

One morning Ben chatted so long his mother finally had to remind him that he'd be late for school if he didn't leave promptly. Ben left, but had a strange, uneasy feeling all day. Right after school he rushed home, ran upstairs, and tapped gently on the door of the master bedroom, expecting to hear his mother's usual cheerful greeting, "Come in—the door's open," but there was only silence. Ben hesitated, then slowly pushed the door partly open and peeked inside. The room was empty.

Ben's mother had been taken to the sanitarium because the doctor said her cough might be caused by tuberculosis. Elma tried to take her mother's place, and Ben spent a lot of extra time working in the store for the next few months. Ole was away from home a great deal, spending every moment he could with his wife. They all tried not to show the younger children they were uneasy or fearful that their mother might never come home.

When there was no birthday party for him and Oliver, Ben knew something was very wrong. His father was especially sad and distracted. Three days later, Ben's mother died. July 23, 1911, was a sad day for the Eielson family, and one from which they never quite recovered. The loss of his wife, when she was just a few months past her fortieth birthday, and with the youngest baby only nine months old, seemed almost too much for Ole to bear.

In later years it was said of Ben that he was far more serious than most for his age, and perhaps a little lonely. Although he never told people the reason for this, he knew it all began on the day his mother died. The family missed her very much.

When it was time for school to begin in the fall, Ben remembered his mother's words: "Be sure you finish high school and then go to college. Education will train you to think, teach you to use your reasoning powers."

In discussing a choice in careers, she had said, "When the time comes to make that choice, something inside will tell you the kind of work you should do in the world."

Although Ben carried a full schedule during his freshman year in high school, he still found time for his duties at the store. The winter following his mother's death, Ben spent long hours in the attic, reading the Bible. When his younger brothers teased him about this, asking him to read to them or entertain them instead, he flatly stated, "You have to read the Bible if you want to understand things."

In later years, his sister Elma said of this period in Ben's life: "We almost thought Ben would end up becoming a preacher, like his uncles, because he loved to stand on the stage in the attic or on a chair in the living room telling us what to do." Had he chosen religion, he would have been following a precedent set by four of his mother's brothers.

During the second winter after his mother's death, Ben concentrated on reading Shakespeare, which added a new twist to the plays he wrote for the younger children's entertainment.

During his junior and senior years, Ben was especially competent as a basketball player. He earned the reputation of being an all-around player who could hold his own with the best.

Ben did not limit his interests entirely to athletics but continued his interest in debate. Hatton's debating team brought honors to the school and figured in the 1914 state finals. Ben's high school speech teacher encouraged his desire to excel in debate, and Ben carefully researched assigned topics and practiced endlessly.

Ole, perhaps feeling that the necessity and regularity of milking would teach the boys the importance of doing chores right on schedule, had purchased a cow. In later years Ben quipped, "I found a captive and attentive audience in Clara Belle, our family cow." During debate season, nobody had to remind Ben that it was his turn to milk. In the solitude of the spacious barn, Ben enjoyed sitting on the milking stool beside the cow, methodically squirting milk into the pail, all the time rehearsing his speech for the current debate. In future years, when people complimented Ben on his speaking ability, he often said that he owed it all to the patience of Clara Belle. "Why, at one time," Ben added, "that cow knew more about aviation than most people did."

The debate on aviation was the one Ben worked on the hardest. Following dinner one evening near the end of his senior year in high school, Ben announced, "If you will excuse me, Dad, I have to work on my speech for debate. On the last day of school we're having a final debate, and I'm one of the members of the affirmative side."

"What did you say the subject was, Ben?" Ole asked.

"Aviation—well, no, transportation. What I mean is that I take the affirmative side in the debate and the subject is 'Resolved: Airplanes are the best transportation for the future.'"

"Well, Son, as I see it, you have the most difficult side of that argument," Ole said. "You'd better get busy right away. I can think of five good reasons right now why airplanes *will not* be the best transportation for the future. But, it wouldn't do for me to explain them; that will be your opponent's job."

Later, sitting in his father's study, Ben became inspired and began writing:

> The first five reasons favoring aviation as the best means of transportation for the future are:
> 1. Airplanes don't run over dogs. [Four dogs had just been killed in Hatton by speeding automobiles. Ben knew that almost everyone liked dogs, so this would be a good point to stir emotions in favor of planes.] 2. Planes can travel faster than cars, and they do not bump into things, for there are no barriers in the air. 3. Airplanes don't need roads or tracks to run on, so they would be good to use in isolated places; they need only a small level landing field. 4. Airplanes can fly anywhere; therefore, people would be able to travel to places they couldn't reach before. 5. It would be fine to ride in a

plane and would save lots of time. Planes will make the world
appear smaller.

Ben wrote that people would get used to flying and learn to like
it, just as they had learned to prefer the automobile over the horse
and buggy.

He remembered a grasshopper invasion years before. All the
crops were destroyed. Although the farmers put out poisoned bait
for the 'hoppers, it was too late. He wondered idly if perhaps the
plane could someday be used for spraying crops from the air. He
suggested this method of pest control. There were so many other uses
for the airplane from the farmer's point of view that Ben began
adding other ideas and kept writing until his father entered the
library and told him that it was past his bedtime.

On the day of the big debate, Ben's initial nervousness wore off
the first time he got up to speak. During the rebuttal period, Ben
forcefully squelched his opponent's arguments one after another. He
was elated when his side won the debate. Later, his teacher told him
that although she didn't agree with him about aviation, he'd done
an outstanding job.

"Thank you," Ben replied, "but it was very easy for me, because
I really believe in all those things I said."

High school graduation marked a turning point for Ben. Along
with three other boys and five girls, he graduated from Hatton High
School in the spring of 1914. He finished with an excellent record as
a scholar, an athlete, a good citizen, and a star member of the debate
team. At the graduation exercises it was said of him that "he made
his high school career one of fruitful activity and did a great deal
toward placing Hatton High School before the public eye beyond
Hatton." For a moment, Ben was sad. He wished his mother had been
in the audience to share his graduation honors.

Just before he entered the University of North Dakota, Ben was
restless and uneasy. He was still uncertain about which courses he
wanted to take. Ben knew that his father had his heart set on him as
his successor in business, along with his brother Edwin. On the other
hand, his high school teachers had advised him that his two best
assets on the debating team—the logic of his attack on opponents

and his coolness under pressure—fitted him well for a career in law or in public service. Ben couldn't choose.

Ben went over the list of studies offered by the university. He decided that the most natural thing would be to enter the school of commerce. He told Ole that he would follow in his footsteps. His father studied him for quite some time before he replied, "That's fine, Ben. I'm proud of your choice. But, remember, if you ever change your mind I'll understand."

Ben had received permission to drive the family Cadillac to Grand Forks to enroll at the university. On the appointed day of his big trip, he was up early. He was much too excited to eat breakfast, but his father refused to excuse him, and Ben sat at the table dutifully picking at his food. Ole finally said, "Ben, I can see it does no good just to make you wait, so perhaps we will see you off and then the rest of us will continue our meal."

The family gathered around the car. With many last-minute instructions ringing in his ears and tearful goodbyes from Elma and Adeline, Ben prepared to leave. He waved goodbye to the family and early-rising friends who had come to witness his grand departure.

As soon as he got to Grand Forks and had completed his enrollment, he wrote the family a letter about the trip, which was read with as much interest as if Ole were reading to them about the adventures that befell Marco Polo.

Idly daydreaming in a college class one day, Ben thought, "Now that Dad agreed to let me drive the car to Grand Forks alone, maybe he'll let me take flying lessons some day." In the next moment, had the professor asked Ben what he was daydreaming about, no doubt he would have answered simply, "The Eielson family will probably be the first in Hatton to have an airplane."

Attending college in Grand Forks was Ben's first venture away from home for any length of time, and he missed the family very much at first. He wrote chatty letters home telling about his studies and his extracurricular activities. Ben's schedule at the university was a heavy one, but he soon plunged into a round of student activities, athletics, and debate. He also played cornet in the band and sang in the glee club. He played forward on his fraternity's basketball team.

During his freshman year, Ben joined the Ad Altiora Literary Society and tried out for debate. The Ad Altiora team defeated the

Hesperians, and Ben won other debate trophies as well. He and Albert Sheets went to Missoula, Montana, to meet the University of Montana's winning team there. When they returned to Grand Forks, Ben was elected to Delta Sigma Rho forensic fraternity.

One of Ben's speech professors used Ben as an example for the class to follow, saying, "Now take Eielson there as an example of the ease we should have in public speaking. He seems as much at home up here on the stage as if he were down in the bookstore talking to the girls."

On his visits to Hatton, Elma often teased Ben about his girlfriends. Ben replied, "Girls are interesting and fun, but I've decided not to get too serious about any one girl until I'm ready to settle down."

Back at the university, Ben's forceful delivery and his outstanding style of oratory continued to find favor with the law instructors on campus, and they kept trying to interest him in law courses for his junior year. In the spring of 1916, Ben was also elected editor-in-chief of the *Dacotah*, the student-managed yearbook and chronicle of school activities. However, he never assumed this position because he transferred to the University of Wisconsin.

Until then, Ben had almost given in to the idea of being nothing more than a successful businessman in Hatton. But a sudden interest in a legal career in his second year at college took him to Wisconsin. There he continued to be a keen student and was involved in extracurricular activities. Yet, Ben was restless.

Interested in politics because of his father's involvement at the local and county levels, Ben also was interested in world affairs. Since 1914, the ugly darkness of World War I had spread in Europe. He often talked with other students and his professors about the war and the upheaval it was bound to bring to the United States.

Ben told his law professor, "I don't know how long I can continue to sit in a classroom. It appears that the United States will be involved soon."

Ben was not destined to complete his law course at the University of Wisconsin, but he did remain there until the end of the first semester.[1]

During the short time that Ben attended the University of Wisconsin, he made a name for himself. He was initiated into Phi Delta

Polar Pilot

Rho, the national honorary legal fraternity. It is significant that in 1929 he was chosen, along with Charles Lindbergh, as one of the 17 outstanding alumni of the University of Wisconsin. That same year he also was selected as one of the 10 outstanding alumni of the University of North Dakota.

ENDNOTE

1. Bob Reeve, another name famous in Alaskan aviation circles, also attended the University of Wisconsin. When Reeve entered the university in 1922, Ben's picture hung on the wall of the Phi Delta Phi fraternity house to welcome him—a daily reminder of the flying life that Reeve never forgot.

Reeve, who had the same intense feelings about aviation that Ben had, was expelled from Wisconsin just six months short of graduation because of "his overriding interest other than education." Undaunted, Reeve spent the next few years searching for any type of job in aviation, including fueling planes, barnstorming, and flying in Central America, which he did for Pan American Airways for three years.

Reeve came to Alaska in the early 1930s to "make a million dollars." He felt that Alaska offered a trio of possibilities—gold, flying, and good fellowship. He arrived with 20 cents in his pocket and remained to pioneer glacier landings and open the Aleutian air routes. Bob Reeve was a name to be reckoned with in Alaskan aviation. In 1972 he was chosen "Alaskan of the Year" for his many contributions to the state.

4

Cadet Eielson

THE EUROPEAN WAR started the year Ben graduated from high school. While working in the Eielson store that summer, Ben listened to talk of the war with great interest. "Neutrality" was the buzz word. Yet, many college students, like Ben, were concerned and asked themselves, "How can America possibly remain neutral?"

Former President Theodore Roosevelt's policy of modernizing the army and the navy had almost ceased by 1914, and the United States was neither emotionally nor militarily prepared for war. Ben idolized Theodore Roosevelt, for he was the first President to ride in a plane. On October 11, 1910, after his term of office, he flew in a plane piloted by Archie Hoxsey, at St. Louis, Missouri. Ben duly noted this event and pasted the news clipping in his scrapbook.

On August 14, 1914, President Wilson issued a proclamation declaring the neutrality of the United States. Yet within six months, six American ships were torpedoed and sunk by the Germans without warning. On May 1, 1915, the American tanker *Gulflight* was sunk without warning. Only six days later, a German U-boat torpedoed and sank the Cunard liner *Lusitania* off the coast of Ireland. The call for an end to neutrality grew louder.

While discussing the incident with his classmates, Ben said, "It will be impossible for America to remain neutral now. I'll have to talk to my father again about enlisting." Ben was especially interested in the fliers who were organizing the Lafayette Escadrille, which later was amalgamated with the French air force.

When Ben's college friends first began volunteering to train for the infantry, he talked seriously to his father about joining them. Ben and Ole had discussed the reports of the Pancho Villa fracas in

Mexico, where planes were a great help to General Pershing. The First Aero Squadron was organized with nine "pusher" biplanes, mostly Curtiss J2s. One pilot made what was then a record nonstop flight lasting 4 hours 22 minutes. When Ben brought this new record to his father's attention, Ole merely shook his head and replied, "Ben, I know you're interested in aviation. I also know that if you enlist it will be in the air service branch. But I wish you would remain in school."

Early in January, Ben talked to his father again, saying, "There's no point in waiting any longer. I'm going to enlist as an air cadet." Ben's decisive statement marked the end to months of uncertainty.

In trying to explain his feelings to his father, Ben said, "Dad, I don't want to underestimate the importance of the infantry in this war. I know their fight is important. But, I want to learn to fly and help fight the war in the air. The men slogging around in the mud in France need the extra help that airplanes can give them. Besides, we're entering a new aerial age, and I want to be part of it."

Ole remained silent, lost in thought, with a far-away look in his eyes. Ben knew he was recalling their first real disagreement over flying, when Ben had defended the Wright brothers.

Ben said quietly, "With Europe at war now, you can understand why Wilbur Wright's aerial demonstration in France in 1908 meant so much more to the people there than Orville's flights at Fort Myers. In Europe, the airplane was not regarded as a fad or a plaything but as a highly important means of transportation and possibly as a weapon."

"Son, I'm not going to stand in your way any longer," Ole said in a tired voice. "I'm not going to argue with you any more. In troubled times like these, every man has to decide for himself what he wants to do. I'd rather see you finish school first, but if you feel it's necessary to quit now and serve your country, then that's your answer."

"I'll be leaving the university at the end of the first semester," Ben stated. "Thanks for seeing things my way, Dad," he added. "I'll be heading for Fort Omaha, Nebraska, on January 15."

As Ben prepared to leave Hatton, the family gathered to say goodbye. Ole stood bareheaded in the January cold and shook hands with his son. "Ben, be careful," he said. "I'm just afraid that if you take this pilot's training, we'll never see you alive again. The planes they're building now aren't considered safe. Just yesterday I was reading what Colonel Billy Mitchell had to say about our planes."

Ben's enlistment in the U.S. Signal Corps, Aviation Section, at Fort Omaha, Nebraska, on January 17, 1917, was a starting point for him. From that day on, he never turned away from aviation. It became and remained the most important thing in his life.

Tension peaked on April 6, when war was finally declared. The American Expeditionary Force (AEF) of 1917–18 was a jolly, singing bunch of young men intent on rescuing the "damsel" France from the wicked German "Hun." Fortunately, the Americans arrived on the western front at a time when a war of maneuver was replacing the deadly and bloody war in the trenches.

The AEF found Colonel Billy Mitchell already there. Mitchell, later to figure importantly in Alaskan aviation history, hadn't waited for war to be declared, either. The aviation enthusiast, who would go on to become General Mitchell, had taken personal leave from his regular army assignment to check on the war in Europe to determine the part aviation would play in that battle. Mitchell arrived in Spain in March 1917. Almost immediately, he called on Major Hugh Trenchard, a British pioneer in military flying.

Born in Nice on the French Riviera on December 29, 1889, when his parents were vacationing there, Mitchell had a special feeling for the French people. Speaking French like a native, he was welcomed to France with tears of joy. Mitchell was rather like a hero. They would later call him "Le General Aviateur Americain."

Mitchell made the rounds in France, checking on aviation. He found that French pilots were encouraged to do all the acrobatic flying possible in order to be alert for possible combat flying, and he approved. He knew that back in the United States, pilots were discouraged from doing acrobatic flying on the assumption it was too dangerous.

Unfortunately, many of the American pilots were being trained by non-flying officers, who failed to realize that when a pilot got into a dangerous position where swift maneuvering was the only way out, he would be incapable of doing so without previous acrobatic training. Mitchell immediately sent word back to the U.S. Army recommending that pilots practice acrobatic flying as much as pos-

sible. Mitchell was not surprised when he saw the great strides aviation had taken in Europe, but he was very discouraged when he
compared those advances with the slow growth and official neglect
of aviation in the United States.

The recruiting posters read: "BE AN AMERICAN EAGLE!" However, many men didn't make the grade. Others were injured or killed
in plane crashes. According to some officials, the training planes used
in the United States were "just two jumps ahead of the freak stage."
Because the aerial age was so new and untried, there was little experience the men could fall back on. Statistics showed that more students and instructors were killed during training in the United States
than were killed in the dog fights over the front lines in France.

On June 10, 1918, Ben transferred to the School of Military
Aeronautics, University of California, Berkeley. There he joined 850
other cadets for an intensive eight weeks of school prior to the start
of flight training.

From the time of his enlistment until he completed training,
Ben was an especially promising student of aviation, and he advanced rapidly. He kept up with the latest news from the war front
in Europe and read everything he could about the role aviation
played in the war effort. After he completed his ground school training at Berkeley, Ben was sent to Mather Field, near Sacramento,
California.

He was just beginning to learn to fly when another tragedy
struck the Eielson family. Shortly before he was transferred, Ben
received word that his older brother, Edwin, was ill. He had planned
to go home as soon as he completed flight training, but a telegram
stating that Edwin was much worse brought his training to an abrupt
halt. Ben reached Hatton shortly before Edwin died from tuberculosis, the same illness that had taken the life of his mother in 1911.

Ben's grief over his brother's death was mingled with worry
about his father. Edwin had always enjoyed working in the family
store far more than any of the other boys and had taken over much
of the responsibility of operating it. Ben noticed that Ole's hair had
become grayer. He felt a twinge of guilt as he wondered how much
of it was due to his choice of a career. However, both Oliver and
Arthur were home, and they took over the store in Edwin's place.
Ben returned to California, saddened and still wondering if he had

made the right move. Ole's parting words rang in his ears: "Son, you took on a big job, and your work isn't finished yet. If you don't go back, there will be no living with you."

The only thing that could lift Ben out of his depression over Edwin's death was flying. On his first solo flight, Ben knew he'd found his life's work. Alone in the open-cockpit plane, controlling the flimsy craft by moving the stick back and forth while the earth fell away beneath him, nothing thrilled him more. Soaring into the upper reaches of his element as unfettered as the wild geese he used to watch and envy when he was a child, Ben couldn't contain his excitement. With the wind whipping his exposed face and no one else to hear, he murmured his disbelief. He vowed to himself, "No matter what happens, I'm never going to give up flying!"

Soon Ben received a second lieutenant's commission in the Aviation Section of the U.S. Signal Corps and then his orders to sail for France. If things went on schedule, he'd be there right after Christmas. He determined to write to his father about his orders immediately so that Ole would be used to the idea before he left.

Since Edwin's death, Ben had been very careful to write home regularly. His father's letters to him proved Ole worried about all the publicity concerning the loss of life during training and the type of planes the pilots used. His brother Oliver wrote: "Dad thinks every letter he gets from you will be the last. When he doesn't hear from you at all, then he really worries."

Ben tried hard to put into words the way he felt about flying since his solo flight and the prospect of overseas duty. After many attempts he merely said that he had received his commission and enjoyed cross-country flights. He looked forward to leaving for France right after Christmas.

Ole read the letter aloud to the family. His voice faltered. The news that Ben would be going to France brought a twinge of fear. He was more certain than ever that he would never see Ben alive again. He turned to Elma and said, "Ben will kill himself in a plane crash—I just know he will. I keep picturing a plane crash and can see Ben."

While waiting to leave for France, Ben and his fellow pilots logged many extra hours of cross-country flying. They even had a few sessions in acrobatic flying in preparation for possible aerial combat, which was then in the spotlight of publicity.

Returning from a routine training mission out over the Mojave Desert on November 11, 1918, Ben circled the field to land. He was puzzled to see a group of men dancing around on the runway. He circled, buzzed the field, and motioned to the fellows to clear the field for landing. Waving happily up at Ben, the men rushed to the outskirts of the field in joyous abandon. Ben landed the plane, wondering what had happened.

Even before the swirling dust settled, his mechanic rushed over and yelled, "The war is over, sir!" Ben pushed his goggles back and unfastened the clasp on his helmet. He pulled it off and heard the mechanic yell again, "THE WAR IS OVER, SIR!"

With the roar of the engine still in his ears, Ben stared at his friend dumbfounded. "The war is over?" he asked in stunned surprise. "Are you sure?" Almost with a feeling of guilt he added, "That's good. Now nobody else will be killed. But what about aviation? What's going . . ."

"Come on, Ben," another pilot called. "We're going to celebrate!"

In the barracks that evening, the chief topic of conversation was the unexpected end of the war in Europe. The swift change of events came so suddenly that the pilots found it hard to believe.

Ben wrote from California telling his family that his orders to sail for France had been canceled. But he explained that he intended to stay in the service until the end of the 60-day period during which the armistice would be in effect and however long it took after that for some agreement to be reached at the peace conference. He ended the letter by saying, "I just can't seem to realize that the war is over. We thought we'd be in France right after Christmas, but now we don't know where we'll be. We're glad, of course, for there won't be any more killing. But the end came so suddenly there's a general feeling of uneasiness among the fellows here."

Those in the air service had kept up with the reports from the various squadrons. By the time of the Argonne offensive, the original aero squadron had expanded to three. The planes were used both for observation and reconnaissance and for bombing behind enemy lines. Eddie Rickenbacker, the American Ace of Aces, had shot down

26 enemy planes. Bearing out Mitchell's prediction, the airplane proved to be a highly effective military weapon. It was during this period of fighting that Mitchell became convinced that the next war could be fought and won by air bombing alone.

By the end of the war, 500 Curtiss float planes were in use. The naval arm helped protect convoys by spying the waters for lurking U-boats. Later, some of the navy's planes were converted to bombers, and navy pilots joined the army air arm in its raids on German military installations—a strategy Mitchell promoted.

At the beginning of the war, the U.S. Army had only 55 planes. When it ended, there were 3,227 Army Air Force DeHavilland 4s, of British design, with 12-cylinder 450-horsepower Liberty engines. A total of 5,460 planes had been shipped to Europe, over 1,000 to the Allies. The planes were of wood construction, chiefly Alaska spruce. Because of the great wartime demand for wood, Alaska acquired a new industry.

Ben remained at Mather Field until January 1919 and was then transferred to March Field, at Riverside, California. During the war, March Field had been a busy flight-training center. By the time Ben arrived there, much of the purpose and excitement was gone. Flying time for the pilots was strictly curtailed. Ben wrote home that he spent more time in the swimming pool than in an airplane.

Walking alone one night, Ben slowly toured the quiet field. He found the sight of the countless planes crammed into the hangars like sardines, many still in packing crates, very depressing. Even on the flight line it appeared that the usual "spit and polish" of flight-ready planes was missing. After he retired, Ben spent a restless night, tossing and turning.

The next morning at breakfast he discussed his feelings with fellow pilots. His voice rose as he exploded, "I hate to see all those planes just sitting there in crates! When I think of all the benefit planes could bring, it makes me sick to realize they might not be used at all."

"I know exactly how you feel," one of his friends said. "They're not the best planes in the world, but it seems a waste to leave them in the hangars."

"I'm trying to find out what the government will do with the surplus planes," Ben said. "Surely they must have some idea of what's going to happen to them. The planes should be put into use. Unless we keep promoting aviation, we'll be going backwards!"

Ben's mechanic joined them and stood listening to the conversation, waiting for an appropriate break so he could deliver a message. Ben looked up and the mechanic said, "Your plane's ready, sir." Ben rose abruptly and strode off toward the field, happy for even the short period of flying time allowed.

When Ben returned from the flight, the mechanic met him. It was easy to see he was excited about something. Ben grinned and asked, "What makes you so happy?"

"I'm going to stick with aviation, sir! I got a letter today. There's a stunt pilot back home who wants me to work for him—you know, keeping his plane in shape, like I do yours."

"That is good news," Ben said. "Stick with aviation!" He added, "There's a big future in aviation, if we can just sell the idea to people."

"It won't be the same as being in the army and working with you, sir," his mechanic said, "but at least I'll still have my hand in the flying business. What are you going to do after you're discharged? Do you know yet?"

"Not really," Ben replied. What I want to do is keep on flying, but I guess that's wishful thinking."

Many other pilots in Ben's outfit were just as uncertain about the future as he was. Eventually, the day came when Ben's mechanic stopped to say goodbye. Ben thought his friend looked strange in his new civilian clothes, his pants carefully pressed, and not a spot of grease showing. He looked a little shorter, quite uncomfortable, and perhaps even a little lonely. "Do you know what you're going to do yet?" the mechanic asked.

"Well, not really," Ben said. "All I know for sure is that I'll be going back to Hatton first and spend some time with my family. I'm certain my father will want me to complete my law courses. Drop me a line in Hatton, and if you're ever around there, stop by for a visit."

On March 4, 1919, Ben was honorably discharged as a Second Lieutenant, Signal Officers Reserve Corps. A short time later he stopped by to tell his commanding officer goodbye. "It's going to be strange not flying every day," Ben said. "I don't know how I'll adjust to being grounded."

"Yes, there will be a big adjustment to make. I wish you luck in whatever you undertake," his commanding officer said. "I think I told you I'm planning to stay in the service. A military career appears to be the best thing for me. Perhaps when you've grown tired of civilian life, Ben, we'll meet again at some army post or another." He knew that Ben had briefly considered staying in the service and couldn't resist teasing him a little.

At the time Ben left the service, there were thousands of trained fliers who would not be needed for actual service or for training other pilots. Ben left the post, as many of the other pilots had, with a feeling of regret and wondering how he would fit his new skills into the earthbound world of civilian life. The only thing that made Ben's separation not quite so final was his choice to remain in the reserve corps.

5

The Struggle of Aerial Pioneers

THE USE OF THE AIRPLANE during World War I had shown many pilots not only that aviation would revolutionize warfare but also that it would change the pattern of commercial transportation in postwar America. It was nearly 20 years after the first powered flight, yet the idea of flying as a practical reality was still almost universally rejected. The ex-army pilots were convinced of the aerial age, but they were nearly alone in that conviction. The history of mankind had been written in two dimensions—the land and the sea. Now, it would be written in three.

The nucleus of trained pilots in the United States remained. These young men, many in their twenties, were tuned to the new dimension. They realized that there had been a revolution in the world, one that began on the sands of Kitty Hawk. To put their efforts into historical perspective, the barnstorming advocates of flight sometimes looked back to the story of the Wright brothers.

However, the Wright brothers were not the first to dream about flying. For centuries, Europeans had done so. Leonardo da Vinci had designed a helicopter and also the parachute. The work of mathematicians and physicists, including Samuel P. Langley, of the Smithsonian Institution, with his 1891 publication "Experiments in Aerodynamics," was basic. However, Langley never constructed a successful flying machine because he relied exclusively on science, not experience.

About the same time, gliders, carrying men aloft in heavier-than-air craft without power, were being experimented with. Before his fatal crash in 1896, Otto Lilienthal, of Germany, had successfully made 2,000 glides.

Writers, students, and promoters started dreaming of man-made flight. They were a band of brothers tuned in to the aerial age. They were unmoved by the belief that God never meant man to fly. Some went to ridiculous lengths to promote aviation. All pioneers of flight studied the flying methods of birds, especially the sea gull, the stork, the albatross, and the condor. Even the humble sparrow contributed to man's knowledge of flying by suggesting the tail-down landing to Octave Chanute.

In the fall of 1908, the crucial time of testing the Wright brothers' planes in both America and Europe had arrived. Wilbur Wright had taken the latest model Wright plane, with a 35-horsepower engine and a payload of one passenger plus 100 pounds, to France. The demonstration in Europe caused a sensation. Because of his perfect control of the plane in all kinds of winds, and the fact that he established a new world record for distance—62 miles in 6 minutes short of 2 hours—and reached an altitude of 361 feet, Wilbur was the toast of the continent.

However, over Fort Myers, Virginia, Orville Wright, demonstrating a two-seater model ordered by the U.S. Army, was not so lucky. After several successful flights, tragedy struck. Thomas Selfridge was killed and Orville was injured. This incident was the one that caused Ben and his father to have their first real misunderstanding.

The dual demonstrations in Europe and in America pointed out that, while flying was readily accepted in Europe, it was looked upon in America as a new and rather dangerous sport.

The planes the pilots used for stunting and for commercial ventures were the same types as those used during the war for combat flying, when loss of life was so great. There is no doubt that the skill and the courage of the pioneer stunt men kept aviation before the public. They can be given a great deal of credit for the development of aviation.

Stunt pilots constantly asked themselves, "How long will people pay to see aerial stunting?" When a news reporter asked one of the most famous barnstormers of the 1920s what the biggest danger in flying was, the pilot solemnly replied, "The danger of starving to death." Indeed, the financial returns for taking aerial risks were skimpy.

However, stunt pilots in increasing numbers became convinced that they must find other ways to use the plane to make it acceptable to the public. Famed instructor and pilot Casey Jones arranged to speed urgent news photos across the country. Other pilots sought employment with the airmail service, which had an inauspicious beginning. On the very first flight, in the early 1920s, a Washington to New York run, the plane started, then stopped. Someone had forgotten to fill the fuel tank! The mail plane finally got off the ground, but the pilot became lost and made a forced landing in Maryland. The flight never reached New York.

In the following years, the mail got through with increasing regularity. However, this was because the mail pilots were extremely capable and heedless of danger. Thirty-one of the first 40 to fly the mail from New York to Chicago were killed in crashes.

Statistics were carefully kept by General Billy Mitchell, who constantly spoke out against the inadequate planes, the lack of landing fields, and the unreliable weather reports. In spite of low wages and of all the odds against them, the airmail pilots took pride in getting the mail through on time.

Promoting aviation was a big job. Mitchell was on the right track, realizing that some startling and spectacular projects would be needed. While Mitchell sponsored various endurance tests and transcontinental flights, ex-army pilots continued to promote aviation by adding innovative and more-daring tricks to their programs. They had a big job ahead selling the airplane to the general public.

6

Hatton Aero Club

KNOWING HIS FATHER'S DISAPPROVAL, Ben was cautious about promoting aviation. And, like the others, he soon found that a much-changed America would make it even harder to stir the public's imagination regarding flying.

They had to be optimistic, but aviation enthusiasts knew that selling aviation to the general public in the unsettled atmosphere of postwar America would not be easy. As one ex-army pilot summed up the situation, "I guess we can all go back home and try to promote flying, but first we have to pick up the pieces of the civilian life we left. From what I hear from my folks, many people think the airplane is a fad or a nuisance. Others say that about all planes will do is help the automobiles ruin the railroads."

Many returning veterans, including Ben, found that there was more of everything—money, leisure, cars, movies, dance halls promoting jazz, and drinking. A popular song asked, "How Ya Gonna Keep 'em Down on the Farm, After They've Seen Paree?" In Ben's case, it was more fitting to ask, "How Ya Gonna Keep 'im Down on the Ground, After He's Been Up in a Plane?"

Ben was determined to promote aviation, but he soon realized that doing so was a full-time job. His return to Hatton was marked by a happy family reunion. "This is better than Christmas," Adeline said. "There've been so many people asking about you." Needless to say, each caller received a lecture on the miracle of the aerial age. Ben's enthusiasm was contagious.

The family realized that Ben was uneasy. It was apparent that he was disappointed that he had missed the coveted opportunity to serve his country overseas. Ben worked at the store, but his most interesting activities were elsewhere. In addition to promoting flying, he took an active part in the organization of the Carrol O. Flesche Post of the American Legion and was a charter member.

It soon became apparent to his family that Ben would be unable to confine the task of promoting aviation to his off-duty hours. Several times when Ole visited the store, he heard Ben discussing flying, even with the ladies, young and old.

There wasn't a plane in Hatton, and many of the customers felt as Ole did about aviation. They recalled that the planes used for combat in France were crude machines, called "flying coffins" or "crates." They told Ben he was lucky to have come through alive and stressed that he should now forget flying.

Instead, in the winter of 1919–20, Ben succeeded in persuading a number of Hatton residents to join him in the formation of a flying club. In contrast to the dismal reports they had read about flying, Ben told his friends a different story. He spoke of the vast possibilities in commercial flying. He stated positively that he believed that a club engaging in commercial flight would be a highly profitable investment. He stressed that aviation would revolutionize transportation and that Hatton should take the lead in promoting flying in North Dakota.

"The first thing to do," Ben said, "is to form the Hatton Aero Club, elect officers, draw up an agreement, and purchase a plane."

Garv Olson jotted down figures on a sheet of wrapping paper. He divided the paper into three columns—"Cost of Plane," "Cost of Delivery," "Cost of Upkeep and Repairs." Ben grinned and said, "You'll need a fourth column, 'Income'!" Ben saw that Garv was sold on the club idea and that he agreed that the members should purchase a plane. Ben was elated.

Hatton's became the first flying club in North Dakota and one of the comparatively few in the entire country. That says much for Ben, Garv, and those who eventually associated with the pioneering project. Ben estimated the price of the plane to be about $2,500—a great deal of money, especially for a project of such an uncertain nature.

After the club was formed and the officers were elected, Ben said, "In order to get contracts to fly at county fairs and various celebrations in the Northwest, we've got to have a well-planned and intensive publicity campaign. We'll need bookings for exhibition flights, and we'll give our customers more thrills than the contracts call for."

One of the fellows said, "Ben, it's fine to talk about flying, but we don't even have an airfield here. Besides that, it will cost quite a bit to buy a plane, and the upkeep will be expensive, too."

"We can use some of the level fields around Hatton for an airfield, maybe even some of the cow pastures," Ben replied. "Of course, we'd have to do a bit of work to get them in shape, but we could do it. Hatton has lots of possibilities for landing fields."

Waving a sheet of paper in the air, Garv said, "Look. I've got it all down in black and white. The plane will pay for itself in no time."

"That's where you'll all be surprised," Ben added, "because we *will* get the cost of the plane back in just a short time. Garv and I figured we can arrange for performances at all the fairs in North Dakota and maybe even Minnesota! We can also take people on joy rides or business trips—and even teach them to fly."

On February 11, 1920, a contract was entered into between the Hatton Aero Club and the Curtiss Northwest Airplane Company, in Minneapolis, to purchase one Curtiss-powered Standard Model J1 Jenny airplane for $2,485. After much delay, a plane was located in Dallas, Texas, and it was immediately shipped to Minneapolis.

When he heard that the exact model plane the club wanted had been located, Ben was elated. He could hardly wait to tell Garv the good news, but he was bothered about telling his father.

Just before dinner the next evening, Elma and Ben were alone in the dining room. As his sister put the final touches on the dinner table, she teased Ben about getting married and settling down. Then Ole came into the room. Sitting down at the head of the table, Ole asked, "How's everything at the store, Ben?"

"Fine, just fine, Dad. You're not to worry about the store. If there's any worrying to be done, you let Oliver and Arthur and me do it!" Glancing over at Elma, Ben added, "That goes for you, too, Elma."

Elma laughingly replied, "Oh, I'm not going to pick out a wife for him. I was just teasing him about settling down. You know how talk gets started."

"Indeed I do," Ole said very seriously. "As a matter of fact, recently I've been hearing a lot of talk around Hatton about flying.

Why, just the other day I even had someone come into the bank to see about financing a plane! He didn't talk to me directly, but I had a report on the conversation. What do you know about that, Ben? I suppose you've heard talk like that, too, haven't you?"

Sighing in relief, Ben said, "Well, Dad, I told you about the Hatton Aero Club we formed in February, remember? Well, we did talk about buying a plane. In fact, we found one in Minneapolis for $2,485. We've made the down payment, and the balance is due as soon as the plane is picked up. It's a Standard Jenny plane. I'll have to pick it up." Ben was so relieved when Ole brought up the matter of the plane that the whole story about the Jenny flooded out.

Turning directly to Ben, Ole asked, "You say the plane is in Dallas now?" He shook his head and added, "I knew when you formed that aero club there would be more to it than studying aviation." After a moment's silence, Ole said, "Son, you know your flying career in the army wasn't very profitable. You don't have a penny saved, do you?" Before Ben had a chance to answer, Ole shook his head again and added, "Just how do you expect to finance the Jenny? How do you ever expect to get your investment back?"

Ben pulled a brochure from his pocket and spread it out on the table in front of his father. Flushed with excitement, Ben said, "Look. This is our brochure. Isn't it great? We're going to write to all of the fair officials in North Dakota. We'll put one in each letter. We'll have a full summer of work lined up even before the plane is delivered. Well, what do you think of that?"

As the rest of the family entered the room, Ole said abruptly, "Sit down. I'll read it to you." He read the caption, "AERO CLUB OF HATTON, HATTON, NORTH DAKOTA," printed in large, black letters across the top of the folded brochure. Ole continued, "Organized to promote interest in aviation in North Dakota."

Ole paused and said, "There's a picture of a Jenny upside down in the center of the brochure. What does that mean, Ben?"

Ben said in a tone of voice showing he wished Ole had never asked about the picture, "That's to show people some of the stunts we're going to do. Remember, people aren't used to stunt flying yet."

"My son's going to be an aerial circus performer," Ole said to no one in particular.

"Honestly, Dad, I don't expect that part of flying to last too long," Ben added. "The plane has lots more important uses. Why, someday we'll be delivering mail and other supplies by plane. It will save lots of time, weeks in some cases."

Without bothering to answer Ben, Ole read on. "Ask for rates for our exhibition flights. Our pilots will give a real acrobatic flight. . . . We do not give a skimpy loop or two and call it an exhibition. We do everything known to aviation. We guarantee to satisfy." He continued, reading what was printed in larger letters: "SAFE PASSENGER WORK. OUR MOTTO: NEVER TAKE A CHANCE WITH A PASSENGER." Across the bottom he read the even larger type: "TIME FLIES, WHEN WILL YOU?"

Ole cleared his throat and opened the brochure. This question appeared in large letters: "HAVE YOU HAD YOUR FIRST FLIGHT?" Below it was the assertion, "A new and pleasant thrill you will remember all your life."

Ole shook his head disapprovingly and closed the brochure. He read the back page: "Aero Club of Hatton, North Dakota's Pioneer Aviation Club." Below this the officers were listed: "Edward Nyhus, President; C. D. Mastrud, Vice President; G. M. Olson, Secretary-Treasurer; T. B. Stavens, 1st Vice President; D. L. Wambheim, 2nd Vice President." Under the list of officers was a drawing of a grasshopper.

Ole tapped his fingers on the brochure and said, "Well, Ben, I must say you've covered just about everything. You're doing a good job promoting your new club."

Ben laughed shakily and replied, "That's something I learned from you, Dad, while helping with the store ads. You always said that if we wanted to sell something, people had to know what we were trying to sell. Well, I'm trying to sell aviation! I want people to know exactly what they'll get for their money and the services they can expect from us."

Ole handed Ben the brochure and said, "Son, I used to think you would settle down and take over the store. Later, I thought you were interested in law and would become a lawyer. I didn't want you to quit school and join the military, but I couldn't keep you from it. Now, you've evidently put in a lot of work on this project. I realize that you tried to keep it from me because you thought I might oppose it. Well, Son, there's no doubt I would have. But, it's plain to see you've made up your mind. But, there's one thing I want you to promise me, Son . . ." Ole stopped speaking and drew a deep breath. "I want you to go back to college and get your degree," Ole stated firmly. "In case this Hatton Aero Club project falls through, or even if it proves to be successful, before you think about doing any more flying, I want you to get your degree."

For the first time since the discussion started, Ben relaxed. Relief came over his face, and he heaved such a deep sigh he startled Adeline. He turned to Ole and said, "That's fair enough, Dad. I'll keep that promise. I won't go back on my word. But, the project will be a success, I know it will."

"Now we will have dinner," Ole said. The family bowed their heads while he asked the blessing.

Afterward, Ole was silent, for he recalled Ben's words on the day he'd returned home from the service. After the family greetings were over, Ole and Ben had had a private chat. Ole told Ben how glad he was to have him home and back on the ground. Ben laughed and replied, "You know, Dad, I wished many times that you could have been in a plane with me. I know you don't approve of flying, but if I could just get you to take a ride in a plane, you'd change your mind."

"It will be a long time before you get me in one of those contraptions," Ole replied, "and I hope it's a long time before you're back in one."

Ben excused himself and started to help Elma and Guri clear the dining room table. Adeline followed him into the kitchen, teasing him about a ride in his plane. Ben led her to the sink and said quietly, "Look, let's not upset Dad any more tonight. Be a good girl and help us out here."

Elma bustled into the kitchen. She looked up at Ben and said, "Oh, Ben, I thought we'd never get through that discussion on flying. Dad took things pretty well, but you've got a long way to go before you sell him on aviation."

Scraping the dishes for Guri, Ben replied, "Well, I'll just have to keep on trying. Now, if Dad would only consent to be one of my first passengers, then I know my troubles would be over. I'll just have to think of some way to convince him that flying isn't as dangerous as he thinks it is."

Elma replied, "Dad's not the only one you've got to convince. There are not too many people in Hatton who are sold on aviation."

Ben said thoughtfully, "Well, let's see. I think I can name them for you. Besides myself and the officers you already know about, there are three more stockholders—Alva Wambheim, M. S. Haakenson, and Selmer Hove. That makes a total of nine people in Hatton who are sold on aviation. Hum-m-m. Now, if I count the other Eielsons in with that group, we have Oliver, Arthur, Adeline, Helen, Hannah, and, of course, you, Elma. That makes a grand total of 15 people in all to cheer us on."

Elma said, "That's not very many."

Ben replied, "When I first got home from the army, there was only one. For a while there, I believe I was the only person in town who thought the airplane was here to stay."

7

Barnstorming

THE USUAL QUIET OF HATTON was shattered by a strange roaring overhead. Many people had anxiously awaited the sound signaling Ben's arrival with the Hatton Aero Club's Jenny. The deserted streets filled with people, shading their eyes, looking skyward. Almost reluctantly, Ole accompanied the shoppers in his store as they rushed outside to join their fellow townspeople.

The little plane, a mere spot in the sky when it first appeared, grew in size as Ben circled the main business section of town, dropping altitude with each lazy sweep. As he passed over the Eielson store, he dipped his wings in a salute, then regained altitude. The plane roared off toward Grimson's pasture, near the edge of town. The stockholders figured Ben should land in just a minute. But he couldn't resist the temptation to show off a bit.

A stir of excitement swept over the townspeople as Ben suddenly whipped the sturdy ship into a series of wingovers, loops, and Immelmann turns. The spur-of-the-moment acrobatics were mostly for the benefit of Ben's family and the stockholders of the Hatton Aero Club. The stockholders stood in Grimson's pasture, the newly improvised municipal landing field, gazing up at the Jenny and cheering.

In the cockpit, Ben was having the time of his life and hoped that Thorval Stavens, his helmeted and goggled passenger, was too. His initial flight over Hatton was almost as thrilling for Ben as his first solo was. He felt he was living again for the first time since he'd left the service.

Cutting the first sky trail from Minneapolis to Hatton, Ben renewed his acquaintance with the toy-train look of the landscape below. Even Tobiason Lake, site of his big camping adventure, looked tiny from the air. "And it looked so huge when we camped there," he thought.

As Ben finished his aerial stunting, he saw several men surrounding the spot they'd leveled in Grimson's field. They were anxiously waiting for him to land. He circled several times and watched the crowd disperse to the outskirts of the field.

In a final fling, Ben zoomed upward and zeroed in on a barn. He put the little plane into a steep dive and didn't pull out until it almost brushed the roof. He climbed back into the sky, then swooped around in circles. He finally came in for a graceful landing. The plane rolled to a stop just short of the end of the leveled field.

Pandemonium broke loose in Grimson's pasture. Almost immediately the plane was surrounded by a group of yelling club members and townspeople. One of the stockholders exclaimed, "Wow! For a minute there, when you headed for the barn, I thought we were going to lose the plane before we even got started!"

Ben laughed and replied, "Just getting in some bombing practice. Spraying crops or destroying enemy ships, it's important to hit the target. Remember, I'm a careful pilot. It's my life, too. Besides, Thorval was with me this time, so I cut the stunting short."

As Ben and Thorval attempted to step out of the cockpit into the waiting crowd, they were lifted to their friends' shoulders. "Three cheers for Ben Eielson!" one stockholder yelled. The men headed for a line of waiting cars and unceremoniously dumped Ben and Thorval into the back seat of an open touring car. In an impromptu parade, with horns tooting in unison, just about every car in Hatton followed behind the open touring car carrying the hero of the day.

Ben protested that he had to go back and look after the Jenny. There were certain things that had to be done.

"No problem with the Jenny, Ben," one said. "Your mechanic is on the job right now!"

"Yes," Ben stated flatly. "The only thing is he's never seen a plane before, and I promised I'd be there to explain everything to him."

The handbills advertising Hatton's first aerial circus had been distributed all over town. The circus was free, and everyone in Hatton and the surrounding trade area was invited. On Sunday morning, Ben was up at daybreak to check the plane. Everything had to go like clockwork for the Hatton Aero Club's first real public performance. Yet, he was back home in time to attend church with the family. He noticed that Ole was especially quiet during the walk to church and again on the walk back home. Without even stopping at the house, Ben turned at the corner to leave for Grimson's field. "See you at the ballpark," he said to his father.

Inside the Eielson home, Elma hurried the younger children through lunch. "Don't waste time," she said sternly. "We must all be at the ballpark on time. They have reserved the best section of seats for us."

Right on schedule, the Eielson family filed in and was seated in the section usually reserved for visiting dignitaries. Ole sat stiffly in the grandstand, trying very hard to be cheerful. He happily greeted friends and neighbors who stopped to chat, and smiled and waved at others who passed. Only Elma knew how Ole really felt. In a quiet voice, he'd just said to her, "Everyone in Hatton is here to see Ben kill himself."

A tiny speck appeared in the distance. A sudden hush fell over the crowd in the grandstand. Craning their necks, the spectators shaded their eyes. There it was—the Jenny!

Clenching his fists, Ole followed each move as Ben put the plane through an intricate series of stunts. While his father watched in well-concealed horror, Ben skillfully did every wild and dangerous trick he'd ever learned in his training days and a few he'd seen other pilots do but had never tried before. These were the spectacular tricks that famous stunt men collected handsome wages to perform. But Ben did them all for nothing for the people in his home town.

In Ben's experienced hands, the little plane seemed alive. It twisted and turned, responding to his every wish. The younger Eielson children, unaware of the potential danger, were thrilled and delighted by the aerobatics.

During the short periods Elma wasn't totally absorbed in the aerial show, she watched her father. For the most part, he sat poised and smiling, but right at that moment she could see that his mind was far away.

In spite of his fears, Ole admired much of the stunting. "Yet," he thought to himself, "there's Ben. He won such high honors in high school debate. In college he showed such promise of becoming

an eloquent lawyer. Yes, Ben has it in him to become a great statesman, but now neither of these things will happen, because Ben is
going to kill himself flying. Maybe not today—the show is almost
over—but . . ."

Then Ben leveled the Jenny out and abruptly did a complete flip.
The audience gasped. He raced the full length of the ballpark, turned,
and raced back. Ole sank wearily onto his seat, clasping his clammy
hands together. What would Ben do next?

Just about the time Ole thought he couldn't stand another minute of the terrible suspense of waiting for something to go wrong,
Ben waved gaily to the crowd in the grandstand. He gained altitude
and made a few lazy circles around the bases on the field. He dipped
the wings in final salute and roared away, heading back to Grimson's
pasture. Ole sat drained, motionless in his seat.

After the family returned home, Ole heard a knock at the front
door and quickly answered it. Elma heard her father say, "That's fine.
Thank you for bringing me the message."

Ole turned to Elma and said, "That was one of the stockholders.
He said Ben landed safely. I made arrangements with him at the
ballpark to let us know about the landing. I was worried Ben would
be dizzy or maybe just too tired to land safely." With a deep sigh of
relief, Ole added, "Well, the aerial circus is finally over for today."

"Ben really put on a good show, didn't he, Dad?" Elma asked,
hoping she could change her father's mood.

"Oh, yes. Ben's a good pilot," Ole replied, "but there's always
the element of chance; he has no control over that . . . He'll kill
himself flying, Elma! That's what he'll do, kill himself!"

After Ole left for his library, Elma said to Adeline, "Oh, I hope
everything goes all right at dinner tonight. I'm so worried about what
Dad will tell Ben."

"You needn't be," Adeline replied. "He sat through the aerial
exhibition in the park. The worst part is over. This morning, right at
the last minute, I thought he was going to refuse to go. When I asked
him if I could go for a ride in the Jenny, he said, 'No!'"

When the girls finished setting the table, Adeline knocked at the
library door. When Ole didn't answer, she opened the door quietly.
Her father was standing at the window. He turned to Adeline and
said, "You saw him today; he loves flying. We'll never be able to keep

him out of a plane. There's nothing we can do with Ben. When he was a boy, we couldn't keep him off the windmill. It won't do any good to tell him to stay out of that plane, either. We're just going to have to learn to live with his obsession."

Adeline saw that her father was in no mood for sympathy, conversation, or extra attention. She hurried off to the kitchen as Ben came in the back door with Oliver and Arthur closely behind. Just about the time Ben starting talking, Ole came into the room. He asked, "Is that the regular act you'll be doing at the county fairs this summer? It seems to me one performance like that is enough!"

Ben replied, "I don't intend to make stunt flying my life's work, Dad. But right now that's the only way to get people interested in flying. Wouldn't you like to see Hatton from the air, Dad? I'd be happy to have you for a passenger. You'll enjoy flying. I won't charge you, either."

Ben's offer took Ole completely by surprise. "Me?" he asked. "You want me to take a ride in that plane? Oh, no, Son, not any day soon, I'm sure of that." In a puzzled tone, Ole added, "Thanks for your offer, anyway, Ben."

Ben said earnestly, "Look, Dad, stunt flying will keep me in practice. Besides, it's important to learn how to maneuver a plane. Later, when I'm doing commercial flying and get in a tight spot, it will help me make a safe landing."

"Commercial flying?" Ole asked in surprise. "Now, do you really think commercial flying will be a paying proposition?" He shook his head and said, "Ben, if Billy Mitchell can't convince people that aviation is important and we need better and safer planes in this country, then how do you think you can? No, Ben, people haven't accepted aviation yet. What in the world makes you think they will listen to you?"

A few minutes later, Oliver and Arthur burst into the room. Spilling over with excitement, Arthur pushed a stack of handbills toward Ben and asked, "Will you autograph these for us, Ben? We collected them from all over town. Some of the kids want to buy autographed handbills from us. We don't know how much we're going to charge, yet, but . . ."

Ole turned to leave the room but stopped to exclaim, "Autographed handbills! WHAT NEXT?" He looked sternly at Oliver and

Arthur. "We've had enough excitement for one afternoon. Please put those handbills away. Now, boys, I'll give you 15 minutes to wash and change for dinner. We're having company, you know." Ole left the room and went upstairs.

Oliver said, "I've been thinking, Ben. It's a good thing you didn't have to crash land on that ballpark today. It's pretty rough in spots. Just think what could have happened to both you and the plane. Guess you both might have retired for good!"

Ben turned to Adeline and said, "If Dad asks about me, tell him I'll be back in a few minutes."

As soon as Ben left, Ole came back into the dining room. He said rather crossly, "This is the last time I'm going to tell you to put those handbills away, Oliver. It's bad enough to have your brother lose his head over flying. The rest of us don't have to follow his example. Your 15 minutes are almost up. Remember what I told you?"

Oliver raced down the street and caught up with Ben. "If you had charged admission today, you'd have made lots of money," Oliver said. "Maybe you just didn't think about that. Well, I'm interested in finances, so maybe I can help you keep books or something."

"Thanks, Oliver, I'd appreciate that. If we come out ahead on expenses," Ben added, "I'll see that you get part of my percentage of the money for your help."

Dinner at the Eielson home that evening was a happy affair. Elmer Osking, who was there to celebrate his and Elma's engagement, was a little nervous at first, but as the evening wore on and Ole treated him graciously and appeared to be in a good humor, things were fine. After dinner, Elma played the piano and the entire family joined in singing.

Oliver and Ben sat at the kitchen table working on the schedule of appearances for the next few weeks. Ole retired early and admonished the children not to stay up too late.

In the days and weeks that followed, Ben found plenty to keep him busy. He found plenty to worry about, too. Just flying from one prairie town to another and locating a safe landing field was quite an accomplishment. Eventually, it proved to be an even greater problem than putting on the two-a-day aerial stunting exhibitions scheduled at each stop. The various fair managers were more than willing to cooperate in staking out a landing strip adjacent to the fairgrounds. Unfortunately, they had never flown a plane themselves, so their idea of what was needed didn't always prove helpful.

After their initial landing in a town, Ben and Garv often had to round up a crew to do additional work on the landing field before Ben could take off for his exhibition. Gradually, as word spread as to what the requirements were, the job became much easier.[1]

Most of the improvised fields were hemmed in by rows of tall cottonwood trees. On more than one occasion, the Jenny dragged its wheels, brushing the tops of the tallest trees. There also were rows of telephone poles and lines to contend with. Landing in the tiny spaces, surrounded by obstacles on all sides, called for steady nerves and split-second timing. Ben was especially conscious of the fact that Garv's life was at stake, too. Garv experienced a few thrills hopping from an uneven cow pasture in one town to an unknown landing field in the next.

The appearances of the Hatton Aero Club at the North Dakota fairs were well received. Ben became a celebrity and acquired a following of fans. It wasn't unusual for his fans to round up a carload or two of aviation enthusiasts and dash off to the next town on the itinerary.

Ole worried all the time Ben was flying, but that didn't stop him from encouraging the children to start a file of newspaper clippings, which grew rapidly. Ole also received clippings about Ben's activities from friends and business acquaintances. Soon, he told the children they could start pasting the clippings in a scrapbook.

Constantly on the alert to find new ways to promote flying, in addition to his usual stunting activities, Ben was elated when he arranged his first commercial flight. Among the clippings he sent home to Hatton, Ole was surprised to find one that read:

> Felix La Page, Walhalla banker, has found a new use for the airplane. With delivery of a large sum of currency from the First National Bank at Walhalla to Morden, Manitoba, rendered exceedingly difficult and hazardous by auto because of rain-sodden roads, and with the possibility that part of the auto trip would have to be made after night, Mr. La Page hired an airplane from Hatton, N. Dak., piloted by Ben Eielson, to

make the trip. . . . The night landing was safely made with the
help of lights from 25 autos parked in a hollow square in front
of the landing field.

Ben took a great deal of pride in his first commercial flight. He
knew his father would consider the event a big step forward. He was
right. Oliver dropped Ben a note telling him that, for the first time,
Ole appeared pleased. He quoted his father as saying, "If Ben has to
risk his neck flying, at least he's doing it for something more useful
than aerial stunting."

Ben's aerial exhibitions at the fairs improved, too. He was the
first to think of stunting from an altitude of 10,000 feet. He and
Garv added an information sheet describing the new style of aerial
acrobatics. It read:

> After we have climbed to an altitude of 10,000 feet, the
> following stunts will be done in succession:
>
> THE FALLING LEAF   IMMELMANN TURNS
> TAIL SPINS   LOOPS   POWER SPIRALS
> BARREL ROLLS   WINGOVERS
>
> By this time, we are near the earth and will put on a
> grass-cutting exhibition, that is, jump over houses, etc. Our
> arrangement of flight is something new. It has never been seen
> in this state. In our main flight, the people are not compelled
> to crane their necks and strain their eyes every five minutes.
> We climb to a high altitude before we reach the fairgrounds.
> Thus, we overcome the climbing delay and at the same time
> show the crowd a ship when it looks like a speck in the air.

As the summer advanced, there was more and more talk in
Hatton about Ben and his Jenny. It was easy to see that the people
had pleasure reading of his exploits.

Ben and Garv added another sheet to the material sent ahead to
each town where they had a scheduled performance. They offered
the fair boards a chance for free advertising. The brochure read:

> The Hatton Aero Club offers to take up free of charge the
> man who satisfies certain requirements which you may make.
> The free ride could go to the man who comes furthest by
> buggy, etc. If you wish, we can allow a passenger to go along
> on the stunting flight. This creates a lot of interest.

One Sunday during July, Ben and Garv flew to Grand Forks and then on to Elbow Lake, where they were scheduled to put on two performances—their first venture in Minnesota. Upon landing at Elbow Lake, they found many of the people in town were at a church picnic honoring Ella Ness, who was leaving to be a missionary nurse in Madagascar. They also learned that Miss Ness didn't have sufficient funds to purchase all the medical equipment she wanted to take along.

While waiting for the people to gather for the stunting exhibition, Ben said, "Garv, let's do some benefit flying this afternoon. You've heard of benefit concerts for this and that; we've had them in Hatton. We'll just fly passengers as usual today, but we'll share our receipts with Miss Ness. We've had a profitable summer so far, and I don't think the other stockholders would mind if we shared our luck. Let's give her two-thirds of our take today. If we have a good afternoon, her share of the money might be enough to purchase the equipment she still needs."

Ben continued, "If anyone objects, I'll take her share out of my part of the profits. Let's get the minister's permission for the benefit flying. He'll have to arrange for Miss Ness to stay around, too. We wouldn't want her to leave before we give her our donation."

The minister was surprised at the offer, but he readily gave his permission.

Ben said in parting, "Please tell Miss Ness I'll give her a free ride in the plane so that she can see her home town from the air."

After the second aerial stunting exhibition of the day, Ben landed and taxied to the front end of the field. Garv grabbed the megaphone and called, "Step right up, folks. See Elbow Lake from the air! First come, first served. The line forms to the right!"

It was a busy afternoon, for there were many residents who wanted to see Elbow Lake from the air. The pastor introduced Miss Ness when it was her turn. Ben handed her the helmet and goggles passengers wore and offered the usual instructions on how to adjust them. Ella appeared to be very timid about taking her first plane ride, but handling timid passengers was nothing new for Ben. As he strapped her in the passenger's seat, he said, "Relax and enjoy the flight."

Garv counted the money while Ben flew. After the flight, he

called Ben aside and said, "Well, there's good news. We said we'd give Miss Ness two-thirds of the money, and that comes to $250." The passenger flights varied from $5 to $15, depending on the length.

The pastor arranged for the presentation ceremony. He called for the attention of the people in the milling crowd and, after a short speech, presented Ella with $250. Her eyes filled with tears.

Several times near the end of the summer, Ben was forced down by engine trouble. At such times, he and Garv found it difficult to locate good landing fields. With split-second timing, Ben was forced to choose immediately. Sometimes they landed in grain fields where old stumps, rocks, and even piles of rocks cleared by the farmers lurked unseen in the lush grass. The cool-nerve control Ben developed that summer making emergency landings perhaps destined him for the world fame he later achieved.

Ben and Garv felt almost like gypsies, always on the move. Garv's help on the plane and his flair for keeping finances straight was invaluable to Ben. Oliver's help with bookkeeping at Hatton proved to be a big asset, also. Oliver forwarded correspondence to the proper town, kept records of payments sent to Hatton, and deposited all money in the special Hatton Aero Club account.

After an especially trying day near the end of the summer, Ben and Garv decided to splurge and checked into a plush hotel. As they had dinner in the hotel dining room, Ben said, "Garv, I'm sorry things haven't always been this fancy. We've spent more time sleeping outdoors under the wings of the plane and eating picnic style. It was lots easier that way because it's more convenient to work on the plane. It didn't really bother me, but I never thought to ask you about it."

Garv grinned and replied, "I haven't had time to give it much thought, but we might as well take advantage of the break we're getting tonight. Sounds as if it will be more of the same gypsy life later."

ENDNOTE

1. The need for landing places in various towns in North Dakota during the summer of 1920 stirred an interest in aviation. On May 19, 1938, a special commission from the U.S. Postal Department made possible an airmail flight from Hatton to Fargo to

celebrate the anniversary of the establishment of airmail service in the United States. For that event the Eielson Cachet Club furnished an unusual cachet for the Hatton mail. The picture on the cachet showed the first mail plane used in Alaska and beside it the first airmail pilot in Alaska—Ben Eielson.

8

It Ended in Climax

Fortunately, the summer passed without too much trouble or any delays. Ben was in such a good mood near the end of July that he decided to make an unscheduled stop on one of the club's tours. About 12:30 P.M., as he and Garv flew low over the town of Portal, North Dakota, Garv pointed wildly to a huge crowd of people already standing three deep around a fair-sized and better-than-average field. Over the roar of the engine Garv shouted, "Look at that, Ben! We'll make a fortune today!"

Garv had completely forgotten what Ben had told him earlier in the month about the importance of being in Portal on July 25. Ben felt a little guilty. He knew that the big crowd wasn't waiting to see the Hatton Aero Club's aerial exhibition. Yet, in an effort to please Garv, he put the Jenny through a few loops and death dips before landing smartly on the prepared field.

A red-faced army sergeant came striding through the clouds of dust. He shouted, "I'll give you five minutes to get that crate out of the way. We've got some real planes and real pilots coming in today, not a bunch of aerial clowns! MOVE!"

Looking beyond the sergeant, Ben saw a detachment of troops standing in line. Ben knew he'd timed his arrival in Portal just right. The delegation on the platform was the welcoming committee for General Billy Mitchell's "Black Wolfe Squadron." Mitchell's proposed flight from New York to Nome, Alaska, made the headlines everywhere. Portal was the squadron's last stop before heading north through Canada to Alaska.

Ben surprised the frantic army guards by asking permission to park the plane. "Go park it," the sergeant yelled. "Whoever expected to see another plane flying in North Dakota, anyway?"

After the Jenny was taken care of, Ben paid the two eager youngsters who had assisted him in tying down the plane 25 cents and hurried to the opposite end of the field. In a few moments he said, "Listen. They're coming now." Off in the distance he'd heard more than one muffled roar. As the sounds grew louder, a hush fell over the crowd. Shading their eyes, the spectators looked skyward.

Shortly after 1:00 P.M., four DeHavillands flying in perfect formation swept over the field. The planes circled three times. Wings wide and wheels seeming to reach for the runway, the lead plane swooped down and landed.

As a cheer went up from the jubilant crowd, the pilot jumped hurriedly out of the cockpit. He waved and smiled, then bent to check the thin rubber tires on the plane. Ben couldn't control his excitement any longer. He said, "Garv, that's Captain Streett[1]—the pilot that just got out of plane number one! I pulled duty with him lots of times. And that's Ed Henriques, his mechanic."

While Ben and Garv were talking, the second and third planes landed without mishap. Now, the fourth plane was bumping and tossing across the field. "Look, Garv. Something's wrong. That plane's in trouble."

"There goes the tail skid," Garv said.

As Ben and Garv watched anxiously, the DeHavilland swerved to a stop, raising huge clouds of dust. When the dust settled, the spectators found that the pilot and his mechanic weren't injured but that damage to the plane was extensive.

A short time later, the four pilots and the four mechanics were lined up on a wooden platform. After the army band played a few stirring marches, the people saluted the flag in unison. A Portal minister asked God's blessing on the "brave Americans" during their epoch-making flight to Alaska, the "Arctic Frontier."

In a hushed voice, choked with excitement, Ben whispered to Garv, "There's Lieutenant Kirkpatrick and Lieutenant Crumrine." Ben stopped talking abruptly. A general stepped forward. He was welcomed to Portal and was introduced to the assembly. In ringing tones, he spoke of the skill and the courage of the young pilots who, in their "sturdy ships," were "blazing new air trails over an uncharted territory." He called Alaska the "outpost of civilization" and wished the pilots well on their "far trail to the north."

Standing in thoughtful silence during the speech, Ben was visibly moved. He pictured the adventures ahead and wished he were one of the pilots heading north to Alaska.

"What's the matter, Ben?" Garv asked. "You act as if your mind is a million miles away."

"Not quite a million miles away," Ben said. "I was just thinking about the air route to Alaska. I understand General Mitchell tried to get permission for the Black Wolfe Squadron to fly from Nome to Siberia, but the officials didn't think it was such a good idea. You know our government doesn't officially recognize the Soviet government, but what a flight that would have been! It's going to be very frustrating for the pilots to be so close and not be permitted to hop across the Bering Strait."

Garv watched the army crew working on the damaged plane and asked, "Do you think they would mind if we offered to help them get that tail skid repaired?"

"Remember the time we fixed ours with a car axle?" Ben asked.

"That's just what I was thinking," Garv answered.

Ben approached the sergeant in charge of the repair crew and asked, "Do you mind if I offer a suggestion?"

"I've got an open mind," the sergeant replied. "Fire away."

"Have you thought about using a car axle for a tail skid brace?" Ben asked.

"We left with a supply of repair parts," the sergeant replied, "but we seem to have been hard on tail skids."

"You'll be here for days if you wait for a part," Ben said. "If there's one thing I've learned in the aerial stunt business, it's to improvise. We take lots of shortcuts, providing they're safe ones."

"There ought to be a spare axle in one of the garages in this town," the sergeant said. He turned to the crew and bellowed, "Let's move, men. Try all the garages and pick up a car axle."

By late evening the damaged plane was repaired. Ben and Garv had worked right along with the army mechanics.

For the next few weeks, Ben was moody. He traced the route of the Black Wolfe Squadron on a map he kept handy in the cockpit. Garv knew that as soon as they landed in a town and the Jenny was taken care of, Ben would rush to the nearest store to pick up a newspaper and search its pages for information on the flight to Nome.

As the DeHavillands gradually made their way across Canada and drew nearer to Alaska, the news reports grew more exciting. Flying through rain and fog, the planes were grounded only when visibility was nil. A series of minor accidents slowed down their progress. Yet, by fixing damaged tires, broken propellers, and torn wings and by repairing smashed undercarriages and tail skids, the adventurers kept flying northward.

Ben read the paper to Garv:

> The four DeHavilland 4-B biplanes, each powered by a 12-cylinder 450-horsepower Liberty engine, left Mineola, New York, on July 15, in an attempt to fly to Nome, Alaska, and return. The planes had frames of Sitka spruce covered with Irish linen, with wingspan of 43 feet and fuselage length of 27 feet. They weighed 4,450 pounds apiece when fully loaded with gas and oil, and the engines, which swung wooden propellers measuring 92 inches from tip to tip, turned up to 1,400 rpm and were described as "making an amazing amount of noise." Cruising speed was 90 miles an hour and top speed was 115 mph.
>
> At 4:08 P.M., plane No. 4 of the Black Wolfe Squadron, U.S. Army Air Service, touched its wheels down on the lumpy surface of Sergief Island in the mouth of the Stikine River, near Wrangell. Three more planes of the squadron landed at intervals of about two minutes.
>
> After leaving Mitchell Field at Mineola, the squadron made stops at Erie, Pennsylvania; Grand Rapids, Michigan; Winona and St. Paul, Minnesota; Fargo and Portal, North Dakota; crossing into Canada at the latter. Canadian ports of call were Saskatoon, Saskatchewan; Edmonton and Jasper, Alberta; then Prince George and Hazelton, British Columbia. [After making 11 stops since leaving New York on July 15,] on Saturday, August 14, the four planes . . . buzzed Wrangell and went on to Sergief Island, where a large smudge fire had been built to send up a beacon of smoke. They were the first planes ever to fly in the area.
>
> At Wrangell, Mayor J. G. Grant had declared Saturday a holiday and a large part of the population headed for Sergief

Island in small boats or aboard the *Hazel B No. 3,* which towed a barge alongside to take care of the overflow.

The fliers spent the weekend at Wrangell, and on Monday prepared to go on to Whitehorse, Yukon Territory, although the weather was somewhat uncertain. Captain Streett in No. 1 went up first for a look at the weather and returned to report it favorable. The other three planes took off, but when No. 1 tried it for the second time, the wheels hit a soft spot and skidded off into a slough and a propeller tip was damaged. The other three planes went on while Captain Streett and Sgt. Henriques remained to repair the propeller.

While Ben had eyes only for news of the squadron, North Dakota's country weeklies chronicled the daring of modest Ben Eielson, aerial stunt flyer.

After one performance, an editor wrote:

The big event of the day was an aeroplane flight by Ben Eielson of Hatton. He started in by rising some 3,500 feet where he began his stunts. Nose diving, grass cutting, and looping the loop were only a few of the things he did, but he touched a spot in everybody's heart that made it stop beating for a moment, and then beat again with renewed vigor.

While Ben willingly paced the plane through the routine of the aerial acrobatics expected of him, he was not an exhibitionist at heart. But, he'd determined if stunt flying was the only flying he could do, he'd settle for that.

One day Ben and Garv flew to Glenwood, Minnesota, where the fairgrounds was the landing field. Recent rains had soaked the ground. Although Ben succeeded in landing safely, the wheels quickly sank into the mud. The area was small and was hemmed on three sides by cottonwood trees and on the fourth side by the grandstand.

All day long Ben tried in vain to figure out some way to get the plane in the air. It seemed impossible. That night he walked in his sleep, flailing his arms as if he were twirling the propeller.

"Ben, wake up," Garv called. Before he could reach him, Ben "twirled the propeller" again and a water pitcher crashed to the floor. The noise woke Ben.

The third day that they were grounded, Ben woke Garv very early

and said, "Get up, Garv. I've got a solution. We'll drain all the
gasoline and leave just enough to get into the air and over to the
solid ground by the depot."

When they reached the fairgrounds, they found a large crowd
had already gathered. Ben told Garv, "We'll just put these fellows to
work today."

The gas tank nearly emptied, Ben turned to the men surrounding the plane. "Give us a lift, will you? And when the engine starts,
get behind and lift and push!"

The engine roared, and the plane, urged on by the muscles of
the doubting men, moved forward. Ben opened the throttle wide,
and the plane lifted over the row of cottonwoods. Its wings brushed
the tops of two trees, while its tail caught and carried away the
topmost branch of the tree between.

Ben landed near the depot and refueled. Garv climbed into the
passenger's seat, and the two were soon on their way to their next
stop. The crew who'd helped them into the air waited and waved
until the plane was out of sight.

In late August, Ben was billed for a day of stunting at Climax,
Minnesota. He landed on a small, soggy field chosen by fair officials.
The field was bordered by the inevitable trees, including some tall
elms, and a railroad track was at the far end, with telephone poles
on both sides of the track.

Many times during the summer Ben wished that he and Garv
had enough money so someone could travel ahead by car and choose
the landing field. Somehow, the "best place in town to land" often
turned out to be the opposite.

Garv and Ben got out of the plane. Ben stood silently surveying
the area. Abruptly, he said, "Garv, we can't stay here. You'd better
not get back into the plane, either. I wouldn't want anything to
happen to you. Not only is this field soggy, but look at the tall trees,
telephone poles, and wires! I don't see anything to do but try to get
out of here. I saw a pretty good spot on the way in; remember when
I pointed it out to you? Well, I'm going to try to make it there. Guess
you'll have to walk. But, believe me, it'll be much safer than flying
right now."

When Ben tried to take off, the mud stuck to the wheels, making
the plane lift too slowly. Instantly, Ben saw that he wouldn't make

it. There was a double row of wires directly ahead. He could see that he would be unable to go above the nearest of the two telephone lines paralleling the railroad grade. He decided to fly under the first wires, over the railway, and then under the second set of wires.

He slid gracefully under the first set of wires and across the grade. Too late, he saw that the telephone pole on the opposite side was not aligned with those on the first side, and one wing wrapped around the pole.

The Jenny careened crazily to the ground, one wing crumpled around the telephone pole, the other intact, and the landing gear demolished. Ben hung on for his life as the plane bounced into the bushes. The telephone wires snapped and tangled in the crumpled wing. Wood flew in all directions.

Garv ran to the plane. He'd heard it fall with a sickening crash. Badly shaken, Ben sat in the cockpit. He heard Garv shout, "Ben, are you all right?"

Ben shook himself and replied, "I think so, Garv, but look at the plane. I sure made a mess out of that! Well, it appears the plane met its end in Climax."

Garv said, "Let's find a place to stay. We'd better get a doctor to look you over, too."

"I don't need a doctor," Ben said. "I think I'm all right. After we report the damage to the telephone company, we'll go to the hotel."

When they reached the hotel, Ben called Hatton, hoping Oliver would answer the phone. He wasn't quite prepared to tell his father about the accident. Luckily, Oliver answered. Ben explained the situation and added, "If you and Arthur can bring the truck, we can haul the plane back to Hatton."

While Oliver was talking, Ben could hear voices in the background and feared that his father would take the phone. After a short pause, Oliver said, "Dad said to tell you that airplanes can be repaired or you can buy a new one—although he hopes you won't—but pilots have to be born!"

In spite of the serious note in Oliver's voice, Ben laughed. "I got the message now," he said, "but what about the truck?"

"We'll be there as soon as possible." Oliver laughed, then added, "Dad said this is one night he doesn't have to lose any sleep worrying about you and your next stunt show, because there's not going to be one."

Ben decided to unload the plane in the Eielson back yard. Ole stood at the kitchen window watching the proceedings. At the first sight of the dismantled and damaged plane, he started to tremble and called Ben. Ben came into the kitchen and Ole said, "Son, it's a miracle you weren't killed. This flying business is dangerous. Next time you might not walk away. Don't even bother to repair it—it's too far gone. What do you plan to do now?"

"Well, I'm going to meet with the Hatton Aero Club stockholders as soon as possible, and we'll decide where we go from here. In the meantime, I'm going to start rebuilding the wing."

Ben went outside and began the slow, patient work of stripping the wing. Ole checked on Ben's progress daily. After breakfast one morning he turned to Oliver and said, "Look at your brother out there. He doesn't know how lucky he is to be alive. All he's interested in is fixing that plane."

Ole went out to look at the plane and admonished, "I never realized how flimsy that plane is built. QUIT FLYING, Ben, or at least wait until they build better and stronger planes."

Ben slid out from under the wing and stood, wiping his hands and looking intently at his father. Finally he said, "It wasn't so much the fault of the structure of the plane this time, Dad. It was a mistake in judgment on my part. I never should have landed where I did, even if they said it was the best place in town."

"There are not enough people flying yet, so there is no need for good landing fields, I suppose," Ole said. "Now, remember your promise, Ben. It won't be long before school starts."

"I haven't forgotten my promise," Ben replied.

Oliver had been helping Ben work on the plane, and after Ole left, he said, "Dad has been upset ever since we got your call from Climax. But he's not used to Elma's being gone, either."

Ben had refused to let the family notify Elma and Elmer, who were on their honeymoon, of the accident. Elma was the only one who could reason with her father and at the same time defend Ben's wish to fly.

"I've never seen Dad remain upset for so long," Oliver said. "Just yesterday, when you were gone to town to meet the stockholders,

Dad said, 'I've got a good notion to burn that plane up before Ben returns with more material for the patch job.'"

"I know it's been hard on Dad," Ben replied. "First, he lost Mother, then Edwin. Although he expected Elma to get married, he didn't realize how much we'd all miss her around the house."

When Elma returned, she visited the home where she'd been the "lady of the house" for so many years. In spite of Ben's advance protests, the first news that greeted the honeymooners was a report of Ben's crash.

Elma surveyed the mangled plane with mixed emotions, saying, "Oh, Ben, you were lucky that time. Why don't you give up flying and go back to your law studies? You're 23 years old, and if you don't finish college now, you never will."

Ben looked at Elma and said, "Well, I told the fellows in the Hatton Aero Club this would be a good opportunity for me. I can rebuild the plane and make it stronger. It'll give me a chance to put some of my own ideas into use. If there were just someplace else to work so that Dad wouldn't see the plane all the time. Someday, each town will have an airfield, hangars, and proper facilities for repairing planes."

"Oh, Ben," Elma said, "you could have been killed!"

Ben threw up his hands. "I give up! Look, we're having a meeting of the Hatton Aero Club tomorrow night to decide definitely what to do about the plane. Until then, let's talk about something more interesting."

The following evening, the members of the club gathered in the Eielson back yard. Some of the stockholders hadn't seen the plane since the crash and were shaken by the sight of it.

Ignoring the expressions of shock and horror, Ben said, "If we sell it, that will be the end of the Hatton Aero Club. As you can see, right at the moment the only thing that we can really salvage is the engine."

One member said, "I hear there's a man from Gardner who wants to buy the engine for his boat."

Another added, "Whatever Ben decides to do is fine with me. I think we all made more money on the deal than we had hoped. Ben and Garv had a busy summer. With the $200 fees they got for exhibitions at the fairs and the $5 fees for joy rides, you can tell how hard they worked. Personally, I don't have any complaints. It was a very profitable summer, and Ben took all the chances."

When the vote was taken to dissolve the company, it won by a narrow margin. The man from Gardner was contacted, and he purchased the engine. Then Ben asked if he could buy the wrecked plane for a salvage price. The members agreed. Ben moved it to a barn in the vicinity and continued to work on it.

Ben reported to his father, "The Hatton Aero Club is now out of business. We sold the engine, and I moved the wrecked plane from the back yard, too. But I'm still rebuilding it. Don't worry, though, Dad. When opening day rolls around, I'll be at the University of North Dakota, ready to enroll."

"That's good news, Son—the best news we've had in a long time," Ole said.

ENDNOTE

1. During World War II, Major General St. Clair Streett was in command of the Thirteenth Air Force in the Pacific.

9

Graduation and
the Barnstorming Finale

AFTER THE ACCIDENT IN CLIMAX, repair of the Jenny became the first item of importance for Ben. He spent all his waking hours rebuilding the damaged wing and the landing gear. When a new engine finally arrived, it was promptly installed.

After his exciting summer with the plane, it was difficult for Ben to start thinking about college. Yet, he re-entered the University of North Dakota, taking the plane with him.

Oliver also enrolled as a freshman. Ole's parting words to Oliver were, "A college education develops a man's mind, teaches him to think, multiplies his capabilities, and helps him make the most of himself. See that you work hard, Oliver." Almost as an afterthought, he added, "I'm glad you're not interested in flying, Son."

Getting back into the swing of an academic life presented many difficulties for Ben. He probably was the first student to have a plane at school with him. He tried to forget that there would still be about six weeks of good flying weather before he had to store the Jenny for the winter.

Ben sought out the handful of other veterans on campus and found a few pilots with whom he could carry on hangar talk. Among his friends were Frank Talcott, who had flown with the Royal Canadian Flying Corps during the war, and Charles W. "Speed" Holman, who had served in the air force. The trio soon became close friends. On weekends, while the weather was good, they joined Ben in performing a few barnstorming engagements, stunting for excited grandstand crowds. Following their exhibit of daring and skill, they padded their pockets by offering three-minute rides for $15 to $25 per passenger. Frank Talcott later became office manager for the Brown and Bigelow Company, in St. Paul, and had many amusing episodes to tell about his flying experiences with Ben. Charles Holman continued his interest in flying after his barnstorming days. Holman Field in St. Paul was named for him.

All of the ex-pilots were eager to hear Ben's tales about his aerial stunting days. Ben explained that he had a very successful summer. The stockholders had made a nice profit. However, after counting his personal expenses, the expenses involved in repairing the damaged plane and in purchasing the new engine, plus the cost of returning to college, Ben admitted that he had little money to show from his wages as the pilot. But that did not concern him.

In addition to flying, Ben also played basketball on a fraternity team. He dated several girls, but when the Halloween masquerade ball came, he fooled them all. He flew to Wisconsin and picked up a girlfriend from his days there. After the dance, he flew her back home.

In the evenings, Ben often took long walks alone. He had difficulty keeping his mind on lessons, for thoughts of flying persisted. One weekend, while visiting home, Ben told his father, "I still would like to make a career out of flying. I keep thinking there must be some way to do it. I guess the only time I'm really happy is when I'm in a plane. Things are just different in the air, Dad."

Shaking his head in disapproval, Ole replied, "Son, keep your feet on the ground long enough to get your degree."

Oliver injected, "Just recently a flock of sheep nearly ruined Ben's plane. It happened when he landed in a farmer's field in one town where he was trying to line up some business for next summer. Ben made his call, but when he went back to the plane, he found that the sheep had eaten most of the linen from one wing. After making temporary repairs, he headed back to Grand Forks. He made it all right, but the plane was a little hard to handle. Now, he still has to cover the wing."

"You shouldn't have taken a chance flying until the wing was properly repaired," Ole added worriedly.

"Oh, the trip back was a little rougher than usual," Ben said, "but outside of that, everything was just fine. But don't worry, Dad. I'll be putting the plane in storage next week."

Not long after Ben's visit home, he received a telegram from one of his ex-army buddies from San Diego, California. The telegram read, "My partner cracked up stunting yesterday. Want his job?"

Ben resisted the temptation to quit school and join his pilot friend. He felt a little guilty because he'd paused long enough to consider the offer. But he did send a return telegram expressing his regrets over the loss of his friend's partner and added that he wasn't interested in the job at that time.

Ben was extremely happy in June 1921 when he received his B.A. degree. He was pleased to be the first in his family to get a "sheepskin." Ole, Arthur, and the girls traveled to Grand Forks to be on hand for the big event. Of all the parents in the audience, none could have been more pleased than Ole Eielson.

After the ceremonies were over, Ole shook hands with Ben and said, "Son, I'm proud of you. Now, perhaps you'll want to take postgraduate courses so you can become a lawyer."

"Don't worry, Dad. That's what I plan to do this fall," Ben said. "But, remember, I told you I'm going to fly this summer. You know, more people than ever before are becoming interested in flying. I don't mean just stunt flying, either."

Now that he had completed college, Ben felt as if a weight had been lifted from his shoulders. Ole seemed happier, too. His mood changed only when Ben left Hatton for his second summer of stunt flying. Things had been in a turmoil for a week as Ben arranged the last-minute details of his summer tour and planned his schedule of exhibitions.

When Ben told his father goodbye, Ole said, "If you're determined to join the air circus, there's nothing I can do to stop you. Just remember to be careful, Son. If you have another accident, perhaps you won't be able to walk away from it as you did last summer. Don't forget you said you'd enroll in school for law courses in September. I'm looking forward to that."

Ben replied, "I've been checking on law schools, and one of the best is Georgetown University, in Washington, D.C. That's where I plan to go this fall."

Ole was pleased to hear the news and added that Ben might become a senator.

"You drive a hard bargain, Dad," Ben said. He grinned at the thought that his father was still determined to keep him on the ground. He turned to Ole and added, "But, remember, this summer is taken care of—all booked up. After that I'll be grounded for a long time."

"It's a strange thing, Son, but before you took up flying, I never looked forward to winter," Ole said. "But now, it's reached the point where I'm happy when summer's over. I'm even happier when November rolls around, for then I know you'll be through flying at least until early spring."

Oliver butted in, "Ben's made a name for himself. We're getting a number of letters requesting repeat performances."

"I hope there isn't a repeat performance in Climax," Ole said curtly. "I don't want Oliver to get a call from someplace this summer to come and pick up the pieces." Then he admonished, "You keep in touch, Ben. Don't forget to write or call, no matter what happens."

Ben stopped talking and stared off into space, then added, "Stunt flying will soon be replaced with commercial flying. They have been setting some new records in long-distance flying, Dad. Over in France they're flying passengers between Paris and London. The Germans are starting airlines out of Berlin. I tell you, Dad, there's nothing wrong with thinking about a career in commercial flying in the United States, either. Why, if the gas tanks were large enough or if plans for refueling in the air materialize, we'll be flying nonstop from New York to San Francisco on a regular schedule. Remember, last year Billy Mitchell arranged a transcontinental flight, but the planes had to make 40 refueling stops along the route."

During the summer of 1921, Ben, Frank Talcott, and "Speed" Holman performed in many daredevil exhibitions. Ole told a Hatton friend, "Ben's doing aerial stunting again with complete disregard for his life."

When the weather was good, even though they had money, the trio preferred sleeping under the wings and eating picnic-style meals. It made it easier to work on the plane. At such times, bedded down on the ground, they looked up at the stars and talked for hours, discussing the future. Ben always had the biggest plans. He liked to talk about long-distance flights, starting a commercial airline, or even flying nonstop from New York to Paris. One night he startled his friends by telling them about his dream of flying around the world!

Ben said, "Frank, I think we three would be flying a plane even if we didn't get paid a penny to do it. I guess we're lucky our act has caught on and we can book engagements at such fancy prices."

Ben was still the chief pilot, but the rotation system worked fine. It was especially helpful to have one of the trio pick the landing fields in advance and then send word back concerning the best place to land in each new community. All three helped keep the plane in condition.

In between scheduled engagements at the various county fairs, the trio made impromptu appearances at smaller towns not on the regular itinerary. Flying low over a town, they depended on the roar of the engine to attract attention. Soon people began to gather. Setting the plane down in the most likely looking spot, Ben called to Frank, "Let's go!"

Frank bellowed over a megaphone to the audience, "Step right up, folks. Get a real ride in a real airplane! This is your big chance to see your home town from the air! Take a dip in the clouds! Special price today, only $5 for five minutes! Line forms to the right!"

One day, near the end of summer, Ben and his friends ran into an unusual situation at one of their regular stops. They had arrived a day early in one of the larger towns. They found that the fair officials had scheduled another stunt act in addition to theirs, but there was a problem. The second act was scheduled to follow each of Ben's performances. However, the plane used in the alternate act had been damaged on the trip over and couldn't be repaired in time for the first show.

That night Frank said, "Tomorrow we're going to have a big crowd of spectators. The people here are treating us like celebrities already. But the other fellows are going to miss their performance unless we help them."

"Help them?" Ben asked. "How can we possibly help them at this late hour?"

"The stunt man wants to work out his new trick with you, Ben. What shall I tell him?" Frank asked hopefully.

"Well, I don't see what I can do to help," Ben said, "but I guess we can at least talk to him."

"Sure thing, Ben," Frank said. "We meet him tomorrow morning out at the field."

The next day dawned bright and clear. Ben pronounced it perfect flying weather. The stunt man showed up on time and with a note of importance in his voice said, "Now, Eielson, all you have to do is fly the plane. After you finish your regular performance, I'll join you. After we're airborne, I walk on the wings, hang by my heels from the struts, and climb down a trapeze that hangs from the undercarriage and swing back and forth. But that's not all. We just added a new trick. Today I'm going to wind up my act with a real hair raiser!"

"What's the big finale?" Ben asked.

"Well, my friend here will drive the car. Now, I'm sitting on the wing of the Jenny. After you gain altitude and do a few loops, you drop down low and fly the plane directly over the car. Then, just about the time the crowd begins to get tired of the plane racing along over the car, you gain enough altitude so I can slip down from the plane to the top of the car. That really gives the spectators something to write home about!"

"Slow down," Ben said. "Now, tell me how much practice you've had doing that stunt."

"Well, not too much, but then it's a new idea," the stunt man added.

Ben stated flatly, "I can see where it would be very easy to break a leg doing that one. You might even fall and be hurt much worse than that. If I swerved the plane just an inch or two in the wrong direction, you'd miss the car below. That trick will require perfect timing. We'll need a lot of practice."

"Practice?" the stunt man echoed. "We don't have time to practice! The grandstand is all sold out for your performance. Our exhibition is an extra bonus. We already have both sides of the road booked solid for our act, too."

"You mean we practice as we perform?" Ben asked incredulously.

"That's about it," the stunt man said. "You're a top pilot, and I'm one of the best stunt men around. Listen, don't worry. It's easy. You just fly over the automobile, see. Then I dangle from a reinforced rope ladder and lower myself to the top of the car. You take off, and

I stay on top of the car a while. Then you buzz back overhead, and I grab the rope ladder again, like a trapeze artist. Next, I climb back up to the wing of the plane and walk over and sit down, right back where I started from. Then you land, and it's all over, and we're a big hit!"

"Well, I don't know," Ben said. "It seems to be pretty short notice. Besides that, we've never worked together before. That might make a difference."

"Listen, I've been reading in all the papers about what a great stunt pilot you are. I'm not worried. Why should you be worried?" the stunt man asked. "Think about it when you're doing your part of the exhibition, and let me know."

Just as the stunt man had predicted, a sell-out crowd packed the grandstand. The people eagerly craned their necks to watch for Ben's appearance. He put the little plane through the routine of aerial antics.

After Ben landed, the crowd went wild. The stunt man called, "What did you decide, Eielson? I'm ready if you are. All we need to do is attach the rope apparatus to the Jenny. It's already been tested. The men are here to get the job done. You already know just what to do."

Ben hesitated for a minute and then saw the anxious look on the stunt man's face. He wondered if perhaps he needed the fee to get the plane repaired. Ben remembered the times he had been hard up for cash for repairs himself. He finally said, "It looks like you're back in business. I'll try it one time, that's all. But I don't want any money; you keep all the money."

Soon Ben was flying low over the speeding automobile. The stunt man sat jauntily on the wing, waiting for his big moment. The speed of the plane was carefully timed to coincide with that of the car.

The stunt man reached under the wing and pulled the ropes that held the special rope ladder in place. It fell, shifting with the wind. Ben knew that when the man's weight was on it, it would hold steady.

The stunt man waved to Ben and started down the reinforced rope steps. Ben lined up the plane over the speeding auto again. He clocked the speed of the plane. The timing was perfect with that of the car. As the stunt man dangled in the air, holding the bottom rung of the ladder, Ben held the plane steady. The stunt man's feet touched the top of the car lightly. He teetered uncertainly for a moment, then flung the rope ladder aside. His body swayed, but he remained erect, balancing himself on the brace that spanned the roof of the car. Ben lifted his plane into the air and circled lazily around over the speeding car. The stunt man stood with arms outstretched, a huge smile on his face. The crowd was ecstatic.

Ben flew over the car again. He banked and retraced his path. On the third sweep over the car, the stunt man grabbed the rope ladder with the reinforcing metal bar and swung loose from the car. He flipped himself up to the second rung of the ladder and then swung back and forth for a minute or two. Ben held the plane steady as the stunt man climbed back up to the wing of the plane and pulled the ladder up behind him. Ben looked over the side of the cockpit. The stunt man waved and smiled.

For the first time since he'd taken off, Ben relaxed. "Never again," he said aloud. Ben thought stunting was fine when a man had only himself to worry about.

That night at dinner Ben and his friends and the stunt man discussed the successful trick. The stunt man said, "Now that I know it'll work, I can practice for the next exhibition. Fortunately, our plane will be ready in time for tomorrow's performance. I certainly appreciate your help, Eielson."

The next day the grandstand was packed again. Ben's aerial stunting proved to be as popular as it had been the previous day. But as Ben and his friends prepared to leave town, they learned that the stunt man had been taken to the hospital. In doing the act with the regular pilot and plane, somehow the timing went wrong. Although the stunt man braced himself for the drop to the top of the car and made a successful transfer, he remained standing for only a moment. The crowd screamed in horror as he slipped and fell from the top of the speeding car. Fortunately, the narrow dirt road was surrounded by tall weeds and grass. The stunt man threw himself sideways and landed on a grassy bank. He rolled over and over, but the tall grass and his padded flying suit helped break his fall.

Ben, Talcott, and Holman reached the hospital just as the doctor prepared to operate on the man's shattered right leg. They talked with the stunt man as he was being wheeled into the operating room.

Ben shook his head in wonder and said, "You're lucky. Things could have been much worse. I'm just glad your accident wasn't even more serious."

"Eielson, I've been stunting for a long time. This isn't the first accident I've had, just the worst one so far," the stunt man said. "But there's no way a man can practice a trick like that unless he just does it. People are getting used to the usual aerial stunting tricks now, and if we don't come up with something new, we won't be able to stay in business."

With a touch of irony in his voice, Ben asked Frank, "What was it that farmer called us the other day, 'brainless fools'? Maybe he was right at that!"

Near the end of August, Ben and his friends ended their summer tour. When Ben returned to Hatton he found a breezy letter from the ex-stunt man telling him that he appreciated his thoughtfulness and concern. He reported that he was still hospitalized, his leg was in a cast, and as soon as he was released he would head for California to take courses in ground school. He ended the letter by telling Ben that he figured he'd probably be walking again by the time he was ready for pilot's training.

Ben told his father, "We had a fine summer, and I'd say it was very successful. The plane's been sold, so I won't have to worry about storing it this winter."

Oliver shook his head and replied, "Ben, I just can't figure you out at all. This is the first time you're acting as if you don't have any regrets about giving up flying."

Chiding Oliver for his skeptical attitude, Ben asked, "Now, can't you just see me flying a plane in Washington, D.C.?"

Oliver started out the door and then turned to add, "By the way, Judge Eielson, we're having a sort of farewell dance at the lake pavilion tonight before all the fellows leave for college. Would you like to join us, or is it beneath your dignity?" He paused. "Mind if we get serious for a minute, Ben? Did you have enough money left for tuition after you paid all expenses this summer?"

"I'm not rich, of course," Ben replied, "but I've got enough for my train fare, room rent, and tuition. Also, I plan to look for a part-time job. It's a good thing I know a little bit about politics. I'm planning to visit with Congressman O. B. Burtness and see if he can help me find one."

"I get the feeling you're rather looking forward to Washington and even law school, Ben. That's good. I know that Dad's happy about it too."

Ben smiled and replied, "Well, it will be more interesting than weighing prunes and selling overalls. Yet, I doubt it will be more exciting than flying." Ben stopped talking and then added thoughtfully, "I mean serious flying, Oliver. My days as an air gypsy are over. I think I learned my lesson these last two summers. We have to get people interested in serious flying."

10

Washington, D.C., and a Changed Life

Wʜᴇɴ Bᴇɴ ᴀʀʀɪᴠᴇᴅ ɪɴ Wᴀsʜɪɴɢᴛᴏɴ, D.C., in the fall of 1921 to enroll in postgraduate law courses at Georgetown University, he immediately sensed an almost electrified atmosphere in the nation's capital. In his letters home, he described Washington's excitement and glamour. He wrote of the city's civic beauty and monumental splendor, which far exceeded his youthful imagination. As he toured the town on foot, his interest in government quickened.

As a young boy, Ben collected books for his private library. One of his first choices was a complete 13-volume set on President Theodore Roosevelt. Roosevelt, a many-sided man—war hero, writer, reform politician, and naturalist—appealed to him. Ben was impressed with Roosevelt's accomplishments while in office and especially his stamp of approval for aviation.

One of the first things Ben did after he arrived in Washington was to call on Olger B. Burtness, the Republican congressman from North Dakota. Ben had first met Burtness when the congressman visited the University of North Dakota while Ben was a student there. Burtness was very cordial to him.

Ben explained that he was looking for a job to help pay his expenses while attending law school. He told Burtness about his two summers of stunt flying, which had helped to promote aviation but were not very financially rewarding to him. Ben further explained that his father wanted him to become an attorney and would have been more than glad to pay school costs but that he wanted to pay his own way. A few days later, he received a part-time appointment to the Capitol Police Force and became a guard in the U.S. House Office Building.

Ben found his law studies challenging. His carefully handwritten notes, entered in a loose-leaf law notebook, discovered by Vi Bjerke in the winter of 1969–70 in the Eielson Museum attic, detailed his daily assignments and the progress of his studies and legal research. Despite the long hours of study demanded by his law assignments, Ben enjoyed the time spent on his guard job because it enabled him to meet many distinguished people, including congressmen, senators, visiting dignitaries, and top U.S. government officials.

Among his new acquaintances was Republican Dan Sutherland, Alaska's voteless delegate to Congress. Ben liked Sutherland, and apparently the feeling was mutual.

Sutherland, a former miner, businessman, and member of the Alaska Territorial Legislature, was impressed by Ben's keen interest in Alaska. Together, they spent many hours discussing the future of Alaska. Ben readily sensed the qualities that set Sutherland apart from other members of Congress. Sutherland still retained a certain spirit of friendliness from his pioneer days in frontier Alaska, a devotion to the outdoors, and a distaste for affectation and artificiality—all qualities that appealed to Ben.[1]

Ben admitted that he had always been interested in Alaska and went out of his way to collect news of the flight of the Black Wolfe Squadron in 1920.

Sutherland told Ben a detailed story of the squadron's flight: By the time the four planes reached Fort Davis, on the Nome River, at 6:00 P.M. on August 23, they had logged 54 hours 50 minutes in the air since leaving Mineola, New York, and had covered 4,320 miles. The squadron finally reached its original destination on October 20. By then, the planes had covered approximately 9,000 miles and had logged 112 hours in the air. The squadron landed, as Captain Streett reported, "with the same crew we started with, the same planes, and even the same spark plugs."

Ben replied that he felt that Mitchell and the members of the squadron had taken a big step forward for aviation. The New York to Nome flight showed the feasibility of long-distance commercial flights. Sutherland added that he thought aviation had a big role to play in improving transportation for Alaska, if the officials would allow it to develop.

Ben and Sutherland also discussed airmail service for the vast territory of Alaska and the inadequacies of the present system. Sutherland told Ben that Alaska mail-team drivers and their sled dogs were in a category of their own. He predicted their place would stand in the history of Alaska and warned Ben that they would be difficult to replace.

Sutherland knew only too well the isolation of Nome residents, who had put up with irregular mail service for many years. He cited the incident of a Fairbanks resident sending a Christmas card to a friend in Nome in the fall of 1918. The next August she received a reply. Her friend in Nome reported: "Your Christmas card reached Nome today, July 1, 1919. Some mail service!"

A clipping from a Seattle paper of May 1920 explains the mail delivery service: "The U. S. Coast Guard cutter *Bear* sailed for the Arctic today taking 25,000 pounds of mail to Nome, the first of the season."[2]

Alaska worked its way into Ben's imagination, and his discussions with Sutherland grew longer and more frequent. Ben was convinced that winter flying in Alaska was feasible, and the thought of it intrigued him. Gradually, he lost interest in becoming an attorney.

In the meantime, Ben continued research on Alaska. He found that while San Francisco was still a village of mud huts, and long before the American frontier was pushed to the Pacific Coast, the Russian traders/explorers had invaded Alaska. Actual penetration of the Alaskan interior by Americans did not take place to any extent until the 1890s, long after the 1867 purchase by the United States.

The more Ben read about Alaska, the more he felt that there were many challenges to be met in that frontier country. He studied the maps of Alaska in Sutherland's office with great care. Where the Bering Sea meets the Arctic Sea, Siberia and Alaska seem to join hands, except for about 60 miles of water. The Little Diomede Island, which is part of Alaska, and the Big Diomede Island, which belonged to the former Soviet Union, are separated only by a narrow strait.

Ben often became so immersed in his reading about Alaska that he found it difficult to get his mind back on his studies at law school. He began spending more and more time in Sutherland's office. One day he said, "After reading all this background information on Alaska, I'm even more sure we are on the right track in thinking the airplane can solve Alaska's transportation problems. Perhaps the plane can succeed in pointing out Alaska's strategic location, just as Billy Mitchell says it can. Of course, the present planes can't carry large equipment and other heavy freight, but someday they will build planes that can."

Sutherland replied, "Ben, if you go to Alaska you'll find the greatest thing you have to overcome is government indifference toward Alaska's problems. But, I'll promise you this: I'll do everything I can on this end to help you in whatever you decide is the best way to begin promoting aviation in Alaska. But your job won't be easy. However, you will find a few in Alaska who will pitch in and give you all the help they can."

One day Sutherland told Ben that there was a job open at the Fairbanks High School for the fall of 1922. He explained that a teacher was needed who could not only teach English and science but also coach the basketball team. Ben listened intently. Sutherland summed things up by saying, "Sounds just made to order for you, Ben. If you go there to teach, you can put your theories about flying into practice."

Ben smiled and replied, "Teaching used to be considered a job fit only for women, but I guess times are changing. Besides, basketball is one of my favorite sports. You've given me something to think about all right."

Almost as an afterthought Sutherland added, "What will your family think if you suddenly decide to go to Alaska to teach school?"

"My father has never been pleased with my interest in flying, especially stunt flying," Ben replied. "The idea of teaching might please him very much."

Sutherland asked, "Do you think the climate will be a drawback? You know, Alaska isn't as bad as most people think."

"After the winters we have in North Dakota," Ben said, "I think I can stand almost any kind of weather."

"Think it over, Ben," Sutherland said. "As I told you, you don't have to make up your mind right now."

During the next few weeks, Ben did a lot of thinking. He knew he couldn't do much of anything until after his first year in law school, anyway. Maybe after that he'd go back to Hatton for a while, talk things over with his father, and decide about the next step.

At the end of the school year, Ben told his Washington friends goodbye and headed back to Hatton for the summer. One of the first things his father asked was "Well, Ben, what will you do now?"

Anxious to see his father's reaction, Ben said, "I think I'll get a job for the summer here in Hatton. Next fall, well, maybe I'll teach school."

Ole looked so pleased Ben almost felt guilty. He knew his father had expected the worst, that he planned to take up stunt flying again. Finally, after a long silence, Ben asked, "Aren't you going to say anything, Dad? Aren't you surprised?"

Ole said, "Son, I don't know what to say. The last thing I expected was to hear you would even consider teaching as a career. But what about your law studies? I thought you were interested in becoming a lawyer. What happened back in Washington?"

Ben replied, "Well, I met Dan Sutherland, Alaska's delegate to Congress. He got me interested in Alaska. I've been doing a lot of research on Alaska ever since."

"Alaska!" Ole exclaimed. "I'd call that a real challenge. Alaska's a place where they need young men with pioneer blood. You have my blessing. If I were younger, I'd like to visit Alaska myself."

When Elma stopped by to welcome Ben home from Washington, he asked, "What do you think about me going to Alaska to teach school, Elma?" Then Ben told her what Ole had said.

"Dad's right," Elma said. "I think Alaska would be just the place for a young man looking for adventure. I don't think you will get restless there. But, Ben, well, . . ." Elma stopped talking. She laughed and added, "Somehow I just can't picture you teaching school."

Ben replied, "Now, listen, Elma. You haven't even heard what I'll be teaching. It won't all be in a classroom. If I take the job in Fairbanks I'll be coaching the basketball team and supervising other sports—hockey, for one. Of course, I'll be teaching English and science, too."

After Oliver entered the conversation, he called attention to the fact that there were no planes in interior Alaska. But he added that the region needed air transportation. Oliver chuckled, "First, he will go in for stunt flying, and then he'll try to put the sled-dog drivers out of business." Oliver stopped talking as Ole returned with a map and the globe.

Elma studied the globe in silence and then said, "Alaska is at the end of the earth, Ben."

Ben spun the globe around and pointed to Alaska. He said, "That's not the way I see it, Elma. I think Alaska is at the top of the world."

"There aren't any planes in Alaska," Ole said happily. "I think Ben will be a fine teacher. Now, let's see what we can find out about Alaska."

Ben took a summer job collecting for two local business firms. But, increasingly, the urge to go to Alaska grew on him. The territory itself held the lure of frontier adventure, and, perhaps with another Jenny, he could get back to flying.

ENDNOTES

1. Dan Sutherland grew up in the East, but in 1898 he heard stories of gold discoveries and was attracted to Alaska. He spent the winter of 1898–99 in Koyukuk and Rampart. In the spring, he moved to Nome.

   The following year, he joined John J. Sesnon in the lighterage business, moving freight from ship to shore, under the firm name of Sesnon and Sutherland. In 1902 Sutherland sold his interest and moved to Council, where he worked a rich hydraulic mining property. He soon had mining interests in other locations and subsequently was put in charge of mining operations on Ophir Creek for C. D. Lane. He was also in charge of mining operations, in a number of locations, for the Liebes family of San Francisco.

   In 1905 Sutherland left the Nome area and headed up the Yukon to booming Fairbanks. He obtained a claim in Cleary Creek and worked it until 1908. While in Fairbanks, he became politically associated with Judge James Wickersham, who was making his first bid for delegate to Congress from Alaska on the Republican ticket.

   While Sutherland was still engaged in mining, he was appointed by President William Howard Taft to be the U.S. Marshal for the First Judicial Division, with headquarters in Juneau. From 1912 to 1920, Sutherland was in the Territorial Senate. In 1920, when Wickersham retired, Sutherland ran for the office of delegate to Congress and won.

2. Between 1924 and the early 1950s, every permanent settlement and most of the seasonal fishing and hunting camps in Alaska started to receive service by the regularly scheduled bush planes and later airlines. Savoogna, on the north shore of the island of St. Lawrence, was the last village to have dog-team mail service. "Ta-pa'-ah-mi," or Chester Noongwook, was the last of the dog-team mail drivers.

11

Ben Teaches School in Alaska

DURING THE SUMMER OF 1922, Ben planned his trip north. Dan Sutherland had been called out of Washington unexpectedly, and without his help, Ben found that getting information on traveling to Alaska was almost as difficult as making plans to go to a foreign country. Alaska was inaccessible except by the water route.

No one seemed quite sure of the best way to get north. But almost everyone agreed that the trip must begin in Seattle. Ben left Hatton by train. Somehow, it was a little easier telling the family goodbye this time. Ole actually seemed quite pleased about Ben's new career.

In Seattle, Ben would board the steamer *Northwestern*. While he waited for its departure, he wandered down to the dock area, which he found fascinating. In addition to the many passengers boarding to head north, tons of supplies were being loaded onto the ship. When Ben mentioned to one of the men working at the dock that he was going to Fairbanks, the man said it was too bad the Alaska Railroad wasn't completed that far yet. The reservation clerk had told Ben that he could reach Fairbanks by traveling over the Alaska Railroad from Seward, terminus of the boat trip.

On board ship, Ben met an old sourdough heading back to Alaska. After expressing surprise that Ben was going to Alaska to teach and not to prospect, the sourdough told Ben stories about what he called the "real Alaska." He ended his stories by assuring Ben that sooner or later he, too, would get involved in gold mining, for it was Alaska's most exciting business.

Ben replied, "I'm going to Fairbanks to teach English and science and to coach basketball at the high school. But what I really want to do more than anything else is fly."

The sourdough shook his head in disbelief and asked, "Fly a plane in Alaska? Every pilot who ever tried it cracked up, except for the fellows in the Black Wolfe squadron. But they didn't stay long." Ben assured the old-timer that he knew all about the squadron.

The sourdough added, "Son, we had a piano teacher in Nome once who wanted to fly a plane. He wanted a plane so bad he built one out of wood and piano wires. He added a rotary engine and hired a pilot from outside to show him how to fly it, but he never got it off the ground."

As they were eating dinner that evening, the sourdough told Ben how he'd gone north to the Klondike in 1898 and then prospected in Alaska for 20 years. He spoke of Fairbanks with real feeling. It was easy for Ben to tell that this was his favorite spot in Alaska.

He said, "Fairbanks used to be an exciting place. Why, Son, the gold fields there produced $22 million in placer gold alone in 1906. Why, there are mining districts within a 150-mile radius of Fairbanks that can be reached in summer only by a water route several hundred miles in length!"

Ben asked bluntly, "Did you ever think about prospecting by plane?" Filled with enthusiasm, he added, "Why, if I had a plane in Alaska I could fly you wherever you wanted to go, or, that is, as far as the gas supply would allow. But we could have gas stored at strategic spots, and we could carry extra cans of gas in the plane."

The sourdough listened quietly and finally said, "If you could do that, Ben, you'd be a real hero. But I'm not sold on that flying business. I think I'd rather travel by boat in summer and dog team in winter and make sure I get where I'm going."

Ben smiled and replied, "Oh, there's no guarantee that there wouldn't be accidents or mechanical troubles. But, then, you could have accidents traveling by boat or dog team, too."

The sourdough nodded and, after a moment's silence, said, "Listen, if you could figure things out so you could haul me and my supplies to a good prospect I know about in the Iditarod country, well, maybe I'd be interested in this airplane business. But, believe me, there are no airplanes in the interior, or airfields either."

Ben replied, "We used level ball fields, cow pastures, and county fairgrounds for landing fields in North Dakota, but now they're starting to build airfields in a few towns."

"Where would you get an airplane?" the sourdough asked.

"The government has a lot of surplus army planes in storage," Ben replied. "Perhaps we could make arrangements to have one shipped to Fairbanks."

"Well, I guess you don't know much about Alaska's freight rates yet," the old-timer said. "The freight will cost more than the plane's worth. But, you'll find out about the freight rates when you get there. Then, of course, there's gas and oil. That's expensive too. Fueling a plane won't be like feeding the sled dogs dried fish once a day. Why, you'd have to ship in a year's supply of gas and oil by boat."

The next day the two visited as they relaxed on the deck. The spectacular scenery along the Inside Passage—the island-sheltered coastline of the Pacific Ocean from Puget Sound north for a distance of about 1,100 miles—kept Ben in constant awe.

The old-timer remarked, "When I see mountains, I always think there's a good prospect on the other side. Canadian and Alaskan mountains acted as barriers to interior explorations until the passes were discovered. The Chilkoot Pass was a tough one. Thompson Pass, between Valdez and Fairbanks, wasn't near that bad. Son, I guess I've been over every river and winter trail in the interior. Alaska is a big place, all right. Travel is mighty tough and slow, but I love every inch of the country."

Just about the time Ben thought the scenery couldn't possibly be any more beautiful, the view was further enhanced by contrasting thickly timbered hillsides carved into intricate patterns by numerous streams and fjords, which extended out on both sides of the passage. The old-timer said that near the northern end of the route there would be monstrous blue-grey glaciers. "They come out of the mountains like huge icy fingers reaching to grab a firm hold on the mountains to keep from spilling into the sea," he said.

The closer the steamer got to Alaska, the more enthusiastic Ben became. The old-timer had an air of expectancy about him. He commented softly, "Every time I come back to Alaska, it's just like a new start. Pretty soon I'll be heading into the Iditarod country. Don't have to walk too far, either, this trip. It's really something to think about, riding that fancy government railroad as far as

Fairbanks. I remember the days we had to walk in over the Richard-son Trail."

Ben smiled and replied, "I guess you might say it's a new start for me, too. I've never taught school before."

Suddenly a worried look crossed Ben's face. He thought to him-self, "What if I stay in Alaska but never get to fly again—never get to feel the slight tremble of the stick in the palm of my hand? What if I can't get anyone to believe in the airplane for Alaska?"

As the ship entered the 20-mile stretch of smooth water called Resurrection Bay, the old-timer stood drinking in the scenery as if for the first time. He turned to Ben, who leaned on the rail, intent on getting a closer view, and asked, "Isn't she beautiful? Yes, sir, once you live in Alaska you'll never be happy living anyplace else. It's like a magnet pulling you back. You'll see, Son—one year in Alaska and you'll never want to go back to that North Dakota country."

Ben and the old-timer were together during most of the voyage. Actually, it hadn't been too surprising that the grey-headed sour-dough miner and the young cheechako teacher hit if off from the very beginning, but they did make an odd looking pair. However, Ben enjoyed his new-found friend with his outspoken ways. Ben, himself, usually spoke right to the point, but his bluntness was tempered by a keen sense of humor.

The old-timer surely had a boundless enthusiasm for Alaska and all things connected with mining. Ben had an equal enthusiasm for aviation and also had picked up some of Sutherland's enthusiasm for Alaska, even if it was remote.

Ben soon thought so strongly about Billy Mitchell and what he had said about Alaska's strategic importance that he turned to his new friend and asked, "Do you know that Alaska is the most strategic place on the globe? The great circle route, the shortest distance between Asia and the United States, is through Alaska."

The old-timer threw back his head and laughed heartily, saying, "Hold on a minute, Son. You're not teaching school yet! You didn't say anything about teaching geography, anyway, did you?"

Ben laughed too. His new friend continued, "Now, it's fine to talk about flying from Alaska to Russia and Asia, but before we worry about that, first we've got to figure out how to get from one point in Alaska to the other without wasting so darn much time. If you'd ever made a trip to Nome, you'd know what I'm talking about. When you're through mushing that treacherous winter trail by dog team, well, after you reach Nome, you wouldn't worry about going any further for a while."

Ben replied, "Sorry, I just get carried away when I talk about aviation. But, remember, someday you'll be able to fly from Seattle to Alaska in just a few hours, although you'll miss a lot of good scenery."

There was no denying that the lengthy boat trip through the Inside Passage was pretty special. As Ben thought back over the scenic route, he decided he wouldn't have missed it for anything.

By the time the boat reached Valdez, there was quite a heated discussion going on among the passengers over whether or not Fairbanks-bound travelers should get off in Valdez and travel over the Richardson Trail or remain on the boat until they reached Seward and there take the train to Anchorage and on to Fairbanks. The confusion seemed to be caused by the fact that the passengers were not quite sure whether or not the Alaska Railroad was officially running trains beyond Anchorage.

Ben told his friend that he was due in Fairbanks a week before school opened and was informed in Seattle that the trains were going through. He asked his friend what he planned to do. The old-timer reported that he knew for sure that at least the work trains were going through but that he doubted if the Tanana Bridge was completed. He advised Ben to stick with him and his original plans of taking the train from Seward to Fairbanks.

"We can always take the ferry across the Tanana," he said, "and get on another train on the other side."

Ben took his advice and arrived in Fairbanks well in advance of the appointed time specified in his contract.

The Alaska Railroad—constructed, maintained, and operated by the government—had a main line length of 470.3 miles. As the old-timer thought, the great steel bridge across the Tanana River at Nenana was not completed, but passengers got off the train and were taken across the river by ferry. The railroad passed through a portion of Alaska that was exceedingly beautiful, including the Kenai Lake region, Girdwood, Anchorage, the Matanuska Valley, Wasilla, the Susitna Valley, Mt. McKinley Park, and the Nenana River Canyon.

Ben found that Fairbanks sat on a section of high land between the small Chena River and the large Tanana River. He felt a surge of excitement as he viewed the busy town. Quaint log cabins outnumbered the more modern buildings. Trees lined the banks of the Chena River, the autumn colors making brilliant splashes against the seared brown tundra. The fall air was crisp and cool. The log houses appeared to be quite comfortable and "settled in." They were surrounded by shade trees and colorful flower gardens. Many of the homes had carefully tended vegetable gardens behind them. Ben even noticed that a few old-timers had cultivated gardens on the roofs of their cabins.

After settling in his room at the Alaska Hotel, Ben toured the main part of town and then headed for the high school. The old-timer had told Ben that Fairbanks was called the "Golden Heart" of Alaska and said that it was noted for its hospitality, which even made cheechakos feel that they were in the midst of old friends. The reason for the friendly spirit, the old sourdough had advised, was that Fairbanks had been the "end of the trail" by boat and by road. With the completion of the Alaska Railroad, it was also the end of the "iron rail."

Ben smiled at this "end of the trail" description and almost added that he hoped to make it the "beginning of Alaska's aerial trails." But he decided the sourdough wouldn't appreciate hearing any more about aviation, as he was headed deeper into the interior by meandering riverboat.

Ben's first glimpse of the school pleased him. In 1922 the Fairbanks High School was a two-story wooden building, complete with a picturesque square belfry. Ben found the door unlocked and walked in. He stopped at the first open door and introduced himself to Mr. Keller [first name unknown], who showed him around the building. Besides Keller and Ben, the two other teachers were Esther Smith and Hannah Sponheim. Ben was surprised to find that Hannah Sponheim, from his home town of Hatton, also taught in Fairbanks.

Mr. Keller said there would be about 48 students in high school that year. Although it was several days before the teachers actually had to begin work, they already were on the job busily arranging for opening day.

Ben located his classroom and began putting away supplies.

After the room was in order, he sat at the desk, daydreaming. He thought, "Well, I must write to Dad tonight. At least he will be happy now that I have my feet firmly planted on the ground, and under a teacher's desk at that." Lost in reverie, he wondered, "How will I ever get a plane to Alaska?"

Ben jumped up from the desk and rolled down the map that hung over the blackboard. He observed it carefully and noted the huge area marked "unexplored." He studied the province of British Columbia and the Yukon Territory, the far-flung parts of Canada located between Alaska and the States. He knew it would be many years before Alaska was accessible to the States by land, because the highway would have to cross hundreds of miles of Canadian territory, much of it tilted heavenward in sharp, rocky crags. Abruptly, he turned from the map and reached for the teacher's edition of the English book at the same time. He was soon lost in another world. Next, he tackled the science book. Silently, he lectured himself about the advisability of forgetting aviation and preparing lessons.

After two solid hours studying and making lesson plans, Ben looked at the clock and found it past the time his landlady had expected him back at the hotel. Ben started walking hurriedly home but slowed down to study the yellow-green hillsides and inspect the beautiful country. He noticed that the fireweed was turning white, making hundreds of balls of cotton. Earlier, the fireweed had been a deep magenta color. One of the old-timers at the hotel had said that when the fireweed turned white, winter wasn't far off.

Ben glanced down a side street and saw two men cutting up a caribou. They waved at Ben, and one man told him that if he traveled far enough out of town, he'd see many hunters. "Alaska," the man added, "is a hunter's paradise."

Ben made several friends during his first few days in Fairbanks. He'd been invited out almost from the very first day he'd arrived in town. Compulsively active, he'd taken long walks in each direction around town, but he couldn't keep flying off his mind. He talked aviation to almost everyone he met. This included business people, the other teachers, people he met at parties or at church, and others he met just walking around town. Of course, he always listened carefully to their ideas about transportation, too. He especially liked to visit with the old-timers and hoped that the one he had met on the trip to Alaska would write after he was settled in the Iditarod country.

The night before school started, Ben went to bed rather late. He'd been busy laying last-minute detailed plans for the first week of school. He decided that everything must go just right. He didn't want to make the mistakes made by most first-year teachers. Ben had listened carefully when the other teachers shared ideas with him.

The next day Ben was shaved, showered, and dressed long before any of the others in the hotel were out of bed. Because he was so early, he took a walk. Finally, he paused on the Chena Bridge and studied the country. When he reached school he found the other teachers arriving. Apparently they had the same idea he did.

It was different in the school that day. There was a feeling of busy importance in the air, missing during the past week of preparations. Some eager students arrived early. Some yelled greetings to each other; others were grouped in pairs, talking. Ben had almost forgotten the eagerness of high-school-age youngsters—the old thrill of getting back to school after a summer's vacation.

The bell rang. Ben suddenly found he was more nervous than the first time he'd participated in a debate. But he shook himself and walked out into the hall. He stood by the door, dignified and smiling, but quaking inside.

During the busy morning, everything went well. Later in the day Ben pulled up short in the middle of the English class. He found that, somehow, the students were talking about flying. He had determined not to mention flying at all. Now he heard himself responding, "Railroads? Oh, railroads are a big help. So are roads. But, we're talking about the many places in Alaska that are beyond the end of the railroad tracks and beyond the present road system."

The class period took wings, but he managed to complete the English assignment just as the bell rang. He told the students, "Now, when you come to class tomorrow, we're going to stick to the English lesson, so please be prepared."

When Ben left school that day, several of the boys he'd had in English class and in physical education class—prospective members of the basketball team—were waiting for him on the front steps. They followed Ben down the street saying, "Tell us more about flying, Mr. Eielson."

Early one morning a few weeks later, Ben sat at his desk waiting for the bell to ring when one of his students arrived early and asked, "Will you tell us more about flying today, Mr. Eielson?"

Ben replied, "Perhaps I'll have you write a composition about Alaska's transportation problems. How would you like that?"

"Oh, I don't mean all kinds of transportation," the boy said. "We wondered if you would just tell us about flying airplanes."

Later, nearing the end of the class period, the subject came up again. Ben said, "Alaska is 586,400 square miles in size. The history of transportation has been written mostly in romantic stories of the Aleut bidarka, the Eskimo kayak and umiak, the shoepac foot travel of sourdoughs, the romantic age of the sternwheeler and the riverboat, the heroic dog team, the plodding pack horse, and, finally, the automobile and the 'iron horse.' Tomorrow, we're going to write a realistic story on Alaska's transportation problems. Now, let's make our story factual and try not to elaborate on just the most romantic phases of travel."

"Are you going to tell us anything about airplanes?" one student asked.

Ben smiled and said, "Perhaps, but not today. Today you're going to tell me a few stories so we can get ideas for our compositions."

The students quickly joined in telling stories of sourdough mushers, who opened winter trails in the interior by following Indian trails of long ago. Others told how the pioneers had cut and chopped their way through the wilderness, blazing trails for others to follow.

One boy told about dog-team travel. He talked about how the mushers prepared dried fish for the dog teams and how expensive good sled dogs were. Ben added, "As early as 1895 and 1896, Sheldon Jackson reported that Indian dogs used for hauling freight along the Yukon sold for $100 to $200 each, and the freight cost 20 cents a pound for a 30-mile haul."

Another student told about the treacherous walking prior to freeze-up. He reported that hummocky, bunch-like grass slipped and overturned, causing travelers to continually walk in water of uncertain depth, making foot travel dangerous and tiresome.

Ben couldn't resist adding, "A pilot would have the good fortune of being able to fly over and above the spongy tundra. But," he admitted, "in case of a forced landing, he wouldn't escape walking home."

One of the students raised his hand and said, "That's the dangerous part of flying. My father said that's why aviation will not become popular in Alaska for a long time."

"We must consider aviation from a practical standpoint, not from the standpoint of its being dangerous," Ben replied. "Its practical aspects must be given priority, even over its potential importance for military operations or its possible use for pleasure-seeking travel."

"Pleasure-seeking travel?" a boy burst out. "Pleasure-seeking travel in a dangerous machine?"

"Let's pretend we're traveling over Alaska in a plane, strictly for pleasure. I can think of several short pleasure flights that can be made from Fairbanks. What about you?" Ben asked.

The students made several suggestions, and then Ben said, "After we discuss your answers tomorrow, I'll tell you how long it would take to reach the various places by plane. Class dismissed."

As the students left the room, Ben overheard one of the boys say, "I think Mr. Eielson is a good teacher, but my dad says that he can't fly an airplane in Alaska in the wintertime."

The following day most of the students brought their lists of Alaskan towns, along with information on the distances between the towns, the various means of transportation needed, and the estimated time for travel. After they compared notes, Ben gave them the estimates of how long it would take to make the same trips by plane, and they were astounded at the big differences.

"Remember, this doesn't include stops for refueling," Ben said. "This is just flying time."

One student said, "The airplane would really speed up mail delivery. Mr. Eielson, do you know how much mail is stacked up in Fairbanks during the time we're in between travel by boat and by dog team?"

"Speaking of mail," Ben said, "I just got a letter from a friend of mine in McGrath. It took three weeks for it to get here. Fortunately, it was just a note about mining, but what if it had been an emergency message?" Ben pointed at the map and said, "Look carefully at the distance between the towns. You see, it's only about 300 miles from Fairbanks to McGrath. A plane could make the trip in three hours."

After school one Friday afternoon, a delegation of the younger boys approached Ben and asked, "Mr. Eielson, will you help us build a model airplane before the weather gets too cold?" Ben was happy to oblige and enjoyed himself. Helping build the model plane reminded him of the day he took his brother, Oliver, to the Prairie Chautauqua just so he could look at a model flying machine.

Ben's conscience bothered him a little when he thought about Oliver. He'd been planning to write his brother a letter for quite some time but kept putting it off. First, there was the rush of work during the first few weeks of school. Preparing lesson plans, organizing the basketball team, and working out a schedule for games kept him busy evenings, too. Then, just about the time Ben thought things had slowed down enough to get caught up on his correspondence, Dan Sutherland came to town and invited Ben to go campaigning with him. Happy to have a chance to get active in politics in Alaska, Ben gladly accepted.

12

Fairbanks—Ben's New Home

O<small>N THE DAY THAT</small> B<small>EN'S STUDENTS</small> finally completed the model plane, he decided to stay home that evening and write to Oliver, no matter what. As he sat at the desk in his hotel room, Ben tried to put into words some of the happenings in his first two months in Alaska. The lengthy letter, dated October 20, 1922, read as follows:

Well, Fairbanks is a pretty nice town. I am having a fine time. I have never seen such hospitable people. I have been invited out on an average of once a day since I got here.

There are about 3,000 people in town. Most of the houses are small and built of logs. There are two roads leading out of town, and, believe me, they are awful. One leads to Chatanika and the other to Valdez. I have driven out quite a ways on both of them.

Everything is very high up here. The smallest coin is 25 cents. The cheapest cigar costs 25 cents; glass of milk, 25 cents; bag of peanuts, 25 cents; to press a suit, $2.00, etc.

My roommate and I pay $50 a month for our rooms—bedroom with twin beds, sitting room, and shower bath. We stay at the Hotel Alaska. My roommate's name is Earl Foster. He is here attending school at the Alaska College of Mines. Very nice fellow. He is two years older than I.

Congressman [Delegate] Sutherland from Washington was up here a couple of weeks ago. He is campaigning. I took him, Judge Clegg, and the political boss of Alaska on a two-day trip while he was here. The judge owns a car but can't drive it, so I take him somewhere almost every day. We went over the summit of the Alaska Range. Climbed it on a road cut into the mountain from which we would fall thousands of feet if we steered too far out. The roads are awful. We went 28 miles straight on low. At one point the grade was so steep that we had to blow into the gas tank to get gas to the carburetor. It would not flow uphill, so while I drove, Sutherland kept blowing into the tank thus keeping the car going. On this trip we went to a dance at Eldorado, a gold mine. We went there on a little train drawn by dogs.

There were 12 women and 35 men at the dance. Could not get more than one dance in three. Every woman was married except one; she was a grass widow. The people were very fine to us. The judge's wife had left calls for us in every town to see how we were getting along. You can imagine my surprise when my name was called on the dance floor to answer the telephone as I did not think I knew anyone for miles, and the telephone is government owned and to be used only by officials. Everybody knew all our names and all about us before we got there. They all wanted to talk about aviation as few up here have ever seen a plane.

Oliver wasn't surprised by Ben's next offhand revelation. He smiled and shook his head as he read, "The city council has offered to put up $1,000 toward getting a plane, and the Commercial Club will probably put up the rest if I want to go into it."

Fully aware of his father's belief that now that he was teaching school in Alaska, there was no need to worry about the possibility he would take up flying in a land without planes, Ben cautioned Oliver, "Do not mention this to Dad as I am not sure yet anyhow, and it would worry him."

Ben then went on to report on another flying offer he'd had in Alaska. He wrote: "I also received a tentative offer to fly for a McKinley Park summer resort and gold mining company for the coming summer. I don't know how much money it will pay yet, but it might be a fancy salary—$150 and expenses."

Ben described Fairbanks as follows:

We have seven hotels, eight restaurants, electric lights, a fine Masonic Club house [Ben was a Mason], a cabaret, and four fine dance halls. The [gold] mines are just closing up, and the people are coming in for the winter.

The only occupations are gold mining, fur trading with the Indians and the Eskimos, and a little agriculture. The farms are placed on hillsides so they can get the maximum of light

and heat through the short season. There are no farms on the
flat banks of the Tanana. Too cold and marshy.

Ben went on to state that he enjoyed his schoolwork and told of
the big part athletics played in his teaching. He also added, "The days
are getting pretty dark, and we turn the lights on at school at 2:30
P.M. The weather is good yet, and we have not had snow on the ground
since the last of August. The weather has not been cold, either."

The letter also included a description of the northern lights.
People new to Alaska are often overcome by their beauty, and Ben
was no exception. He described the Aurora Borealis for Oliver: "You
should see the northern lights up here. The lights on Broadway, with
their shimmering signs, are like a man with a match by comparison.
They're all colors of the rainbow and traveling back and forth across
the sky with a swish that sounds like a silk shirt. At one moment
they are gone entirely, and the next they are spread all over like an
explosion."

Ben's letter to Oliver also included a little information on his
social life:

> They have some very fine dances up here. As nice girls
> and good dancers as you find anywhere. I went to a dance the
> other night where every girl (about 100 of them) wore evening
> gowns. Much better dressed than they are at home. However,
> most of them are married. I am going around some with a
> graduate of the University of Washington—Gamma Phi Beta—
> pretty keen!

Ben's letter ended with these comments: "I would like to have
our Cadillac or my airplane up here. I hope you are getting along
well and remember, do not take things too seriously."

Ben's statement to Oliver about not taking things too seriously
was a reference to the big difference in the way the brothers felt over
the matter of money. Ben never worried much about money and,
greatly to Oliver's disgust, did not have a healthy balance in his
savings account in the Hatton Bank.

Oliver remembered that when the Hatton Aero Club started
operating, Ben told him, "Look, I don't want to worry about money
all the time. Make the financial arrangements to suit yourself. Just

be sure that I have enough money to buy gas and oil and to keep the engine in top condition. Give me enough cash for daily living expenses, and we'll worry about my wages later. In the meantime, deposit all the money in the bank account. If I have to think about making good wages, it will take all the excitement out of flying."

Of course, after Ben had taught in Alaska for a couple of months, he wished he'd been more careful about saving his money. He didn't have enough money to buy another plane. However, even though he had no immediate prospects of buying a plane and shipping it to Alaska, his interest in aviation had not diminished in the least. He decided that he would have to work on some project to help finance a plane.

By early November, his students had become greatly interested in the new course in aviation that Ben had added to the curriculum. Aviation was even becoming quite interesting to the other high school teachers. It was strange how often the subject of flying popped up in their classes now.

Perhaps it was the feeling of isolation that gripped Fairbanks residents when the deep snow blanketed the land. In the hold of winter's frigid cold, the rushing streams were stilled, becoming huge expanses of ice. Daily Ben witnessed the arrival and departure of the dog-team mail drivers. He spent many hours visiting with them and discussing their routes.

In an after-school discussion, one of the teachers said, "The airplane is ideal for use by those whose economic condition permits such luxury. But in Fairbanks dog-team travel is the accepted way of life."

Ben did not agree, and his fellow teacher replied, "Given a means of locomotion that gladly and tirelessly carries the traveler from 20 to 30 miles per day, over an uneven trail, in fair or foul weather, and that subsists on two pounds of dried fish per dog per day, the inevitable law of economics renders dog-team transportation se-cure."

Ben nodded and agreed that the dog teams would be difficult to replace but added, "The airplane will be useful in conducting busi-ness and will also help save lives. When calamities strike the residents of isolated villages far removed from medical assistance, then the airplane will represent the difference between life and death. Perhaps this great need for medical assistance will prove to be the selling point for aviation in Alaska."

Everyone in town was waiting to see what W. F. Thompson, the local editor, would have to say about Ben's ideas on flying. Ben had met Thompson at the suggestion of one of the sourdoughs at the Hotel Alaska. The old-timer felt certain that the editor would put the young teacher in his place concerning his idea of flying in Alaska in the winter. Instead, Ben found him to be one of the most stimulating people he met in Fairbanks and a real supporter of aviation.

Ben found that the crusty editor of the *News-Miner* had a unique combination of the most contradictory and paradoxical qualities possible. Although Ben's political beliefs were completely different from Thompson's, the two hit it off from the very first. Thompson, a dapper man with a gray Vandyke beard, had a genuine love for Alaska. Although he limped, he was remarkably active for a desk-bound editor, and there wasn't much that happened in Fairbanks that escaped his attention.

Even before Ben met Thompson in person, he read the local paper and found the column "In Our Town" one of its most interesting features. One never knew who or what would be the next target for Thompson's barbed comments. His writing was witty yet had a self-revealing charm. Ben sensed immediately that Thompson had a real capacity for understanding what was best for Fairbanks.

Some of Thompson's "enemies" told Ben that the editor wrote best when "flamed" with the proper spirit. During those Prohibition days, when he came out with an especially daring editorial or column, people said that he had found another "cache" of home brew.

After telling Ben that he should discuss aviation with the editor, the old-timer at the hotel sat back and waited in anticipation, fully expecting to read some sarcastic report in the paper about flying in Alaska in the winter. Instead, Thompson began writing articles supporting aviation.

After the editor and the young teacher became acquainted, they spent many evenings sitting in the newspaper office, often drinking home brew and talking flying. Although Ben was not a confirmed drinker, he was not opposed to taking an occasional drink. He told Thompson that he hated to see a man drunk in public but had no quarrel with taking a social drink now and then.

During their first conversation, Thompson repeated the story Ben had heard from the old-timer on the boat about the piano teacher in Nome who set out to build the first airplane in Alaska in 1912. He said that Henry Peterson, the Nome piano teacher turned inventor, spent months putting his flying machine together. As he sawed and hammered away in his shed, the Nome residents watched in amused silence. By the time Peterson had a rotary engine ready to mount in his homemade plane, he had acquired an even larger audience of skeptics.

Thompson added that Peterson eventually became used to being watched as he worked but repeatedly told the curious children never to touch his airplane. Usually, the youngsters just stood in curious wonder as Peterson patiently strung the piano-wire bracing in place. As the project neared completion, Peterson was so confident the rig would fly that he advertised for a pilot from the States to come to Nome and fly his plane on the test run.

He engaged a team of horses to pull the plane about two miles out of town to the crest of Gold Hill. Merchants and miners, who had openly made fun of Peterson, couldn't resist the temptation of being on hand for the trial flight. Peterson's invention just might fly, after all, and if it did, they didn't want to miss the big event. Prior to the trial flight, ribbon badges announcing the momentous occasion sold in Nome for $1 each.

The pilot appeared to be a trifle uneasy. He climbed into the cockpit and pulled his flying helmet and goggles into place. He instructed one of the men just exactly how to spin the propeller. The proud volunteer starter gave the wooden propeller a mighty heave. The engine growled to life. The wings shook from the vibrations, but the plane did not move.

The pilot hopped out of the cockpit and checked over the plane. He was trying his best to earn his advance payment for "piloting" the ship. He positioned some of the men at the rear of the plane and along the sides and gave them careful instructions. He then vaulted back into the cockpit and yelled for the men to push the plane. The plane just plowed through the snow, much as an automobile would.

The following day, when those who weren't already aware of the failure of Peterson's rig to get airborne heard the story, Peterson was the laughingstock of Nome. With ill-concealed disappointment,

Peterson ignored the laughter and quietly arranged to have the horses haul the flying machine back to his workshop. He thanked the pilot for his efforts. Still convinced he could succeed in building a plane that would fly, he doggedly continued his experiments.

When Thompson finished his detailed story about Peterson's unfulfilled dream of bringing aviation to Nome, Ben shook his head and said that he could sympathize with the inventor. He knew how difficult it was to convince people of the plane's worth. He said he felt that Peterson might have succeeded if he had had a level field to use to start the flight.

As Thompson continued his chronology of Alaska's exposure to aviation, he next told Ben about James V. Martin, another of the misunderstood early-day inventors. Martin was luckier than Peterson because he succeeded in getting his planes into the air. He invented numerous aeronautical products and manufactured both planes and cars in his factory at Garden City, Long Island. In 1911, Martin set a new world speed record of 70 miles per hour in his personally designed airplane.

Ben said that there was no doubt that aviation took a big step forward when Martin became the first pilot to fly an airplane in Alaska. Thompson explained that Fairbanks merchants had first heard about Martin's activities in the States and then decided to invite him to bring his plane to Alaska.

Prior to confirming Martin's aerial appearance in Fairbanks, the merchants scheduled many minor events, including foot races, horse and bicycle races, rock drilling contests for the miners, and a host of other special activities. When Martin accepted their offer to journey north, they were elated. They spread the word that they now would have the same type of popular attraction that was sweeping the States—a real aerial exhibition!

Earlier in 1914, Martin had made special appearances in Seattle in a plane he had designed. Not only did he take off and land on dry ground by using the plane's wheels, but one of the highlights of his exhibition came when he attached floats (pontoons) to his plane and astounded people by taking off from the bay, flying several minutes, then landing on the water.

In Fairbanks, the merchants were in a quandary over how much money to offer Martin to ship his plane north and put on a show.

They settled on $1,000. After Martin wired his acceptance, he elected to take the Klondike Trail north.

Martin, his wife (the former Lily Irvine, the first English aviatrix), and his mechanic were in charge of the many loadings and reloadings of the crated plane during its circuitous trip from the States to Skagway, over the famed Chilkoot Trail to Whitehorse, and by steamship the rest of the way.

The steamer *Alaska* finally reached Fairbanks on Saturday, June 21. The trio were met by a huge welcoming committee. The plane was unloaded in Fairbanks and hauled to the ballpark. Then the job of reassembling the fuselage, putting on the skis, and installing the 100-horsepower Gnome rotary engine began.

In preparing for their sponsorship of the aerial exhibit, the local merchants had organized under the name of the Fairbanks Amusement Company. Prior to Martin's arrival, they roped off the ballpark and planned to utilize the bleachers to accommodate the huge crowd of people expected to witness the big event. An advance ticket sale was organized, with tickets priced at $5.00 for the best seats and $2.50 for the others. By selling all the tickets they had printed, the merchants hoped to cover the cost of Martin's $1,000 fee. But people soon realized that they did not need bleacher seats to watch the air show.

As Martin prepared to take off, the improvised airfield was the scene of frantic activity. Having no tachometer to check the revolutions of the engine, Martin had rigged up an ice scale, tied a rope to the tail skid, then tied the rope to a stake driven in the ground, tethering the plane. He instructed the mechanic to watch the scale. When it read 40 pounds, he was to cut the rope and release the plane.

Helmeted and goggled, Martin climbed into the cockpit, his silk scarf waving in the breeze. The mechanic spun the propeller, bringing the 100-horsepower engine to life. Then the mechanic rushed to the back of the plane. When the scale pressure reached 40 pounds, he signaled Martin and cut the rope. The plane surged forward.

As the plane rolled down the field, Martin waved gaily to the crowd, but the plane did not get airborne. Martin found it necessary to make three runs before he was confident the engine was warm enough for the takeoff.

On the fourth try, the plane lifted into the air. Martin climbed to an altitude of 400 feet, making lazy circles over the ballpark. In spite of the fact Martin hovered over the ballpark and didn't attempt to fly very far, the odd-looking ski-equipped biplane was a sight to behold. It was actually flying!

The crowd cheered wildly. Many of the old-timers had been very skeptical and doubted that Martin would get the strange rig off the ground, but even their cheers added to the din. There was no denying that they were disappointed because the plane was merely making circles over the main part of town, but it was flying!

For a total of nine minutes, Martin circled the ballpark; then he landed. The chairman of the merchants' committee made an elaborate ceremony of presenting Martin with the $1,000 fee.

The *News-Miner* reported that the plane had achieved a speed of 45 miles per hour and a height of 400 feet over the ground. "It rose in the air as beautifully as a monster bird. Many of the sourdoughs were extremely skeptical about the machine and its ability to fly, but by the time Captain Martin went over for the third time, all were yelling and throwing their hats into the air."

Martin's biggest problem was gasoline. He had brought two cases of high-test gas north with him to Whitehorse but was not allowed to take the fuel on the *Alaska*. Finally the gas was placed aboard the *Julia B.*, but the boat had not yet reached Fairbanks. The engine of the plane did not run satisfactorily on the product available locally. "Higher-proof gas is needed," reported the *Fairbanks Times*.

The Fairbanks Amusement Company, which already had a considerable investment in the venture, spent $200 more to charter the *Loew Victor*, a speedy launch, and sent it to meet the *Julia B.* By the following morning the *Loew Victor* had arrived with the aviation gasoline, and Martin made two more flights, one of 14 minutes and the other 6 minutes. He made a final flight the evening of July 5, then advertised the plane was for sale, but found no takers in Fairbanks. With the help of his mechanic, he dismantled the plane, crated it, and loaded it aboard the steamer for the return trip over the gold rush trail and back to Seattle.

In a final long-winded article in the *News-Miner*, Thompson reported on the flights again and ended his story with these words: "Regarding the possibility of flying through the atmosphere with heavier-than-air craft, the minds of many sourdoughs of Alaska have been set to rest."

When the editor ended his story about Martin's adventures in Alaska, Ben said, "That was quite a feat for Martin in 1914. But even more important, it showed a strong interest in aviation by Fairbanks merchants."

Almost without a pause, Thompson continued his narrative: "What little flying Alaskans have experienced won't be much help in selling winter flying. We had our first look at military planes in August 1920. After a long delay, the Black Wolfe Squadron finally got here, but they didn't stay long. I really had myself some fun writing about that trip. Of course, the squadron had the whole government behind them. Alaskans can't afford to put up money like that to get aviation started.

"I guess you remember hearing about Clarence Prest, too," Thompson said. "He was supposed to show up in Fairbanks for sure this summer, but he never made it."

Thompson then went on to relate the story of Prest's second attempt to fly to Nome and then across the Bering Strait to Russia. After his ill-fated trip in 1921, Prest began preparing for his second try at a hop to Russia. In 1922 he got a Standard plane and christened it the *Polar Bear*. This time, Prest decided to begin his trip in Alaska and had the Standard crated and shipped to Juneau. He took off from the beach in Juneau, heading for Dawson, in the Yukon.

The city council in Fairbanks had heard about Prest's new plans to fly from Alaska to Siberia and decided it would be a good idea to have him for a star attraction at the town's big Fourth of July celebration that year. They sent a telegram offering Prest $1,000 if he could get his plane to Fairbanks in time to do stunt flying on the Fourth of July.

Although Prest was anxious to get there, he had trouble during the entire flight. Four times his engine quit; four times the Standard crash-landed in the bush; four times Prest doggedly made repairs, and each time he hopefully took off again.

Prest eventually made it to Dawson, where he did a few stunts and landed safely on a river bar. Sourdough miners passed the hat to help him with expenses. He made it to Eagle almost out of gas. However, Eagle residents had gained a smattering of experience with planes when the Black Wolfe Squadron visited them in 1920. They told Prest it would be a simple matter to add ether to motorboat fuel and liven it up enough so he could fly.

As Prest prepared to leave Eagle, the helpful residents gathered around. In true Alaskan style, they presented him with many gifts, one of which later saved his life. Among the presents donated were a cake and a pistol. The sourdoughs told Prest the pistol was to be used to shoot game in case he crashed again and got hungry while repairing the plane. The cake was donated to provide instant energy in case he had to go hunting.

Intent on a safe arrival in Fairbanks so he could collect the $1,000 fee for stunt flying, Prest was not prepared for more problems, but they came. His engine quit before he reached Circle, Alaska. In the Seventymile River area, the *Polar Bear* crashed for the last time. Prest was shaken up although not seriously injured. But he was stranded in the middle of a boggy swamp. Dispirited and hungry, he couldn't even eat the cake because it was soaked with gasoline, so he took his gift pistol and went hunting. He shot a caribou, cleaned it, and packed it back to the downed plane. He made a temporary camp and cooked some caribou.

Prest then packed some of the cooked meat in a shoulder pack and started walking. The only hope he had for rescue was from search parties. Soon it began to rain. He stumbled along downriver for four days before he was rescued by a riverboat operator who took him to Tanana.

The smashed plane eventually was recovered and taken to Fairbanks. Though records are vague, this may have been the plane Ben used in the winter of 1923 to do flying out of Fairbanks.

Thompson had reported the story of Prest's hard luck in the *News-Miner* and wise cracked, "Next time, his airship will probably knock the top off Mt. McKinley and create a site for a summer hotel." Prest did not return to Alaska.

The discussions between Thompson and Ben about aviation dominated their meetings in the office of the *News-Miner* and gave Ben the idea of organizing the Farthest North Airplane Company.

13

Wings Again

Soon INTEREST WAS HIGH ENOUGH that the Farthest North Airplane Company was formed. As the first planned flying project in interior Alaska, it attracted attention all over the Territory. Many Alaskans felt that with the solid backing of Fairbanks residents and the dedication of a man like Ben, it had to succeed. Ben was elated at the prospect of having wings again. At his urging, the company ordered a war surplus Jenny from a salesman in Sacramento, California, who offered a good used one for $750. One day after school Ben and Thompson discussed the order.

"The freight on the plane will cost more than the plane itself," Thompson said. "We'd better figure about $800. High freight rates are a way of life in Alaska."

"That's about what I figured," Ben replied. "But I guess we can scare up enough for the down payment between the two of us and worry about financing the balance later."

Thompson thought for a minute and then asked, "How long do you think it will take before we make enough to pay for the plane plus the freight?"

Ben replied, "Well, you said the city council would pay $1,000 for stunt flying on the Fourth of July. That alone will more than cover the cost of the plane. If we advertise and line up enough work between now and the time the plane arrives, it shouldn't take more than 10 days to earn enough more money to pay the freight. That's not counting operating costs, of course."

"There's talk about President Harding coming to Alaska," Thompson said.

"If he really does, we can put on a special aerial stunt show for

103

him," Ben replied. "If we order the plane now, we can certainly do that."

After the order was sent, the weeks seemed to drag. One night Thompson said, "No use having you worry yourself sick, Ben. We'll just do some checking on that salesman. It wouldn't be the first time an Alaskan was taken for a ride by a salesman from outside."

Thompson enlisted the aid of a detective, who located the plane salesman in Kansas. The detective found that the man was honest but that he'd had so many orders for good used planes that he couldn't fill them quickly.

Satisfied that the salesman would soon have a Jenny for them, Ben relaxed a little. When school activities permitted and he wasn't chauffeuring Judge Clegg someplace, Ben dressed for the cold weather and explored the two roads leading out from Fairbanks. He knew he would have to study the surrounding terrain as carefully as possible. Once he started flying, his life would depend on how well he knew the country.

During his trips with Judge Clegg, Ben realized that in winter, with the ground blanketed in white, the country would be hard to read from the air. Fairbanks was circled by low hills and stands of birch trees. Countless small lakes and streams that doubled back and forth across the countryside, with loops in all directions, cluttered the landscape. Sometimes the streams nearly touched, then arched away again. With the streams frozen and covered with snow, they all looked alike. Even on a clear day, the vast frozen expanses of Alaska's hinterland would confuse any pilot.

Ben spent many hours talking to the sourdoughs at the hotel. They drew accurate maps for him as far out as they had prospected and explored. He also spent hours talking to the mail-team drivers, who were excellent authorities on the country. Even his students knew he was interested in topography and spent leisure hours with him, pouring over his growing collection of printed and hand-drawn maps. They also told him about old-timers who had traveled in sections of the bush other than those he had already mapped. Ben called on the old-timers as soon as their names were made known to him.

After a delay of several more weeks, Ben received notice that the Curtiss JN4 was available. Excitedly, he dashed off to tell Thompson.

"Well, it looks like we're in business," Thompson said. "But now we've got another problem. It's time to round up the balance of the money. We'll just go down to the bank and talk to Dick Wood."

Even though it was after closing time when the two arrived at the First National Bank, they were ushered into Wood's office. Seated in comfortable chairs in front of the banker's desk, Ben and Thompson soon were deep in conversation about Alaska's transportation problems and how use of the airplane would solve them. Although Wood had often listened to lengthy discussions on aviation from the two and was a stockholder in the Farthest North Airplane Company, he knew there must be another reason for their visit.

Wood smiled when Thompson abruptly switched to finances and talked glowingly about the quick money they would earn by commercial flying out of Fairbanks. Ben also spoke eloquently and convincingly on the extra month or more that use of the plane could add to the usual mining season.

Wood listened in silence through most of the discussion. Just as it appeared he was ready to speak, Thompson stood up and shook his finger at Wood, saying, "You know I'm right about this money deal. Now, the total cost of the plane will be over $1,500, including freight. With the $1,000 the city council will pay us for an aerial stunt show, that leaves us only $500 left to pay."

Wood said, "Of course, there will be other expenses."

Ben quickly added, "Yes, that's true. We'll need to do some work on the field. We have to build a hangar. Then, there's the cost of gasoline and oil."

Wood asked sharply, "What about a mechanic? Besides your wages as pilot, Ben, it's going to cost an extra salary for a mechanic to keep the plane operating, isn't it?"

Ben realized with a start that he'd completely forgotten to think about wages.

"You're giving up a teaching career to become a pilot," Wood said. "Are you willing to take a cut in wages? I would think you'd expect much higher wages. There's no comparison in the two jobs as far as risking your life is concerned." At that time, high school teachers in the interior were paid about $1,350 to $2,250 annually.

"I'm willing to pay my share of the money in advance," Wood said, before he was cut short again.

"Good," Thompson replied hurriedly. "The professor here also took some law courses. We'll be back tomorrow with the contract. Might have another partner by then, too." Then he added, "When we're here tomorrow we can arrange to borrow the rest of the money we need from the bank."

As the editor and Ben shook hands with Wood and turned to leave, Ben said, "Thank you for your time, sir. We'll be back tomorrow right after school."

"Yes," Thompson announced loudly, "we'll be here to take care of the little matter of borrowing about $500 each, maybe more. See you tomorrow, Dick."

Thompson laughed as he and Ben walked back to the newspaper office. "Thought I'd wait and spring that part about the loans right at the last minute. No sense shaking him up too soon." After a moment, he added, "Pratt is interested in our venture too. Maybe we'd better take him in with us, and then we'll have four trustees."

Once inside the newspaper office, Thompson handed Ben a sheaf of papers. Ben began writing and repeating aloud, "The Farthest North Airplane Company, Richard D. Wood, C. B. Eielson, William F. Thompson, and H. E. Pratt." Ben suddenly paused and said, "I could borrow the money for my share from my dad and not bother Dick Wood about borrowing from his bank. Of course, it would upset my father if he knew the loan was for another airplane, but . . ."

Ben suddenly stopped talking because Thompson wasn't listening anyway. He appeared lost in thought and abruptly tilted his chair back, put his feet up on the desk, and said, "The Farthest North Airplane Company. That sounds great. The words have a real ring to them." He looked at Ben and added, "Don't worry about borrowing a little money from Dick's bank. You'll pay it back in no time. No need to upset your father."

Thompson continued, "Yep, we'll show those fellows back in Washington, D.C., a thing or two. Fairbanks will soon be in the big time!"

Ben said that he knew Dan Sutherland and Billy Mitchell would be pleased to hear the news. Thompson reported that he was sure they would too. He added that he was glad there were at least two men in Washington who cared. He went on to say that the steamship people might not be very happy. "When we really get this air transportation going, it will break the old monopoly they've had. Professor, the Black Wolfe Squadron made the first aerial connection from the States to Alaska back in 1920. Now, how long do you think it will be before we get regular airline service between the States and Alaska?"

Ben replied, "Well, Roy Jones has already made a good start in southeastern Alaska by flying from Seattle to Ketchikan, but a great deal will depend on the interest of the people in Alaska and the financial help the pilots can get. Alaskans waited nine years before the railroad was completed. It will be even longer before a highway is built to connect Alaska to the States, because of having to deal with Canada."

Thompson interrupted Ben to add, "Some of the government officials make a career out of ignoring Alaska. But I suppose we'll have to prove that it's possible to fly planes year-round in interior Alaska before we can get any help from the big boys."

"We'll just have to prepare the plane and the pilot for cold-weather flying the same way Alaskans prepare their homes for the cold," Ben added.

Fortunately, Alaska's sub-zero winter weather was no handicap for Ben. He was used to cold weather. The first deep cold came to Fairbanks in November, but by then the log cabins were securely chinked. Wood for fuel—in many cases sawed by hand and neatly stacked—was piled high in convenient locations. Meat and other supplies were stored for the winter. Fur parkas and mukluks made their appearance in late November and the first part of December.

Ben told Thompson, "Every time I look at the piles of wood around town it reminds me that we must order a year's supply of gasoline and oil from the Standard Oil Company so we can have it shipped up and stored ahead of time." Then he asked, "Did you know gasoline prices are about 100 percent higher here than they are on the east coast?"

"That's right," Thompson replied. "That Jenny won't go anyplace on dried fish. The dog-team drivers have it all over us there. They have a strictly local fuel supply."

There didn't seem to be enough hours to get everything done. Ben's first winter in Alaska was anything but monotonous. In addition to carrying on the regular schoolwork, he devoted many hours to developing a championship basketball team. His efforts were not in vain, for the Fairbanks High School team won the 1922–23 championship. Ben sent a picture of the team and the cheechako coach home to Hatton. He also developed a good hockey team and skated with the students in the old armory at every opportunity.

Ben didn't confine his activities entirely to school functions. He also was active in the Lutheran church, the Masonic lodge, and the American Legion. He was intrigued with the sled-dog races, the most popular spectator winter sport, and he was popular at social events.

He respected the Alaskan cold, where temperatures could drop to 50 degrees below zero and hover there for days. A man's bare hand would freeze to an exposed metal surface on contact. In two hours number 10 weight oil would congeal so it resembled the heaviest grease. A plane, if allowed to sit outside in such temperatures, would become difficult even to tow, since the tires would freeze flat on the bottom.

Coupled with the weather problems on the ground, a pilot faced the characteristics of the flight route—jagged peaks and miles of uninhabited tundra. Alternate emergency landing sites would be few and far between.

Determined to get started on winter flying as soon as possible, Ben wrote for permission to fly the mail from Fairbanks to Nenana, 58 miles by rail. He planned the trip for about the middle of February, when the weather would moderate. He decided to wear an Eskimo parka and mukluks for a flying suit to help fight the bitter cold he would be exposed to in the open-cockpit plane. He had heard many stories of early-day prospectors who suffered needlessly during winter's cold because they refused to adopt clothing suitable to the climate.

Ben told his friends that he would have the Alaska Railroad tracks to follow and insisted that the Fairbanks to Nenana flight would be an "easy run." He was right. On February 21, 1923, he prepared for the big hop to Nenana, using a borrowed plane. The temperature was about 5 degrees above zero, and there was no wind. A group eagerly gathered at the ballpark. It appeared that all Fairbanks took an interest in the proposed flight. When the sound of the plane revving up reached local ears, others hurried to the ballpark, ready to watch or to assist his takeoff. He was making history.

Earlier in the day there was no shortage of assistants at the ballpark, for all the mechanics in town were on hand. They helped Ben check over the plane, helped heat the oil before pouring it in, and even took turns watching the firepot set to heat the engine. These precautions that Ben took against the cold were used by many bush pilots in succeeding years.

When the big moment came to spin the propeller, the men tossed a coin to see who the lucky starter would be. Ben carried 500 pounds of mail and express packages to Nenana. Records are not clear as to what plane Ben used on the flight. Some sources say it was a DeHavilland brought to Alaska by an English adventurer. Others say that it was the rebuilt Prest plane. At any rate, the flight was reported in the *Congressional Record* as having taken place on February 21, 1923, a year to the day before his first official flight in the DeHavilland furnished him by the government.

There were no problems during the flight. The people in Nenana treated Ben like a hero. When he got back to Fairbanks, there was another big celebration.

"Things will be even better," Thompson said, "when we've got our own plane."

Almost before Ben realized it, winter was over. Fairbanks experienced a true Alaska spring. In the north there is no April such as lyric poets write about, for in Alaska spring comes like a charge of dynamite. The lawns that yesterday were covered with white turned green. All over town people were busy in their greenhouses. By Memorial Day they were busy planting gardens with plants they had started inside.

There was the usual surge of mining activity, which came every spring, and the old-timers left for their claims. With only about 100 days to wrest gold from the ground, the miners usually worked their claims 24 hours a day in 8-hour shifts.

The closing days of school were hectic. The weather was moderating, the days were growing longer, and the students were getting restless as they looked forward to vacation. Ben was impatient, too, waiting for the Jenny to arrive. He made many trips to the depot to check the freight cars, always looking for the oblong crates.

School ended with a rush in May. As Ben stood in his classroom watching the students hurry off, he was sad. It had been a good year, better than he had expected for his first year of teaching. He hoped the school people hadn't been too disappointed in his work. He actually felt a little lonely saying goodbye to Mr. Keller, Esther Smith, and Hannah Sponheim.

Hannah asked, "What are you planning to do this summer, Ben? Are you going back to Hatton?"

"Well, I'm . . ." Ben stopped. He shrugged. What was the use of explaining again that he was waiting for the Jenny so he could get started in commercial flying. The statement would trigger another series of polite questions and answers, and maybe Hannah still wouldn't believe he was serious.

"Well," Ben repeated, "I'm not really sure of my plans yet. But I hope you have a nice vacation."

"When are you leaving Fairbanks?" Hannah asked.

"Oh, I'll be here for some time," Ben replied. "You know I wouldn't miss President Harding's visit."

Over two weeks after school officially ended for the teachers, Ben walked to the narrow bridge spanning the Chena River. He listened for the whistle of the inbound train and finally heard it far off in the distance. Just as he turned to walk toward the depot, a truck screeched to a halt on the bridge. The driver leaned out the window of the cab and yelled, "Ben, there's a telegram for you down at the Signal Corps office!"

Ben started running. The telegram had to be about the plane. He just knew it. Suddenly, he thought about his family, then shook his head. It couldn't be bad news from home. He had just received a long letter from his father. No, it had to be about the plane.

Ben arrived at the telegraph office almost out of breath. He opened the door and burst into the small room. After claiming his telegram, he drew a deep breath. He read, "Airplane shipment left Seattle today, steamer *Northwestern*. Will arrive Seward 27 June. Please make necessary arrangements railroad shipment Seward to Fairbanks."

Ben felt like throwing the telegram in the air and cheering, but, instead, he walked sedately out of the office. Once outside, however, he said aloud, "She's on her way! I'm going to fly!"

Ben hurried to the office of the *News-Miner*. He rushed inside, waving the telegram, and related the news to Thompson.

"That's great," Thompson replied, "but we still have a long wait. That slow steamship! Well, we've been waiting this long, I guess another week or so won't hurt us. It's almost as exciting as waiting for President Harding. We have a lot to do before and after the plane gets here so we're ready for the President's aerial stunt show."

Harding's visit had been a favorite topic of conversation in Alaska for over a month. His visit would mark the first time a President of the United States set foot in Alaska. Alaskans had waited for years for a President to get a firsthand glimpse of the Territory and looked forward to showing off their beloved Alaska to him.

When news of the President's proposed visit first spread over the vast Territory, a presidential reception committee was formed in each community to lay plans for his visit. Each town tried to outdo the other by providing a spectacular reception with extra-special events. The President wasn't due in Fairbanks until after he participated in the golden spike ceremony in Nenana marking the official completion of the Alaska Railroad. But in Fairbanks, they weren't worried about being overshadowed. After all, Ben would be putting on his aerial stunt show. Who could top that?

When Ben and Thompson discussed the proposed aerial circus, Ben said, "I just hope nothing goes wrong. I was talking to an old-timer the other day and he said that sometimes the spring rains are really bad. He said we might even have some washouts along the railroad."

Thompson replied, "Well, Ben, I wasn't going to bring up that subject now. But as long as you have, just imagine how the railroad people feel. They're expecting the President on July 15, and if the floods hit at the usual time, I don't know how they'll get the roadbed back in shape for his visit."

Ben shook his head and replied, "If the trains aren't operating, how will we get the Jenny here in time to get it assembled? We'd better come up with some alternate plans. The way our luck has been running, the old-timers will be right. I could go to Chitina by car and get the Copper River train to Cordova, then get the boat and go to Seward. No trouble is expected with the railroad at that end. I could have the plane loaded on the train in Seward and then, if I had to, I could get off at Anchorage, unload the plane and assemble it there, and then fly it to Fairbanks. Except, there isn't an airfield in Anchorage."

During the next few days the weather was unseasonably hot, with temperatures reaching 90 to 95 degrees. Nervously, Ben watched the weather reports. Then, true to prediction, the rains came. Day after day heavy rains pelted down from Broad Pass to Fairbanks. High water in all the rivers and creeks in the area, especially between Cantwell, at Mile 320, and Brown, at Mile 383, made things even worse. Officials and repair crews of the Alaska Railroad were very uneasy.

Then their worst fears were realized. The bridges over the Cantwell River and Windy Creek were seriously damaged. A portion of the bridge over the Nenana River at Mile 370 was carried away in the rushing waters. Even bridges at the Healy River coal spur were heavily damaged. Ben heard each new report of disaster with a sinking heart. He next heard that considerable track on the Alaska Railroad had been washed out between Windy and Mt. McKinley Park. Then, the bank at Mile 353.2 slid out. Repairmen rushed there and found a 200-foot trestle would have to be rebuilt. There was no doubt that the railroad repair crews had a tremendous job ahead of them.

Talking to the man in charge of the Fairbanks depot, Ben found that it would not be possible to ship the plane by rail from Anchorage to Fairbanks for an indefinite period of time. The agent said that the Jenny could be loaded aboard the Alaska Railroad at Seward and brought to Anchorage, but with bridges out and the slide at Mile 353.2, service to Fairbanks was temporarily cut off. Although the target date for completion was an optimistic one because of President Harding's visit, nobody cared to set a specific time.

Ben couldn't stand sitting in Fairbanks doing nothing. He and Thompson again discussed alternate means of getting the Jenny to town. The Jenny had a limited range of about 300 miles. Ben wouldn't be able to fly it from Anchorage to Fairbanks unless he could refuel.

Although a plane had never made the flight from Anchorage to Fairbanks, Ben knew that it would be fairly easy because he had the tracks of the Alaska Railroad to follow. He told Thompson, "There are two ways to solve our problem of limited range. If I can get some bigger gas tanks built in Anchorage and have them installed, that would work. If I can't arrange for that, maybe I can refuel at Curry.[1] I know the trip can be arranged some way. Of course, there's still the big problem of finding an airfield in Anchorage and a place to assemble the plane."

Ben's worry over the lack of an airfield in Anchorage was a real one, because in the spring of 1923, Anchorage did not have a field or any planes in town. However, perhaps because they heard that Ben might have to assemble his Jenny there if the railroad repair work wasn't done, Anchorage residents decided to do something about building an airfield.

On a bright spring morning the whole town of Anchorage turned out. Equipped with horses and tractors and with axes, shovels, rakes, and other hand tools, they set to work. In record time volunteers cleared 16 acres of stumps and undergrowth for a municipal airfield. The *Anchorage Daily Times* applauded the work:

> Never in the history of the community did such a spectacle present itself as was enacted at the aviation field yesterday. Men from every walk of life, every nationality, and various races worked shoulder to shoulder. . . . Characteristic of the spirit of Alaska, there were no degrees of ranks, just one big family of enthusiastic men and women inspired with a great purpose.

After another day of waiting and another unfavorable report on the repair work, Ben asked Thompson, "Why don't I go and talk to Bobby Sheldon again?"

Bobby Sheldon operated the auto stage over the Richardson Trail from Fairbanks to Valdez. After making several inquiries around town, Ben located Sheldon at one of the garages. He explained his Anchorage plane assembly idea to Bobby.

"I'll be happy to take you along for company," Sheldon said. "I'm leaving at 2:00 P.M. today." He grinned and added, "Get ready for a rough ride. They call the Valdez-Fairbanks road the 'Richardson Trail' and trail it is!"

Promptly at the appointed time, Sheldon pulled up in front of the hotel, and Ben hopped into the five-passenger Model T. The two headed down the Richardson Trail. Sheldon explained that he was well prepared in case of a rough trip. He had four cases of Red Crown gasoline, a pick and a shovel, plenty of rope for a Spanish windlass in case they got stuck, plus the supplies ordered by various people along the route.

It was 317 miles to the Willow Creek fork to Chitina, where Ben could catch the train to Cordova. The Model T bumped and rattled along the rough road. About every two hours Ben asked, "Do you want me to drive, Bobby? I'll be glad to relieve you if you're tired." However, Sheldon seemed a little hesitant.

All along the route, crews were repairing bad sections of the road. Ben said, "There's still some talk that President Harding will leave the train at Fairbanks and drive over the Richardson Trail. If arrangments can be made and time permits, he will make the trip. Guess that's why there's so much activity today."

A few miles further down the road, Sheldon stopped the Model T and said, "All right, Ben, she's all yours." The two men quickly changed places. Ben needed no instructions for driving the car, as it was just like the one he used in Hatton for deliveries.

"You'll be one of the first to get a ride in the Jenny after I get it to Fairbanks," Ben assured Sheldon.

As they bumped along the rutted road, Ben asked, "When did you make the first trip from Fairbanks to Valdez, Bobby?"

Sheldon laughed as he recalled, "Back in 1913. When I first suggested the trip, the old-timers thought I should either be given a lunacy test on the spot or be shipped directly to Morningside Asylum in Washington."[2]

Ben retorted, "I know from experience that it's not easy to suggest something new. How did you make out on that first trip?"

"If you think we've been over some bad sections today," Sheldon replied, "you should have seen the trail then. It was terrible, but I managed to drive a Ford all the way from Fairbanks to Valdez. I proved what I set out to prove. Now the Richardson Trail is a motorway, but there were many people who thought it would always remain a trail. There's been a lot of work on it since 1913. Ever since 1920 it's been called the best dirt road in America."

When the two finally reached the Willow Creek fork to Chitina, they parted. "Thanks very much, Bobby," Ben said. "I'll catch the train to Cordova here."

As Sheldon prepared to leave, Ben called, "Don't forget, Bobby, you have a free plane ride coming. I'll see you back in Fairbanks soon."

The timing was perfect. Ben boarded the Copper River and Northwestern Railroad immediately. He arrived in Cordova just in time to board the steamer *Northwestern* there. When the boat arrived in Seward, Ben supervised the unloading of the crated plane and had the Jenny reloaded on an Alaska Railroad freight car. There were rumors in Seward that trains soon would be running through to Fairbanks.

At the depot in Anchorage, Ben heard that the rumors were true. The repair work was completed on the stretch between Cantwell and Fairbanks. Ben was a little disappointed, for in his mind he was prepared for the flight between Anchorage and Fairbanks. He knew Anchorage people would be disappointed, too. Yet, he also knew that it would be much faster to assemble the plane in Fairbanks as originally planned. But he assured people in Anchorage that their field would get much use later.

Ben decided to double-check with the railroad agent, who reported that all of the repair work was completed and standby crews were stationed at critical points. He said that the weather was clear in Fairbanks, and even if more rain came, there was little danger of washouts. The depot agent added, "I think you're more excited about getting that plane to Fairbanks than you are about President Harding's visit."

Ben grinned and replied, "As a matter of fact, I am. I have to assemble the plane before the President's arrival. I'm scheduled to put on an aerial stunt show when he visits Fairbanks."

As the train pulled out of the Anchorage depot, Ben sat back and relaxed for the first time since he had left Fairbanks with Bobby Sheldon. Barring any further trouble, the plane would be assembled on schedule.

ENDNOTES

1. Curry, Mile 248.5, was the halfway point between the coast and the interior on the Alaska Railroad. Passengers spent the night in the Curry Hotel, operated by the railroad. The hotel had excellent accommodations for 150 guests. After a day of traveling on the Alaska Railroad, most guests were nodding over dinner and in a

hurry to get upstairs to bed and fall instantly asleep to the murmur of the Susitna River.

2. For many years Alaska did not have its own insane asylum. All mental patients were shipped outside to Morningside Asylum in Washington. Alaskans were fond of saying there were three sides to Alaska—inside, outside, and Morningside.

14

Wings over Fairbanks and Nenana—1923

THE TRAIN WITH THE CRATED JENNY pulled into the Fairbanks depot on July 1, 1923, but there was no time for rest. Ben rushed to supervise the unloading. Thompson, Dick Wood, and Ira Farnsworth, one of the best mechanics in town, were all at the depot to help. They had rounded up a crew of men to haul everything to the ballpark.

Thompson stated loudly, "Now that the plane is here, our problems are all solved. We've got two whole days to get the Jenny assembled. Oh, I forgot to tell you, Ben, the folks up at Nenana already have tickets printed because I assured them you would be there on the Fourth of July to put on a little stunt show. Well, I'll see you fellows later. I'm going to the office and write a story about this. Keep me posted!"

The ballpark was bustling all day. First, the men carefully assembled the undercarriage, attached the wheels, and connected the wheels to the fuselage. The fragile wings were mated to the body. Sturdy guy wires were laced between.

"She's beginning to take shape," Farnsworth said, "but the biggest job will be mounting the engine and bolting it in place."

The men struggled and strained, but with the help of a block and tackle, the heavy engine was lifted, and Farnsworth bolted it into position.

Anyone watching the scene at the ballpark might well have thought that assembling a plane was an everyday occurrence, but there were hecklers who took bets on the plane ever flying. Turning to look at a man who bet against a successful flight, one of the high school boys, who by now all but idolized Ben, said, "Excuse me, sir, but Mr. Eielson said the plane is going to fly, so I know it's going to fly!"

Ben smiled and kept on working, but after a momentary silence, he added, "It's a used war surplus Jenny, but she'll fly all right."

On the night of July 2, the completely exhausted men finally called a halt. Ben was so keyed up he was unable to sleep. After pacing back and forth in his hotel room, he wrote out a list of things to be done. Instead of going to bed, he went back to the ballpark. The sight of the almost completed Jenny was reassuring. He sighed in relief. Suddenly, much of the tenseness of the past weeks disappeared, and he realized how tired he was. Since there was no reason to return to the hotel—it was almost dawn—Ben stretched out under the wing of the ship, his head pillowed on some wadded-up packing material. He used his jacket for a blanket. Just before he dropped off to sleep, he thought about the many times he had slept by his first Jenny during his barnstorming days. He smiled as he recalled some of his needless worries then.

The next thing he heard was Farnsworth's voice calling, "Ben, wake up!" Ira was shaking him vigorously by one shoulder and repeating, "Wake up, Ben. We've got a lot of work to do today."

Dazed, Ben sat up and rubbed his eyes. Farnsworth asked, "What are you doing here, anyway? You needed a good night's sleep."

Ben stretched, yawned, and replied, "Well, I did get a couple of hours of sleep. I'll have to go home and change now."

Soon sidewalk superintendents arrived. One of the men studied the huge gas tanks and in a disdainful manner asked Farnsworth, "After you get those bulky tanks filled with gas, how much additional weight can the plane carry?"

Striding up behind the speaker, Ben overheard the question and answered, "The plane will lift 400 pounds besides me."

Sometimes Ben explained facts about flying to the hecklers. "There's room for one passenger plus freight. Once we actually get our commercial transportation business started, we can add an extra gas tank to increase our range. Then, of course, if we are short of freight on some trips, we can carry two passengers, if they don't weigh too much."

Soon Thompson appeared and said, "Yesterday I wrote in my

column, 'Lieutenant Eielson will surely fly tomorrow! Tomorrow sometime, the flier intends to fly the Jenny over OUR TOWN.'"

"I read that," Ben said, "and the day's not over yet. Don't give up so easily." Ben ended the conversation abruptly and ducked under one of the wings to check the fuel line connections.

"Listen, don't any of you realize the importance of this occasion?" Thompson asked. "This is the first locally owned plane to be assembled in Fairbanks. . . . Now, Ben, you've got to finish that plane so you can practice for the Fourth of July exhibition in Nenana. I tell you, boys, Fairbanks is taking the lead in this aviation business."

Ben and the crew had hoped to be finished by 6:00 P.M., as a baseball game was scheduled then, but the men were still working on the Jenny. Earl Borland, a mechanic who worked for the road commission, joined them. When Ben noticed the uniformed members of the rival teams coming for the game, he said, "Let's get the Jenny rolled back in the outfield out of their way. I wouldn't want someone to hit a home run and damage one of the wings."

The spindly Jenny was banished to the outfield. After a few minutes of practice, the two teams started to play. During July, Fairbanks has almost 22 hours of daylight, so there were no problems connected with working on the plane or playing baseball.

After the game ended about 8:30 P.M., curious baseball fans drifted over and gathered around the Jenny. They were just in time to hear Ben say, "All right, she's just about ready."

A few minutes later they heard Ben call, "Let's push her to home plate; then I'll take her for a trial spin."

"I'll go get Mr. Thompson and Mr. Wood," one of the youngsters said. "They don't want to miss the takeoff." He headed for town on the run.

"I'll spin the propeller for you," Farnsworth said. "Let's hope she starts the first time."

"Good," Ben said, then added, "Before you spin the prop, be sure the spectators are out of the way. I'll take off toward left field."

As the people fell back, Ben called, "No, don't all of you leave. We need some help to roll the Jenny out to the beginning of our runway."

The men surged forward and rolled the plane into position. Ben tucked in his shirt, wiped the sweat from his face, and vaulted into the pilot's wicker seat in the open cockpit. He put on his helmet and just before he pulled his goggles down called, "All aboard for the first flight of the Farthest North Airplane Company!"

Ben nodded and straightened his goggles. Farnsworth spun the prop. The OX-5 engine coughed and died.

"What did I tell you?" a man's loud voice questioned, breaking the silence. "He'll never get that rig off the ground."

Farnsworth took a deep breath and swung the propeller again. The engine chugged and died.

"You want to add another $10 to that bet?" called the pessimistic gentleman to his friend, who happened to be one of Ben's ardent supporters.

"How about making it $25?" Ben's friend asked.

Ben signaled to Farnsworth, who swung the prop again. The engine roared to life. With his head cocked forward, Ben held the throttle, listening to the steady throb of the engine. As he pushed the throttle forward, the engine quickened. The entire fuselage trembled, and the Jenny lurched forward.

After checking the controls, Ben finally raised his head and waved gaily. He again adjusted his helmet and goggles as the Jenny started to roll down the improvised runway. Ben glanced from side to side, making sure everyone was out of the way. He fed full power to the engine, and the little Jenny leaped into the outfield, bounced, skidded, and, on the second run, lifted and surged upward. With his hand firmly on the stick, Ben guided the little plane into a gradual climb.

The Jenny gained altitude, and Ben circled the ballpark. The wind whipped through the open cockpit, sweeping away the last of his anxieties. He wondered idly why he had ever thought he could just teach school.

The plane picked up speed as Ben guided it toward the two-story red schoolhouse. He circled the school and dipped first one wing and then the other in salute. Ben was elated. He felt the Jenny was equal to any plane he'd flown, not as big and powerful as a DeHavilland, but airworthy nonetheless.

He kicked the rudder, and the Jenny went into a sharp skidding turn. He hit the stick and nose-dived downward. Then he gained altitude and circled lazily around the edges of town.

Ben roared back over the ballpark and looked down at the tiny figures in the park. He flew back and forth over the main street. Soon he noticed other figures scurrying from the stores and log homes in the next block. Most of them pointed upward, gesturing wildly, their white faces turned skyward.

In that instant, Ben remembered the constant heckling and sarcastic remarks of the doubters. Ever since the crated Jenny was first unloaded, some men with opposing views had been having a heyday. There were only a few, but they'd kept insisting he would never get the plane to fly.

Ben suddenly dipped the plane down into a steep dive. It looked as if he would surely crash. Abruptly, at the last possible moment, Ben pulled out of the dive. The Jenny gained altitude. "That rig will never get in the air," skeptics had said. "Well," Ben said to himself, "this time I'll show them."

He headed straight for the Chena Bridge, where there was no traffic. Ben plummeted downward. Again at the last moment he pulled out of the steep dive and roared upward, gaining altitude for yet another dive.

As a spur-of-the-moment extra, Ben swung in a wide circle. Holding the ship steady, he pulled tight pylon-eights around the twin smokestacks of the Northern Commercial Company. He saw another group of people running toward the ballpark.

He climbed aloft once more with lazy spirals, as if climbing a staircase. He swooped low over the ballpark, and the cheering spectators scattered in all directions. By now he felt almost guilty, sure the stockholders were scared sick the plane would crash. He decided to save the rest of his tricks and put the Jenny into a turn, held it to a slow glide, and then set it down gently on the rutted grass of the ballpark.

A large group of people came running toward the Jenny, everyone talking and shouting at once.

"That was quite a show!" Dick Wood exclaimed. "For a minute there I thought I had lost my investment before the Farthest North Airplane Company even got into business."

One of the mechanics asked, "How can that frail plane stay in one piece when you throw it around like that?"

"These ships can take a lot of punishment," Ben replied, "but there are some things we have to check out yet. The Jenny's left-wing heavy. We'll have to take a couple turns on the turnbuckle on that side."

Ignoring the mechanics and the discussion underway, Thompson questioned in a loud voice, "How does this sound? At 9 o'clock on the third day of July 1923, Professor C. B. Eielson went aloft in his airplane. His machine had never been flown before; the engine never turned over; the wires and wings never tested off the ground. . . ."

Ben wasn't listening. He walked slowly over the improvised runway, along with several of the men. Ben pointed out the ruts and rough spots. He asked, "I wonder if the baseball players would mind if we widened and leveled our 'runway' a little more. That should take care of most of the bad spots."

"I'll stay here and guard the plane," one of the high school boys volunteered. "You'd better get something to eat. You haven't had anything yet today."

It wasn't until Ben was seated at the table with his steak in front of him that he realized how exhausted he was. He picked at his food and finally said, "I guess I'm too tired to eat. I'll go check at the ballpark again and then get some sleep."

At the ballpark Ben found that two of his former students had decided to sleep by the plane. He laughed and said, "There's really no need for two of you to guard the plane all night, you know. But if that's what you want to do and your parents know where you are, it's all right with me."

Ben returned to the hotel for the night. The next thing he knew it was morning and there was noise in the street. It was the crew decorating for the Fourth of July. He peered out the window. "Perfect flying weather for the Nenana trip," he thought. He dressed hurriedly and left to collect some shovels, hoes, and rakes.

When he arrived at the ballpark, the boys were still fast asleep. He began shoveling to level the biggest humps. "Unless I get some help," he thought, "I'll still be here when the show is set to go on at Nenana."

In a few minutes Farnsworth showed up with a gallon of white paint and a brush. The day before, in a surge of civic pride, he had lettered "FAIRBANKS" in huge letters across the side of the Jenny.

Farnsworth waved to Ben and called, "I think I'll get the paint on my sign first so it can be drying, and then we can check the plane."

Soon Farnsworth was busy painting. He called to Ben, "Now, this sign is going to show up fine. If you get lost, at least the people will know where you're from."

Then several businessmen appeared. "Let me give you a hand with the leveling, Mr. Eielson," one of them said. "Pilots shouldn't have to shovel dirt. Anybody can do that."

As the volunteer staff increased, Ben divided the men and boys into two crews, and the work went even faster.

For the afternoon Fourth of July performance in Fairbanks, Ben was billed as "THE GREATEST LIVING FLIER, THE AERIAL DARE-DEVIL" who was to give Fairbanks residents their first Alaska aerial circus.

The Fourth of July was always one of Alaska's biggest celebrations, but this Fourth was extra special. By the time the Jenny was ready to take off, a huge crowd filled the bleachers. There were miners, trappers, merchants, fishermen, Eskimos, and Indians. The eager crowd spilled over onto the ball field.

Ben finished checking the plane. He climbed into the cockpit, Ira spun the prop, and the OX-5 engine sputtered to life. Earl Borland, the other mechanic who had helped Ben to gain experience with airplane engines, grinned in delight.

Ben guided the Jenny down the newly leveled runway. He fed gas to the engine; it roared. The Jenny raced forward, bounced, and took off. For the next 30 minutes Ben did every trick he knew. He looped, dived, and spun the plane all over the Alaska sky. When he swooped low in a nose dive, he could hear faint cheers from the ballpark. He could tell by the way the crowd waved and the spectators followed each maneuver that they enjoyed it.

He looped and then flipped the Jenny right side up and circled the ballpark lazily. He made a sharp turn and came in for a landing. Pushing his goggles up over his forehead, he sat quietly in the cockpit. The people of Fairbanks were wild with excitement. Then Ben climbed out of the cockpit, and their cheers grew louder as they rushed to greet him.

Dick Wood hurried forward, waving a telegram from Nenana. Ben looked at his watch; the sun was still high. There would be plenty of time to fly there, put on the show, and be back in Fairbanks before the sun went down.

"How about flying to Nenana with me, Dick?" Ben asked. "I need someone to handle the finances."

Wood looked at the Jenny and started to shake his head. Then he glanced at Ben. After a pause he asked, "Will you land the plane and let me off first before you start doing all your fancy stunts?"

"If that's the way you want it, Dick, that's the way it'll be," Ben replied.

"Well, I suppose someone has to show these people that our airplane company can carry passengers too. Give me a few minutes to think about it, Ben."

A short time later, after the plane had been refueled and checked, Ben again climbed into the pilot's seat. "All set for the flight to Nenana," he called.

Dick Wood nodded. He was already sitting in the passenger's seat. According to Thompson, Wood had decided to make the trip after he was "well fortified with Alaska mule." The Jenny lifted gracefully.

Fairbanks friends who witnessed the event later reported that it was a little disturbing to see two of the best men in town, sitting one behind the other in a rig not much wider than a canoe, preparing to lunge skyward.

Ben circled the ballpark and dipped his wings in farewell. The crowd watched until the Jenny disappeared into the spaceless sky. They would hear nothing further until Nenana residents wired that the plane had arrived safely.

Earl Borland shivered. He thought, "If we don't get good news, we might never know what happened." He turned to Farnsworth and said, "I think I want to get into airplane mechanic work. After the past few days, my job at the Alaska Road Commission will seem pretty dull. Then, someday, I want to take pilot's training and learn to fly."

Before the two left they advised the others that they would spread the word as soon as they heard from Nenana. The crowd finally dispersed.

True to prediction, Ben had an easy run. Quite a distance out of Fairbanks he spotted the excursion train slowly crawling along heading for Nenana. He swooped low over the train. Ben shouted to Wood and throttled back, timing his speed to that of the train (a trick he had learned during his barnstorming days). Ben flew the length of the train, turned, and flew back alongside the train, window high. He lifted his hand in greeting to the scores of surprised faces pressed against the windows. Abruptly, he climbed back up.

"Dick," he yelled, "how do you like flying?"

There was no answer. Ben looked at Wood, who was slumped in his seat. All Ben could see was Wood's tie standing up in the slipstream. With a guilty start Ben realized that although he had cautioned Wood carefully about buckling the safety belt and helmet securely and properly fastening the goggles, he also had promised not to do any tricks until after Wood was out of the plane. He really hadn't planned the stunt with the train.

In Nenana, the eager residents crowded the ballpark field. Ben's initial flight on February 21, 1923, marked itself deeply into Nenana history. The result was that advance ticket sales for Ben's Fourth of July appearance were tremendous; the show was sold out. Programs were printed billing "Benny Eielson, the world's greatest airplane pilot" as the main feature of the big celebration. Such an occasion was made of Ben's appearance that officials planned to issue certificates to those present so they might go home and prove that they had witnessed the performance.

Nenana was at the foot of a bluff at a point where the big Tanana River made an abrupt turn. The corkscrewing Tanana, bigger than all the other streams, made patterns on the greenish tundra. The day was perfectly clear, and sighting the bluff and the bridge, Ben started his landing pattern. No matter what the field was like, it couldn't be much worse than the one in Fairbanks.

Ben circled the field, lowered the ship carefully at each turn, and glided the Jenny in for a smooth landing. Wood, reaching over the cockpit, offered his hand to Ben, saying, "Nice work, Ben. Thanks for one of the most thrilling experiences of my life."

The reception committee gathered around the Jenny and greeted the air travelers warmly. After a round of welcoming speeches, the head of the committee said, "Professor Eielson, we're going to have President Harding here in Nenana in a couple of weeks to drive the golden spike on the Alaska Railroad. Some of us decided that it would be nice to have you come back for the dedication ceremonies and do a couple of stunts for the President."

Before Ben could answer, Wood stepped forward and said, "We've already arranged for Eielson to put on a special stunt show in Fairbanks."

The head of the committee laughed and replied, "We might have known you'd try to top the golden spike ceremony we're having in Nenana."

Ben turned from his work on the plane and added, "Sorry I can't make it for the dedication ceremonies here, but keep me in mind. I'll be doing commercial flying out of Fairbanks this summer. Maybe we can accommodate you some other time."

One of the committee members handed Wood $500 and said, "We're not expecting anything bad to happen to you, Mr. Eielson, but we thought it would be better if you knew we'd paid in advance."

"Yes," Ben laughed, "I know what you're trying to say." He turned to the blushing Wood and caught a look of pure panic on the banker's face. Wood grabbed his arm and said, "Look, Ben, this $500 is peanuts. If you think there's any danger, well, maybe two aerial stunt shows in one day is just too much."

Ben laughed and replied, "That's what I did barnstorming—two shows a day. Everything will be fine."

A young man stepped up and offered to help refuel and check the plane. Ben smiled and shook hands. He was glad the man happened along to break the tension.

"My name is Freddie Moller, Mr. Eielson. I'm mighty pleased to meet you. I'm going to learn all about airplanes because someday I'm going to fly one of my own when I go prospecting again."

"Thanks," Ben said. "I'll give you a rundown on what needs to be done, then she's all yours, Freddie, until I'm ready to take off again."

Sensing that Freddie was reliable, Ben had no qualms about turning the plane over to him. He had found another good Alaskan aircraft mechanic in the making.

After a rousing piece from the town band, the master of ceremonies introduced Ben and Wood. An expectant hush fell as he announced the big event of the day.

Ben taxied down the length of the runway, the exhaust pipes

spitting thin blue columns of smoke. Wood, surrounded by Nenana civic leaders, showed his pride as the Jenny circled the field. "There's no doubt about where that plane is from," he announced, looking at the huge white letters spelling "FAIRBANKS" against the dull-colored cloth fuselage.

For the second time that day, Ben put the Jenny through the familiar and intricate series of stunts. He did whip stalls, Immelmann turns, spins, loops, power spirals, falling leaves, grass-cutting, and all the stunts he had done earlier in the day in Fairbanks. Suddenly, he realized that he had been cavorting in the air for almost an hour and knew that it was time to land.

On impulse, Ben streaked toward the Tanana River and then flipped the plane upside down directly over the ball field. Clearing a low cabin roof with only inches to spare after a power dive, the plane shot upward again. Finally, Ben settled the Jenny down on the runway.

The cheers of the spectators were deafening, but Ben appeared not to hear. He thought to himself, "I'll never teach school again, but I won't be a stunt flier always. There's more serious flying to be done."

Freddie came up, sputtering, "Can I learn to fly?"

Ben gripped his hand and said, "You can if you want to badly enough."

Ben chalked up another Alaskan convert to aviation and laid on the encouragement. He was anxious to begin the ground chores, but Freddie took over, saying that he "remembered it all." Escorted by the reception committee and a beaming Dick Wood, Ben was led to the head table. After a round of speeches and many words of praise, the head of the committee signaled that it was time to eat.

Much later, Freddie arrived. He managed to squirm his way through the crowd and squeeze himself into a seat next to Ben. He monopolized the conversation and Ben as he told of his dreams. "The Arctic holds great riches. My friend, Alfred Brooks, the chief geologist for the United States government in Alaska, and I have talked about it for years. Yes, sir, Ben, the most inaccessible places in Alaska hold the biggest promise. That's why I've got to learn to fly. What's the best way for me to get started?"

It began to look as though several of the people waiting to meet

Ben were about to move Freddie bodily if he didn't stop talking. Freddie jumped up and said, "I'm leaving, I'm leaving." But he added one last remark: "When I learn to fly, the only passengers I'm going to fool around with are prospectors!"

The head of the Nenana civic group took Ben's arm and said, "Now, Mr. Eielson, we've got a lot of people waiting to meet you and some big entertainment planned. We're having a banquet and a dance tonight, so let's get started. We've already wired Fairbanks and told them not to expect you until tomorrow afternoon." Ben and Wood enjoyed a festive evening.

Evidence of how pleased Nenana folks were with Ben's aerial circus appeared when the *Nenana News* came out the next morning. The report read:

> There were somersaults, nose dives, spins, and a variety of other feats which kept the spectators in a state of tense excitement. The excitement assumed the proportions of a panic when the plane came swiftly across the field straight at a nearby cabin. Collision was cleverly avoided, however, by a slight movement of the wings which tilted the plane over the house.

The next day when Ben and Wood landed at the Fairbanks ballpark, they found many people had come to the field just to see how Wood looked and what he would say about the trip. Wood was not only very much alive, but he spilled over with enthusiasm.

During Ben and Wood's absence, Thompson was busy inserting several large ads in the *News-Miner.* One ad read:

> STARTING TODAY
> TO TAKE PASSENGERS UP
> FIRST COME FIRST SERVED
> LT. C. B. EIELSON, AVIATOR

One ad asked:

> TIME FLIES? WHEN WILL YOU?

It continued:

> A THRILL YOU WILL REMEMBER ALL YOUR LIFE!

Another ad read:

During the next few days, Ben had customers lined up at the ballpark at all hours waiting to take joy rides. Charges were as high as $50 for eight minutes of flight. Sometimes, those who waited the longest for a ride were the most rewarded, for as the lines thinned out each day, Ben extended the length of the flights a little.

Although Ben tried to be fair with everyone, the temptation to fly over new territory sometimes took precedence over concern for payment. Ben's passengers noticed that he constantly jotted down things in his notebook. He marked various landmarks and, as soon as he landed, hastily improved on his original sketches. He memorized the names of scores of little creeks hidden in the gullies and low hills north of Fairbanks. He became especially familiar with the Fox and the Chatanika areas. He had the Jenny in the air every minute possible.

One day Ben met Bobby Sheldon on the street. Sheldon later reported on the incident: "Ben approached me with his usual broad grin. I knew he was going to offer me a ride. I began to sicken."

Ben said, "Bobby, I haven't forgotten my promise to you, and tonight about 7:00 P.M. I'll take you on that plane ride. First, I will give Dorothy and Florence Roth a ride. When you hear the plane coming in, I want you to come over."

Shortly after 7:00 P.M., Ben landed, helped the Roth girls out, dumped a five-gallon can of gasoline in the tank, and motioned for Bobby to get in. Sheldon's wife cried as he kissed her and the baby goodbye. Then Sheldon climbed aboard the Jenny, as nervous as any passenger Ben had ever had.

Seated in the cockpit, Sheldon remained anxious. One reason may have been that he expected Ben to do some stunting, and he wasn't wrong. When they finally landed safely, after more than a half-hour in the air and a complete survey of the Tanana Valley, Sheldon was cured of wanting to be an aviator.

One day after Ben landed, Farnsworth admonished, "Ben, we'd better slow down on these joy rides and get the Jenny in shape for President Harding's exhibition. Everything must go exactly right."

"Don't worry," Ben said. "I've been doing a little planning myself. But, you're right; we'd better get the Jenny in tiptop shape. Of all my stunt shows, this one must be the best!"

15

The First Commercial Flights

AFTER THE HISTORIC HAMMERING of the golden spike by President Harding in Nenana, the party continued on to an eagerly waiting Fairbanks. Things started in the afternoon when the President made a speech to a huge crowd at the ballpark. The temperature stood at 94 degrees. During the speech, three people collapsed from heat prostration. President Harding frequently mopped his brow and remarked that his party suffered more from the heat in Fairbanks than it had at any time since it left Hutchinson, Kansas. "It is something we scarcely expected to encounter this far north," he said with a smile, indicating that one more of his preconceived fears had fallen away.

An aerial stunt show by Lieutenant Eielson was announced as the highlight of the day. Ben was determined to prove any boast that Thompson had made. He felt truly an Alaskan while performing his death-defying stunts over Fairbanks. He realized that he was taking part in more than just a stunt-flying exhibition. He was heralding the beginning of a new chapter in the history of transportation for interior Alaska. With the official dedication of the Alaska Railroad now history, he must prove the airplane's capabilities to Alaskans.

On that memorable afternoon, Ben put the little Jenny through all the intricate maneuvers he had ever used in aerial exhibitions. The stunt show was one of the most daring and technically perfect he had ever performed. The huge crowd went wild.

After the President and members of his official party shook hands with Ben and congratulated him on his performance, one official said, "Mr. Eielson, if today's performance means anything, we'll be hearing a lot more about you."

In the group of officials on the Fairbanks field that day were several men Ben had already corresponded with concerning the need for airmail service in Alaska. Since their arrival, Ben had personally contacted those to whom he had written letters.

When Ben finished his exhibition for the President, he experienced the usual letdown. Yet, even before he had time to finish servicing the plane, Wood, in company with a portly gentleman, rushed over to meet him. The gentleman was R. F. Roth, the attorney for the Stewart-Denhart mine on Stewart Creek. There had been a breakdown at the mine, and every hour it was shut down cost the company money. Wood said, "Roth wants to know if you can fly him over there today with some machine parts. The company wants you to pick up the mail that's been piling up for the past month and take that over, too. I told Mr. Roth that judging from our trip to Nenana, it would probably take about an hour to fly there. If we can't fly the parts there, it will take six days to ship them by boat."

Roth hesitated a moment and then asked, "How about it, Mr. Eielson. Can you leave today?"

"Well, we can't leave until the ball game is over." Ben stopped and asked, "How about a landing field or a level spot near the mine?"

Roth replied, "The fellows at the mine already know about you and your Jenny, and they've cleared a good landing strip near the mine."

Ben nodded and said, "Let's go look at my map."

"Oh, you won't need a map, Professor Eielson, I mean Lieutenant Eielson. I'll be glad to show you the way."

Eielson grinned when he heard Roth call him Lieutenant Eielson. He knew this was another of Thompson's ideas. The old editor had decided that the head pilot of the Farthest North Airplane Company surely rated a fancier title than The Flying Professor.

Ben laid out his map on the workbench in the improvised hangar where the Jenny was being worked on and said, "I'm sure we can find the mine."

"But I already know how to get to the mine," Roth interjected.

"Have you ever seen the country from the air?" Ben asked.

Tracing the route to Stewart Creek very carefully, Ben jotted down the mileage. He noted aloud that with no head winds and the Jenny's engine turning over smoothly, it would take between 1 hour and 1 hour 15 minutes to reach the mine. He told Roth his margin of safety would be very slim. He studied for a minute, then retraced the route, pointing it out on the map to Roth. He said, "We could make an emergency landing here at Munson if we had to. I know there's a supply of gas there if we need it."

"I figured you'd fly in a straight line," Roth said. "Guess I didn't stop to think about the need for refueling or an emergency landing place."

"How much do you weigh?" Ben asked suddenly.

"What?" Roth asked in surprise. "Why do you need to know that?"

Ben could tell that Roth plainly considered this last question impertinent. He tried to explain by adding, "I'm sorry. I should have explained something first. If you and the machine parts and the mail don't gross over 400 pounds, that's fine. If the total weight is over that, we'll have to leave something behind and make two trips. We might as well figure it out right now."

"Oh, I see," Roth replied sheepishly. "Well, I weigh about 205 pounds."

Ben nodded and asked, "Why don't you have the parts delivered here so we can get them loaded?"

"I know that mining country like the back of my hand," Roth added. "We'll make it in fine shape." Then he left to get the machine parts. Ben finished checking the Jenny before he rejoined the presidential party and watched the ball game.

When the game ended and the teams cleared the field, Ben supervised the loading of the freight. Farnsworth called, "All aboard," and spun the prop. The heavily laden ship took off sluggishly.

Roth was seated in the passenger cockpit holding on as if his life depended on the strength of his grasp. He said aloud, "Whew, I didn't think we were going to clear those trees."

If Ben heard him, he didn't answer. The Jenny climbed slowly, but Ben was pleased. Even with a heavy load, it cleared the scrub trees.

Ben began feeding gas to the laboring engine to achieve maximum efficiency. Looking from one side to the other, he checked every curve and twist in the streams as they flowed past under the canvas wings. He mentally compared the aerial view of the landscape with the penciled route he had traced earlier in the day. The paper map and the scene below certainly bore no resemblance to each other.

Ben smiled and looked carefully at Roth. He was planning to shout and ask Roth if the country he'd reported he knew like the back of his hand looked at all familiar from the air, but Roth was still hunched low in the passenger's seat, hanging on.

The day was bright and clear. Ben was so elated over his first commercial flight that he didn't even feel the strain of the past 10 days. The engine ran smoothly, and the Jenny made good time.

About an hour later, Ben heard an excited yell from Roth. He looked down and saw smoke curling up from a tiny clearing on the left. Raw earth was heaped in thick piles beside gaping holes in the ground. A tram car was poised on a set of wooden rails. It looked like a child's toy from the air. From the way Roth waved his arms, Ben was certain that they had reached the Stewart-Denhart mine.

Peering intently over the side of the pilot's cockpit, Ben saw tiny figures running toward a small clearing. Making a low pass over the area, Ben found that he couldn't land in the spot prepared by the miners. Almost in the center of the clearing three stumps pointed upward like jagged miniature mountain peaks.

Gunning the Jenny, Ben lifted it high over the surrounding trees and began circling the area off to one side. He picked out a small sandbar about a quarter mile from the mine, where the surface looked smooth. The swift waters of Stewart Creek swirled on both sides of the sand strip. When Ben flew over the sandbar, two of the men from the mine ran beneath the plane. They frantically cleared rocks and debris from the area while Ben circled above.

Ben decided the sandbar, although not completely cleared, was better than the prepared landing site. He circled again and dipped his wings so that the men could clear several of the bigger rocks out of the new runway he'd chosen. Finally, he brought the Jenny in. The wheels touched the sandbar, the plane bounced, and then it stopped less than 3 feet from the water. Soon the miners were running through the underbrush along the shore shouting a welcome to Ben and Roth.

Roth climbed awkwardly out of the plane and said, "Fine landing, Ben, although," he grinned, "I didn't expect to land here."

"This sandbar is lots better than the strip back by the mine," Ben replied. Checking his watch, he added, "Right on time."

The miners unloaded the parts and the mail into a small boat while Ben and Roth hopped ashore. At the request of one of the men, Ben walked to the strip the miners had prepared to inspect it. Several of the men followed him. "Too rough, is it?" the man asked. "This is the first time we've tried to build a landing field."

Ben could tell that the men were disappointed he'd landed on the sandbar instead of using their clearing. He knew preparing the field represented many hours of hurried and hard work.

"If you'll clear these stumps out of the center here," Ben said, kicking the offending stumps to emphasize his point, "I'll be able to land here next time."

"That's good," the man said, "because we want to make sure there is a next time. We'd like to set up regular plane service between the mine and Fairbanks. We'll fix this place any way you want it."

"Good," Ben replied, "and don't feel too bad about your landing strip. You should see the ball field we use in Fairbanks. It's only 1,200 feet long! You fellows did a pretty fair job at that. A little dynamite under those stumps and the clearing extended a few more feet, and this will be a good place to land."

"Before very long I guess you'll be landing in many out-of-the-way places," the man added. "Lots of small isolated settlements will demand air service soon."

Roth appeared at the clearing and asked, "You'll be flying here regularly, won't you, Ben?" He hesitated a minute, then added, "Dick Wood said to talk to you about drawing up a contract for regular service. I guess the men already told you they'll improve the strip to meet your specifications."

"I'll work on a contract as soon as we get back," Ben replied. "I'm sure we can arrange a regular schedule."

"Let's go have a cup of coffee," a miner suggested. "Lawyer Roth has to complete his legal work, and the mechanics are already busy installing new parts. One of our mechanics wants to help you service the plane, too."

"I'll be back for that coffee when we finish working on the plane," Ben said. "Keep it hot."

One of the men at the mine worked with Ben. Later, the coffee break gave the miners a chance to get caught up on the latest news from Fairbanks. Finally, when Ben was ready to take off, his crew of helpers had grown to three. The men lined up holding hands; the one on the end spun the propeller. After one false start, the Jenny roared to life. Ben guided the ship down the narrow sandbar. Emptied, it lifted easily. Roth and Ben waved to the miners, who stood in a semicircle on the shore, waving until the plane was out of sight.

All during the return flight the frail Jenny bucked head winds. For the first time since the plane was assembled in Fairbanks, the OX-5 engine seemed too tiny to Ben. He looked at Roth and imagined that his passenger was a little uneasy. The portly lawyer was bent over almost double. In spite of himself, Ben laughed as he thought, "Roth probably thinks we'll never see Fairbanks again."

Looking to each side of the plane, Ben mentally checked off the landmarks. The homeward flight was anything but smooth. An hour passed. Ben knew that he and Roth would soon be home. In a few minutes he sighted the twin stacks of the Northern Commercial Company. Turning the Jenny slightly to the left, Ben sped low over the Chena slough. He circled the ballpark, fishtailing in over the birch trees. The little ship rolled to a stop. They had been in the air 75 minutes on the return flight.

Ben stretched and rubbed his hands together. He had been up since 6:00 A.M. It had been a full day. Roth heaved a sigh of relief as he straightened himself and climbed shakily out of the plane. "It was a great experience, Ben," he said weakly. "I'll check with you soon, and we'll get a contract and schedule worked out to suit you."

Ben smiled and asked, "Are you feeling all right?"

"Fine, just fine," Roth replied, "but I liked the flight over much better than the one coming back."

The stockholders of the Farthest North Airplane Company arrived at the field, anxious to hear the details of the trip.

Soon, the news of the first commercial flight in interior Alaska went over the military telegraph wires stretching along the banks of the Yukon, leapfrogging to Unalakleet, St. Michael, and Nome. The message tapped out in isolated relay cabins along the trail read: "History was made today in interior Alaska with the first commercial payload carried aloft in a plane. Lt. Ben Eielson piloted his plane from Fairbanks to Stewart Creek, carrying passenger, freight, and mail. More flights are planned in the future."

Thompson, bubbling over with enthusiasm for aviation, wrote in the *News-Miner*:

> Lawyer Roth was loaded into the Jenny—200 some pounds of him—and with mail and machinery parts Lt. C. B. Eielson made the first commercial trip out of Fairbanks to the Stewart-Denhart mine. After paying Eielson more than he asked for the trip, Stewart and Denhart figured . . . that it had cost them $450 less to get their lawyer and supplies from Fairbanks by air than it would have cost them over the trail, and they were served by the airplane in an hour where it would have taken six days by trail. The Farthest North Airplane Company (Dick Wood, Lt. Eielson, . . . Bill Thompson, and [H. E. Pratt]), residents of OUR TOWN, are pioneering this district with this airship to the old-timers in the camps near here, and it may be noted in passing that their faith in their gamble was not misplaced, for the financial returns show it.

The very next day, Ben received a wire from Livengood, 65 miles from Fairbanks. The wire read: "Bring me by airplane one carton six ounce snuff from N. C. Company today."

Ben dashed over to the Northern Commercial Company, then hurriedly returned to the ballpark with the snuff. The Jenny was readied, and Ben took off for the mining camp near Livengood. He circled to check the prepared landing spot. It looked okay. Upon landing he had a royal welcome. Ben presented the bill for the snuff—$12—and then the bill for the delivery—$85. The mine owner didn't bat an eye and immediately paid cash for both bills. Pretty costly snuff? No, not in that Scandinavian community, for the rule was "No snuff, no work." If the mine owner had waited for the steamer to arrive with his parcel of snuff, the outraged miners would have hollered for their precious mixture for 25 days. Unhappy workers without snuff would certainly have cut their productivity. The miners didn't demand many luxuries. The owner told Ben that he considered the snuff delivered by plane a good investment.

Ben made enough money in 10 days to pay for the plane, F.O.B. Fairbanks. Acting as chief pilot, navigator, and mechanic (although he was assisted by several of the top mechanics in town), Ben set many records in his first flights.

Alone in Alaska's sky, he was the first to cast the moving shadow of a plane on vast stretches of uninhabited land. He flew over un-mapped wilderness. The strange landscape, the pattern of rolling hills and level country, was an intricate abstract of curves. Since there was no subsoil drainage, the waters gathered in innumerable lakes of all sizes that drained off into a maze of sloughs and rivers, taking such unbelievable windings and doublings that sometimes Ben's goggled eyes could not follow them.

Some of the lakes were black, some rusty red, while others appeared bright green from algae and moss. A few were sparkling blue, taking on the color of the sky. The scenes were breathtaking. The deep green of the hills contrasted with the wooded lands, the lighter greens of the moss making streaks of contrasting green. The streams made long sweeping loops, cutting so close together it ap-peared a man could take one step across the land between.

On a far horizon stood Ben's only beacon, the hazy blue-and-ivory mass of Mt. McKinley. He tried to tell his father about Mt. McKinley. Towering high in the clear spaces or hugged with clouds, the peaks of Mt. McKinley, capped with snow even in summer, were the most awesome sight of all. His fantastic aerial views of the mountain far exceeded the best oil paintings he'd seen of it or the lavish praise writers had heaped on it.

Ben found it impossible to describe the waterways, too. The huge interior rivers cut with directness and purpose past the intricate wanderings of many smaller streams. Tiny clusters of cabins and mounds of machinery appeared at intervals, marking the mining settlements that appeared so incredibly tiny and remote from the air. Often, the places where humans wanted to be or could maintain themselves were lost in the vastness of the land. With the winds whipping around him in the open-cockpit plane and singing past the struts, Ben was free to daydream. At such times, travel in Alaska other than flying seemed nonsensical.

Ben wondered if roads would ever cut across the as yet roadless sections of the wilderness or if waterways and skyways would be enough. He wondered how many years it would be before planes took to the air during the long, harsh winters in sufficient numbers to make the tedious toiling trips by dog teams over Alaska's frozen trails a thing of the past.

In the summer's heat, he shivered when he thought of the big job ahead, because he was still alone in the Alaska sky. No one could really spell out the years of effort that would make his daydream complete.

During Ben's first summer of flying in the North, Alaskans gladly provided many jobs for him and his little Jenny. Miners were the first to realize what the plane could do for them. As the owners of the Stewart-Denhart mine learned, Ben could cut the delivery time for supplies, machinery, and mail. They could measure time in minutes and hours instead of days and weeks. The savings in time meant added comforts and conveniences and extra money for their summer's work.

The little Jenny proved to be a welcome addition to other modes of travel in 1923. Ben often carried sick people to St. Joseph's Hospital, in Fairbanks, and took doctors into the bush. The time spent on mercy flights meant far more to him than the days he'd spent stunt flying.

One day after Ben had rushed a sick miner to the hospital, he told Thompson, "The doctor said that patient couldn't have lasted another day without medical help. Some of the trips I've made in the Jenny have actually saved lives. My dad would have been very pleased if he'd heard what the doctor said today. Dad thinks it's a big step forward since I switched from stunt flying to commercial flying."

In a letter sent home to Hatton about this time, Ben enclosed a snapshot entitled "Our Only Competition." The picture showed a group of five youngsters standing before their model Jenny made out of surplus wooden packing cases, smiling proudly and wearing helmets and goggles just like the real pilots did.

Before the summer was over, Ben's fame spread to even the most remote settlements in interior Alaska. He carried a variety of freight, including gold, fish, furs, machine parts, and wild game meat. He laughingly referred to himself as an errand boy with wings.

Working skillfully, with boldness and foresight, Ben eagerly accepted the challenge of pioneering aviation into the interior. Yet, flying the old army Jenny presented many problems, the biggest of which was the limited flying range. In discussing this problem with Wood, Ben said, "The ship and I are tied to a string that reaches out about 150 miles from Fairbanks. If the folks in the mining camps didn't have a supply of gas on hand, we'd have to worry even more. What we really need is a bigger plane. If we have any major problems with this plane, we don't even have a spare ship to use until the Jenny's repaired and ready to fly again."

Wood was sympathetic, but, having lived in Alaska for so many years without air transportation, he was more impressed with the accomplishments they had made with the Jenny than with its limitations.

"One thing at a time, Ben," he replied. "We've been waiting a long time to have a locally based plane operating out of Fairbanks. Our little ship is a good beginning."

But Ben thought about the many calls he had received for trips he couldn't make because of limited range. He knew that the miners out in the lonely camps wanted to be assured of regular service. One plane couldn't possibly do the big job ahead.

Several days later, when the subject of limited range came up again, Ben told Wood, "I want to be able to serve the people in Nome and on the Arctic Slope. I want to fly north to Barrow and over the top of the world. Someday planes will make regular flights across the Polar ice cap."

"What in the world are you planning now, Ben?" Wood asked in surprise. "You lost me somewhere in Nome."

Ben laughed and replied, "Sorry, Dick. Didn't mean to confuse you. But I read in the papers yesterday that Eddie Stinson flew the first nonstop flight between Chicago and New York. He made it in $8\frac{1}{2}$ hours and carried three passengers. You know that the Jenny doesn't even have the range to make a trip from Fairbanks to Anchorage unless we install auxiliary gas tanks or refuel along the route."

Wood shook his head and added, "I know it's not easy for you to be patient, Ben, but we've got to work with what we have."

"Eddie Stinson was flying a Junkers," Ben replied, "a big ship, and he had THREE passengers. I can't carry that many. We're losing business every day."

Unable to provide all the services requested from isolated points,

Ben became more determined than ever to get a bigger plane. No matter where he was, he continued to talk aviation. In the remote mining settlements, the miners gathered around to listen. As the only pilot in interior Alaska, he made many friends for himself and for aviation as well.

Ben continued to be a mailman, an ambulance driver, and a traveling salesman who delivered machine parts, groceries, and medical supplies. He quickly became the confidant of the people, serving as news bearer in both directions. He delivered news from Fairbanks to the bush and brought messages from the bush to Fairbanks.

Ben's personality made people trust him instinctively. When he hauled out gold to the banks, the miners weren't pessimistic about the possibility of the plane's cracking up and their gold never reaching its destination.

Back in Hatton, Ole Eielson was busy trying to keep up with his son's commercial flights. He told Oliver one day, "Well, Ben will be home for the winter, I'm sure. He's already put on aerial stunt shows in Nenana and Fairbanks. The Jenny's range won't permit him to extend his aerial exhibits. In a land without airfields and reliable weather reports and with only one open-cockpit plane in operation, Ben doesn't have much choice."

"Don't count on Ben coming back to Hatton, Dad," Oliver retorted. "I'm sure he has other ideas."

Ben kept the Jenny in the air every chance he had, and the last thing on his mind was returning to Hatton or to law school or getting into any business other than flying.

16

Flights in Interior Alaska—1923

THOMPSON BUSIED HIMSELF writing glowing accounts of Ben's commercial flying and reported one day, "He's demonstrating what aerial traffic can do for this country." That was certain. Settlements well beyond the range of the Jenny sent wires requesting aerial service, and Ben hated to turn them down.

One such request came from Norman Wimmler, a placer miner. He wanted to arrange a charter flight to Circle, originally called Circle City, over 160 miles from Fairbanks. The Indian village and mining center was 50 miles south of the Arctic Circle, beyond the Jenny's flying range. Ben had often talked about flying to Circle because he had heard so many interesting stories about the town. Gold was discovered on Mastodon Creek in 1894 by two prospectors sent to the district by an early trader named Harper. In a short time, Circle was a camp second only to Fortymile.

By 1898 Circle had a library, a hospital, and an Episcopal church. In 1897–98 the great gold strike in the Klondike, of the Yukon Territory, drew off most of Circle's population. But during the winters, when food was scarce in Dawson, the miners drifted down the river to Circle and survived.

In 1902 the Fairbanks gold rush took many of the Circle residents, but many old-timers, content to continue small-scale mining around Circle, were still mining there in 1923.

Ben wasn't worried about finding a level landing field. He knew that at Circle the Yukon widens into many shallow channels, a section known as the Yukon flats. At any rate, Wimmler reported that the miners were preparing a level strip for him.

When Ira Farnsworth first talked to Ben about the request to send a pump to Circle to prevent one of the mine shafts from being flooded out entirely, Ben said, "Let's put in that auxiliary gas tank."

As Ben inspected the lashings on the pump, he said, "Well, this Jenny has really had a workout this summer. The engine's been pretty faithful, but sooner or later we're bound to have serious engine trouble. What we need is a new engine or a bigger plane."

The owners all agreed that the Jenny was due to be replaced. Bouncing up and down on the ballpark field with each takeoff and landing, and bumping to a stop on many hastily cleared strips in remote areas, had taken its toll. The landing gear had been repaired many times. On each trip, the cockpit was crowded with mail, machine parts, and numerous other items, large and small. The hours piled up on the OX-5 engine, but Ben gave it excellent care. For every hour that he was in the air, at least two hours were spent on maintenance.

After the pump was loaded aboard the Jenny, the lighter supplies were piled in. The mail was loaded last. Farnsworth yelled, "All ready!" Ben smiled and waved. When the prop was spun, the engine roared to life.

The first part of the trip was uneventful, the engine purring steadily along. Trained by his years of barnstorming, Ben watched the country intently, unconsciously looking for places to land. This trip was no exception. He had just noticed a good landing spot near Birch Creek when almost immediately the overworked engine began to sputter—the sound he'd been dreading. Ben swung the Jenny around and headed back to the level strip beside the creek. He slipped to a landing and sat for a few seconds in the cockpit, but there was no time to waste.

Hopping out of the plane, Ben hurried to the front. He checked the engine and made several adjustments. While he worked, swarms of mosquitoes traced his movements, enjoying the rare chance to feed upon a human in the wilderness.

When he completed work on the engine, Ben rested a minute. He wished heartily that it was sacks of groceries he was transporting to Circle instead of a heavy pump. Had his cargo been groceries, he could measure his chances of survival against cans of meat, beans, and fruit. Then, in the event he couldn't get the plane started, he could take a pack of food and hike to Circle. He checked the map closely. It was about 20 miles to the mine. "We'll make it," he said aloud. In the quiet of the wilderness, his voice sounded strange to him.

Next, Ben double-checked the engine. He had to start the engine and get the pump to the mine in time to prevent a major disaster. He rechecked the lashings and then walked along the stretch of beach he would use for a runway, shoving boulders and fallen trees out of the way. He went back to the plane and got his axe and hunting knife. He cleared brush and a few stunted trees from the far end, stacking them in a neat pile.

Then he walked back to the plane, reached over the side of the cockpit, and set the magnetos. Running to the front of the plane, he chinned himself on the propeller. Nothing happened. He dashed back to the cockpit and checked the spark, then rushed forward to spin the prop again. The engine popped to life.

Ben vaulted into the cockpit and gave one last whack at the mosquitoes before he pulled his helmet and goggles into place. He lined up the Jenny on the short stretch of level beach. The plane rolled forward as he pulled back on the throttle. The Jenny lifted into the air, the wheels just brushing the tops of the surrounding trees. Ben breathed a sigh of relief. Barring any further trouble, he should be in Circle only 45 minutes later than he had originally planned.

About 15 minutes later Ben sighted the buildings of the old mining town. He almost cheered as he spotted several tiny figures waving a welcome. The men eagerly pointed in the direction of the prepared strip. Ben circled and brought the Jenny to a bouncing halt just short of where they stood.

Dozens of miners gathered around the Jenny to welcome Ben. They listened in amazement while Ben reported the reason for his delay. "Delay?" one asked in surprise. "We thought you made the flight in record time."

Ben smiled. He'd almost forgotten that Alaskans were more used to delays in delivery than any other people. He told them that the Jenny probably would need repairs. They assured him he could get all the help necessary. Ben instructed one of the men how to assist with the routine service on the Jenny. The others left to work on the mine pump.

Much later, the foreman said happily, "Come on, now, let's

celebrate. The pump's been installed; we'll take care of the big repair on the plane later. You're going to spend the night here, anyway. Let's go up to the mess hall and have some dinner." As they started toward the mess hall, he turned to ask, "How about my cigars? Did you get my message in time to pick them up?"

"Right here," Ben said. "Kept them safe all during the trip. But I'll admit I was tempted to break open the box back there at Birch Creek."

Dinner at the mining camp was a festival. The miners told Ben over and over that the pump had prevented a disaster at the mine. One of the men came to report that the flooded portion of the mine was now pumped free of water and work could proceed on schedule. He told Ben that the Jenny would soon be repaired, too.

After all the work was done, Ben and the miners talked long into the night. At bright dawn the following morning, Ben was up to check the plane. The miners prepared a list of supplies for him to deliver on his next trip. After a hasty breakfast, he headed back home. On the uneventful return trip, Ben took advantage of the exceptionally clear weather to study the new trails opened by the added fuel tank.

There was a crowd at the ballpark when Ben landed in Fairbanks, because everyone was anxious to hear about his forced landing. Ben told Thompson, "Sooner or later, that engine's going to conk out, and that will be the end of the Farthest North Airplane Company."

Thompson asked, "Did you have any luck when you tried to order a new engine?"

Ben answered, "I even have trouble keeping a supply of spark plugs in stock here. I'm still waiting for the ones I ordered last month. I've written to friends in North Dakota and Minnesota to see what they can do."

"Oh, well," Thompson said, "the manufacturers probably don't pay much attention to orders for plane parts from Alaska. I imagine they think we hibernate up here right after the Fourth of July. Send them a reminder, anyway."

The next day Ben received a telegram from Brooks requesting that Dr. Aline Beegler be flown there to attend an emergency medical case. The wire also reported that Ben could land on the new airstrip, which the people had chopped out of the brush. The strip was described as "level and containing no stumps."

Despite strong north winds tearing at Ben and his passenger, the trailblazing trip to Brooks with doctor, medical supplies, and mail was completed without incident. A few days later Ben received word that Mrs. J. J. Dwyer and her two small children wanted to fly from Brooks to Tolovana. At Tolovana, a passenger was waiting to go to St. Joseph's Hospital in Fairbanks. Before leaving Fairbanks, Ben stopped at the hospital to relay the message about the incoming patient. He was becoming a familiar figure there.

St. Joseph's Hospital had 50 beds and 20 private rooms in the three-story building. It was founded in 1906 by the Sisters of Charity of Providence, a Catholic organization, and was called the mercy base for the interior. Ben joked with the nurse on duty about extending the area served by the hospital by adding the auxiliary tank to his Jenny. He also picked up a list of instructions from the doctor. The detailed report concerned first aid prior to the flight, during the flight, and in case of a delay.

Ben flew to Brooks without any problems. He picked up Mrs. Dwyer and her two small children and transported them to Tolovana. Mrs. Dwyer was very grateful, as the plane trip had saved her 25 days of weary travel by riverboat with two youngsters. At Tolovana, Ben loaded the sick miner aboard. A nurse in the village had calmed the patient's fears and assured him the plane trip would be uneventful. After the patient was aboard, the nurse called Ben aside and said, "I just told him the same things you did earlier. He's suffering so much I think he welcomes the thought of flying. He knows he doesn't stand much chance by staying here."

Ben made good time on the flight from Tolovana. An ambulance was waiting, and Ben rode with the patient to St. Joseph's. After the miner was admitted, the nurse at the desk said, "People are beginning to depend on your plane."

The next day Ben received a message that there was a very sick miner at Tofty, too sick to be transported to Fairbanks. Ben hurried to the hospital and consulted with the doctor on duty. The nurse at the desk said, "Your patient from Tolovana is 100 percent better today. He had an appendectomy. He said to tell you he's indebted to you for life."

The nurse added that the doctor would meet Ben at the ballpark as soon as he finished his rounds. The Jenny was serviced, and when the doctor arrived, he and Ben were on their way.

While waiting for the doctor to visit his patient, Ben wandered around the Tofty mining camp. He and the doctor stayed overnight because the doctor wanted to remain with his patient. The sick miner was better the following morning, and Ben and the doctor returned to Fairbanks. The doctor sat in the forward cockpit in thoughtful silence. After they landed in Fairbanks, he asked Ben to meet him for dinner at the Frisco Cafe.

After dinner, while the two relaxed over coffee and cigars, the doctor said, "Ben, the fact that I could charter a plane and visit the sick miner was the only thing that saved his life. Someday I may try to get a plane of my own. Airplanes are really needed in this country, if for no other reason than to help the sick and the injured. If you ever leave Fairbanks, Ben, we'll be right back where we started. People sometimes die needlessly because of the isolation of the mining camps and lack of medical facilities in the bush."

"I'm not planning to leave Fairbanks," Ben replied, "but we've got to do something about getting another plane or two. I've been talking to Jimmy Rodebaugh. He's interested in organizing another commercial air transportation company. Sometimes I get two requests for service at once, and then I have to make a choice."

"When both your charter requests are for medical help, I can see where you have a problem," the doctor replied. "I suppose sometimes it appears to be a matter of life or death for either party. If you have to decide which patient is to get top priority, that calls for real courage. The next time I see Jimmy Rodebaugh, I believe I'll talk to him about his plans to form a company. I'm convinced we need another plane or two besides yours."

Not long after Ben's conversation with the doctor, a smallpox epidemic struck an Indian village on the Yukon River. Once again, the call for help came to Fairbanks. Ben flew the doctor and supplies for vaccinating the people to the village. When they returned to Fairbanks, the doctor said, "Ben, we never would have made it in time if we had not had the plane. Do you realize how many lives you've saved already by using this single airplane?"

Ben added, "I keep thinking about what would have happened

if that village had been just a few more miles from Fairbanks. We never would have been able to reach it. We need bigger planes and ones that will fly in the winter. A DeHavilland would be an improvement."

In discussing the matter with Thompson later, Ben said, "Many of the interior settlements are demanding air service. We can't be held to the limits of the Jenny. Even with the auxiliary gas tank, we're still tied to Fairbanks with a string that's too short. Someday we'll get an emergency call from a place beyond the Jenny's range. Then what will we do?"

Thompson replied, "If that Indian village where you delivered the vaccine were a few miles further, it would have been just like Fairbanks during the flu epidemic."

Thompson stared off into space. A few minutes later he said, "Yes, it was a terrible time. When I think back on it now, I always picture what it would have meant to Fairbanks to have had air transportation then."

Ben was shaken by the naked feeling in Thompson's words. He'd heard stories of the flu epidemic before, but not from Thompson. Ben mused, "No wonder he has been so enthusiastic about aviation."

Ben and Thompson talked on about their plans for a bigger plane. Ben said, "I've written to Dan Sutherland and also to the officials in the Post Office Department. I'm trying to get an airmail contract, and I've asked that they supply a DeHavilland."

"Alaska's so far away, Ben," Thompson said, "that officials find it easy to forget us. Now, if Harding had only lived, I think things would have been different. He found out the truth about Alaska when he was here. He knew our problems first hand. . . . His death marked a sad day for Alaska."

"Yes, I believe you're right about that," Ben said thoughtfully. "But some of the members of his cabinet were here, too," Ben added. "That should mean something." He continued, "I sent letters to all of them. That's what I've been doing in my spare time. The last time I wrote I even mentioned what a big help improved mail service within Alaska would be to officials back in Washington. I told them President Harding was all for giving aviation a chance here. . . . If I don't hear something definite pretty soon, I'm going back to

Washington, D.C., and call on a few of the key people we need to win over."

Thompson laughed and replied, "If I were younger, I might go with you. They'd better be thinking bigger planes for Alaska, because people here certainly are. Why, I heard the other day you were planning to fly over the Arctic ice pack to the North Pole."

"Why not?" Ben asked. "With the right plane that trip would be no problem at all. But, at the moment, I'm more interested in getting airmail started. I told Dan Sutherland that first we need to get a mail contract for Nenana and McGrath. Later we'll want to extend the mail route to Nome."

September came, and Ben missed the long hours of summer daylight. Temperatures dropped at night. Heavy fogs often hung like a blanket over the town, and there was smoke from forest fires burning in the interior. He tried to arrange trips so he would get home before dark. If that wasn't possible, he'd wire word back to Fairbanks not to expect him until the following day. On some of his overnight trips, he sometimes arranged short flights into the remote areas to check a prospect for a miner or deliver supplies. Venturing out from mining settlements where he had gas and oil stored enabled him to see new country.

As each autumn day passed, Ben drove himself harder than ever before to keep the Jenny in the air. He hated the thought of ending his first summer of flying in Alaska. He had put in 145 hours of flying and had covered over 12,000 miles. It was a miracle that he had experienced no serious engine problems. Although he had had some narrow escapes and some mighty rough landings, he had avoided personal injury or injury to any of his passengers. After his forced landing at Birch Creek, Ben had expected more trouble but was happy that none came.

Because Ben's Jenny was the only plane flying in interior Alaska, everything he did made news. He and the Jenny were becoming a favorite topic of conversation even in the remote mining camps. While Alaskans looked on his work with pride, Ben was impatient because of his limitations. As each day passed and there was nothing new or promising in the letters he received from Washington, Ben grew restless.

Late in September, workmen began setting up protective

wooden boxes around the exposed fire plugs. Next, they filled the boxes with sawdust. The air had a definite chill. The lush green of the tundra country turned a seared brown.

While the birch trees were still yellow with vivid fall color, the first snow came. With their first white coating of "termination dust," the hills beyond Fairbanks took on a softer appearance. Ben remembered the first time he'd heard snow referred to as "termination dust." In his first month in Alaska, one of the old-timers at the hotel announced that at the first sign of "termination dust" the tourists and the seasonal workers ended their visits in Alaska and headed outside. But, in the fall of 1923, the sight of the snow meant more than that to Ben. It meant his flights were numbered and would soon end completely.

One chilly November morning, while Ben and Farnsworth worked on the engine prior to a flight to Stewart Creek, the latter said, "Well, I guess it's about time for us to put the Jenny up for the winter. Are you sorry you didn't go back into teaching this year?"

"Oh, I'm not really sorry, although I will miss the students," Ben replied, "but I'm not planning to leave Alaska."

Farnsworth was plainly worried. He knew that it wasn't like Ben to keep his plans so secret. Finally, Ben stated with determination, "I hope to keep on flying right here in Fairbanks. What do you think of that?"

"Keep flying after November?" Farnsworth asked incredulously. "What in? We can't do much more to keep the Jenny in the air, Ben. She's like a tired old woman. She's seen her best days, I'm afraid."

Ben answered, "I'm going back to Washington, D.C., and sell the politicians on the idea of a bigger plane. Did you ever go skiing, Ira? That's what I've been thinking about for winter flying—skis. We can get someone to build us some."

Farnsworth shook his head. "I'll be anxious to hear what kind of a reception you get in Washington. Be sure and keep us posted."

The two friends parted. Farnsworth returned to his shop, while Ben hastened to check his mail before picking up the supplies for the mine. There was a letter from Washington, D.C., that read: "Thank you for your letter written in August concerning air service for the Territory of Alaska. At this time, the department cannot consider furnishing a plane. Perhaps at a later date. . . ."

Ben carefully folded the letter and put it back into the envelope. On the return from the post office, Ben stopped to visit Farnsworth. Without telling him about the letter he had in his pocket, he said, "Ira, I just stopped by to tell you we're going to fly a plane THIS WINTER in Fairbanks. We're going to continue air service. It's needed NOW, not at some vague date in the future!"

Farnsworth agreed but was puzzled by Ben's remarks. "That's about what I figured we'd decided this morning."

"Well, when I get back from Stewart Creek this afternoon, we'll store the Jenny in the warehouse. Then I'm going outside, and when I come back to Fairbanks, I'll have a bigger plane."

Farnsworth interjected, "I can't see how you're going to convince Washington to furnish a plane. . . . I keep thinking if you don't get the plane you might change your mind and not come back."

Ben replied, "To be absolutely honest with you, I don't even know what kind of a plane I can get, but I'd like one of the flying coffins—the DeHavillands. A few improvements have been made on them since the war. They are much better planes than our little Jenny."

The word had already gone around town that the Jenny would be making its last flight of the season, and a sizeable crowd gathered at the ballpark. Everyone was anxious to watch Ben take off. "Almost as many people and as much excitement as when the Jenny made her first flight," Ben remarked to Farnsworth.

After the Jenny was airborne, Farnsworth stood dejectedly, looking skyward, squinting his eyes against the sun until the Jenny disappeared. Only then did he turn and go into the warehouse. Several of Ben's friends followed him.

"Might as well get this place cleared out and ready to store the Jenny," he said. "We'll just build some shelves back in the corner out of the way. We'll sort our tools out, too. Won't be needing them here after today."

"What's Ben going to do?" one of the men asked.

"Ben's going to Washington, D.C.; then he's coming back to fly a mail plane out of Fairbanks this winter," Farnsworth replied with much more conviction than he really felt.

Soon they had a space cleared for the Jenny, tools sorted, and odds and ends carefully stacked on newly erected shelving in an expanded storage area. "Don't throw any parts away," Farnsworth admonished. "We might need them for the Jenny later, just in case we don't get a bigger plane."

As Ben prepared to leave Stewart Creek, the men at the mine were reluctant to see him go. The Jenny was heavily loaded with supplies and personal belongings that the men wouldn't be using for the rest of the season. The miners lined up to shake hands with Ben. He joked with them about some of the more amusing incidents of the past summer. He promised he'd see them back in Fairbanks after he returned from the States.

After the Jenny was airborne, the men stood silently, looking upward until the plane disappeared. As the men turned to go back to work, the foreman said on a hopeful note, "Well, our first summer of air service is over. Let's hope it's not the last."

Late that evening, Ben and his friends pushed the Jenny into the old warehouse for storage. Ben was touched when he returned and found the men had cleared a space for the Jenny and the spare parts. "You don't know how much I appreciate all your help," Ben told them.

After the plane was stored, Farnsworth turned to leave and said, "The old Jenny's going to hibernate just like a bear. She's like everything else around here in winter."

Ben ran his hand affectionately over the hood of the Jenny and said, "She deserves a good rest, but she still has a few good miles in her, too."

Just then Thompson appeared. "Judge Clegg called me, and I told him you probably were out here mooning around over the plane. Cheer up. When we get a bigger plane, we'll be busier than ever. But cutting the government red tape will be harder than flying a plane in the winter. Just as soon as you get word about the plane you're going to have shipped here for the airmail service, send me a wire. I've got the headline planned already. How do you think this sounds: 'MAIL SERVICE FOR KUSKOKWIM THROUGH AIR! Word was received today from Lt. C. B. Eielson and Dan Sutherland that . . .'?

"What's Judge Clegg so interested in talking to you tonight for?" Thompson suddenly asked.

"We had quite a conversation about 'winged justice' the other night," Ben replied. "You know how the 'floating courts' have been used in Alaska for years. Well, I was trying to work out an aerial schedule for Judge Clegg so that I could present it in Washington when I'm there. The judge makes his rounds to places off the highway by steamboat, gasboat, and rowboat in summer. In winter, he goes by dog team or snowshoe. His itinerary takes in the Yukon towns of Eagle, Circle, Ft. Yukon, Rampart, Tanana, and Ruby, the Iditarod mining region, and the Kuskokwim River district. He needs the use of a plane to get around. First, we need to get the Justice Department to authorize it. I'm working out a schedule to show that government expenses will be reduced and time and money saved."[1]

"Well, I might have known you had something planned to add to your request for a plane besides the need for airmail service," Farnsworth said. "That's a good thing to tell Washington about. Court cases drag out here for months. I guess if the government can have a revenue cutter for a 'floating court,' we ought to be able to get approval for a plane."

As the time approached for his trip to Washington, Ben found that he was reluctant to leave. He wished there was some way he could get a plane shipped to Fairbanks without leaving, but he knew there wasn't.

ENDNOTE

1. The Territory of Alaska was noted for its unique judicial institution called the "floating court." The Territory was divided into four judicial districts, but the districts were so large and the towns so far apart that Judge Wickersham made a trip to Washington, D.C., to obtain approval for a "floating court." The government detailed a revenue cutter and a court with attendants, bailiffs, clerks, criers, and representatives of the marshal's office and the district attorney's office to move from place to place to transact business that needed to be brought before the court. When airplanes took over, they were called Alaska's "flying court," and the phrase "winged justice" became more than a figure of speech.

The first official court trip by air was made in 1926, when the Department of Justice authorized the use of an airplane to carry court officials to Wiseman, in the Koyukuk region, about 150 miles within the Arctic Circle. No term of the District Court had ever been held there, owing to the isolation of the region. The plane left Fairbanks at 8:00 A.M. on July 2 and landed at Wiseman $2\frac{3}{4}$ hours later. Had a riverboat been chartered for the exclusive use of the party, the trip would have taken two weeks.

By 1928 the airplane had come into general use in connection with court business in the Fourth Division of Alaska. In November 1928, a deputy marshal flew from Fairbanks to Ruby and brought back an insane woman in six hours actual flying time. The same trip by dog team would have taken 22 days and would have been far more costly.

17

Airmail Service for Kuskokwim

Bᴇɴ ᴡᴀs sᴀᴅ ʙᴜᴛ ᴇxᴄɪᴛᴇᴅ as he packed to leave for the States—sad because he still did not have a plane for winter flying but excited over the prospects of obtaining one from the government. He packed only the bare necessities, as he didn't plan an extended trip. As he walked toward the depot, he paused to shake hands with a former student who had expressed his desire to fly. Ben said, "Don't give up on your plans to become a pilot. I'm very proud of your decision to learn to fly. If I can help, just let me know."

A large group of friends gathered at the depot to say goodbye. One man handed him two packages, saying, "Here. A few of us got together and . . . well, . . . have a good trip."

One of the packages contained a box of cigars and a book on Alaska. The other contained issues of the *News-Miner* that described the flights Ben had made that summer.

Ben's journey to Seattle was uneventful, except that he met several Alaskans on the boat from Seward to Seattle who either knew him or knew someone he knew in Fairbanks. It surprised him to see how many Alaskans were really interested in aviation and how Alaskans from other parts of the Territory had already heard about his pioneer flights in Fairbanks.

Several days later, as the train pulled into the Hatton depot, Ben saw his father, brothers, and sisters gathered on the platform to meet him. That evening, the Eielson home rang with laughter and gay conversation. Promptly after dinner, several of Ben's friends stopped by to visit, including some of his former partners in the Hatton Aero Club. All were anxious to hear reports about Alaska and the activities of the Farthest North Airplane Company.

Eventually, Ole got up and said, "Ben, it's time for bed now."

Before he dropped off to sleep, Ben noticed the trophies he had won in debate still standing on the shelf over his desk and thought, "When I get to Washington, D.C., I'll have a chance to use my debate training."

The next morning after breakfast, Ole said firmly, "Ben, we did a lot of talking about the future while you were gone. Now that you've decided not to teach school in Alaska, we'd like to see you settle right here in Hatton. Oliver has a good head for business and a real interest in the field of finance. We thought you could go into business together."

Ben replied, "But, Dad, even if I'm not teaching in Alaska, I already have my business there—the Farthest North Airplane . . ."

"That's just it," Ole said briskly. "We think you should get out of the flying business. It's only seasonal, anyway. If you don't want to go into business in Hatton, you can always go back to Georgetown University and complete your legal training. That's the main reason you're going to Washington, isn't it, to check on classes?"

"Well, no, not really, Dad," Ben replied. "But, of course, I might be stopping at the school to see a few of my friends."

Ole hesitated for a moment and then said, "Well, Son, I was afraid your trip to Washington had something to do with flying. I was looking over the newspapers you brought home from Alaska. I read where you'd been talking about flying the mail this winter."

Ben looked around at the members of the family and replied, "I wish I could say I had enough money saved so you could all go on a trip to Alaska, but I haven't. If you could visit there, then it would be a lot easier for you to understand why I like Alaska."

"Well, there wouldn't be much point in visiting there in the winter," Ole said. "If I ever do go to Alaska, I'd rather go during the summer. But don't get your hopes up too high, Ben. The government might not supply a mail plane. If no one else has ever flown there in winter, how will you manage it?"

Ben retorted, "Don't worry about the plane. I've got other plans in case the government refuses our request."

In a few days Ben headed for Chicago and then Washington. It hadn't been too hard leaving the family this time, as he promised to stop at Hatton on his way back to Alaska, regardless of how things went.

Ben had a few hours to spend in Chicago. He grew restless as he walked around the big, noisy city, and decided that Fairbanks was more his style.

In Washington, after Ben registered at a hotel, he called on Dan Sutherland. The two quickly got around to the latest on the airmail contract. Sutherland said, "The people in the Post Office Department probably are tired of seeing me. Ever since you started flying the Jenny, I've been sticking pins in them. You're getting famous, Ben. Since the cabinet members returned from their tour of Alaska, they've been asking a lot of questions about your flying there."

Next, Ben met with governmental officials. He implored them, debated them, submitted factual data on Alaska and a complete report of his aerial work in the Far North, and then waded through a maze of red tape trying to pin the officials down to a contract.

One morning Ben arrived at Sutherland's office a little earlier than usual and found him very excited. "I've set up some final appointments with the Post Office people," he said. "After yesterday, I think we're all set. I'm sure we'll get a contract for 10 round trips from Fairbanks to McGrath, twice each month, starting in January or February. It looks like we'll get a DeHavilland, with a 400-horsepower Liberty engine too! I hope everything goes right this morning. I just have a feeling this is it. But, the department wants to pay you only $2.00 a mile for the first five trips and $1.50 a mile for the remaining five trips. That's less than half what the contractor receives for delivering the mail by dog team."

Ben shrugged and replied, "If the Post Office Department only knew it, they missed a bargain."

"What do you mean?" Sutherland asked.

"I mean I'd have flown the mail for nothing, just to prove that flying is feasible in Alaska in the winter. When we get final approval, the first thing I'll do is send Thompson a wire. Do you know he was so confident of our ability to cut red tape that he has the headline ready for the newspaper?"

True to Sutherland's predictions, final approval was given that day, and Ben rushed to the telegraph office.

Ever since President Harding's trip there, Alaska had been very much in the national headlines during 1923. In a speech in Seattle, the President called for large appropriations for agriculture and roads, for conservation of timber, fish, and other natural resources, and for continued government operation of the Alaska Railroad. "We must," he said, "regard life in lovely, wonderful Alaska as an end and not a means and reject the policy of looting Alaska as the possibility of profit arises."

What President Harding had seen and heard in Alaska had thoroughly aroused him to the needs of Alaskans. He concluded his Seattle speech by saying, "Our adopted program must be development of Alaska for Alaskans. To plan for well-rounded development into a permanent community of homes, families, schools, and an illuminating social scheme, we must give all encouragement."[1]

Ben returned to Fairbanks with new haste, added firmness, and a streak of stubbornness that enabled him to see the difficulties ahead in the winter of 1924 as just so many evils to overcome.

During February, the sun rose only briefly over the horizon, but for those engaged in promoting aviation in Alaska, the long, dark days were busy ones. A heated hangar for the government DeHaviland was built at the ballpark, but extreme cold weather caused a delay in construction. The plane was not moved into the building until February 18. The big Liberty engine was assembled at a local machine shop and delivered to the hangar. By February 20, Ben and his dedicated helpers had the plane ready. Excitement mounted, for the next morning Ben was to make his first trip from Fairbanks to McGrath with the U.S. mail.

When the postal officials in Washington plotted the course, so little was known in advance about the mail-route country that they consulted three maps of the region, no two of them alike. McGrath was located about 300 miles southwest of Fairbanks at the confluence of the Takotna and Kuskokwim rivers. The principal activities were freighting, mining, and trapping. It was the transfer point for freight bound for the upper Kuskokwim. McGrath dated back to exploration by the Russians as early as 1840. Its residents of the Alaskan interior looked forward to airmail delivery.

McGrath had no landing field, so Ben planned to use the frozen Takotna River until spring ice breakup. The ballpark at Fairbanks was covered with 2 to 3 feet of snow as preparations were completed for the flight, but because the snow was light, dry, and powdery, it didn't pack well.

Ben was the only one who had done any experimental flying in interior Alaska in the wintertime. Not much research had been done on icing in frigid weather or on how the engine would perform in such temperatures. He would soon find out.

The eagerly awaited flight in the government DeHavilland took place a year to the day after Ben made his initial flight to Nenana with the mail, which he did to prove to government officials that it was possible to fly in Alaska in the winter. That shorter flight on February 21, 1923, had helped Ben obtain the 1924 contract.

Ben knew that when the time came to take off for McGrath, he might be challenging death. But it was his friends who expressed the most concern. Laughing at their dire predictions, Ben said, "Don't worry. I'll come through all right. I'll be back in Fairbanks right on schedule."

The DeHavilland's gas tanks were filled with domestic aviation gasoline. The thrust bearing was filled with Mobile B oil. Clearances were checked, and the engine was inspected. Many eagerly joined forces to push the plane out of the hangar. On the snow-covered field the plane stood awkwardly on its bulky, 300-pound, flat-bottomed homemade skis.

Ben waited impatiently while a dog team was driven alongside the plane. Shutters clicked as the musher, representing the era of dog-team mail delivery, and Ben, the new era of airmail delivery, posed. After the first picture, Ben busied himself supervising the stowing of 164 pounds of mail destined for McGrath.

In addition to the mail, Ben carried a full set of tools, a mountain-sheep sleeping bag, 10 days' provisions, five gallons of extra gasoline, extra Mobile B oil, snowshoes, a gun, an axe, and some spare parts. His clothing included two pair of heavy woolen hose, a pair of caribou socks, a pair of mukluks reaching over the knees, one suit of heavy underwear, a pair of khaki breeches, a pair of heavy trousers of Hudson Bay duffle over the breeches, a heavy shirt, a sweater, a marten cap, goggles, and over it all a loose reindeer-skin parka, which had a hood with wolverine fur around it. (Wolverine fur is the best kind of fur to have around the face because it does not frost.) On his hands he wore a pair of light woolen gloves and a pair of heavy fur mitts over them. He was well protected for open-cockpit flying.

After the plane was loaded, the photographers were determined to take more pictures, but noting Ben's impatience to take off, the mayor finally cut the speech making short. Shutters kept clicking until Ben waved his hand and called, "Ready to take off."

It was 5 degrees below zero, and there was no wind. The sky was about two-thirds overcast with clouds at 4,500 feet. The weather report as telegraphed from McGrath was good. Ben's friends stood shivering as they watched him climb into the plane. They wondered how he could endure cruel winds in the open cockpit. They watched as Ben warmed the engine, raced it to full power, then throttled back.

The ship quivered violently but didn't move. The skis were stuck and had sunk about 1½ feet into the snow, making it impossible to taxi. When Ben got the engine to about 1,300 revolutions per minute, the skis broke loose from the snow. The plane traveled about 800 feet before it lifted from the snow-covered field. It was 8:45 A.M., and the first official Alaskan airmail flight was underway.

Ben busied himself checking the instruments. The Liberty never missed, but the air speed indicator didn't work. Later, he found that the tachometer worked erratically, and the compass deviated as much as 40 degrees because of the magnetism of the engine. He was well acquainted with the country and did not depend on the compass except for relative readings taken by pointing the plane at some known landmark. It didn't really bother him that the compass was off, for he was used to contact flying in daylight.

For the first 50 miles, Ben followed the Tanana River, knowing it would provide a fair emergency landing field, even though the ice was a little rough in spots. He reached Nenana at 9:21 A.M. The entire town was out to cheer for him, so he descended and circled to wave.

At Nenana, he left the Tanana River and steered across country. Ben veered to the left of a straight course in order to follow the flat country and stay near the roadhouses, which were located on the mail trail at intervals of 35 miles. After about 1½ hours, he spotted Lake Minchumina on his right. He was then almost halfway between the lake and Mt. McKinley, each of them probably about 30 miles away.

As he sped along in the Arctic haze, he watched for signs of ice on the wings. There were none. His mind raced with all of the details he had to remember. Looking down intently, he saw the dog-team trail below. Then, suddenly, he spotted a black moving spot. He figured it probably was Fred Milligan, the mail driver, and his dog team on the well-worn mail trail. Milligan was no novice at mushing. He'd traveled the trail for many years, carrying mail to small isolated towns like Diamond, Roosevelt, Ophir, Iditarod, and Flat.

Milligan came to Nome in 1907 and had carried the mail by dog team in the Nome area and also over the Tanana, the Kuskokwim, and the Yukon rivers. He knew every dip and curve along the route to McGrath and beyond. On this chilly February day he had been mushing since early morning. Mile after mile, the silence of the frozen North was broken only by the sound the dogs made, the swishing sled runners, and the creaking sled.

Just as he started to cross the 16-mile stretch of Lake Minchumina, Milligan's dogs tensed. Turning their heads abruptly, they looked behind them. Impatiently, Milligan urged the team onward, but the leader stopped dead in his tracks. The dogs looked upward, and Milligan, hunched on the sled runners, looked up too. Miles away, Milligan saw the mail plane. Soon the strange-looking wooden contraption, with its narrow body and cloth-covered wings, came roaring directly over Milligan and his team.

Milligan recalled that the Eskimos first saw a flying machine in 1920, when Mitchell's Black Wolfe Squadron came to Nome, and they had named it "Tingun," or "Bird of the Tundra." As Milligan excitedly reported later at the roadhouse, "It flew right over us! The pilot leaned out and waved at me. He was flying just above the tree tops!"

Milligan knew that Ben was on his way to McGrath with the first batch of airborne mail. His dog team took from 18 to 22 days to make the trip. It hardly seemed possible to him, but Milligan knew that Ben planned to make the trip to McGrath and return to Fairbanks the same day. The round trip of 600 miles would take only six or seven hours of flight time.

Milligan sighed deeply. He did not resent the intrusion of competition but felt a kinship with Ben on the lonely trail. After all, they were fellow mail carriers in the wilderness. Although Ben and Milligan may not have given it more than a passing thought, they were participating in a historic moment—the beginning of the end of the long era of dog-team mail delivery.

Milligan later said that he had felt sorry for Ben, exposed to the elements in the open-cockpit plane, high above the ground and at the mercy of the bitter winds. "At least," Milligan thought, "I can hop on the runners and bury my head in the ruff of my parka. The dogs know the way. Ben can't let up for one second."

Milligan wondered idly if the government would renew Ben's experimental mail contract. Many mushers considered flying the mail a risky business and spread that story. They said that the mail was much safer on the ground. Milligan also knew that the trappers and the roadhouse keepers resented the fact that the mail plane wouldn't be breaking trail for them. The only place Ben would land would be at the clearing on the river at McGrath.

Roaring along high above the dog-team trail, Ben did mental arithmetic, estimating his time of arrival at McGrath, and wondered if his projected figures for gas and oil consumption were correct. He realized that if he landed safely at McGrath, he would make it back over Lake Minchumina before Milligan had crossed its entire length. That should set some kind of a record. He'd never paced a plane against a dog team before. Soon he spotted the main Kuskokwim River, which he followed to McGrath. He found there was about a foot of snow on the Takotna River.

After circling the area twice, Ben came down smoothly, sliding about 500 feet after the 300-pound skis first touched the snow. As he had plenty of room, he intentionally made a fast landing. The skis made by Charlie Schiek, of Fairbanks, stood up just fine under the jolt of landing.

It was 11:35 A.M. It had taken only 2 hours 50 minutes to cover the 315-mile course. On a straight shot, it would have been 280 miles, but the way Ben had come, via the dog-team trail, he had covered 35 extra miles.

All of McGrath and the visiting Indians, who had camped nearby in great anticipation of the "man bird's" arrival, were on hand as Ben landed. The mail was transferred to a waiting sled, and a dog team finished the last short lap of the historic journey.

Ben covered the engine with a large canvas hood for warmth. He filled the gas tank with the fuel he'd brought from Fairbanks—

domestic aviation gasoline—about 62 degrees B Test. He added 3 gallons of Mobile B oil to what was left in the sump. He had planned a complete oil change at McGrath but found the stock he had ordered last fall had missed connections and there was no extra Mobile B there.

McGrath residents were extremely excited and could hardly hold themselves in as Ben went about the routine work. Several offered their help. Ben was elated, too, but there was work to be done. One of the leading citizens finally insisted that he join him at a banquet prepared in his honor.

Ben hesitated. Knowing the shortness of the February days, he'd planned to stop at McGrath only long enough to exchange mail. But he could see the excited crowd had other ideas, and he promised to join them at the roadhouse. First, he dug out his little fire pot, hired someone to stand watch, and put it under the canvas hood to help keep the engine warm. He told his helper that he would have to drain the oil and then heat it again before pouring it back.

Barely able to control his impatience to get started for Fairbanks, Ben tried to act like a guest of honor. When the speeches finally were over, the Indians present sent a delegate to talk to Ben. He was touched when he learned that the Indians wanted to adopt him into their tribe and make him their new chief, a great honor for a white man. An Indian spokesman promised that the ceremony would be performed during one of his future trips when he had more time.

It was 2:00 P.M. before Ben could tear himself away. He supervised the loading of 60 pounds of mail and made the final preparations for the return trip. He was a little apprehensive, for he barely had enough time to reach Fairbanks before dark.

Several McGrath residents tried to convince Ben that he should stay overnight, but Ben knew that it might be too difficult to start the engine after the plane had stood out all night in the cold. There was no head wind, and Ben felt that he could return in better time with a higher ground speed and a straighter course.

Ben knew that his fuel and oil calculations were correct. On the trip over he'd burned about 20 gallons of fuel per hour and used about 1¼ gallons of oil. At McGrath, he'd been warned to keep to the dog-team trail. One old-timer said, "The Kuskokwim country is no place to be lost in winter. Even if you make a successful forced landing on those big skis, you might not be found for days, weeks, or even months."

Ben had trouble starting the Liberty engine alone. He finally got a man to hold back the plane while he swung the propeller. As there was no one in the cockpit, when the engine coughed, Ben dashed madly to the control board. By the time the engine started, Ben was perspiring freely. Things would be easier on the next trip, for he'd already started to train a helper.

At first, the skis dug into the snow. Ben turned the engine to 1,450 rpm. He made a long run on the frozen river before he got off the ground. Once airborne, he cut the engine to 1,300.

During the first part of the trip over the Appel Mountains, the DeHavilland ran smoothly. In 1 hour 15 minutes he reached Lake Minchumina, the halfway point. So far, he was right on schedule, but it was almost dark. The air grew colder. The long fur of the parka hood whipped against his face, blurring his vision.

Down on the dog-team trail, Fred Milligan neared the end of Lake Minchumina. Out of the stillness, for the second time that day, Milligan heard the roar of the plane's engine. He cocked his head. The lead dog tensed. This time, Milligan thought it sounded as if the plane was some distance off the trail. Peering upward in the dusk, Milligan could see nothing, yet he knew that Ben was somewhere up in the darkening sky. Ben had already delivered the mail at McGrath and was on his way back to Fairbanks. Milligan later reported, "I decided right then and there that Alaska was no country for me to keep running dogs on the mail route."[2]

Milligan was correct in his judgment that the plane was not directly over the trail on the return trip, for Ben had decided to fly a compass course to Fairbanks. It was too dark to do anything else.

In a few minutes, Ben passed over a stream that was not on his map. He thought it might be the Kantishna River, but it wasn't. Later, when he reached the Kantishna River he thought it was the Tanana River. It was time for him to be nearing the Nenana Bluff. It was almost impossible to see anything. Then he noticed a river going around a bluff. He was positive that this was the Nenana River because he saw another river, which he thought must be the Tanana, entering it. The spot where the rivers joined appeared to be where the town of Nenana should be located.

Ben struck out for the bluff but found that the town of Nenana wasn't there. He knew he must have veered to the left, so he started up what he thought was the Tanana to find Nenana. He followed it for 50 miles. By this time it was pitch dark. Ben shook his head. He couldn't believe he had traveled 50 miles off his course after the same compass course had brought him to Lake Minchumina, the halfway point, exactly on course.

He flew blindly on. Landing was out of the question. His plight was critical. The sky was entirely overcast; not a star twinkled. Any pilot knows how dangerous it is to fly "contact" over strange country at night. Only a fool or a desperate man would do it. Ben was no fool, but he was getting desperate.

As the land slid beneath the DeHavilland's wings, Ben's mind raced with random thoughts. He recalled that the Indians along the Yukon thought so much of his ability as a pilot that they'd named him Brother-to-the-Eagle. But, on this dark night, he felt more like a lone eagle in the chill of the winter sky.

Suddenly, Ben saw a faint beam of light. He cut his altitude and circled around it. He figured it must be the light from an oil lantern in a trapper's cabin on the Chatanika River. He was sorely tempted to set the plane down and at least have a place to sleep and the companionship of another human. Still, he hesitated to land. He knew that he might wreck the plane and with it the chances of getting permanent airmail service for Alaska.

Feeling that permanent airmail service was the most important consideration, Ben flew on, though his gas supply was getting dangerously low. On a hunch, he turned left. If he was correct, he would be over the Chena River. Suddenly, he saw a flare of light in the distance. He headed for the light like a homing pigeon. He was right; it was home field!

In spite of a snowstorm, many people had been waiting at the field since 4:00 P.M. So great was the interest in Ben's flight that earlier in the afternoon a jury locked up in a court case was dismissed by the judge so jury members could join their fellow townspeople at the ballpark.

Darkness fell with still no sign of the "flying professor." Ben's friends thought that the plane could have tangled with a mountain peak or skidded into a precipice. When he failed to appear by

5:30 P.M., even a few of his staunchest friends grew fearful. The field was a sad scene. Some of the women cried openly. More than one of his former students joined them, unashamed of their tears. Thompson loudly told them to be quiet, for their sobs would prevent him from hearing the sound of the engine.

Just before he left for McGrath, Ben had recommended that if it got too dark before he got back, the field should be lighted with flares in empty drums. Thompson soon directed the men to fill the drums. When the drums were filled, the men set them in a single row down the center of the field. Because most of Ben's flying had been done during the long days of summer, there had been no need to worry about lights for the field, so the men weren't quite sure where the drums should be. Instead of placing them around the edges of the field to mark the boundaries, they mistakenly chose a center row. At least the frequent flares illuminated the ballpark and the strained faces of the crowd, which had grown to about 1,500 people.

Thompson looked at his watch and called out, "It's 6:30 P.M." A wire from McGrath said that he had left there at 2:45 P.M.

Suddenly someone cried out, "LISTEN, LISTEN!"

A hush fell. In it, the crowd heard the faint sound of the Liberty engine. Some shouted for joy. A few people who had given up and were on their way home turned and ran back to the field. Coming in to land, Ben kept far enough away from the center of the flames to give himself clearance, figuring he would hit the prepared runway in the center. But too late, he realized the flares were not at the edges of the field. Ben found himself descending on a patch of shrubbery near two stunted trees. Ben couldn't quite clear one of the trees. As he hit the tree, he heard a loud crunch and knew that he had broken a ski. He gave the ship the gun to pull it over. It barely cleared the other tree, shearing the top. Finally on the ground, the DeHavilland rocked gently over onto its back. In addition to the ski, the landing gear was broken and the propeller was smashed.

When they found that Ben was not hurt, just dazed, the people spilled over the field to greet him. Exhausted but happy, Ben gripped Thompson's hand and said, "I checked the gas gauge not too long ago, and there was only about a gallon of gas left."

Ben glanced at his watch. He found he had been in the air 4 hours 10 minutes on the return trip, most of it flying after dark.

Ben said, "We've got to get the plane into the hangar."

The men laughed. "Don't worry about the plane," Farnsworth called. Instead, Ben was hoisted on the shoulders of his friends and carried into the hangar.

With Thompson's help Mayor Marquam called the assembly to order. On behalf of the people of Fairbanks, the mayor presented Ben with a diamond-studded Swiss watch inscribed, "C. B. Eielson—Pioneer Alaska Trail Blazer—Fairbanks to McGrath—February 21, 1924." Attached to the watch was a gold chain on which hung a gold nugget. At the other end of the chain, a diamond-studded knife was attached.

By the time the mayor finished his presentation speech, all eyes were trained on Ben. He swallowed nervously and thought, "These blessed Alaskans had this planned weeks in advance." He was too filled with emotion to speak. He looked around the hangar and finally said, "I . . . well, . . . I can't tell you how . . ." He stopped. He tried again. No one seemed to mind that he was at a loss for words. Then Thompson asked, "What time is it, Ben? Some of us have been here since 4 o'clock."

Ben grinned broadly. With a flourish, he took his new watch out of the jeweler's case and reported happily, "It's exactly 7:30 P.M.!" Then, after a short thank you, Ben held up his hand and said, "I've got to check the plane. You know, I must send a report to Washington, D.C., right away."

Farnsworth appeared to assure Ben that there was nothing wrong with the plane that couldn't be fixed right in Fairbanks. "Charlie Schiek says that it will be easy to rebuild the ski and the landing gear, but you'll need a new prop." That cost Ben $424.

Once the plane was inside, the McGrath mail was unloaded and taken to town. The lateness of the hour didn't matter. After all, as Dick Wood reported, "The mail is still 20 days ahead of schedule."

Many of the crowd gathered at the Frisco Cafe for a late dinner. Ben calculated that he had been in the air that day for seven hours. He'd covered a distance of 600 miles, farther than from Fairbanks to Siberia, Point Barrow, or Juneau.

The big talk in Fairbanks for many days was the comparative differences in speed for the airplane and for the dog team. Those favoring the airplane could point with pride to the fact that Ben flew against a gale, delivered the mail at McGrath, attended a banquet in his honor, made a long list of commissions he was asked to attend to in Fairbanks (for it seemed everyone in McGrath wanted something that would be delivered on the next trip), prepared the plane for the return flight, and flew back over Lake Minchumina before Fred Milligan and his dog team had finished crossing the lake.

Thompson dug up statistics on the dog-team mail route and printed them. A report prepared in 1923 and 1924 by E. Coke Hill, winter mail contractor between Kobe and Flat, stated that the Kobe-McGrath section of the winter mail trail was in excellent condition. Hill, a former U.S. Commissioner at Ruby and assistant U.S. Attorney at Fairbanks, noted that much of the trail was in condition for use by four-horse bobsleds. There were 10 roadhouses in cabins along the 254-mile route. In 1923 Hill contracted to carry the mail from Kobe to McGrath and then on to Flat once each month between November 1 and April 1.

In another show of recognition for an idea that had come to its time, the Fairbanks Igloo of the Pioneers of Alaska conferred an honorary membership upon Ben, with a formal initiation ceremony, for his blazing of Alaskan airmail trails. Ben signed his name upon the Igloo honor roll directly under that of President Harding, who had received the same honor in July 1923.

ENDNOTES

1. Although there was every reason to believe that the ultimate success on the contract was in no small part because of the President's trip to Alaska, there was also good reason to think that Billy Mitchell's constant references to Alaska's strategic importance and the need for developing aviation in the Territory had triggered a favorable attitude.

Mitchell was still in the thick of arguments with Congressional committees, always appearing to plead for appropriations for more and better planes. Following President Harding's death, Mitchell told his closest friends that he saw less hope for his air policies than ever before; soon he said so in public.

Calvin Coolidge, who succeeded Harding, publicly stated that airplanes could be used only for scouting purposes and that the use of planes during the war actually had proved nothing. Shortly after, he asked for less controversy on aviation, and Mitchell released new statistics and statements to the press.

The President let it be known that he was irritated because the "air squabble" was getting so much coverage in the press. Mitchell's closest friends began to steer clear of him in order not to endanger their own positions. His crusade for air power was shrinking to a one-man job.

Not expecting any help from President Coolidge himself, but feeling that someone in his administration might be favorably inclined towards aviation, Mitchell watched the changes being made in Coolidge's cabinet. He said of one of Coolidge's appointees who would have some authority over aviation, "How Coolidge happened to pick that bird is one of the fascinating mysteries of his administration. He must have known less about airplanes than the peanut vendor in front of the White House."

In spite of all the reprimands and calls for silence, Mitchell continued to send copies of his written appeals to various agencies. His attention was centered on proving the need for better planes, a separate air force, and immediate defense plans for Alaska.

2. Heeding the times, Milligan gave up dog mushing for airplanes. He became a flight mechanic for Pacific International Airways, which was taken over by Pan American Airways (PAA) in 1933. He retired as mail superintendent with PAA in Seattle in 1956.

The home of Carl Ben Eielson, Hatton, North Dakota, now the Hatton Eielson Museum, October 23, 1991. (John Borge)

Eielson children, ca. 1907. L–R: Elma, Arthur, Carl Benjamin, Adeline, Oliver, Edwin. (Hatton Eielson Museum, hereafter HEM)

Eielson in military uniform, 1918. (State Historical Society of North Dakota, hereafter SHSND)

Letterhead of Aero Club of Hatton, 1920–21. (HEM)

Aero Club of Hatton
Hatton, North Dakota

ORGANIZED TO
PROMOTE INTEREST IN AVIATION IN NORTH DAKOTA

ASK FOR RATES FOR EXHIBITION FLIGHTS.

OUR PILOTS WILL GIVE A REAL ACROBATIC FLIGHT. ANY STUNT THAT ART SMITH
DID AT THE SAN FRANSISCO EXPOSITION AND SOME HE DID NOT KNOW HOW
TO DO. WE DO NOT GIVE A SKIMPY LOOP OR TWO AND CALL IT AN
EXHIBITION. WE DO EVERYTHING KNOWN TO AVIATION.
WE GUARANTEE TO SATISFY.

SAFE PASSENGER WORK
OUR MOTTO "NEVER TAKE A CHANCE WITH A PASSENGER"

"TIME FLIES WHEN WILL YOU?"

Flyer promoting Aero Club of Hatton, 1920–21. (HEM)

Original Jenny, purchased by the Hatton Aero Club, used for barnstorming in 1920. (HEM)

Probably the eight original investors of the Farthest North Airplane Company, 1923. Eielson center front. (SHSND)

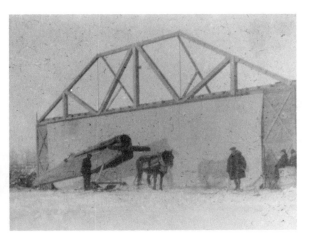

Borrowed Jenny used on the initial flights from Fairbanks to Nenana, being towed to storage at Fairbanks hangar, 1923. (HEM)

Flyer promoting Ben's appearance at Nenana, July 4, 1923. (HEM)

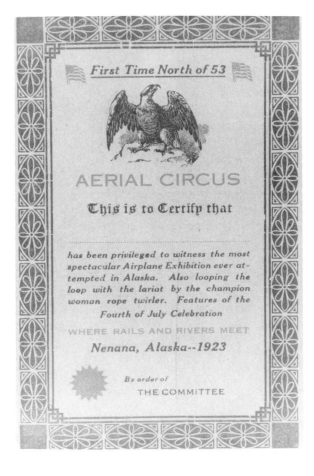

First Time North of 53

AERIAL CIRCUS

This is to Certify that

has been privileged to witness the most spectacular Airplane Exhibition ever attempted in Alaska. Also looping the loop with the lariat by the champion woman rope twirler. Features of the Fourth of July Celebration

WHERE RAILS AND RIVERS MEET

Nenana, Alaska--1923

By order of
THE COMMITTEE

Eielson's history-making airmail flight, February 21, 1924, from Fairbanks to McGrath. Pictured is the DeHavilland DH-4. Note dog team and sled in foreground. (SHSND)

Harry Watson sent a letter to himself, Fairbanks-McGrath-Fairbanks, on the first flight, February 21, 1924. (HEM)

Ben landing at McGrath, February 21, 1924, first airmail flight. (HEM)

Fairbanks from the air, Eielson photo, ca. 1924. (SHSND)

Mt. McKinley, Eielson photo, ca. 1924. (SHSND)

Eielson's Jenny JN4 at Fairbanks, 1925. (SHSND)

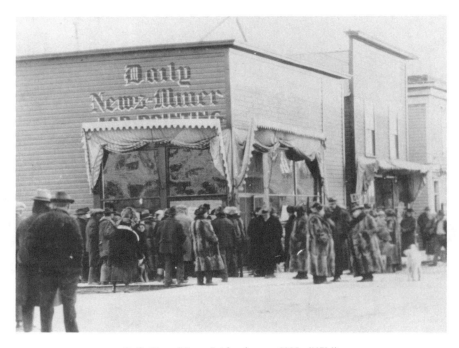

Daily News-Miner, Fairbanks, ca. 1925. (HEM)

Kenny Lake Roadhouse, typical of stopping places found along the dog-sled trails. (HEM)

Bennett-Rodebaugh Company, Fairbanks, 1926. (HEM)

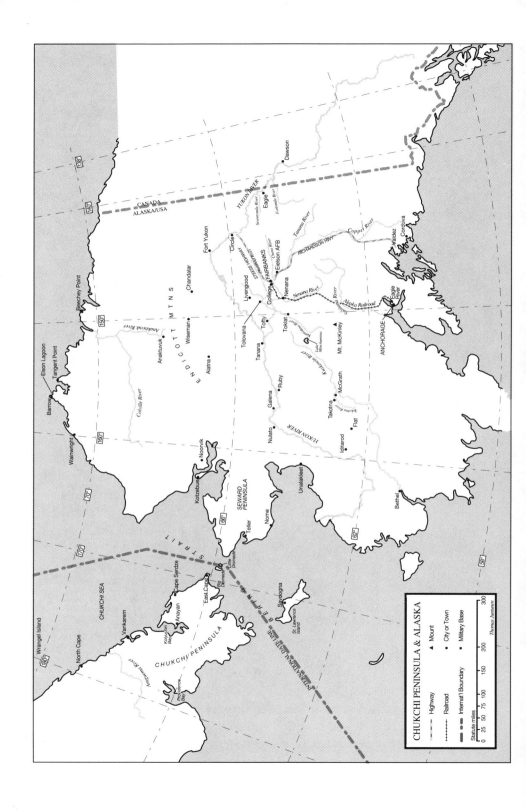

CHUKCHI PENINSULA & ALASKA

18

Moose Ptarmigan Ben

THERE WAS AN APPEALING BRAVADO in Ben's determination to complete the first round-trip airmail flight successfully. The same spirit had marked his friends during their long hours of waiting in the cold and the snow at the ballpark. After the flight, many people asked the same question Dick Wood had asked, "Did you have any trouble keeping warm?"

Ben said that he did not suffer from the cold. He explained that if he hadn't already been sold on the native parka and mukluks, he would have been by the time the trip was over. On the advice of old-timers, he had first adopted the Eskimo parka and knee-high moccasins, more commonly called "mukluks," on the flight from Fairbanks to Nenana on February 21, 1923. During that trip, he found that his native clothing was comfortably warm in the open-cockpit plane.

Prior to moving to Alaska, Ben had used the fur jumpers then in general use in the States for open-cockpit flying. But in case of a forced landing in the States and the necessity of walking any distance for help, the pilot always removed his fur jumper, as it was too heavy for walking. If a pilot in Alaska walked in leather boots for a prolonged period of time, he was virtually sure to have frozen toes or feet. As many cheechako prospectors had discovered, leather boots and winter treks didn't mix.

Old-timers in Alaska had early adopted the hand-sewn fur parkas and mukluks, which had been used for centuries by the Eskimos for protection from winter's blasts. Enlightened explorers had also adopted and widely used native clothing while making extended walks in the Arctic and the Antarctic. The use of native clothing and

169

methods of travel enabled explorers Peary and Amundsen to have successful expeditions. Peary established the principle that northern voyages should begin in mid-winter and end before the spring thaws. He preferred erecting snowhouses to replace tents formerly used.

Another famous explorer, Vilhjalmur Stefansson, from North Dakota, also adopted native clothing and methods of survival. His theory was that the Arctic was friendly to those who understood it. Ben found Stefansson's books helpful in planning for his own survival in the event of forced landings.

A unique feature of Ben's special flying parka, lined with wolverine fur, was that it also had a wide fringe, or ruff, of wolf fur, coarse and long. In windy weather the long hairs in the projecting ruff whipped across his face constantly, stimulating circulation and keeping away frostbite.

Ben was especially pleased with the warmth and the comfort of the mukluks in cold weather. Because they were not stiff, like leather boots, Ben found that he could feel the rudder at all times and had better control of the plane.

When Ben reported on his first flight to the Second Assistant Postmaster General, he was still so enthusiastic over the cold-fighting properties of the native clothing that he urged its use by all airmail pilots in the States.

He wrote:

> I found that I could fly in 40 below weather in perfect comfort with parka and mukluks using the engine heater. Even when I had the exhaust heater turned off, I found that I had too much clothing on. At five below zero, I was too warm. On my second trip I cut out the caribou socks, the duffle trousers, and the heavy fur mittens and I was entirely comfortable.

He went into great detail to prove that native clothing was the lightest, most durable, warmest, and cheapest for cold-climate flying.

His return flight from McGrath, over uncharted land in the early darkness of a winter night, was an experience even novelists would have had difficulty describing. Yet, Ben wrote about it in a matter-of-fact manner to postal officials in Washington, as follows:

> By this time it was pitch dark. I could not believe that I

had traveled 50 miles off my course after the same compass course had brought me to Lake Minchumina. I could not see the lights of Nenana, so I left the river going east. I thought I must have gotten on Kantishna River and that I was following it back to Mt. McKinley, as the country looked flat in the pitch darkness.

The sky was entirely overcast; not a star showed. I wandered around completely lost for over an hour. Then I knew that the river I lost was the Tanana. I saw a light. . . . I was tempted to set the ship down . . . but I would wreck it if I did. I went back to the big river [and then] saw a light in the distance. . . . It turned out to be my home field.

Ben's report on the first airmail flight in the government plane was of such interest that it was read aloud at a cabinet meeting. After hearing the report, President Coolidge, Secretary of Commerce Herbert Hoover, and Postmaster General Harry New were impressed. The President sent Ben a personal letter congratulating him on the success of his flight. Postmaster General New and Secretary Hoover, who had met Ben in July 1923 in Fairbanks when he put on an aerial stunt show for President Harding and his cabinet, also sent letters of commendation. Hoover's letter read in part: "I congratulate you on the conspicuous success of your undertaking. Your experience provides a unique and interesting chapter in the rapidly developing science of aerial navigation."

Ben's second airmail flight from Fairbanks to McGrath was on March 1. The early morning weather report from McGrath stated: "Temperature nine below zero, calm, clouds to the south."

Everything worked. Ben flew a straight course going over, veering to the left on the return trip in order to follow the flat country. He had decided that this course was the most practical in case of a forced landing. On the return flight the sky was overcast, so he could glimpse the mail trail only at a few points. His report to Washington on the second trip read:

Time on the trip over, 3 hours 15 minutes. Time return trip, 4 hours 20 minutes. Poor time on the return trip due to head winds. Left Fairbanks at 8:15 A.M. and carried 252 pounds of mail; arrived at McGrath at 11:30. Left McGrath at 12:55 P.M., arrived Fairbanks 5:15 P.M. The danger of losing the course is small and in case of forced landing, I am always

within striking distance of a roadhouse. There are quite a few
lakes and rivers for emergency landing. The ground is covered
with scrubby trees. On one side is the highest mountain range
in North America and on the other is a low range. I use 20
gallons of gas per hour at ordinary speed and about 1¼ gallons oil.

The skis are excellent for landing, smoother than wheels,
but easier to break. The engine exhaust heater keeps the cockpit entirely warm. We are indebted to the U.S. Signal Corps
for excellent weather service and reports on progress of flights,
furnished by radio. Have received finest cooperation from
Captain C. Burkhead, U.S.A., and Warrant Officer Davis, both
of Fairbanks.

When Ben landed at McGrath on his second trip, the helper he'd
started to train was there, eager to begin work. After the mail was
unloaded, Ben left to deliver personal packages that he'd been asked
to pick up. During lunch at the roadhouse, he again was besieged
with requests for goods from Fairbanks. He cheerfully obliged, a
practice that most other bush pilots continued through the years.

The third trip called for a stop at Nenana to deliver and to pick
up mail. Because of pressure applied by Nenana residents and those
beyond Nenana, arrangements were made with postal officials to
include Nenana on the airmail route so that town, too, could benefit
from the improved mail service under terms of the experimental mail
contract. The "landing field," which Ben had previously examined
at Nenana, was on the frozen Tanana River.

On March 12 Ben arrived in Nenana at 9:25 A.M. He unloaded
the mail from Fairbanks and loaded the 200 pounds of Nenana mail.
Four minutes later, he took off for McGrath. The balance of the trip
from Nenana to McGrath was uneventful, except that Ben spotted
many good winter landing places on rivers and lakes and at roadhouses to add to those he already had listed.

He landed at McGrath at 11:45 A.M. After the mail was unloaded,
Ben unloaded wire for the Takotna radio station. After lunch, he left
McGrath at 1:30 P.M. carrying about 170 pounds of mail in addition
to the Nenana mail.

The engine temperature on the trip over was only 65 degrees, a
little too cold for greatest efficiency. The shutters had been closed

all the way, so on the return trip the radiator was partly covered under the shutters to keep the engine warmer.

Ben landed in Fairbanks at 5:20 P.M. after being in the air for 3 hours 50 minutes. The temperature was 15 degrees above zero. In his report to postal authorities on the third trip, he wrote:

> We have been experimenting with different shaped skis for the tail skid. The ordinary skid buries itself completely in the snow. The first ski we put on was about three feet long, curved to fit the skid, and bolted on. We found this unnecessarily cumbersome. We are now using a board bolted on the skid and curved to fit. The board is six inches wide. It seems to work fine. If the snow is only a foot deep, this is not needed.

The fourth airmail flight was made on March 26. This was the coldest trip yet attempted, for the temperature stood at 10 degrees below zero with a light wind. Ben left Fairbanks at 7:40 A.M., landed at Nenana at 8:27 A.M., and departed at 8:52 A.M. As he landed at McGrath at 11:35 A.M., he struck an overflow on the Takotna River, which was covered by snowfall the day before. The plane broke through the thin ice and stopped in 6 inches of water. The ice below was solid, but the impact of landing and the jolt through the thin ice cracked one ski. With the help of several local men, temporary repairs were made.

When the mail was opened in McGrath, the postmaster showed Ben a newspaper that had been delivered from Washington, D.C., in only 14 days. Prior to the airplane service, the trip on the trail from Nenana to McGrath would have taken that long.

Ben departed at 1:05 P.M. The weather was clear when he left McGrath, but at Lake Minchumina he was slowed by a snowstorm. Later, he ran into a fog, but he was able to maintain ground contact.

The fifth trip was made on April 9. The temperature in Fairbanks was 12 degrees above zero, and skies were clear with a wind from the east. Ben left Fairbanks at 7:00 A.M. Owing to radio trouble, he received no weather report from McGrath. He landed at Nenana and departed five minutes later with about 300 pounds of mail. The trip from Nenana to McGrath was beautiful and clear.

At McGrath, a large delegation of Eskimos waited to meet him.

When he landed, they gathered around the plane, and a solemn spokesman informed Ben that they had prepared a potlatch celebration in his honor.

Ben was someone very special to the natives of Alaska. He was a strange combination of bird and man. After an elaborate feast, featuring many special native foods, the Eskimos presented Ben with a fine new parka. They adopted him into their tribe and gave him the title "Moose Ptarmigan Ben." After they presented the parka, the natives told him the meaning of his title. To the natives, the moose was the biggest animal known. Ben was the biggest man they had ever known, not in stature, but in achievement. The ptarmigan was their swiftest bird. Ben was both, hence the title "Moose Ptarmigan."

Ben was unable to speak for a few minutes, but then he thanked them for the potlatch, the parka, and his new title. He immediately changed into his new parka and then left to look over several spots for summer landing fields.

In his report to Washington on the fifth trip, Ben discussed the sites checked for landing fields and noted, "A lot of work will be required before we have a landing field in McGrath suitable for wheels."

There was a mix-up that day on the return flight. A snowstorm had developed in Fairbanks, and a wire was sent to Ben advising him to spend the night in McGrath. However, he left McGrath at 1:00 P.M. without receiving the message. He fought head winds and the storm on the return trip, which took four hours, but he landed without mishap at Fairbanks.

The sixth trip, made on April 23, was his fastest so far. The temperature at Fairbanks was 10 degrees above. It was partly cloudy, but there was no wind. Ben left at 6:50 A.M. and landed at Nenana at 7:13 A.M., where he picked up 365 pounds of mail and departed by 7:20 A.M. At 9:27 A.M. he landed at McGrath, for a total flying time of 2 hours 30 minutes.

The mail he brought to McGrath on the April 9 and April 23 flights would not have been delivered there for 2½ months by dog team because the spring thaw made travel impossible. The last dog team departed McGrath before April 9, and the first boat would not arrive before June 20. The month of April gave the airplane a chance to prove its all-weather superiority over established transportation systems.

When Ben landed at McGrath on the sixth trip, a delegation of miners from the Takotna mining camp, a few miles south of Ophir, met him at the plane. They had carried a very sick man, William "Hosie" Hummel, by dog team so Ben could fly him to Fairbanks. The miners had already contacted Dr. Joseph Herman Romig, physician for the Alaska Railroad, at Anchorage. After Romig received their wire, he advised them to take Hummel to McGrath so that the airmail plane could take him to the Fairbanks hospital. Romig would travel there.

Ben explained the regulation against carrying passengers on the mail plane. He also said that it was unfortunate that officials in Washington couldn't realize that the great distances in Alaska were a real hardship. Ben had two choices—refuse to carry the patient and run the risk of his dying, or carry him and jeopardize the mail contract. It didn't take long to decide, and Ben announced, "Hosie can ride in the back with the mail sacks. Just be sure you strap him in properly."

At 11:30 A.M. the silvery wings of the DeHavilland lifted skyward on their way to medical assistance. Before leaving McGrath, Ben warned Hummel that he expected trouble landing at the Fairbanks field, for the ballpark was soggy. A drainage ditch had been dug around the field, but it soon overflowed onto the field.

When the DeHavilland, with the extra weight, landed on the soggy runway, the standards on one ski broke. The plane skidded along the drainage ditch, then nosed over, snapping the propeller.

Ben climbed out and rushed to the aid of his passenger, who dangled upside down held by the safety straps. Slightly shaken but uninjured in spite of the unorthodox landing, Hummel was taken to the hospital where Dr. Romig waited.

In Ben's report to Washington, he stated:

> In McGrath it was explained to me that a very serious hospital case had developed and there was no doctor within several hundred miles. . . . Mr. William Hummel, was brought by dog team from Takotna and I took him to the Fairbanks hospital. . . . The trail is very bad now and the doctor here has since advised me that it was probably a case of life or death.

> For a report on the case you may write to Dr. Joseph Romig, Surgeon for the Government Railroad, Fairbanks, Alaska. The trip was made without compensation. We left McGrath at 11:30 A.M. and arrived in Fairbanks at 2:50 P.M. The patient stood the trip very well.

Ben also reported on the damages to the plane and added, "Damage was caused by poor judgment in attempting too quick a turn on the ground with skis. The plane has been repaired again and is ready to go. So far no trip has been postponed on account of weather and every trip, 600 miles, completed on the same day."

The seventh trip passed without incident, except for the usual problems at the Fairbanks field. The DeHavilland zoomed down at 60 miles per hour, much faster than the Jenny, and the 1,400-foot field, with stumps and a woodpile at one end, proved dangerously short.

Ben's eighth trip, the second one made in May, was ill-starred. He carried another illegal, but ill, passenger— Charlie Nystrom, from Iditarod. After they landed in Fairbanks, the plane hit a soggy spot and the wheels sank deep into the mud. The plane crashed sideways, then nosed over. Ben was disheartened. Once the government learned of the accident, it canceled the contract for the two remaining trips, but his friends predicted that the unexpected cancellation would not dim his enthusiasm for flying. They were right. After the first shock wore off, Ben went to work for Jimmy Rodebaugh, joining pilots Noel Wien and Art Sampson.

Jimmy Rodebaugh was a railroad conductor who thought that there was money to be made promoting aviation. He believed that flying was the fastest-growing business one could get into. He had enough money to buy two planes and planned a trip outside to buy them and look for a couple of pilots. In the spring of 1924, he ordered a stock of aviation gas in 5-gallon cans and launched his company with two Standard planes. He hired two young farm boys from Minnesota—Art Sampson and Noel Wien—as pilots. Wien had only 500 hours in the air and Sampson had less, but they were aviators, and Rodebaugh offered them $300 a month and paid their boat fares north.

The increased demand for planes meant that the best planes Rodebaugh could buy in the States cost him $5,000. The two Standards had Curtiss OX-5 engines that cruised little faster than autos and had to come down every 100 miles to refuel. But Rodebaugh had extra gas tanks built and replaced the engines with more powerful 150-horsepower water-cooled Hispano-Suizas, called "Hissos." Rodebaugh originally had planned an eight-hour-a-day operation, but business was good and he wanted to expand.

The first miner Ben carried was Jack Tobin, who wanted to land near Copper Mountain in Mt. McKinley National Park. The history-making trip was uneventful. (Later, Copper Mountain was renamed Mt. Eielson in honor of Ben, and the visitors' center there now provides a magnificent view of Mt. McKinley.)

While Ben was flying for Rodebaugh, he never forgot his dream of six airmail routes for Alaska. He contended that Nome needed to be served by plane, and he visualized air service from Alaska to Europe. Ben had a world view of things, and that appealed to many in Fairbanks. In the meantime, he, Sampson, and Wien hauled meat, sled dogs, gold dust, and whatever was needed by those living on the frontier. In one day Wien took in $1,500. The planes earned one-third of their cost the first summer by carrying joy riders at $10 a ride and miners at $1 a mile. Alaskans wanted to fly.

Although the Standards were profitable, Ben felt that bigger planes were needed. But he was convinced that government airmail contracts were the key to getting airlines established because the steady income from such contracts was essential. Rodebaugh did not believe that any money would come from the government. Alaskans didn't want to wait, and Rodebaugh felt that aviation was a sure-fire deal.

Ben continued to research the types of planes available interna-tionally. He had extensive correspondence with the Fairchild Aviation Corporation in New York. After he learned that his winter flying had attracted attention outside, he laid plans for private financing in New York in case the mail contract became a reality.

In an article written about the time of Ben's eighth trip, Vilhjalmur Stefansson stated:

> His second year in Alaska (1924) Ben Eielson received the
> first Alaskan airmail contract for winter flying. He made his
> trips regularly 600 miles every two weeks forward and back

between Fairbanks and McGrath, on time and without a hitch.
But that was a small part of his flying. He carried sick people
to the hospital, medicines to remote camps, and miners to
their work. . . . He had several forced landings, but the natural
landing fields were so numerous that he always came down
safely and took off safely after repairs. He was learning that
however bad the Arctic was for raising pineapples, it is about
the safest and easiest place there is for flying, especially in
winter, when every river and every little lake is a safe and
smooth landing field, or at least safer and smoother than you
can find almost anywhere else.

Ben kept busy sending letters and wires to all Federal and Territorial officials, stressing the need for airmail service for Alaska and
asking for an appeal of the decision of postal officials. The replies
were far from encouraging. The only hopeful news Ben received was
from Dan Sutherland, who reported that he was working toward
getting a bill introduced in Congress permitting the use of airplanes
in Alaska for mail delivery. Sutherland told Ben that he expected to
have the bill approved before the Post Office Department called for
new bids for mail delivery in Alaska. Ben promptly replied that he
had prepared a proposal on a network of six routes.

19

Billy Mitchell Tries to Help

WHILE BEN KEPT HIS HOPES HIGH for a permanent mail contract, an unexpected blow to Alaska's brightening aviation reputation came from a project pushed by General Billy Mitchell, a vociferous proponent of both aviation and Alaska. Among the reasons Mitchell felt his round-the-world flight was needed was that it would draw attention to the strategic importance of Alaska. But the flight came at a time when many in high government offices still considered aviation a fad and not one to be taken too seriously.

Ben told his friends not to pay too much attention to Mitchell's expedition because of the adverse publicity. He added that if he had the proper equipment, he could fly across the Arctic Ocean. He mentioned that in 1923, Roald Amundsen, in a foreign-built Junkers plane, attempted to fly from Wainwright, Alaska, over the North Pole.

The four planes used by Mitchell were designed and built by the then relatively unknown Donald Douglas. The single-engine Douglas World Cruiser biplanes were powered by 450-horsepower 12-cylinder Liberty engines. They were open-cockpit planes with interchangeable landing gear, wheels, or pontoons. The flagship was named the *Seattle*, and the other three planes were the *Boston*, the *Chicago*, and the *New Orleans*.

The worldwide race for the first country to fly around the globe was too much of a challenge for Mitchell to ignore. He could not sit and watch while British, French, Portuguese, and Argentine airmen performed that spectacular, but dangerous, venture. He upset many when he insisted that the United States should get into the competition, but, eventually, the United States joined in the race.

The round-the-world flight squadron left Santa Monica, California, on March 17 and arrived in Seattle, Washington, on March 20. There, pontoons were substituted for wheels.

The original schedule called for the squadron to reach Sitka, Alaska, on April 2, 1924, simultaneously with the opening of the Alaska American Legion convention. Bad weather and a minor accident to Major Frederick Martin's plane, the *Seattle*, caused a delay. On April 5, as the planes prepared to leave Seattle, it was discovered that one of the metal wing tips on the plane's propeller was broken. As it was being replaced, a wrench was dropped through a pontoon, making a new float necessary.

On April 6 repairs were completed and the flight got underway, with three of the planes finally getting into the air after engine trouble. But the *Boston* was unable to take off until its load was lightened. Yet, all four planes made it to Prince Rupert, British Columbia, before dark. Prior to landing there, Major Martin put the *Seattle* into a steep dive and broke two wing struts. On April 10 the squadron arrived in Sitka.

The planes were to fly to Cordova, but gale-force winds threatened to end the entire expedition. On April 13 they landed at Seward after 7 hours 38 minutes in the air. On April 15 they took off for Chignik, where three planes arrived on schedule, but the *Seattle* did not.

Two navy destroyers, the *Hull* and the *Corry*, performing a line of soundings for a new submarine cable, were both diverted to search for the *Seattle*. The *Hull* found it at Portage Bay. A hole in the crankcase had caused a forced landing. The other three planes reached Dutch Harbor on April 19.

On April 25, after a new engine was installed, the *Seattle* took off for Chignik. On April 30 it left Chignik for Dutch Harbor and disappeared for the second time. Coast Guard cutters, a survey ship, and all available cannery tenders, fishing vessels, and other small craft in the area searched the shores on both sides of the Alaska Peninsula and adjacent islands but were unsuccessful in locating the *Seattle*.

On May 3 the other three planes flew to Atka. On May 10 they left for Attu. By then, they had completed 4,690 miles in 61 hours 53 minutes of flying time since leaving California on March 17.

On May 8 the North American Newspaper Alliance offered a $1,000 reward to anyone finding Major Frederick Martin and Sergeant Alvah Harvey, but the two men rescued themselves. On their way to Dutch Harbor they crashed into the side of a mountain in thick fog, wrecking the plane completely, but neither man was seriously injured. With survival gear, they walked for seven days before reaching a trapper's cabin on the shore of Port Moller. At the cabin they found food and shelter. They rested there for three days, regaining their strength. Unfortunately, Major Martin's crash caused the Territory to later be condemned for air travel.

In the meantime, the *Boston*, the *Chicago*, and the *New Orleans* left Attu on May 17 for the 870-mile flight to Paramushir Island, in the Kuriles, where they put down safely after eight hours of flying.

Leaving Paramushir Island, the three planes headed for Japan and then to India, to Europe, and across the Atlantic to the United States. The *Boston* went down in the Atlantic off the coast of Greenland, but the pilot survived and was provided with a substitute plane. On September 28, 1924, after covering nearly 28,000 miles in 371 hours of flying time, the *Chicago* and the *New Orleans,* along with the replacement for the *Boston,* completed the journey by arriving back in California.

The national publicity from the expedition should have proved beneficial to Alaskan aviation. But Martin's crash had some effect on the cancellation of Ben's mail contract. Alaskan aviation enthusiasts hastened to point out that the crash of the *Seattle* had occurred in the Aleutian Islands in a fog-ridden coastal area between Chignik and Dutch Harbor.

In indignation, Thompson wrote: "With all other means of transportation flagrantly inadequate, the plane is a heaven sent chariot in Alaska. It's used to aid the wounded and sick far from doctor and hospital, to transport judges, bishops, mining engineers, miners, and fur farmers."

Yet, the adverse publicity connected with the round-the-world flight left its mark. Requests for parts to repair the mail plane were turned down, and appropriations for airfields were defeated. This made it difficult for Ben to promote an airmail contract for Alaska.

During an interview in Alaska, Major Martin tried to help mat-

ters, but perhaps some of his statements only made things worse. He
said:

> You can take it from me, Eielson has a worse game to
> plan than ours. In the army's round-the-world flight, there
> were four machines and eight men. We had supply bases scat-
> tered all along the route, with accurate maps of the whole
> course. But Eielson is flying alone, in a strange country, with-
> out proper facilities for repairing his plane. We have to hand
> it to him; one slip and he's gone.

Ben grew impatient with the apparent postponement of a decision on airmail service for Alaska. He again headed for Washington.
Together, he and Dan Sutherland made the rounds of the government
offices. One high-ranking official told them that it was impossible
to operate a plane in winter in Alaska because the temperature
dropped to 70 degrees below zero. Officials completely ignored the
fact that Ben had flown in Alaska in the winter and had already
demonstrated the feasibility of winter flying. None of the men opposing a new mail contract for Alaska had ever set foot there or even
flown a plane!

Later, Ben learned that a few postal employees in Alaska had
written to Washington to say that too great a risk was involved in
sending important papers by air. They overlooked the fact that the
mail had been lost many times while being delivered by dog teams.

After a second trip around the circuit of offices to check on
progress, Ben was discouraged but not undaunted. He decided that
if he could get private financing for planes, he would submit a
prospectus and bid on the mail contract.

Although Ben was unknown in New York and unfamiliar with
the financial world, he set about the job with the same spirit that
sent him cruising Arctic skies. Entering the financial maelstrom of
New York City, he went from office to office, determined to get the
backing he needed.

After his initial calls in New York, Ben was much encouraged.
He stopped in Washington to talk to Sutherland again, but with
things at a temporary halt in Washington, Ben decided to take
advantage of the lull for a visit with his family in North Dakota.

20

Nome—A Spotlight on Alaskan Problems

BEN FOUND IT GOOD to be back in Hatton. After a huge family reunion dinner, he had a long talk with his father. As he briefed Ole on his eight winter mail flights, he could tell that his father was proud of his pioneering in airmail delivery in Alaska. But it also was plain that Ole still feared that Ben might meet an untimely death while flying. Earlier that evening Oliver told Ben that Ole was haunted by the thought that Ben would lose his life in a crash far from family and friends.

Ole pleaded with Ben to return to school and earn his law degree. At first the thought of an indoor academic life was revolting, but Ben finally yielded to his father's persistent pleas. Soon Ben was on his way back to Washington to enroll at the Georgetown University Law School.

Ben tried hard to concentrate on his law courses. Three weeks passed, and he reached the limits of his endurance in the new world of no flying. About that time, an officer in the Army Air Service contacted Ben and offered him a chance to participate in experimental work connected with cold-weather flying. Although he knew that his father would be displeased, Ben sent a wire home: "Have joined the Army Air Service. Send uniform and Sam Browne belt."

Ben followed the telegram with a letter explaining that the three weeks of law school had convinced him that flying in Alaska would always come first from now on. He explained that having a part in establishing aviation in Alaska meant more to him than a law degree. The Army Air Service gave him such a good offer that he couldn't resist.

The army was experimenting with airplane skis, and Ben was given that assignment at Langley Field, Virginia. Here, he designed skis that were strong yet light weight. If he'd learned anything by flying with the skis that Charlie Schiek had whittled for the DeHavilland, it was that they were too clumsy and weighed too much.

In late October 1924, Ben went to McCook Field, Dayton, Ohio, for experiments with his new skis. During his stay there he decided to visit all the officers he could to plug Alaska. By the end of his stay, he had talked to every officer there.

First, Ben told the officers about his experiences in Alaska and then suggested the establishment of an airmail route from New York City, across Alaska, to Peking, China. But Ben knew as he talked to them that nothing would come of the idea at that time. Yet, most of the officers listened sympathetically.

Ben didn't rest until he got an interview with General Billy Mitchell, who was stationed at McCook Field. He was so excited after that event that he rushed back to his room to write W. F. Thompson about their discussion. He ended his letter by saying:

> Mitchell is a good friend of Alaska. I suggested to him and other officers in the Chief's office what could be done in the way of mapping, photography, gathering data, and transporting government agents in Alaska. . . . I have been doing nothing else but explaining why Alaska needs government planes and I received the best encouragement. . . . I shall never be satisfied until I get back there.

However, unfortunately for Alaska, within a few months things were going badly for General Mitchell. The fiery advocate for air power was in danger of being court martialed for his constant and continuing criticism of U.S. aviation policies.

In November, Ben experimented with lighter flying clothes for Arctic weather—a fur suit connected to a tube that supplied fresh air heated from the exhaust of the engine.

Ben's contract with the Army Air Service expired at the end of the year. Then, he planned to submit his prospectus before the Appropriations Committee and bid against the dog-team mail contractor. He and Dan Sutherland planned an all-out effort.

In early 1925 events were not good for regular airmail service in

Alaska. However, Ben's plans for private financial backing of commercial air transport using Fairchilds were looking up. And Thompson continued his blistering editorials concerning the federal shortsightedness. In the meantime, in far-away Nome, a disaster was pending. A diphtheria epidemic in that isolated community made worldwide news.

In January 1925, Nome's only doctor, Curtis Welch, found two unusual cases while making house calls. He was puzzled by the illness of two Eskimo children, whose symptoms he was unable, or perhaps unwilling, to diagnose. These two cases set the stage for a dramatic episode—a life or death struggle. They also made Dr. Welch's name a byword of courage, and the Alaskan dog mushers the heroes of the hour. The event also proved very frustrating for backers of aviation in Alaska.

On a cold day in mid-January, Dr. Welch visited a small, dimly lit house in the Eskimo settlement on the sand spit west of the Snake River, where two Eskimo children lay sick. Dr. Welch examined the children, who had already been sick for three days. They both had high fevers, and their throats were so sore they were unable to open their mouths wide enough for a thorough examination. Dr. Welch wished, as he so often did, that he had a good laboratory available where he could send specimens or a throat swab for analysis. At one point in his examination, the thought of diphtheria occurred to him. The symptoms were there, but he felt that it was highly unlikely. He hadn't seen a case of diphtheria in 20 years in northern Alaska. Also, he reasoned, it was a contagious disease that required a carrier, and Nome had been isolated since the sea froze over in the fall.

Despite the doctor's efforts to treat them, the children got worse. In discussing the case with his wife, Lulu, Dr. Welch said, "It's very strange. Children don't die from sore throats or tonsillitis, but the fact is they are DYING!" The two children died the following day.

On January 21, Dr. Welch was summoned to the Stanly home to examine six-year-old Richard, with the same symptoms. Following his examination, Dr. Welch admitted that he recognized almost immediately what he'd feared to find—the patches of diphtheria membrane.

With only 75,000 units of diphtheria antitoxin on hand. Dr. Welch and his wife realized the terrible implications of his diagnosis. Unless checked, diphtheria could spread in Nome with devastating speed. In the summer of 1924, Dr. Welch had ordered additional supplies of antitoxin from the U.S. Public Health Office in Seattle, but, for some reason, none had been sent. Now, it might be too late.

After advising Mrs. Stanly of his findings, the doctor rushed home to pick up the antitoxin for Richard. But it was too late; the child died during the night.

Dr. Welch acted quickly, notifying Mayor George Maynard and asking that he convene the city council at once to create a Board of Health to enforce quarantine regulations and to handle the mechanics of combating an epidemic. Explaining that the antitoxin on hand would only help check the spread of the virulent disease and help save those who had been infected if the symptoms were caught in time, Welch added, "We must have more serum. We must find out if there is more antitoxin in Alaska. If we have to wait for serum to get here from Seattle, it will be too late."

The mayor suggested that if serum could be located in Alaska, perhaps it could be flown from Fairbanks to Nome. But Alaska's most daring pilot, Carl Ben Eielson, was in Washington, lobbying for airmail service for the Territory. With an epidemic threatening Nome, everything depended on how fast medical supplies could be obtained.

None of the men at the meeting had to be reminded of the seriousness of an epidemic. The predominately Eskimo population had little or no immunity to the white man's diseases. During the 1918–19 flu epidemic, entire villages were wiped out. Even in Nome, where the population was served by a doctor and medical care was available, the epidemic left 91 flu orphans.

The councilmen finally decided to first send wireless messages through the Army Signal Corps office, telling Alaska communities of the serious situation and the urgent need for antitoxin. Within seconds, Dr. Welch's message flashed out across the wilderness. Signal Corps operators monitoring shortwave radios in Alaska's scattered towns and small cities were soon listening intently to Sergeant Jack Anderson, keying Nome's call signal.

Dan Sutherland was notified in Washington, and he received full cooperation from the U.S. Public Health Service. Some Alaskans later said that perhaps the agency was trying to make up for the failure to stockpile the expensive serum in Nome as a safeguard against just such an emergency.

In Alaska, there was widespread relief when it was learned from Dr. J. B. Beeson, at the Alaska Railroad Hospital, that he recently had received 300,000 units of the life-saving serum and that he would send it to Nome. He said he knew it was not enough, but it would help.

Fairbanks residents bombarded Governor Bone and Delegate Sutherland with telegrams asking the okay to carry the serum to Nome by air. Rodebaugh's company had already dismantled the two Standards and stored them for the winter, but without waiting for official approval, Rodebaugh gave orders to ready a plane for flight. He then searched for a pilot. Former navy pilot Roy Darling, an agent in Alaska for the Justice Department, and mechanic Ralph Mackie, a former Royal Canadian officer living in Anchorage, volunteered to attempt the flight.

Governor Scott C. Bone was showered with advice from many people, but he ruled in favor of using dog teams. He said that there was a better-than-even chance the Standard airplane could not make it to Nome and that, if the plane crashed, the serum would be lost. With it would go Nome's chances to avoid a runaway epidemic. Explaining his decision to Territorial officials, Bone stressed that the existing Standard airplanes in Fairbanks were inadequate and that only a relatively unskilled flier was available.

After arranging for a number of mail teams to carry the serum, the governor telegraphed Wetzler (first name unknown), a U.S. postal official in Nenana, to arrange for additional teams to be assigned to the trail so the race down the Tanana and Yukon valleys to Nome could be run in shorter relays.

The word was quickly passed to all Signal Corps stations. Before receiving the message at his station that a team bearing the serum was approaching, a Signal Corpsman would strap on snowshoes and head for the nearest native village to request that its best team and musher assist regular mail drivers along the route.

"Wild Bill" Shannon, the first musher in the relay, was standing by at Nenana on January 27 to begin the run to Tolovana. The temperature was 40 degrees below zero. The train pulled into the

Nenana depot at 11:00 P.M., and the conductor passed the serum package to Shannon. The great serum run had began.

At 6:00 A.M. January 28, Leonard Seppala, the best musher in Alaska, received instructions to leave Nome and start at once for Nulato, on the Yukon. Seppala thought he was to meet a driver there and return to Nome, over 600 miles.

In the meantime, at Tolovana, Dan Green waited for Bill Shannon to arrive. By the time Shannon got to Tolovana, 15 new cases and 4 deaths were reported.

Green read the instructions for care of the serum and went into the roadhouse to warm it for 15 minutes. The package was then lashed to his sled, and he started for Manley Hot Springs, 31 miles away, where Johnny Folger and his dogs waited.

When Green arrived, the serum was warmed, and Folger was on his way to Fish Lake, 28 miles down the Yukon. At Fish Lake, Sam Joseph and his team took the serum and headed for Tanana, 26 miles away. At Tanana, Titus Nickoli carried the serum 34 miles farther west to Kalland's. The mushers averaged five to eight miles per hour.

In the States, many of the media realized that they could sell papers with colorful stories of the dramatic race against death. With few facts available, they let their imaginations run wild. Howling winds and minus-60-degree temperatures along the entire route made good reading.

At Kalland's, Nickoli passed the serum to Dave Corning, who kept up the relentless pace, averaging 8 miles per hour for the next 24 miles. At the Nine Mile shelter house, Edgar Kalland warmed the serum before beginning the next run to Kokrines.

Darkness had fallen again on the trail on the ice of the frozen Yukon. At the Kokrines relay point, 30 miles away, Harry Pitka waited to pick up the serum. At Ruby, another 30 miles, Bill McCarty waited for Pitka. McCarty took the serum to Whiskey Creek, 28 miles down the river.

It was 10:00 P.M. when Edgar Nollner met McCarty at Whiskey Creek. The temperature registered minus 40 degrees, but within minutes the 21-year-old Nollner was pushing his nine dogs as fast as they could go the 24 miles to Galena. There he met his older brother, George, who took the serum to Bishop Mountain, 18 miles down the trail.

Young Charlie Evans was waiting at Bishop Mountain with a team of nine dogs. As Evans waited for Nollner, the weather turned bitterly cold. When George arrived at Bishop Mountain, Evans warmed the serum for almost an hour, afraid the piercing cold would freeze the serum otherwise.

When Evans left the warm cabin and headed for Nulato, it was 5 o'clock Friday morning, 54 hours since the serum had started its journey from Nenana. The temperature was minus 64 degrees.

At the section of the trail where the east mouth of the Koyukuk River flowed into the Yukon, Evans came to open water. He slowed down the team and carefully skirted the overflow and the open leads of water. Dense ice fog also lay along the trail. Evans pulled into Nulato at 10:00 A.M. after a cruel 30-mile run. Two of his dogs had frozen groins and later died.

At Nulato, Tommy Patsy was waiting to take the serum to Kaltag, 36 miles away. Patsy lashed the warmed serum to his sled and, with the best dogs in the village, dashed onto the river ice for the final leg before the trail headed cross-country for the Bering Sea.

Trail conditions were ideal; the snow was packed and the light good. Patsy made the 36-mile run in only $3\frac{1}{2}$ hours, averaging better than 10 miles per hour, the fastest individual time in the serum run.

From Kaltag, the nature of the epic race changed gradually. The trail, that for the first 390 miles followed the Tanana and Yukon valleys, now swung southwest into the hills and away from the rivers. For the next 75 miles, it followed the undulations of small streams, climbing and then descending until it reached the Bering Sea at Unalakleet.

In the meantime, on January 31, the *S. S. Alameda* sailed from Seattle for Seward with 1,100,000 units of diphtheria antitoxin aboard to back up the first shipment of 300,000 units being rushed to Nome by dog team. The Department of Justice and the Navy Department also wired permission to Roy Darling, who wanted to attempt a flight to Nome, that he could fly if he wished, without expense to the government. But by then, so much time had elapsed that it was apparent even to the most partisan flying boosters that the Rodebaugh plane would not be off the ground before the serum reached Nome by dog team. However, with unquenchable enthusiasm, the airplane proponents went ahead with plans to carry the second batch of serum, due in Seward on February 7, to Nome.

In Nome, Dr. Welch and his dedicated nurses at the missionary hospital continued to fight their own grim battle. The dreaded first symptoms of diphtheria were appearing in more and more people. Then panic struck. To escape the quarantine and the disease, frightened residents started to slip away from Nome by dog team to other villages.

As conditions in Nome became more critical, the Board of Health decided to add additional dog teams to aid Seppala along the trail. To speed the relays even more, health officer Summers sent a wireless message to Charles Traeger, storekeeper at Unalakleet, to spare no expense in arranging for additional dog teams to carry the serum north until it could be transferred to Seppala's sled.

Over the huge expanse of western Alaska, the dog teams then carrying the serum inched ever closer to the Bering Sea. Jackscrew, an Indian musher, urged his dogs to greater speed as they climbed higher, into the sloping valleys of the low mountains between Kaltag and Unalakleet. Darkness had fallen, and it started to snow before he reached the mail cabin, 22 miles from his destination at the Old Woman Shelterhouse.

Victor Anagick, a full-blooded Eskimo, picked up the warmed serum at Old Woman and headed for Unalakleet, 34 miles away. He was driving Traeger's excellent 11-dog team. Anagick reached Unalakleet at 3:30 Saturday morning. In six hours he had carried the serum 34 miles.

At Unalakleet, Myles Gonangnan took over, and at Eban, 25 miles later, Gonangnan warmed the serum. He was only 15 miles from Shaktolik, but the wind was blowing hard, and the snow was drifting. Despite warnings, he pushed on.

At Shaktolik, Henry Ivanoff waited. The serum was transferred. But Ivanoff ran into trouble when his dogs picked up the scent of reindeer on the trail and tried to break away to follow the herd. Ivanoff drove his steel two-spike sled brake into the snow to halt the half-crazed team. Immediately, two of his dogs got into a fight. As he waded into the fray, swinging the butt of his whip to restore order, he saw a dog team coming.

Ivanoff recognized Seppala and his distinctive Siberian Huskies.

He waved and yelled at Seppala, but Seppala didn't hear his shouts and only waved back. The second time Ivanoff shouted louder, "Serum! Turn back!"

At first Seppala thought he'd misunderstood the stranger. According to the original plans, he still had 140 miles to go before he reached Nulato, where he expected to pick up the serum. Seppala had been out of communication with Nome and didn't know of the added teams on both ends of the relay.

However, Seppala stopped and turned around. He had left Issac's Point on the north side of Norton Bay that morning and had already mushed 45 hard miles to near Shaktolik. Both men knew that although Ivanoff's dogs were fresh, Seppala's championship team under the guidance of their veteran driver would make much better time through the gathering storm. The two men transferred the serum to Seppala's sled. Seppala shouted to his lead dog, Togo, and the team started back toward Issac's Point. It had been four days since they left Nome. Seppala had driven approximately 30 miles the first day and 50 miles each day since then.

Because of the unfavorable news about the spread of the epidemic, Seppala elected to take a short cut to Issac's Point. He ran into overflow on the ice and open leads of water, but his well-trained team skirted the obstacles and kept going. On his return trip across the ice, Seppala averaged an extraordinary time of seven miles per hour. When he pulled into the kennel at Issac's Point, his team had traveled a total of 84 miles without stopping to rest.

Seppala asked the Eskimo there to build a fire. He undid the package of serum, placing it as close to the fire as he dared. He staked out his team in the dog barns and finally stretched out to rest by the fire, hoping the blizzard would moderate.

Early Sunday morning Seppala hitched his dogs to the sled and lashed the serum in place. The weather hadn't improved. With the temperature at minus 30 degrees and the blizzard still raging, Seppala took off again, heading to Golovin. When he reached Golovin, Charlie Olson was waiting to take the serum to Bluff. The antitoxin was now only 78 miles from Nome.

Olson waved goodbye to Seppala at 3:15 Sunday afternoon. He soon was swallowed up in the blizzard as he headed west toward

Nome. He estimated the wind at 40 miles per hour and prayed that his dogs would be able to make the 25 miles to his Bluff Roadhouse.

As Olson came to Golovin Lagoon, storm gusts funneling through the valley of low hills struck with such force that the sled, the dogs, and Olson were lifted physically from the trail and half buried. Olson righted the sled, checked the serum package, and was soon underway again. Time after time, Olson and his team were forced off the trail. But the veteran musher stubbornly drove on toward Bluff. There, Gunnar Kaasen waited to take the serum on the next relay. Before Kaasen had left Nome, he had chosen Balto, Seppala's champion dog, for a leader.

At 7:30 P.M. Kaasen heard Olson's team pull into the roadhouse. Olson brought the serum inside and warmed it. Olson said that his fingers had become either frostbitten or frozen. It had happened when he stopped to blanket the dogs during the worst part of the blizzard. He also said that he thought two of his dogs might have frozen their groins. Both animals later died.

Fumbling in the darkness, Kaasen tied the 20-pound package of serum to his sled. For the first few miles he made good time. Five miles from Bluff he had to put on snowshoes and break trail around a drift for the stalled team. Farther down the trail the storm grew worse. Soon hurricane-like winds overturned the sled. When Kaasen righted the sled, he discovered that the package of serum was missing. He groped in the snow, searching frantically for the precious package. The serum had traveled over 600 miles by dog team, and Kaasen didn't want to be the one to lose it. Suddenly, he stumbled onto the package in the drifts. It was intact. With a prayer of thanks, he once again lashed it carefully to the sled.

For some reason Kaasen bypassed the cabin at Pt. Safety, where he knew Ed Rohn was waiting to take the serum to Nome. The Board of Health had sent a message to Solomon and Pt. Safety instructing Rohn and Kaasen to wait until the blizzard blew itself out. But, when Kaasen didn't stop at Pt. Safety, he didn't learn of the order. Kaasen's decision to bypass Ed Rohn was the cause of a controversy that lasted for many years.

The trail from Pt. Safety to Nome followed the beach, where snow had drifted heavily, but Seppala's Balto plowed through the heavy drifts. At 5:30 A.M. Monday, February 2, Kaasen swung up from the beach onto Nome's main street. No one was around. Nome residents did not expect the serum to be delivered until after the blizzard abated. Kaasen knocked at the door of Welch's office. A surprised Dr. Welch answered the door. Kaasen handed him the fur- and canvas-covered package. It had come the last 53 miles in 7½ hours. By noon on February 2, Dr. Welch was inoculating the well with the lifesaving liquid.

However, a moment of panic occurred when Dr. Welch first opened the serum package and found that the entire 300,000 units were frozen solid. A radiogram to the U.S. Public Health Office brought the immediate response that the antitoxin was not harmed by freezing.

Altogether, 19 dog teams had traveled 674 miles from Nenana to Nome in 127½ hours to bring to Nome the lifesaving serum. In less than a week the diphtheria epidemic was under control. Governor Bone eventually issued the drivers a citation for their part in the serum race.

Two good results came from the publicity surrounding the serum race. First, everywhere in remote areas, known antitoxins were stockpiled against such emergencies as Nome's. Second, the need for airplanes in Alaska was brought to the attention of officials in Washington with a rude shock.

The day after the serum arrived in Nome, the Associated Press, under a Washington dateline, reported the diphtheria epidemic had spurred the Post Office Department into immediate plans for airmail service. Ben hoped it was true, because he was about to submit his new bid for six routes running out of Fairbanks. After proving to postal officials inside and outside of Alaska that commercial aviation was possible and logical in interior Arctic regions, Ben went to New York City to arrange financing for Fairchild planes.

Later, he wrote to friends in Hatton and in Fairbanks: "It was the toughest job I ever had. But I managed to raise the capital for my company. Of course, the financing is contingent on our getting the mail contracts. With aviation gas costing as high as $1.80 a gallon and pilots' salaries hitting the $1,000.00 a month mark, we had to have those airmail contracts."

At the last minute, Ben revised his prospectus to include a

statement about the diphtheria epidemic in Nome. In an added paragraph he stated:

> Carrying the Alaskan mail by airplane would be but another step forward by the Post Office Department. It would give better service from the start with the probability of lower cost in the future. The Alaskans will have better and cheaper transportation than by the present method, and the airplane will prevent the reoccurrence of such incidents as the Nome diphtheria crisis in 1925.

Vilhjalmur Stefansson had strong words to say about the needless loss of life in the diphtheria epidemic. In an article written for *The Outlook Magazine*, he said:

> It was marvelous luck for the thrill seeking public that Eielson had come down to Washington to lobby for Congressional support of Alaskan flying when the diphtheria epidemic broke out in Nome. Had he been in Fairbanks, the authorities would simply have paid him so much per pound per mile to carry the antitoxin through to Nome, and you might have seen a three-inch notice of it on the inside page of some city newspaper. But he was in Washington, and so the dogs got their chance to race against death, "across the treeless, pathless, uninhabited, frozen wilderness, 700 miles from Nenana to Nome." Of course, there were in reality roads or trails, some of the route was through forest, and there were roadhouses on the average of every 30 miles. But the public did not know these things, and so they had their thrilling "Race with Death," which as we said, they could not have had if Eielson's air taxi had been there to carry in the serum at the regular mileage tariff.

In Alaska, Thompson did considerable writing about the epidemic, in words that were ahead of their time:

> The epidemic which has taken such deadly toll at Nome should serve to rouse the federal government from its lethargy regarding things Alaskan to a sufficient degree to render the reoccurrence of such a condition impossible. Just so long as the United States maintains, in Alaska, its present form of paternalistic government, the citizens of the Territory are justified in expecting paternalistic protection.

Had a trained Arctic flier, such as Ben Eielson, been in Fairbanks, the stricken and isolated people of Nome would have soon had the precious antitoxin serum which would have meant life to many. But our Government is intent on petty economics. . . . Airmail service is too expensive for Alaska, however, even though the stupendous value of such service in just such crises as the present one was pointed out to the Post Office Department at the time of the discontinuance of the service.

We have plenty of fliers and plenty of planes. . . . Why not station a plane, a couple of fliers, and a mechanician or two at each of the radio stations in Alaska for emergency duty? It would do no harm to train a few fliers for Arctic service.

The Prospectus of the Alaskan Air Transport Corporation was submitted in conjunction with the Fairchild Aviation Corporation of New York. Most of the groundwork was done while Ben was in Alaska.

After postal and other government officials read the comprehensive prospectus, there was not much they could do except advise Ben that they would accept a regular bid for airmail service for Alaska. They told Ben that, of course, this did not mean he would get the contract. They expected that the present holders of the mail delivery contract in Alaska, the dog-team contractors, also would submit bids. They told him that the contract would be awarded to the party making the lowest bid.

On December 8, 1925, Ben submitted his ambitious bid to service the six different routes in Alaska. Should the government accept his proposal, the mail would be transported from Nenana to Nome in 2 days instead of the 56 days required by dog team.

21

The Detroit Arctic Expedition

WHILE WAITING FOR A REPLY from the government, Ben returned to Hatton, where he took up work selling bonds. The incongruous job was set up by Oliver, who was a bond broker in Minneapolis. Oliver was happy in his work and made good money; he persuaded Ben to join him. The two brothers traveled extensively in northeastern North Dakota selling bonds. The routine work almost sent Ben silly, and Ben's dislike of selling nearly drove Oliver to distraction. But Ben stayed with it, only to please his father. The life of a bond salesman, Ole thought, was great for Ben. It paid well, was steady, and, most important, kept him on the ground. Fortunately for Alaska and aviation, Ben was bored to the danger point by bond selling when news of an Arctic expedition came.

While Ben sat in a barber shop in Langdon, North Dakota, a messenger from the telephone office came in to say that Ole had called from Hatton and wanted him to return the call immediately. A telegram from Captain George Hubert Wilkins had arrived stating that he was looking for a pilot to go with him on an Arctic expedition. Ole explained that Vilhjalmur Stefansson had recommended Ben as the pilot with the most experience in Arctic flying. Ole told Ben that if he wanted the job, he was to wire Stefansson immediately and then meet with Wilkins in New York. Ben promptly wired Stefansson that he was interested.

Early the next morning Ben boarded the train, looking impatiently toward his meeting with Wilkins. He told Oliver that he thought the job might be the most exciting one he'd ever been offered. When Ben arrived in New York, he immediately called

Wilkins. From their first meeting and handshake, Ben knew he'd found a like spirit in Wilkins.

For more than a decade, Wilkins had refused to abandon his goal of exploring the Arctic by airplane. Ben told Wilkins he thought flying in the Arctic was entirely feasible. Then he explained that his main reason for taking the job was to get back to flying and to save money so he could finance his company.

"Eielson," Wilkins declared, "the air is the only practical mode of travel for the interior of Alaska."

Like most explorers, Wilkins was able to choose his personnel from scores of applicants. If Ben proved to be all that Stefansson said he was, Wilkins planned to make him the head pilot. As commander of the expedition, Wilkins would be the navigator on the proposed flight to the "inaccessible" North Pole.

Both Wilkins and Ben knew that during the next six months the Arctic promised to be so full of airplanes that the polar bear in that unknown area between Alaska and the North Pole would have little privacy.

Preparations were being made by several nations, including the United States, to solve the last remaining mystery of the North— whether or not there was land within the million square miles marked "unexplored." All the great nations of the world were fully aware of the potential value of any land that might exist in the Arctic, particularly in view of the rapid approach of the age of commercial aviation.

Three American expeditions would do their reconnoitering by air. Norway also was sending an expedition, and France another, to find and to claim title to possible land between Alaska and the Pole. It also was rumored that Japan, the USSR, and Germany were hastening preparations in an attempt to be the discoverer. The announcement of plans for the Arctic expeditions revived an interest in exploration that had lain dormant since Robert E. Peary discovered the North Pole on April 6, 1909.

Soon there was much nationwide publicity about Wilkins' projected expedition into the unknown. Ben sent his family several clippings about the proposed expedition, for he didn't want Ole to worry about the more spectacular media descriptions.

Wilkins told Ben that he hoped to make the flight from Barrow, the northernmost point on the North American continent, on March 21, 1926. By starting before the season of dense and impenetrable fogs, Wilkins hoped to accomplish in two weeks that which explorers had dreamed about for two centuries.

After he had visited with Wilkins several times, Ben decided that Wilkins probably was the best qualified person to conduct an expedition. Ben found that Wilkins had more experience in aviation than any other explorer and a broader training in both Arctic and Antarctic exploration than any other aviator. Not only did Wilkins have some experience as a pilot, but he also was an outstanding navigator. In addition, he was a motion picture photographer of note and an expert on the internal combustion engine.

Wilkins was born in South Australia. After his education he was a photographic correspondent with the Turkish troops in the Balkan War of 1912–13. He was with Stefansson's Arctic expedition when World War I started. He returned to Australia to join the army as commander of a squadron of six photographic airplanes. He won the British Military Cross for extraordinary heroism during the war and was mentioned several times in dispatches.

After World War I, Wilkins was a navigator on one of the airplanes that flew from London to Australia in 1919. He was second in command on the British Imperial Arctic Expedition of 1920–21. Then he joined Sir Ernest Henry Shackleton on a voyage to the Antarctic and was with Shackleton when the explorer died in 1922. Following that, he went on an Australian expedition under the auspices of the British Museum.

The idea of reaching Arctic lands by air was not new. It had occurred to farsighted men long before flying had developed enough to make such a project practical. Solomon Andree's balloon flight in 1897 from Spitzbergen was as bold as it was brilliant, even though it ended in disaster. The first successful airplane flights in the Arctic were credited to a Russian, Lieutenant Nagursky [first name not found], who was based at Novaya Zemlya.

Wilkins said that his expedition would mark the first comprehensive and determined effort to reach the inaccessible Pole and explore the polar basin from the air. Other modern explorers (notably Stefansson, MacMillan, Nansen, and Storkerson) had traversed the fringe with the most modern means at their disposal—dog teams and sleds—but no one had ventured near the center of the unknown region. Peary, in his successful journey to the North Pole, was on the opposite side, as were Amundsen and Ellsworth on their then-recent polar flight.

From the popular view of polar travel, Wilkins and Ben would be trying to reach the most inaccessible place in the Arctic. It was a spot most distant from all points heretofore reached by other explorers. It was in the center of the frozen ice pack.

The Wilkins expedition obtained the best flying equipment available: two Fokker monoplanes of Dutch design, one with three 200-horsepower air-cooled Wright engines, modern airplane mapping cameras, and special instruments for navigating in the vicinity of the Magnetic Pole. It was sponsored by the city of Detroit. Among the donors were Detroit businessmen, 185,000 public school children, who collected pennies, and the city council. Wilkins contributed his entire fortune—$15,000—to the effort. Detroit backed Wilkins because it wanted to become known as the aeronautical center of the world in addition to being the center of the automobile industry.

After he concluded his agreement with Wilkins, Ben continued his search for financing for his proposed Alaskan airline. He was interviewed by a New York financier, John A. Hambleton. The two talked long and often, and Ben secured financial backing for an aviation company to handle all airmail contracts that the Postal Department approved.

While he was in New York, Ben also visited Vilhjalmur Stefansson, a man he had admired ever since his high school days. His debate instructor, Oscar Erickson, had first told Ben about the great explorer and author from North Dakota.

On his first visit, Ben thanked Stefansson for recommending him to Wilkins. Ben learned that Wilkins had served as Stefansson's chief assistant for three years on his third Arctic expedition. Stefansson added, "I found it difficult to induce the press to pay any attention to Wilkins or to any of the other men who helped bring us success under difficult circumstances."

After more conferences with Wilkins, Ben learned that the original plans for the expedition were already much expanded. In the beginning, Wilkins had insisted that all he needed for the blind-spot exploration was one plane and one pilot. But at Detroit, this simple thought was replaced with plans on a much grander scale. The Detroit Arctic Expedition eventually acquired the additional sponsorship of the Detroit Aviation Society, the American Geographical Society, and the North American Newspaper Alliance (NANA).

Detroit wanted three planes, and soon the personnel of the expedition grew to such a number that Wilkins was dismayed. Experts from all fields were gathered—mechanics, superintendents, photographers, correspondents, wireless operators, supply depot men, and assistants. Accompanying the expedition as unofficial observer for the War Department was Major Thomas G. Lanphier, Commandant of the First Pursuit Squadron of Selfridge Field.

Since Wilkins was a native of Australia, his right to claim for the United States any land he might discover was questioned. For this reason, Major Lanphier was granted a four-month leave of absence from the Army Air Service to accompany Wilkins and claim any new land discovered for the United States.

There was also a snow-motor section of the expedition, whose job it was to haul aviation gasoline, equipment, and two wireless radio sets from Nenana to Barrow. Malcolm ("Sandy") Smith, a famous sled-dog musher, was to assist this section in finding the trail. The motor-powered sleds were slated to make the journey over the dog trails to speed up delivery of supplies and airplane gasoline to Barrow, which would serve as takeoff point for the explorations.

The latest Fokker, with its three engines, was capable of cruising 2,500 miles nonstop. Furthermore, if one engine should fail, the remaining two could carry the plane with a full load. If two should stop, the third engine could keep the plane in flight for a sufficient length of time to make a safe landing. It also had dual controls. The other, smaller Fokker was equipped with a single water-cooled Liberty engine of 400 horsepower.

Wilkins explained that the flights of the two planes would also be a practical test of the relative efficiency of air-cooled versus water-cooled engines in cold weather. Each machine had a much greater flying range than Amundsen's or MacMillan's flying boats used in their unsuccessful attempts to reach the North Pole in 1925.

The single-engine plane was equipped with extra gasoline tanks and could outfly the big Fokker with a nonstop range of 3,000 miles.

The distance from Barrow to Spitzbergen was approximately 2,200 miles. The oil tanks and the magnetos of the airplanes were warmed by heat from the exhaust pipes. After the planes were tried out in Alaska, the airplane which Wilkins would select for the long flight to Spitzbergen would be equipped with a Fairchild aerial camera.

The third plane slated for the expedition was to have been a beautiful monoplane built in Detroit and donated by Henry Ford. But the day after its completion, the plane was destroyed by fire. Wilkins was somewhat shaken by the loss of the plane, but he was more concerned about accommodations in Fairbanks, so he sent Ben ahead to make arrangements for the huge party that would follow.

There was only one blot on Ben's return to Fairbanks. W. F. Thompson had died during the winter. But even without Thompson, there was a crowd of friends at the depot, and before Ben was settled at the hotel, invitations to dinners and parties were showered upon him.

Dr. Charles E. Bunnel, president of the university, at College, insisted that Ben reserve time to make a speech about the expedition. A few days later, Ben stood before the faculty and the student body and told them that the chief purposes of the Wilkins expedition, officially known as the Detroit Arctic Expedition, as outlined by Wilkins, were (1) to explore as much as possible of the million square miles of unknown area; (2) to claim for the United States any land that might be found; (3) if land was found, to establish bases for exploration and compilation of scientific data; (4) to demonstrate the feasibility of a short commercial route over the top of the world; (5) to reach the North Pole by air; and (6) to fly to Spitzbergen over the top of the world.

Ben explained that any land that might be discovered would have the same strategic value for the army and the navy that Hawaii had and that within the next 25 years the Arctic would be covered with a network of airways even more intricate than the network of steamship lines that now covered the Atlantic and the Pacific. He challenged those in the audience to dwell on the undiscovered and undeveloped resources in the American Arctic.

While the Detroit Arctic Expedition was a scientific one, it was likely that the members would encounter their share of adventures. There were many accounts of vessels having been abandoned in moving ice packs, but they may have escaped the crushing forces of the floes. If so, they could be sighted from an airplane at a distance of 25 miles. "It may be possible," Ben said, "for us to land on the ice pack and read the log of one of the whaling ships caught fast in the ice many years ago." He added that he and Wilkins would have to test the theory that it was possible to land on the ice pack.

Reports filtered back to Fairbanks concerning troubles being experienced by the snow-motor section of the expedition. In Nenana, Ben first heard reports that confirmed his original doubts about the usefulness of the motor-powered sleds. Many predicted that even the intrepid musher, Sandy Smith, would be unable to get the snow-motor section over the Endicott Mountains to Barrow. To those who knew the overland trail, the sled dog was still king.

When questioned about what the expedition would do if the motor section failed, Ben casually replied, "If sleds can't deliver the aviation gasoline to Barrow, Wilkins said we'll have to fly it there."

In answer to the continued comments that he would be flying to his doom, Ben replied, "Even if we should be forced down somewhere, we can always live off the land. Wilkins has plenty of experience in that line. Instead of loading the plane with surplus food supplies, we'll have a 'nigsik' along to catch seals. We can build snowhouses for shelter any time a storm comes along. So don't worry about us."

He also told one of his friends, "When we come back from a trip like that, I won't have any trouble getting financing for six airmail routes in Alaska." Ben's real motive for taking such chances was clear.

Ben was elated to learn that Jimmy Rodebaugh's company was doing well. The company had no trouble getting local financial support, as merchants and clerks up and down Main Street all dug into their pockets. Financial backing even came from miners and traders in the outlying areas. In addition to his two Standard planes, Rodebaugh soon had $28,000 in cash. The company abandoned the treacherous ballpark and leveled a larger field on a vacant lot near the edge of town. Next, they built a hangar with lumber salvaged from an abandoned railroad roundhouse.

Noel Wien was sent outside to search for a large-cabin plane. He found that Alaska was far ahead of the rest of the nation in demands for bigger and better planes. He located a Waco, but it hadn't yet been tested for stress. He found a Bellanca under construction, but it wouldn't be ready for six months. The Fairbanks managers wired Wien to continue his search.

Wien found a used Fokker at Curtiss Field, Long Island, and wired the directors a description of the plane. He said that it had a 54-foot wingspread and was large and spacious, with upholstery as fancy as a car. It had a heavy 180-horsepower BMW German engine and cruised at 90 miles per hour. However, Wien also cautioned that the Fokker was rather large for Alaska. Although there weren't any regular airfields, the Alaskan managers were determined to have a big plane. They voted to pay $9,500 for the Fokker and $400 for freight to have it shipped by boat through the Panama Canal.

Thompson had written in the *News-Miner* that the great ship "would annihilate space and protect all interior Alaska against railroad washouts, strikes, and delays in transmission of humans and freight, render first aid to the injured . . . and make Fairbanks the center of aviation."

Unfortunately, the Fokker was a dud for Alaskan flying. When it finally arrived in Fairbanks, Wien was the only pilot who would fly it. Other pilots refused to fly it at all. They called it a "haywire foreign rig." They said it had a dangerous cockpit arrangement and was too big to land on a river bar, and river-bar landing was a certainty for any pilot flying the bush country. Also, their new field was too short for the Fokker. But Wien was stubborn and made the first flight between Fairbanks and Nome.

In June 1925, the Fokker was chartered by Norman Stine and his two secretaries to carry them to Nome. Stine was an engineer who conducted surveys for the U.S. Smelting and Refining Company. There was great excitement at the new field when Stine, the two secretaries, and 500 pounds of mining papers and books were loaded aboard the huge Fokker. Noel Wien was the pilot, and his brother, Ralph, accompanied him as a mechanic. Stine eagerly paid the $1,000 for the 7½-hour charter, because the circuitous journey by boat would have taken 6 weeks.

Wien ran into trouble just out of Ruby because of a bad storm. Although there was no landing field there, Wien knew he didn't have enough gas to get back to Fairbanks and had to land. He circled and studied possible landing sites. When Wien finally picked one, Stine could scarcely believe his eyes. A seasoned air traveler, Stine was appalled at the sight of the only possible landing spot—a short hillside that sloped up at a 30-degree angle, leveling out into a small baseball diamond. It looked like suicide to Stine.

Wien proved his skill as a pilot as he touched down on the point of a stall and hurtled over the hilltop and down the other side. The big, fast-landing, brakeless ship nosed up and rocked crazily over onto its back. Fortunately, neither the Wien brothers nor their three passengers were injured in the unorthodox landing.

When Stine and the two secretaries arranged for passage on a boat, Noel and Ralph decided to complete the trip to Nome anyway, but they had to wait for a new propeller. After making needed repairs and installing the new propeller, the Wiens took off for Nome.

In spite of difficulties because the new propeller was not properly tuned for the BMW engine and vibrated very badly, Noel and Ralph reached Nome. The Nome people were overjoyed with the aerial connection to Fairbanks and gave the two air travelers a rousing reception. Stine and the two secretaries arrived much later. As a result of Stine's work in Alaska, huge gold dredges were later built for use in Fairbanks and in Nome.

Noel Wien's trail-blazing flight between Fairbanks and Nome marked another big step forward for aviation in the interior. The reception in Nome pointed out the great need for air service out of that isolated community on the shores of the Bering Sea. Wien realized the need for plane service in Nome was great and could be a financial success, so he established an airline there.

Ben also learned that there were two new pilots from San Diego stationed in Fairbanks. Rodebaugh advertised outside for pilots and hired both Joe Crosson and A. A. Bennett. Crosson and Ben hit it off from the first, and the two spent many hours together.

Crosson gave Ben a detailed report on the Fairbanks aerial happenings from his vantage point. He said that, when he first arrived in Fairbanks, business was good for his employers but that he was without a plane. As with most new companies, the young airline had many problems. Crosson said that Bob Lavery, manager of the company, was sometimes too busy in his grocery store to attend to airplane business.

Bennett and Crosson were both hired by telegram. Bennett, a tall ex-logger and go-getter salesman, arrived in Fairbanks first and appropriated the only flyable plane the company had. When Crosson arrived, he was forced to repair the other Standard.

Crosson had mixed feelings about his new job. When he decided to head north, he'd terminated a partnership in California with his sister, Marvel, who also was a pilot. The two had done barnstorming together for several years. When Crosson gave this up to accept the flying job in Alaska, he never dreamed he'd have to repair a wrecked plane before he could fly. But Crosson worked diligently over the Standard as he enviously watched Bennett making charter trips.

Crosson's impatience to make his first Alaskan flight soon overrode his better judgment. Crosson arrived at the field early one morning and found Bennett nowhere around. However, the Standard that Bennett always flew was ready to go. The temptation was too great. Crosson impulsively climbed aboard the plane Bennett claimed for his own and took off. For a brief time he enjoyed his new-found freedom, making a few wide circles in the sky over Fairbanks. Bennett was wild when he arrived at the field.

Crosson soon had a chance to make his first cross-country charter flight carrying a miner and his supplies to his claim. The miner, Van Curler [first name unknown], wanted to charter a flight immediately to his claim on the Upper Chena, 75 miles out of Fairbanks. Crosson said that they would leave as soon as he checked out Ben's Jenny, which was in storage. He had inspected it several days before, and it appeared to be in fine shape.

Crosson didn't bother to get permission from the company manager. He soon was on his way with Van Curler, none the wiser, sitting unconcerned in the passenger's cockpit. The flight to the Upper Chena went fine, but landing was a different story. The old-timer casually told Crosson there was a good field right by his claim. "Ben's landed there several times," he added.

As they circled the landing site Van Curler had pointed out, Crosson was dismayed. The site was about 350 feet long, uneven, and right in the middle of the river. Crosson started to yell to Van Curler that a landing was impossible, but he remembered the repeated assurances that Ben had landed there several times without any trouble. Crosson decided that he must meet the challenge. However, he landed too short, and the Jenny nosed over onto its back. Van Curler and his groceries and supplies spilled out of the plane.

Embarrassed but uninjured, Crosson crawled out and helped his passenger get his footing. He saw Van Curler's wife hurrying to the downed plane in a boat. Crosson was mortified anew. It was bad enough to crash land on his first charter flight, but worst of all, he was being rescued by a woman. Yet, Crosson reported his female rescuer was very efficient. "Did you ever see a Spanish windlass?" Van Curler's wife called to Crosson. Then she added, "We'll have her upright in a few minutes."

Mrs. Van Curler got two poles and some cable out of the boat. The men tied one end of the cable to the tail and the other to a large stump. Crosson stayed by the plane, and Van Curler went ashore and began winding. With the ship almost half over, the cable snapped. On the second try, Mrs. Van Curler manned the crank, and the men succeeded in righting the plane. Then Crosson discovered that the gas had all leaked out of the tank. Undaunted, the Van Curlers brought 10 gallons of lamp oil from the storage shed.

Next, they worked over the bent steel propeller, hammering it out against a log. The top of the rudder was broken, and the cabane struts were mashed over, but Crosson figured the Jenny would still fly.

After a last minute check, Crosson vaulted into the cockpit, and Van Curler spun the prop. Although he had a rough trip to Fairbanks, Crosson landed on the field and quickly stored the Jenny before Bennett got back. From then on, in his spare time, when not repairing the Standard, Crosson worked on the Jenny, too.

Ben and Crosson also discussed water-cooled engines versus air-cooled engines. Crosson reported that after every trip, it was necessary to pull the bank and grind the valves, but still the water-cooled engines often boiled over and conked out in the air.

Crosson told Ben that so far in the winter of 1926 he'd flown 30 hours, crashed 3 times, and spent 20 days waiting to be rescued or walking out.

Ben and Crosson discussed the added danger of the longer flights to Barrow and then over the Arctic Ocean. Ben said that for such flights he preferred the single-engine Fokker over the tri-engine Fokker.

After all the arrangements to accommodate the expedition were completed, Ben grew impatient for the planes and the last members of the expedition to arrive.

On the morning the Fokkers were due, weatherwise sourdoughs predicted a new low of minus 20 degrees. But, in spite of the cold temperature and the snow blanket, there was a great deal of local interest, and many hot arguments ensued over whether or not Wilkins would succeed.

22

Blazing Air Trails to Barrow

POLAR EXPLORATIONS have always stirred imaginations as people hear of expedition encounters with ice and snow. The NANA (North American Newspaper Alliance) wanted exclusive and exciting stories. Stefansson, Dr. Isaiah Bowman, and the other directors wanted the Detroit Arctic Expedition to be the biggest and most successful aerial exploring party ever sent to the region. Wilkins was more interested in the scientific end, while Ben was more interested in the chance to get additional Arctic flying experience and an opportunity to finance an airline in Alaska. Although their desires varied, all were eager for the expedition to begin.

Even with the large number of men connected with the expedition, Wilkins realized that he still needed extra help to unload the planes. When Ben called for help, Fairbanks residents flocked to offer their assistance in hauling the crated ships to the hangar used by Rodebaugh's company. After the planes were in the hangar, supplies and aviation gasoline had to be unloaded and stored.

The next job was to assemble the planes for the flight to Barrow. No one before had used a radio on long-distance flights, but Wilkins had a light wind-driven shortwave set installed in each plane so that it would be possible to maintain contact with the base. By using radio, interest could be kept alive, and Wilkins ran less risk of the expedition's being forgotten, as had happened with early expeditions when nothing was heard from them for months.

Wireless also made good journalistic copy of the flight possible, forcing the news agencies to compete for rights to the hastily telegraphed reports. Polar exploration always made good raw material for the news, and with radio, it would be even better.

One of the most enthusiastic promoters of the expedition was a young reporter, Palmer Hall Hutchison. The NANA supplied much of the money for the expedition, and Hutchison, the NANA correspondent, insisted that as soon as the planes were assembled, he wanted to give them names and have a christening ceremony.

Spilling over with enthusiasm, Hutchison made grand plans. There was more excitement in Fairbanks that winter than the town had known since gold rush days. Alaskans from valleys around arrived daily to welcome explorer Wilkins and Ben.

On March 11, 1926, when both planes were finally assembled, Hutchison arrived at the field with a large group of dignitaries to begin the christening ceremony. Wilkins wasn't pleased with the elaborate ceremony, as he considered it forced publicity. But Hutchison bustled around, energetic and obliging, arranging places for the mayor, five clergymen, the Salvation Army representative, and even the leaders of the Theosophists and the Free Thought groups in Fairbanks.

After the speeches were over, two young ladies, dressed in fur parkas and mukluks, assisted by the mayor's wife, christened the three-engine machine the *Detroiter* and the single-engine Fokker the *Alaskan* by cracking bottles of gasoline over the propellers.

Newspaper photographers had a field day. Nearly everyone from Fairbanks was there. Hutchison, jovial and boyish, dashed around. Ben had observed earlier that Hutchison was exactly the opposite of some of the experts in the party, who never seemed to be on hand when their services were needed. He had especially noted that the airplane engine expert appeared to abhor manual labor. When his services were needed the most, he was always the hardest to find.

When the lengthy christening ceremony was finally over, Wilkins dispersed the huge crowd, telling them that everything was over for the day. But when the crowd was gone and the weather continued calm, Wilkins decided to take the *Detroiter* on a trial flight. The newspaper men had already left, but Wilkins sent word to Hutchison that he intended to make a short test flight. If he hurried back to the field, he could get an exclusive story for the NANA.

In just a few minutes, Hutchison arrived. He found the men warming the engines of the *Detroiter*. Wilkins warned Hutchison, who knew nothing about aircraft, not to come too near the plane while the engines were being warmed.

Just before Hutchison returned, there had been much speculation about which pilot Wilkins would choose for the test flight. Ben felt that Wilkins would pick Lanphier, because he'd heard comments from others that an Alaskan bush pilot couldn't handle such a huge machine.

Finally, the mechanics rolled the three-engine *Detroiter* to the starting point. As Ben had anticipated, Major Lanphier was at the controls. Wilkins climbed aboard. Ben and the others watched intently from the sidelines, with Hutchison beside them. Then the mechanics shouted, "All clear!"

Ben could tell something was wrong. Lanphier was having trouble steering the big plane. It was the first time the cheechako pilot had taken off from such a poor field as in Fairbanks. Before he got the plane off the ground, and only about 100 yards down the runway, the wheels swerved into a snowbank.

When the *Detroiter* halted, the trained mechanics rushed out to stamp down the snow to make a track for the wheels—a very dangerous job since the propellers of the two auxiliary engines, whirling at 1,500 rpm, were directly in front of the wheels.

The mechanics worked from the rear, too, pushing on the tail and the undercarriage. Suddenly, Hutchison, who couldn't resist the temptation to help, rushed out to join the mechanics. He apparently had already forgotten Wilkins' warning and a second warning just given him by Ben and others.

As Ben saw Hutchison at work by the plane, his heart sank. The reporter appeared heedless of the danger of the spinning metal blades, turning so fast they were invisible. Ben's warning cry to Hutchison to stand back was drowned out by the second call of all clear.

But Hutchison didn't leave when the other men did. He stayed by the whirling blades. Ben prayed silently that Hutchison would realize his danger as he and the others, who knew the danger, ran toward the plane. In desperation they kept shouting, but the roaring engines drowned them out.

Suddenly, the plane moved forward quickly. As Hutchison straightened up to get out of the way, he was caught by the propeller.

There was a sickening thud, and Hutchison was hurled to the ground, decapitated. With a sinking feeling, Ben and the others realized that Hutchison had, in effect, given his life for the expedition. Lanphier was nearly in shock. Ben helped Wilkins make arrangements to remove Hutchison's body from the field.

Although Wilkins remained outwardly calm, Ben could sense that he was stricken by the accident. In the uneasy silence after the body was taken from in front of the plane, Ben helped the other men push the *Detroiter* back into the hangar. After the tragedy, no one felt quite the same about the big plane.

It was ironic that the day after the Hutchison disaster, when the mechanics were doing their routine job of warming the engines, Lanphier narrowly missed walking into the fast-spinning blades, but the tip of the propeller only nicked through his fur parka before he got clear of its path. Many of those connected with the expedition were still sick over Hutchison's accident. When they saw that Lanphier had almost met with the same fate, some considered withdrawing from the expedition.

In spite of his attempts to forget the accident, Ben kept remembering how eager Hutchison had been to help with all phases of the project. He had looked forward to being the first man to report for certain whether or not there was solid land in the Arctic Ocean north of Point Barrow. Shortly before his death, he had written a story stating that 50 years earlier a whaler had insisted that he saw a shoreline, which had become known as Keenan Land. Later, the renowned Robert E. Peary returned from the North to announce that he had named Crocker Land in the same area. Stefansson, in his journey over the Arctic ice to Banks Island in 1914, had not come upon land. Thus, proof as to the presence or absence of land in the region was still lacking.

Knowing that his father would read about the tragedy in the papers, Ben wrote home immediately. He added a note at the bottom of his letter saying that he planned to stay on with the expedition.

A week after the accident, Wilkins decided to try another flight from the improved field. With Ben at the controls of the *Alaskan*, Wilkins sat silently, watching him. The two waited to take off. Spectators at the field were uncommonly quiet and subdued. Even Ben was apprehensive. He remembered the two setbacks already experienced—the loss of a plane by fire and Hutchison's death. Ben asked himself what this new test flight in the *Alaskan* would bring. Suddenly, he shook himself to gun the engine; the takeoff was perfect.

Ben and Wilkins circled the outskirts of Fairbanks for 40 minutes, getting the feel of the plane. Finally, Ben heard Wilkins' happy voice above the roar of the engine. "She's a great plane, Ben! We can start for Barrow tomorrow! Let's go back to Fairbanks!"

Because Wilkins had expressed faith in his ability as a pilot, Ben tried hard to do everything just right. The daily papers all over the States quoted Wilkins as saying: "Other excellent pilots will accompany the expedition, but I know I shall disappoint them when I say that Lieutenant Eielson will make the main flight. Nowhere is there a man who has his flying experience in the Arctic. Nowhere is there a pilot better fitted by temperament for the work I have in mind."

As he came in to land on the 1,200-foot Fairbanks field, with snowbanks on each side, Ben's mind whirled with thoughts. Everything went well until he was low over the runway. Then the engine stalled. Ben shoved the throttle wide open, but there was no time to restart the engine. When he saw he was going to crash, he used one of his bush-pilot tricks to ease the crash. He came down, smashing the landing gear and skidding along belly-buster style. The *Alaskan* went through a fence and twisted the propeller like a ram's horn.

Shakily, Ben and Wilkins climbed out of the plane to sadly survey the wreckage. Wilkins said nothing, but the accident looked bad to the other members of the expedition. Ben was heartsick. This was a bad beginning for him.

Although one or two of the men connected with the expedition censured Ben, there was no word of rebuke from Wilkins. Yet, Ben was frustrated. He almost wished Wilkins would say something about the accident, even a rebuke. It might put an end to his guilt.

With much outstanding Alaskan flying to his credit, Ben had experienced his first serious crash and was unfortunate enough to suffer the glare of publicity and hostile fire of jealousy that were turned in his direction. But Wilkins continued to comment that he had not lost faith in Ben.

Ben's enthusiasm for the expedition hadn't dimmed, either. In a letter from Hatton, he received a report of Richard E. Byrd's proposed flight from Spitzbergen to the North Pole in a Fokker monoplane, the *Josephine Ford*. From his clipping service, he also received publicity about Roald Amundsen's preparations in Norway for a flight in the dirigible *Norge* from Spitzbergen to Alaska. When he read of the old Viking's plans, Ben's heart lifted. He remembered that in 1925 this Norseman had flown to within 150 miles of the North Pole but had trouble with the two planes in the expedition and failed to reach his goal. Yet, Amundsen had not given up. In 1926 he was ready to try again.

In the meantime, the *Alaskan* was hauled into the hangar, and the slow repair work began. Ben volunteered to help.

Wilkins reported the bad news to the sponsors and received a telegram from them that, in effect, said, "Get rid of the bush pilot Eielson." Wilkins read the telegram but still didn't say a word to Ben. Not knowing what Wilkins was thinking, Ben expected to be fired any minute.

There was a great deal of pressure on Wilkins from the sponsors of the expedition. The NANA had purchased the exclusive story in advance, and instead of having sensational news to report to the thrill-seeking public, its only news from Alaska dealt with one disaster after another. Ben also realized that, although Wilkins was not so much interested in sensational headlines as he was in scientific exploration and the possible discovery of land to establish a meteorological station, he had to please the sponsors, too.

In the meantime, Byrd and Amundsen received most of the sensational publicity. Still, that did not trouble Wilkins. He planned to do something much more important and dangerous than just fly to the Pole and back.

Finally, Wilkins declared that the field was ready and that the *Detroiter* was in shape for the test flight. Ben knew that he would not be the pilot chosen to take it up. The tri-motored plane was the largest plane Fokker had built up to that time. It was 75 feet long and considered experimental. Wilkins made no secret of the fact that he now hoped to do most of the freighting work from Fairbanks to Barrow with the *Detroiter*.

The snow-motor section of the expedition was still bogged down on the dog-team trails, the sleds loaded with aviation gasoline, supplies, and the two wireless sets that were already supposed to have been set up at Barrow. This latest bad news meant that all the necessary equipment was still more than 200 miles from where it was needed.

Word filtered back to Fairbanks that on March 5, Smith had decided to hire 70 sled dogs and some Alaskan mushers to haul the equipment, but not the aviation gasoline, to Barrow. He planned to leave the gasoline in a cache beside the trail, hoping to pick it up later on.

As soon as Wilkins heard the latest report from the stalled motor section, he decided that he would begin hauling aviation gasoline to Barrow immediately without even a test flight. The huge ship was almost loaded. But while the men worked, Ben overheard one of the crew tell Wilkins, "This time you'd better not pick that Alaskan bush pilot to fly the plane. He can't handle such a big plane." Wilkins didn't answer.

On the morning the *Detroiter* was to take off, Wilkins chose Lanphier as pilot. Ben stood uneasily on the sidelines, watching Wilkins and Lanphier make their final preparations. After all the previous delays and accidents, it was hoped that the takeoff and the trip to Barrow would be perfect. But as soon as the plane got up speed, the watchers knew that there was trouble.

Wilkins discovered that the controls were not quite balanced, and one engine gave more throttle than the other two. The plane swung toward the greater torque and charged straight at a snowbank beside the cleared runway, narrowly missing a bystander. Lanphier pulled the throttle slightly just in time to clear the snowbank and the *Detroiter* zoomed into the air.

Lanphier circled around Fairbanks several times, but both he and Wilkins realized that it would be impossible to fly on to Barrow. There was so much vibration in one engine that the entire plane shook violently.

In a repeat performance, the engines of the *Detroiter* quit as Lanphier came in for a landing. Within a few feet of the spot where the *Alaskan* had crashed, the tri-motored *Detroiter* did also.

Neither Wilkins nor Lanphier was injured, but the undercarriage of the plane and all three engine mounts were smashed completely. The *Detroiter* was damaged far more extensively than the *Alaskan* had been the day before. The big machine couldn't possibly be repaired in time to haul aviation gas to Barrow. Several men quit on the spot.

Again, Wilkins did not show how he felt about the latest disaster. He didn't even speak about it. While some of the men speculated about the future of the expedition, Wilkins ordered the *Detroiter* hauled into the hangar for repair. He informed the group of men huddled about the wrecked Fokker that he would carry aviation gasoline to Barrow in the *Alaskan* as soon as it was repaired.

In a conversation with Ben and the others, Wilkins also expressed his approval of Smith's switch to dog teams to haul the stranded equipment to Barrow, but Wilkins never mentioned who would pilot the *Alaskan.*

The loss of the two planes, worth more than $100,000, within 24 hours weighed heavily. Even harder to bear was the realization that the work laid out for the expedition couldn't possibly be completed that year. The good-weather season in the Arctic was just too short. The only bit of good luck the expedition had was that sufficient repair parts were found in Fairbanks to get the *Alaskan* flying again.

The hardest thing of all, perhaps, was that news of the latest disaster must be wired to the outside world, which was watching expectantly. What had originally appeared to be a race between three expeditions to cross the Arctic by air had apparently been whittled down to a race between two. Yet, a few messages of condolence and encouragement came to the ill-fated expedition party. But one day a lengthy telegram of the opposite type arrived. Wilkins reluctantly read it to Lanphier and Ben. It was from the backers in Detroit demanding that Wilkins immediately discharge the two pilots involved in the accidents. When he finished reading the telegram, Wilkins shook his head. He folded the telegram carefully, put it in his pocket, and never mentioned it again.

Word of the request sent by telegram spread among the men working in the hangar, bringing resentment and indignation. By now the men had less criticism of the Alaskan bush pilot because Lanphier, an ace among army aviators, had encountered the same problem as Ben.

The next afternoon Ben was busy repairing the *Alaskan* when one of the mechanics near him stopped work. He'd seen Wilkins approaching, and when he stopped and stood by the plane, the mechanic said bluntly, "If you're planning to fire Eielson, I've got a few words to say, first! If you're here to tell us that new pilots have been hired . . ."

"New pilots?" Wilkins asked sharply. "What new pilots?"

"Well, we heard you have orders from Detroit to fire the two pilots connected with the expedition."

"I'm not planning to fire Eielson or Lanphier. As you know, Lanphier is merely on loan from the army, but both are competent men. I'm surprised that anyone here could believe I would consider replacing either."

When he finished speaking, Wilkins stalked away indignantly. But suddenly he turned and caught sight of Ben, standing on the opposite side of the *Alaskan*. Ben still had a strange look, so Wilkins walked up to Ben and threw his arm around his shoulder, saying, "Ben, I hope *you* never thought for a minute that I planned to fire you. We're in this thing together. I hope you have the same confidence in me."

Ben shot out his hand to grip Wilkins' and said, "Thank you, Captain Wilkins. You can count on me!"

Although deeply disappointed in the continued bad luck, Wilkins decided to at least clear the snow from the field while the men worked on the planes. He knew the narrow runway, dug through deep snow, only increased the difficulties of taking off.

The weather had warmed up somewhat, and the snow was wet and heavy. Wilkins arranged to rent every machine in Fairbanks for clearing the field. Before the field was clear, Lanphier was driving a road scraper and Wilkins was handling a grader.

The men also worked around the clock repairing the *Alaskan*. Before any exploration work could be done, a base had to be established at Barrow. They raced against fogs they knew would soon settle over the Arctic ice. Although it took a couple weeks to repair the *Alaskan*, the wireless equipment Wilkins needed in Barrow was still on the dog-team trail.

With the new engine installed and a propeller from a Jenny fitted to the *Alaskan* (it took six weeks to order a new propeller from the outside), Wilkins decided to take off without any weather reports. He was determined to make at least one or two trips out over the Arctic Ocean that year so the expedition wouldn't be considered a complete failure.

The *Alaskan* was built to carry 300 gallons of gasoline, but in order to have enough for the round trip of 1,000 miles and still be able to leave some gasoline at Barrow, Wilkins ordered the plane loaded with 750 gallons of gasoline.

On March 31, when the *Alaskan* finally was loaded, Wilkins abruptly informed Ben, "You're taking the *Alaskan* to Barrow." His firm words broke the weeks of suspense and speculation.

Ben's spirits lifted immediately. Although no one had ever flown the approximately 500 miles to Barrow before, Wilkins had given the order very matter-of-factly. No plane had ever crossed the dreaded Endicott Mountains or the unexplored tundra beyond, but Wilkins and Ben would now attempt the flight, and without weather reports. In addition, no plane on wheels had ever landed on snow. Yet, Wilkins assumed there would be no problems with a wheel landing in Barrow.

Wilkins ignored the talk about not having weather reports. He'd been in Barrow in 1913 with Stefansson's expedition and was confident that a wheeled landing was possible there because the snow was packed hard enough by Arctic gales to hold the wheels on the crust.

Ready at last, Wilkins and Ben climbed aboard the heavily loaded *Alaskan*. The normal load of the plane was set at a ton, but Ben managed to get it into the air with 3,500 pounds of weight aboard. The *Alaskan* climbed steadily upward to 5,000 feet to cross the first range of hills north of Fairbanks. Then it headed north.

Ben found heavy fog in the Yukon Valley, but he knew that somewhere beneath the fog were his regular landmarks. He mentally ticked off Livengood and other known sites.

Flying through thick fog was bad enough, but less than an hour out of Fairbanks the two found themselves in a terrific blizzard that covered everything. Luckily, the blizzard provided a tail wind for them. The instruments measured an air speed of 90 miles an hour, but Ben was flying blind, relying on the instruments and Wilkins' skill as a navigator.

When they approached the Endicott Mountains, the blizzard stopped and the fog lifted. The *Alaskan* flew at 5,000 feet, the altitude indicated on their map for the Endicott Range, yet the jagged peaks loomed far above that.

Ben was puzzled. But it soon was apparent that the men who

had drawn the maps did not know the true height of the mountains. Just as Ben started to climb, Wilkins shouted, "Better go up!" Yet, Ben was afraid the heavily loaded plane wouldn't climb much higher.

Ben pushed the *Alaskan* slowly upward, carefully weaving through a narrow pass. He was thankful that the weather was clear, providing unlimited visibility. Wilkins was silent, watching as Ben flew cautiously between the towering rocks. At times it appeared certain that one of the wings would touch one side of the peaks or the other and bring disaster. Once Ben almost swore the wheels touched the snow drifted high in a narrow pass, sending clouds of snow spiraling at each side. He drew a deep breath and flew on. There was no place to turn back. Finally, the *Alaskan* was in the clear. Both men breathed shuddering sighs of relief when the mountains were behind them.

Wilkins later reported, "Eielson was a steady, deliberate, reasoning pilot. He met all emergencies calmly. He summed up every situation and looked at it from all angles and then, whenever there was a chance, he went ahead."

On their map, the entire vast area between the Endicotts and Barrow was blank. Wilkins, a trained navigator, charted the course as they flew. Hour after hour Ben continued flying north over the desolate expanse of territory where few white men had penetrated even with dog teams. The area was mostly uninhabited, except for a few widely scattered tiny native settlements.

Suddenly, the *Alaskan* was again streaking through a gray bank of clouds. Even though there was an occasional rift, Ben could see nothing below. He settled back and trusted Wilkins' navigation. After an hour in the gray misty world, Ben found himself praying for a break in the clouds, a break that would disclose some dark spot or even a faint outline on which he could rest his eyes. He looked at Wilkins, busy with his instruments and oblivious. Ben checked his watch. They had expected to make the trip to Barrow in eight hours.

Flying through the clouds, they could see nothing outside the cabin. Ben was slightly bored, something very unusual for him when flying. But there was nothing for him to do except watch the instruments, keep the plane at the same altitude, and maintain a fixed direction toward Barrow. He'd been spoiled by his contact flying in the interior, where there always was a herd of caribou, a trapper's cabin, or a mining settlement to break the monotony.

Two hours had passed since they'd left the Endicotts behind. Suddenly, the sun shown dimly on one side of the plane. Ben was elated. On the opposite side appeared two rainbow circles, not bows such as Ben had seen many times bridging rain-washed skies over North Dakota, but complete rings of color. In the center of each was the phantom shadow of the *Alaskan*. It was an eerie sight, but a rare and awe-inspiring one.

Finally, after what seemed like ages, they reached the edge of the cloud mass. Four thousand feet below, Ben saw splattered cakes of ice marring the smooth surface of level pack ice. He saw upended blocks of ice with captured snowdrifts between. With a start, Ben realized that they were beyond the Arctic mainland and out over the Arctic Ocean.

Wilkins also studied the landscape intently. He knew from the character of the ice ridges that they'd missed Barrow, passed the coast, which would have been impossible to distinguish from the skyline in the gray world, and were out over the Arctic Ocean.

They had already covered over 600 miles and crossed a shoreline, but it was impossible to find the shore. Ben looked carefully at Wilkins, who appeared engrossed in his thoughts, busy checking his map.

Keenan Land was the last northward island marked on Wilkins' map. As Ben flew above the place where it was supposed to be, Wilkins motioned for him to look below. There was no trace of an island. For Wilkins, all the problems connected with the expedition melted away. The existence of Keenan Land had been doubted by many, but now the Detroit Arctic Expedition flight had proved that it didn't exist.

During the next hour Ben flew steadily on, outwardly calm but growing anxious. Yet, Wilkins made no move to change course, until finally he passed a note to Ben: "If you look ahead, you will see 100 miles farther north in this area than any man has ever seen from the air until today. We are 100 miles out over the Arctic Ocean. What do you say to going on half an hour longer, just to make good measure?"

Ben smiled and called, "Whatever you think."

Ben knew that the longer they flew out over the Arctic Ocean, the more gas they'd use and the easier it would be to land at Barrow. He assured himself that, even if they did have trouble and didn't reach land, he'd be able to provide the answer to one more question that explorers had been arguing over for several years—whether or not a plane could land on the moving ice pack.

Later Wilkins signaled Ben to turn around. A sudden blizzard had blown up, and soon the two were navigating by dead reckoning, searching for Barrow.

After two hours of tedious flying they reached a great blanket of clouds enveloping the mainland. Ben dropped to 2,000 feet. He could see a howling blizzard lashing the coast. Both men searched for Barrow in the blowing snow. Wilkins later wrote, "I could see houses and villages everywhere. If I'd followed my inclination and every impulse of the moment, we would have been flying in circles." Almost simultaneously, Wilkins and Ben sighted a bluff.

In the meantime, at Barrow, Charles Brower, long-time resident and called "King of the Arctic" by many explorers who'd visited there, had given up expecting the plane. With one of the worst blizzards of the year raging, he thought it would be impossible for a plane to fly. The storm in Barrow was so fierce that not even the Eskimos left the shelter of their tiny homes to check their trap lines. Only one hardy Eskimo was out in the blizzard. Ben and Wilkins later learned that he had seen them through the clouds on their way north over the ice pack and had been puzzled over their strange actions. From this man's evidence, they learned they had passed directly over Barrow. They had flown from Fairbanks straight to their target.

Brower first learned a little of Wilkins' plans when he received a wire from New York, dated November 13, 1925. The telegram asked that Brower reserve all the aviation gasoline at Wainwright. It was signed by Hubert Wilkins.

Brower had met Wilkins when he was with Stefansson in 1913. At that time Wilkins spent several weeks in Barrow. Wilkins' reference to aviation gas had Brower stumped, until he suddenly remembered that he had once mentioned to Stefansson in New York that he had several drums of aviation gasoline at Wainwright that belonged to Roald Amundsen's expedition. But Brower didn't know why Wilkins was interested in aviation gasoline.

Soon another wire arrived telling Brower that Wilkins would arrive in Barrow by plane by the end of February and asking that he mark out a landing field and have fur clothing ready for three men.

Brower marked out a field and gathered fur for parkas, but the end of February came and went, and still there was no sign of Wilkins. Just about the time Brower had given up, Earl Hammond, a representative of Wilkins who had been sent out on the sea route, arrived from Kotzebue by dog team with a load of supplies for Wilkins. Hammond told Brower that Sandy Smith, Pathé cameraman Earl Rossman, and others were coming overland from Nenana by snow motor.

Nothing else transpired for three weeks. Then, on the day of the worst blizzard in years, the *Alaskan* came roaring in from the northeast and landed in fine style, coming to a stop a few feet from the bank of a small lagoon south of Brower's trading post.

The little village of Barrow, low and bleak, was almost hidden in the swirling blizzard. Only a few Eskimos were there to witness the landing. Then, as if by magic, everyone soon gathered round the strange looking rig to greet the two fliers.

Most of the older Eskimos, attracted by the noise of the engine, rushed from their homes to see the huge monster bird, which had dropped down from the sky. To them, the plane was nothing to be feared. It was just a curious sight. One old Eskimo reached up and ran his hand over the wing. He shouted, "How can it fly? It has no feathers." Yet, the inquisitive Eskimos readily accepted the strange rig and the men who stepped out of it. One of the village's best skin sewers poked one of the wings with the tip of her finger and noted wisely, "I could sew one of those out of skin easy." A few of the oldest Eskimos stayed inside, fearful of the "evil spirit that had come flying in out of the storm."

Wilkins mentioned to Ben that very little had changed in Barrow since his last visit in 1913. He said that the people then were very hospitable and interested in Stefansson's expedition. Barrow residents were still welcoming them when Ben begged to be excused so he could take care of the plane.

Several of the Eskimos offered to help him, and he was grateful.

He drained the oil and put a tent over the *Alaskan's* engine. To help keep it warm, he hired an Eskimo, Panuzak, to stand watch and tend the tiny oil stove he placed under the tent. Proudly, the Eskimo took over his new job. Finally, the men walked to Brower's trading post. The cook, Fred Hopson, had hot coffee and huge slices of homemade bread and jam ready for them. Brower pointed to a choice spot in his store for their sleeping bags.

After they finished their coffee, Wilkins told Brower that he wanted to set up his small wireless set and try to send a message back to Fairbanks. Immediately, there was new excitement in Barrow, for the people there had never been able to send a message to civilization before. Everyone followed Wilkins and Ben back to the plane to get the set and then watched as they set it up.

When Wilkins had first planned the expedition and decided to use Barrow as a base, he'd asked the United States government to consider installing a radio station at Barrow. The government officials reported that radio communications with Barrow would be impossible. Ships' operators had said Barrow was a "wireless blind spot."

Wilkins proved the government officials wrong. On March 31, 1926, Wilkins sent the first wireless message from Barrow back to civilization, with Ben cranking the handle. Two-way communications were soon established.

When Wilkins told Brower that the purpose of the Detroit Arctic Expedition was to fly out over the Arctic Ocean and try to discover new land or, failing that, to fly across the Arctic and land at Spitzbergen, Norway, Brower shook his head and replied, "Both of those accomplishments appear unbelievable to me."

Wilkins explained that the most immediate thing that concerned him was the delay in the arrival of Sandy Smith and those with him. According to the last report he had, they were still in the John's River Pass area. Wilkins told Brower that the men would bring a motion picture outfit and the wireless sets, one specifically for use of the NANA. Wilkins said that he thought they'd get through all right but that he wasn't sure when they would arrive. Brower asked, "What about the snow motors?"

"They worked fine back in Michigan where they were built," Wilkins said. "The snow there is wet and soft, but they're not equal to the dry snows of Alaska. However, the men will make it now that they have finally switched to dog teams." It was believed that they were about 150 miles from Barrow.

"They must be almost out of food by now," Wilkins said. "Still, there are reindeer and caribou for meat, and they can fish through the ice. But I'm afraid that not all of the men know how to live off the country."

Ben added, "We estimated it would take 30 days overland to make the trip from Fairbanks to Barrow and cost about $3,000, but now, we don't know how long it will take."

"If they're not here soon," Wilkins said, "perhaps we can organize rescue teams from this end. Maybe Hammond can take off from here and backtrack until he meets them."

Knowing that their visitors planned to take off the next morning, everyone in Barrow got up early. When Ben and Wilkins woke up, the chairs around the stove were filled with Eskimos watching them. But the blizzard still raged, and Brower predicted that it would last for several days. "You'll have time for a good rest," he commented.

While they waited, Ben and Wilkins decided to dig out a runway several hundred yards long, down to solid ice. With time out during the worst parts of the stormy weather, and with a great deal of help, the task took three days.

To Wilkins' surprise, during the three days that they were storm-bound in Barrow, he and Ben were drawn into a veritable social whirl. There were four white men and six white women in the village. Miss Edna Clair Wallace, a writer, was spending the winter there to gather material for a novel about the Arctic. The school teacher's wife was there with her sister. Also, there were two nurses at the hospital and the wife of Dr. Newhall [no first name available], the missionary doctor.

The women gave bridge parties, teas, and dinner dances. Everyone danced to phonograph records or to accordion music furnished by one of the Brower or the Hopson children. So, while the blizzard howled outside, Barrow residents and their first air travelers from Fairbanks danced and partied.

Ben also had time to get caught up with his correspondence. He owed his sister, Helen, a freshman at St. Olaf College, a letter. Early one morning he sat at the big table and wrote:

I am writing this in a little trading post situated at the farthest north tip of Alaska. Captain Wilkins and I landed here with the plane *Alaskan* on March 31. We left Fairbanks at 7:30 A.M. reaching the Arctic Ocean at 11:00 A.M. We kept on flying for an hour and a quarter, so I have been farther north into the unexplored area than anyone else except Captain Wilkins. We flew out on the ice for 125 miles north of Point Barrow, then turned around and landed here at 3:00 P.M. . . . Yesterday we went out by dog team to the edge of the ice pack. We also visited a couple of Eskimo homes. I had my first taste of Muktuk (whale skin and fat) and also seal fat. I can positively state that it is not as palatable as roast turkey. I can taste it yet. . . . The trading post is run by a white man named Charles Brower. He has an Eskimo wife and 14 children. So you see we have a very nice family gathering for meals. Wilkins and I sleep on the floor in our sleeping bags. . . . Save the envelope of this letter, as it is the first airmail letter out of Point Barrow, so will some day have a value.

Next, he wrote to his friend, Walter Schlosser, of Grand Forks:

We landed here in a regular North Dakota blizzard, which has been raging ever since, so we have been unable to return to Fairbanks. We hope it will let up by tomorrow so we can start back as we have a lot of flying to do to get our supplies in, owing to the failure of the snow motors to get over the mountains. Our large wireless set has not arrived though it has been on the way from Fairbanks for over a month. Doesn't it seem strange to think of 11 men and 70 dogs struggling along for a month and a half to get here when we get over so easily by airplane in four hours? The distance is 500 miles. . . . Day before yesterday we were out 125 miles further into the unexplored area than anyone else has ever been. From 7,000 feet we could see about 75 miles further but we sighted no new land. As soon as we get more gas we will make a long trip out to see if we can't find some tropical valley with mermaids and everything!

By the time the weather cleared on April 6, the runway was fairly well completed. But snow had drifted around the *Alaskan,* and the wings were covered with ice. Although Ben had expected this, Wilkins later reported that in all his years of Arctic work, this was the only time that he'd seen such a situation occur.

Ben, Wilkins, and their helpers dug away the snowdrifts and roped the ice from the wings. Then Ben and Wilkins told their Barrow hosts that they would see them again soon. After three unsuccessful tries because of the short field, Ben finally got the *Alaskan* into the skies above Barrow. From an altitude of 4,000 feet he could see a great cloud bank obscuring the mainland.

The people in Barrow were no different from others in isolated spots as far as wanting to order things from Fairbanks. When the men finally left Barrow, they carried many letters and packages. They also had commissions to buy a variety of items for Barrow residents, including a case of eggs for the young writer. Nearly everyone wanted something that could be brought to Barrow by plane.

Wilkins busied himself with charts and navigation instruments as Ben guided the plane for nearly 300 miles above the cloud bank to the Endicott Mountains. Without the heavy gasoline cargo, Ben was able to skim across the mountain tops at an altitude of 11,000 feet.

On the first part of the return trip, all went well, but as they neared Circle, the engine began to miss. Ben noticed that the oil gauge indicated a fast-dropping pressure. He was concerned that they would have to make a forced landing on the river ice, which was weakened by warm weather. He struggled to keep the plane in the air until he spotted a river bar about a mile beyond Circle. Ben circled, then brought the *Alaskan* down safely on the snow-crusted sandbar.

Ben and Wilkins hopped from the plane to examine the engine. Suddenly, they were attracted by the noise of someone crashing through the underbrush. They looked up to see a woman running frantically toward them along the shore of the frozen river. When she had almost reached the plane, she stopped suddenly and said loudly, "Oh, the dinner!" Without another word, she turned and ran back in the direction from which she'd come. Ben shook his head and continued working on the engine. In a little while the breathless woman came rushing back, carrying hot food in a pail.

Upon her return, Ben and Wilkins found that the woman lived about a half mile from where they'd landed. She was cooking her husband's dinner when she saw the plane circle and land. She could hardly believe her eyes at first. She had never seen a plane before, and the shock of seeing one land almost in her back yard was quite a thrill. She promptly forgot all about her husband's dinner, which she had left cooking on the stove, and rushed out to meet the strangers and find out why they had landed their plane on her river bar. Then it dawned on her that she had left the dinner cooking on the stove, so she ran back home. "I took the food off the stove," she said, "then started back here again." She flushed, then added, "Well, then I turned around and went back and packed up the hot food for you. Here it is."

The woman excitedly explained that anyone flying a plane must surely be exhausted and starving. She added that her husband could just wait until later, and she would fix dinner again. All three laughed.

Ben and Wilkins thanked her for her thoughtfulness. The way things turned out, they really appreciated the food. Darkness fell long before they got the engine repaired. They slept in the cabin of the plane, but they were up early the next morning and soon completed the repair work. They reached Fairbanks without further trouble.

A royal reception awaited them when they landed in Fairbanks. Everyone wanted to hear about the first trip to Barrow by plane and get the latest news about the snow-motor section.

In spite of the accidents and delays, at least for the time being Wilkins and Ben held top-place honors for having made the longest nonstop flight in the Arctic. This news was a welcome relief. Plagued with bad luck from the beginning, Wilkins was pleased to send the sponsors the good news about the Barrow trip. Ben was happy, too, that he had fulfilled Wilkins' faith in his ability as a pilot and hoped that the sponsors would look upon him more favorably.

Ben told one of his friends, "This Barrow trip will show the Post Office Department what a plane can really do for the people of Alaska. Now I'm sure they'll give me an airmail contract!"

While they waited for weather that would permit a second trip to Barrow, Ben and Wilkins searched for news from outside concerning the two other polar expeditions. Wilkins found the *Detroiter* was still far from ready for ferry trips with gasoline, so he ordered the *Alaskan* put in good shape for the second trip. Everyone connected with the expedition knew that when the time came for the second trip to Barrow, Ben would be at the controls.

In the meantime, Wilkins and Ben learned that the steamer *Chantier* carrying the Byrd expedition had started across the Atlantic Ocean to Spitzbergen. They also learned that Roald Amundsen soon would be at Spitzbergen with the dirigible *Norge*.

23

Supplying the Barrow Base

THE RESIDENTS OF BARROW waited impatiently for Wilkins and Ben to return. The northernmost hamlet of Alaska consisted of three clusters of huts stretching for two miles along a low shore and had served as the jump-off point for many Arctic expeditions as well as headquarters for search parties looking for lost explorers.

Originally, Point Barrow, 12 miles north of the "white man's Barrow," had an entirely native population. The white man's Barrow served as a trading center for the isolated Arctic coast residents. It had a store, a Presbyterian mission, a federal hospital, and a school. Located "on the edge of nowhere," it was the natural headquarters for the many expeditions heading into the Arctic.

The original native village was called Nuwuk—"the point"—by its Eskimo inhabitants. But when it was first visited by white men, they couldn't pronounce the native name. Therefore, while exploring in the area in 1826, Captain Frederick Beechey, of the British Royal Navy, named it Barrow, for Sir John Barrow.

In 1818 the town's namesake had succeeded in having Parliament offer a reward to the mariner discovering the Northwest Passage, which triggered new interest in the centuries-old project. Throughout his life, Barrow was responsible for encouraging explorers and helped outfit many polar expeditions, including Sir John Franklin's and Sir William Parry's.

In 1837 Simpson and Dease, of the Hudson's Bay Company, had traced the coastline from the mouth of the Mackenzie River to Point Barrow, or Cape North. After the failure of Franklin to make the Northwest Passage in 1845 and the loss of his expedition, many

British and American relief expeditions during the next several years greatly increased knowledge of the Arctic.

Eskimos living at remote points often assisted in searches for the early explorers. Now, the exploration of the Arctic by air opened a whole new chapter, and Point Barrow's Eskimos were prepared to help. They contributed a great deal to the work connected with the Wilkins expedition.

Earl Hammond was well rested in Barrow and, when requested by Wilkins, went in search of the others, taking several Eskimos with him. Hammond found the party, and after giving them food, he took Waskey (first name unknown), a wireless operator, and one of the two wireless sets and sped back to Barrow. Smith, Rossman, and their companions, with the remaining supplies, could not travel as fast.

After arriving in Barrow, Hammond and Waskey told Brower that the others in the party were somewhere on the Anaktuvuk River and would be in later. That evening, Waskey erected the wireless set, and Brower proudly sent his first wireless message to Wilkins at Fairbanks. He told of Hammond's and Waskey's arrival and added a weather report so that Ben and Wilkins had some idea of weather conditions.

After his initial success in sending the Fairbanks message, and with appropriate feelings about a shrinking world, Brower sent a second message to San Francisco. It was a momentous occasion for Brower, an Arctic denizen for over 40 years. He always missed being able to communicate with the outside.

Charles Brower had gone north in June 1883 at the age of 21 as an employee of the Pacific Steam Whaling Company. The party was going to Arctic Alaska to investigate certain coal veins and also to trade with the Eskimos for furs, whalebone, and ivory. It also planned to open a new whaling station at Barrow.

Brower later said that ladies' corsets brought him north, for without corsets, there would have been no demand for whalebone and no need for a whaling station at Barrow. The site proved to be a good location, and the operation lasted until the 1920s, when whalebone for corsets was replaced by steel stays.

When the demand for whalebone ceased, the H. Liebes Company, of California, took over all whaling stations along the coast, including the one at Barrow, and converted them to fur stations.

Brower, who had managed the whaling station for many years, stayed on to manage the fur station. There was some question about whether or not the Liebes Company would continue to operate the Barrow fur station. Brower had grown to love the Arctic. He married an Eskimo woman and knew he'd never leave.

On the morning after Brower sent his first wireless message to Fairbanks, the weather cleared and Barrow residents started watching for a moving speck in the sky, hoping to spot the *Alaskan*. Ben and Wilkins took off that morning from Fairbanks carrying 4,000 pounds of aviation gasoline, extra food for the snow-motor section, mail for Barrow, and personal items they had promised to pick up in Fairbanks.

With such a heavy cargo, they would be able to get through the Endicotts only by way of the Anaktuvuk Pass. North of the Endicotts on the great tundra stretching toward the Colville River, they hoped to spot Sandy Smith's dog teams and drop 250 pounds of food and emergency rations for them. By now, the men were desperately short of provisions.

Right out of Fairbanks they ran into a heavy cloud cover, which cleared by the time they reached the Endicott Mountains. They made it safely through the pass and soared out across the vast stretch of tundra and immediately ran into low-hanging clouds blotting out any possible sight of the Smith party. The clouds lifted slightly, and they landed safely on the Barrow Lagoon.

They planned to return to Fairbanks at once, but shortly before they were ready to leave, Smith, Rossman, and their party, badly snow blinded, stumbled into Barrow without the remaining radio. Smith and Rossman immediately started a hot argument with Hammond. Smith and Rossman accused Hammond of leaving them stranded on the trail short of food. They claimed that he hadn't left enough food for the sled dogs, let alone the men.

Wilkins had his hands full. Ben and Brower kept out of the way. Both realized that frayed nerves, snow blindness, and physical exhaustion all caused emotions to be high. It took every ounce of Wilkins' diplomacy to calm the bitter men. Smith finally promised that as soon as his eyes were better, he would start back with Waskey for the wireless still stranded on the trail.

After a semblance of peace was restored, and 10 hours after they had first landed at Barrow, Ben and Wilkins took off for Fairbanks. But Wilkins' troubles weren't over. Prior to takeoff from the Barrow Lagoon, as he helped roll the plane forward, his right mitten caught in the wheel. He felt a sharp pain in his wrist but thought it was nothing but a slight sprain, so he climbed aboard and gave Ben the signal to start, leaving the rest of the pushing to the Eskimo ground crew.

After Ben and Wilkins were airborne, Wilkins' right arm bothered him more and more. Soon, he couldn't use his right hand at all. He gave directions to Ben writing notes using his left hand. Ben noticed that the handwriting was very poor, the messages were much more brief than normal, and the meaning was somewhat vague. He wondered if Wilkins had become ill, but he was too busy trying to keep the plane on course to worry about it.

They passed over the Endicotts without any problems but flew into a fog. At the junction of the Alatna and the Koyukuk rivers, Ben realized they were off course. Wilkins shouted loudly, "Ben, there's supposed to be a village down there," but there was no village. Suddenly, one appeared on the opposite side.

Ben circled the village. Attracted by the roaring engine, the entire population gathered, looking skyward. "It's on the wrong side of the river," Wilkins shouted. "Circle again. I'll drop them a note."

Using his left hand, Wilkins hurriedly wrote a note asking, "What's the name of your village?" Ben lowered the plane for the drop. One of the men promptly retrieved the note and read it, and almost without pause the people stamped "Alatna" into the snow.

Wilkins was puzzled. He looked at the map again. It showed the river Alatna nearby, but there was no village of that name on the map. He shouted loudly, "Drop down again, Ben."

Ben lowered the plane once more, and a second note asking "Which direction is Fairbanks?" dropped to the ground.

After the note was retrieved, the obliging people quickly lined up to form a human arrow pointing toward Fairbanks.

Ben circled the village again and waved his thanks. He swung the plane around and headed it in the direction they'd pointed. By now, Wilkins experienced a throbbing pain in his right arm. The pain grew steadily worse, and his wrist was beginning to become discolored.

Wilkins suspected that he had a broken bone. Soon, he found himself idly wondering about the possibility of running out of gas and having to land in unmapped country and how useless he would be with a broken arm.

It was needless to worry, for in 1½ hours Ben set the *Alaskan* down perfectly at Fairbanks with less than a gallon of gas to spare. It wasn't until they both crawled out of the cabin that Ben learned the reason for Wilkins' almost illegible handwriting. He was shocked at the sight of his off-color arm, and they dashed to the hospital.

Ben told Wilkins to get some rest and he'd get things ready for their third flight to Barrow. The skies cleared two days later, and everything was ready.

On this trip, the *Alaskan* was loaded with 4,750 pounds of gasoline. By now, Ben knew that whenever the *Alaskan* was to be flown, Wilkins would pick him to fly it. Ben felt a growing bond between himself and the Australian. They were not only friends but also a team.

When they reached the Endicotts, dense clouds obscured the valleys that burrowed into the mountains. With their extra-heavy load of gasoline, it appeared that they might not be able to climb high enough. The altimeter registered 9,000 feet, and some of the summits were still above them.

Ben flew through the edges of the clouds that hung on the summits, searching for the pass. Suddenly Wilkins yelled, "Rocks on my side! Keep over!"

Ben yelled back, "Can't. Rocks on my side, too!"

Out of the corner of his eye, Ben saw Wilkins frantically piling cases of gas forward to gain every climbing advantage. In the next instant, the plane hit rough air and was tossed. Wilkins fell, injuring his right arm again. Ben tried to pull the nose up, but the overloaded plane barely responded.

The clouds thinned. Ben looked ahead. He tensed as he saw two walls of rock forming a gorge that looked narrower than the wingspan of the *Alaskan*. Even worse, it was choked with a snowdrift.

Ben prayed. He took a tight grip on the stick and flew straight ahead. There was no room to turn back. With scarcely a foot to spare on either side, the *Alaskan* roared through the narrow rock gateway.

Wilkins watched the wingtip on his side. He drew a deep breath as the wing barely missed scraping the granite cliff. Then he looked down and saw the wheels spinning. With his good hand, he wiped cold sweat from his brow. He realized that they'd squeaked over the ridge by inches and that the wheels had actually dragged in the snow at an altitude of 9,000 feet. Silently, Wilkins thanked his friend Vilhjalmur Stefansson for recommending Ben to him as a pilot.

Safely through the rugged pass, Wilkins was soon at work roughly sketching the unexpected height of the range they'd just crossed. Among their new discoveries in the higher mountains was a lake more than 30 miles long and 10 miles wide, possibly icebound the greater part of the year. The lake was a welcome sight. It meant that they had found their first emergency landing field—probably the only one—in the Endicott Range.

A few minutes later, they discovered a herd of hundreds of caribou feeding in the foothills. Wilkins quickly made a note of their location so they'd know where to find food if forced down in that section of the Endicotts.

The ordeal of crossing the mountains over, Ben flew steadily onward. The trip ended safely in Barrow. When the roaring engine stopped, Wilkins put his good hand on Ben's shoulder and shouted, "Nice work, Ben. You saved our lives back there."

Ben shook his head and replied, "We had more help than that!"

The Eskimo helpers appeared and were eager to learn how to take care of the plane. Wilkins followed Brower to the station, where Brower dressed his arm. During his years in Barrow, Brower had learned to be a pretty good doctor. Before the hospital was built, he was the first-aid dispenser. Even after the hospital was built, Brower continued to assist with medical problems.

Disregarding the doctor's advice, Wilkins told Ben that he was ready to start on their second flight of exploration over the ice pack, but foul weather interfered. Ben made no secret of the fact that he was glad they were held up. Wilkins needed to let his arm heal.

On Monday, April 19, the weather cleared. They went to the lagoon and prepared to take off, but the engine was too cold. In the bitter cold, Ben worked over the engine until his hands were numb, then gave up. Before they left to go back to the trading post, Wilkins scolded the Eskimo, Panuzak, for not keeping the stove hot enough.

A short time later, when they were drinking coffee, they heard wild yells. Suddenly, an Eskimo rushed into the station and called, "The plane's on fire! THE PLANE'S ON FIRE!"

Ben and Wilkins ran to the plane. Panuzak had stoked the stove with so much seal blubber that it overheated. One of the Eskimos had already jerked the hood off and threw it on the ground, stamping the flames out. Another threw snow on the plane, but in spite of their efforts, Ben found the propeller so hot that it was still smoking, the varnish blistered.

Ben climbed into the plane and started the engine. Except for the propeller, everything seemed to be all right. The engine kicked right off. Wilkins climbed aboard and told Ben to take the *Alaskan* up so they could see how it handled. Both men now feared their exploration trip was off because of the condition of the propeller. After they landed, Ben told Wilkins that he didn't know if they could even make it back to Fairbanks.

The weather turned bad again, and fog rolled in across the tundra to a height of 4,000 feet. Wilkins shook his head and asked, "What else can happen?"

"Maybe we can get a propeller from Fairbanks," Ben said hopefully.

Wilkins brightened. He radioed Fairbanks and ordered the *Detroiter* sent north with a load of gasoline and a new propeller for the *Alaskan*. Lanphier radioed back that the *Detroiter* couldn't possibly make the trip to Barrow. Wilkins said, "I can't understand it. After all, we brought the *Detroiter* to Alaska purposely to do long-distance flying. I'm still puzzled about Lanphier's message."

When Ben and Wilkins finished their coffee, both went back to the lagoon. They climbed aboard the *Alaskan,* and Ben took off. Both were hopeful that they could at least make it back to Fairbanks.

Shortly out of Barrow, they flew into a layer of gray and were unable to see outside the cabin. When they reached the Endicotts, a higher cloud layer at 9,000 feet lowered to meet the 4,000-foot layer. It was like flying inside a bottle of milk.

Without saying a word, Ben turned and headed back to Barrow. Wilkins handed him a hastily scribbled note reading, "You had no choice, Ben."

Early the next morning, Ben and Wilkins again climbed into the plane. A few minutes after they gained altitude, the engine began to vibrate and the propeller clattered nosily. Ben shut off the engine. The vibrations ceased. He carefully glided the *Alaskan* to a stop on the Barrow Lagoon, glad the trouble had come on so close to Barrow. It was discovered that the laminations in the propeller, seriously weakened by the fire, had grown weaker on the flight the day before.

Wilkins left Ben to take care of the plane. He hurried to the station to send another message to Fairbanks, planning to order Lanphier to fly the *Detroiter* to Barrow with gasoline and a new propeller. He was in no mood to take no for an answer, but he found that the generator had burned out and he could not contact Fairbanks.

The Arctic's season of mists and fogs, making exploration work impossible, was beginning. With the radio out of commission, outside help couldn't be expected. It was doubtful Ben and Wilkins would have time to fix the propeller, fly back to Fairbanks for another load of gasoline, and still make it back to Barrow in time for one more exploration trip over the ice before the impossible weather set in.

"Things aren't so bad," Ben said. "There's no reason we can't get started repairing the propeller right away. Charlie has some brass. We can cut it into strips and shore up the prop. I think we can get it fixed tonight."

Soon Ben and Brower were painstakingly cutting the brass into strips and wrapping them carefully around the propeller. After adding several brass strips, they decided to wait until Ben tested the plane before they did any more work.

The next day, after warming the engine and installing the propeller, Ben took the *Alaskan* on a trial flight. He found that the prop was not properly balanced. He landed and the men went back to work fitting more brass bindings in place.

All the time they watched for Smith and Waskey, hoping they would arrive with the other wireless set. They also watched for Earl Hammond, who had gone with a fast dog team to see if he could locate Smith and Waskey and give them a hand.

At 6:00 A.M. on April 28, Smith, Hammond, and Waskey mushed into Barrow. They had the long-awaited wireless. Waskey told about the food shortage and the hardships suffered on the trail from Nenana to Barrow. Supplies had run low, and dogs had died of starvation.

The men in the party were weakened and suffered from snow blindness.

As Ben listened to Waskey describe the hardships on the overland trail, he compared them to the experiences he and Wilkins had had on their trips to Barrow by plane. Aside from Wilkins' arm injury, neither of them had experienced any physical discomfort. They'd worn snow glasses and hadn't been bothered by snow blindness. The savings in time had been tremendous.

After the wireless was set up, Wilkins again radioed Fairbanks asking that Lanphier fly the *Detroiter* to Barrow. Lanphier again sent a negative reply. He said that the *Detroiter* couldn't possibly fly across the mountains. He also added that he didn't think the tri-motored plane could reach Barrow without refueling along the route.

Wilkins was still convinced that the *Detroiter* could fly to Barrow. He knew Ben could fly it. He had also promised certain officials in the States to use pilots Major Thomas Lanphier and Sergeant C. M. Wisely for at least one flight to Barrow.

The next day the weather cleared. Ben and Wilkins climbed aboard the *Alaskan*, even though both knew that it was risky to trust the damaged, brass-bound propeller, and prepared to leave for Fairbanks. Ben tested the engine carefully and said, "With luck, we'll make it back to Fairbanks safely."

They did, but by the time they got there, the Fairbanks field was a sea of mud. Ben managed to land safely, but he knew he'd not take off again until the field was drained.

That evening Wilkins gave the men in the expedition a pep talk. He stated firmly, "I'm going to make the first landing that's ever been made on the ice pack and take soundings out there to find out how deep the Arctic Ocean is. Time is running out. Now, let's get this field in shape."

Although Lanphier still claimed it was impossible to fly the *Detroiter* to Barrow, he cheerfully helped with the work on the field. He was out early every morning, singing songs and telling stories and jokes while everyone worked. Ben worked alongside him but didn't take part in the fun. Wilkins watched from the hangar and later said that he liked to select quiet men for an expedition. He explained that after a month or two, even the most entertaining fellows ran out of material and still had months to go. Wilkins didn't elaborate, but everyone knew what he was talking about.

When work on the field was completed, Ben and Wilkins climbed aboard the *Alaskan*. On the first try the plane refused to lift. On the second try it was hard to steer and swerved into the brush at the side of the field. Ben managed to get it stopped just short of a deep ditch and some stumps. He and Wilkins were thrown forward but not injured.

They climbed out of the plane and began to unload the cargo so that they could drag the plane free of the stumps and the brush. Ben was worried about a case of eggs in the rear of the cabin that Wilkins had promised to the novelist Edna Clair Wallace.

When Ben reached down and grabbed the case of eggs and began to unload it, he thought he saw something move. As he reached all the way down to touch the floor of the cabin, his hands grasped a head covered with long, black hair. Surprised, he gained a firmer grip and pulled. A young woman giggled as she slid along the plane's floor. Ben recognized her as Laddie Kyle, an artist and musician, now intent on a career in writing. The young lady immediately begged Ben not to tell Wilkins that she was in the plane. Sheepishly, she started to crawl out of her sleeping bag.

Ben laughed. Wilkins looked into the rear of the cabin. He saw the now furious young woman half in and half out of her sleeping bag. In a few minutes, people would be flocking around the stranded plane. Ben warned the attractive stowaway to be quiet and quickly closed the door. Both men hoped that they could get the plane back into the hangar before the others knew the embarrassed young woman was aboard.

Little by little, they pieced the story together. The night before, the people of Fairbanks had given a dance for the members of the expedition. Laddie Kyle had danced with Wilkins and told him teasingly that she had made two attempts to stow away in the *Alaskan* so that she could write an illustrated story about life among the Eskimos. She confessed that both times she'd sneaked out of the plane, fearful of what Wilkins would do if he caught her before he and Ben took off. She told him that she was tired of routine work and was seeking adventure. She added that one way or another, she was determined to get to Barrow.

Wilkins had merely brushed aside her threat by telling her that there already was a writer in Barrow doing an exclusive story of life among the Eskimos. He told her that the dangers of flying over the Endicotts would be nothing compared to what would happen if Wallace found out that he and Ben had brought her competition to Barrow, along with her case of eggs!

After the dance was over, the aspiring author climbed out of her hotel window, wearing breeches, boots, and a fur parka. In addition to her sleeping bag, she carried water colors, drawing paper, writing paper, and an extra pair of woolen stockings. Long before anyone else was out of bed, she stowed away in the rear of the plane and bedded down in her sleeping bag.

Except for the accident at takeoff, she might never have been found until the plane reached Barrow. Ben told Wilkins that it was possible that the girl's added weight had made the vital difference between a successful takeoff and the crash.

The *Alaskan* was checked over and reloaded. The old brass-bound propeller was put back on, as it seemed to work better than the new one. When everything was ready, Ben taxied down the runway for the second time that day. The field was in bad shape. Just as Ben was getting up lift speed, one wheel hit a deep depression, and the plane bounced with a resounding thump. The right wing split from the fuselage and sagged to the ground. The *Alaskan* skidded forward. Suddenly, it upended, its nose buried in the soft ground, its tail sticking in the air.

Wilkins was standing in the doorway of the cockpit. When the plane nosed up, 50 five-gallon cans of gasoline piled onto him and blocked the door. Ben, trapped in the cockpit, looked out the window and saw gas spurting from the tanks in the right wing, splashing down onto the hot engine exhaust.

"She's catching fire!" Ben yelled. "Get out quick!" But Wilkins was pinned in the doorway.

"I can't move!" Wilkins yelled back. "See what you can do."

Eventually, Wilkins got free. The ground crew rushed in and dragged cans out of the way. Others beat out the blaze by the engine and kept the plane from catching on fire.

After Ben and Wilkins had looked over the wrecked wing and landing gear, they knew there was no hope of repairing the *Alaskan* for use any more that year. Careful inspection showed that the broken wing had been weakened in its frame for a long time. The sharp jolt when the wheel hit the depression was enough to finish it.

Wilkins called Lanphier, Wisely, Ben, and all other members of the expedition to a conference. Wilkins stressed that the *Detroiter* was repaired and, with the *Alaskan* out of service, there was nothing to do except transfer the cargo and the equipment to the *Detroiter* and take off for Barrow. Neither Lanphier nor Wisely appeared anxious to make the trip, but Wilkins ordered the *Detroiter* made ready.

The next morning Lanphier was at the controls of the *Detroiter* when it took off, with Ben watching enviously. With the flight underway, Lanphier appeared to be in fine spirits, even pulling a stunt or two over the field. He told Wilkins that he just wanted to prove that a machine the size of the *Detroiter* could be looped. Wilkins immediately vetoed any more tricks. It was plain that he was in no mood for horseplay.

Wilkins was greatly concerned, because he knew the season for flying successfully over the ice had probably already passed. In May, the Arctic was covered with low clouds and fog, which made it impossible to make observations from the air. Yet, he was determined to attempt at least one more trip over the ice once they got to Barrow.

Not far out of Fairbanks, the *Detroiter* ran into a cloud bank. At one point during this part of the flight, Wilkins was shocked to see the two pilots arguing and fighting over the controls. Apparently Lanphier wanted to return to Fairbanks, but Wisely wanted to go on to Barrow. Wilkins settled the argument by ordering the plane on. The trip continued in an uneasy silence. When the *Detroiter* landed on the Barrow Lagoon, Wilkins breathed a sigh of relief. He told Brower that he had been nervous all during the flight.

Wilkins immediately sent a wireless message to Ben in Fairbanks advising him that the *Detroiter* had arrived safely. He reported unrelenting fog spread out over the Arctic Ocean.

As the men sat about the stove in Barrow that evening, Brower talked about Roald Amundsen's planned trip in the *Norge*. The men argued about the proper etiquette for receiving dirigibles. They all looked forward to seeing the *Norge* at Barrow after its trip from Spitzbergen.

The next day word came that on May 9, Byrd had left Spitzbergen and supposedly flown to the North Pole and returned safely, beating Amundsen in the race to be the first to fly over the North Pole.[1]

The Barrow group speculated about whether or not Amundsen, financed by the NANA, would still make the trip. On May 11, it was announced that he, Lincoln Ellsworth, and Umberto Nobile had left Spitzbergen for Nome in the Italian dirigible *Norge*. Only 4½ hours later Norwegian, American, and Italian flags were dropped over the North Pole.

Not knowing exactly when to expect Amundsen, Brower set up a regular watch. On the evening of May 12, at 7:30, a native rushed into the station yelling, "Airship! Airship!" Wilkins, Lanphier, Wisely, and Brower joined the villagers as they watched, spellbound, when the *Norge* sailed past. The weather had been cloudy all day, but now the northern sky was clear. Silhouetted against it, the silvery gray dirigible floated silently above an open lead of water about six miles from shore. As it slowly drew closer, the men could tell that Amundsen didn't plan to land. There had been some talk that the *Norge* would land in Barrow to pick up a passenger, so everyone was disappointed and longed to know who the passenger was.

During the hour the *Norge* remained in sight, everyone stayed outside watching it. The *Norge* planned to land at Nome, but a storm forced it down at Teller. The wireless transmitter was out of order, and it was several days before the world learned of the airship's fate. The *Norge* was deflated and eventually shipped outside. It had flown 3,391 miles across the top of the world in 72 hours. The flight basically established that there was no land in the Arctic Ocean over which the *Norge* had flown.

Two days later, while Wilkins and Lanphier waited for the weather to clear, a *London Times* correspondent, Lyons [first name not available], arrived in Barrow by dog team after traveling 900 miles to cover the flight of the *Norge* and also to report on the Detroit Arctic Expedition.

Lyons was the passenger the *Norge* was supposed to pick up in Barrow, but he told Brower that he was approximately 30 miles from Barrow when the airship passed. He said that he stood looking after it, sure that the men had recognized him. Leaving his dog team with the guide, Lyons ran far out on the ice to be picked up, but the *Norge* sailed over him and soon was out of sight.

Another mix-up added to Lyons' difficulties. He'd brought radio equipment, complete except for a motor. In Seattle, where he purchased some of his equipment, he was told that the missionaries at Barrow had purchased a motor two years ago. At Barrow, he learned that the motor had burned out long ago. Wilkins would gladly have allowed him to use his radio equipment to send a story, but the NANA officials overruled him.

At any rate, Wilkins had already sent the story of the flight of the *Norge* outside 48 hours before Lyons reached Barrow. He had scooped the world on the news of Amundsen's spectacular flight. However, his story was so far in advance of others that some people didn't believe it.

The excitement of seeing the *Norge* appear over the Arctic ice served as a shot in the arm to Lanphier and Wisely. Under Wilkins' urging, the two made repeated attempts to get into the air just long enough to search for land. Brower later reported that never did a man try harder than Wilkins, but the *Detroiter* wasn't slated to make the exploration trip. The plane was continually forced out of the track the men made for it in the deep snow, even though it was longer and wider than the one made for the *Alaskan*.

Lanphier and Wisely tried to get the *Detroiter* into the air so many times that Wilkins finally declared that there wasn't enough gasoline left to keep trying and still have enough fuel to get back to Fairbanks. But before they could take off for Fairbanks, Wilkins decided that they must build a new runway. He put a large crew of Eskimos to work shoveling a runway about 40 feet wide and over a mile long. However, the weather turned bad before they could use it. When a favorable weather report came from Fairbanks, he told the two pilots, "It's now or never!"

Brower had watched Wilkins, Lanphier, and Wisely try to take off so often that he didn't have the heart to make another trip to the lagoon. Instead, he climbed on top of the warehouse and watched the proceedings from there.

When the *Detroiter* was ready for takeoff, everyone breathed a sigh of relief. Hopefully, the spectators at the lagoon watched. The Eskimos pushed. The *Detroiter* moved slowly down the runway, gathered speed, but appeared to be short of lifting power. At the very end of the runway it managed to get off the ice, narrowly missing a tall rack used for drying bear skins. Then the plane circled once and headed southeast through a hole in the clouds.

Brower, standing on top of the warehouse, relaxed. He wondered if the flight of the *Detroiter* back to Fairbanks would mark the end of Wilkins' attempts to fly out over the ice.

As soon as Wilkins got to Fairbanks, he radioed Brower that he would be back to Barrow in the spring. He said he'd have a new supply of gasoline shipped up by boat and asked Brower to store it for him. True to his word, when the ship *Charles Brower* arrived in July bringing the annual supplies for Barrow, it also brought Wilkins' gasoline and oil.[2]

Although Amundsen's dirigible had flown over the top of the world, it had not followed the route Wilkins planned for his expedition. Wilkins still felt that few of the scientific goals of the expeditions were achieved. Much information of meteorological value was still needed because clouds had hidden the whole area during the *Norge's* flight, leaving the secrets of the region unknown for another year.

Lanphier was unhappy, for he and Wilkins had had a serious disagreement. The next day Wilkins met with all members of the expedition. He summed up the bleak situation by telling them that the expedition was $30,000 in debt, the *Alaskan* was almost a total wreck, and the *Detroiter* was not in satisfactory condition. Personally, he thought a single-engine plane, like the *Alaskan*, was best for exploration flights and the proposed hop to Spitzbergen. He had flights scheduled to complete his work and stressed that a new plane was his greatest need. Wilkins asked Ben to stay on as chief pilot for 1927. He made no specific offer to Lanphier, who was still on leave from the U.S. Army.

Following his argument with Wilkins, Lanphier left Fairbanks accompanied by Frederick Earp, Sandy Smith, Earl Mason, and Sergeant Wisely. In a later interview Lanphier blamed the failure of the expedition on the late start and the lack of sufficient gasoline, which made it impossible to make more than one flight into the Arctic wastes in search of land.

Ben was assigned to stay on in Fairbanks while plans were completed for 1927. Wilkins and the others left Fairbanks in June, planning to go to Detroit, but Wilkins received a telegram in Seward directing him to return to Fairbanks and await further orders.

Wilkins returned, and he and Ben were entertained often. One night Wilkins told their hosts that not in the last 15 years had he remained in one place as long as he had in Fairbanks. Previously, his explorations had prevented him from remaining more than a month in any one town.

Many Fairbanks residents came to appreciate the scientific nature of the expedition. They admired Wilkins for his persistence and endless patience, even in the face of many setbacks. They also knew that the members of the governing board in Detroit had no real idea of the conditions in Alaska. They felt that Wilkins was in much the same position as Alaskans were—governed from afar by men who knew little of conditions in the North.

Wilkins wasn't back in Fairbanks long when he began talking about one more attempt to fly out over the Arctic ice. Since he'd been ordered back from Seward, he felt that the board of directors might still consider the 1926 work a big disappointment. But Ben didn't agree with Wilkins' desire to make one more flight.

Wilkins eventually changed his mind about the extra flight, but he vowed that he'd succeed in exploring the blind spot even if he had to walk back from it. Wilkins told some friends, "With my experience in the Arctic, I'm willing to risk walking back if an accident occurs. I doubt there are 10 people in the world who have this confidence and would be willing to attempt such a thing. I know I can get back."

Ben and Wilkins both knew that many people outside failed to understand exactly what they had accomplished. On the four flights to Barrow and the flight over the ice pack, they had actually flown three times the distance flown by Richard E. Byrd and had covered a larger area.

Wilkins and the Detroit Arctic Expedition were still very much in the news nationwide. A story from the news service reached Fairbanks that Lieutenant Commander Noel Davis, of the U.S. Naval Reserve, planned to fly across the Atlantic in the *Detroiter* monoplane, if, he told reporters, he could purchase it from Wilkins.

Raymond Orteig had put up $25,000 in prize money for the first pilot to make a nonstop flight from New York to Paris, a distance of

3,600 miles. The only serious contender up to the time Davis made his statement about using the *Detroiter* for the proposed flight was Captain Rene Forack, French Ace of Aces, who planned to make the hop in a Sikorsky biplane then being built.

Wilkins and Ben were both surprised to hear that Davis was interested in purchasing the *Detroiter*, for Wilkins had sold two of the engines and most of the spare parts to Rodebaugh's company.

After a great deal of discussion with Ben, Wilkins wired Detroit to find out what was going on. Later, H. G. McCarroll, assistant manager of the Detroit Arctic Expedition, reported that "we have no intention of disposing of the Fokker monoplane the *Detroiter*." McCarroll denied the report that Davis or anyone else had negotiated for its purchase. In his statement to reporters outside, McCarroll said, "The *Detroiter* is still in Fairbanks and will be used for further flights in connection with the Detroit Arctic Expedition."

Ben tried to cheer Wilkins by saying, "Even if the rumors are true, a big plane like the *Detroiter* is too heavy for what we want to do. For exploring, we need a light plane like the *Alaskan*." He added, "And that's exactly what I need for airmail service, hospital service, and everyday use in Alaska. Flying nonstop from New York to Paris is the least of my worries."

"That's what we'll try to get for next year, Ben. What I want to know is this: Can I count on you to be the pilot again?"

Ben grinned and replied, "I'll be ready to go any time you are, Captain. You can count on me. I guess flying in the Arctic is more my style, anyway."

ENDNOTES

1. Even at the time of this writing, there is still controversy surrounding who was the first to fly over the North Pole. Commander Richard E. Byrd left Spitzbergen on May 9, 1926, in a tri-motored Fokker piloted by Floyd Bennett and was gone more than 15½ hours. Upon his return, he reported passing over the North Pole. There is another claim that the time was 16 hours 55 minutes, putting it more in line with the capabilities of the Fokker.

The controversy was given renewed emphasis on December 14, 1971, when Bernt Balchen, who had been Byrd's pilot on many missions, including his flight over the South Pole, stated that Byrd was not telling the truth when he claimed to have flown over the North Pole. He stated that Byrd would have had to cruise at 105 miles per hour to make the round trip to the North Pole and back in 15½ hours.

It is still to be decided whether or not Byrd's place in the record books on Arctic history will remain as the first to fly over the North Pole or whether the honor belongs to Roald Amundsen, the grand old man of Arctic and Antarctic explorations.

2. The first ship in port that year brought an even greater surprise for Brower. His company asked him to come to San Francisco. Brower left Barrow in August, wondering about the future of the fur station.

24

Alaska—Florida—Alaska

Bᴇɴ ᴅɪᴅɴ'ᴛ ᴍɪɴᴅ the extended stay in Fairbanks, for he rather enjoyed the spring weather. He was dating one of the Fairbanks school teachers, Marie Banks, and was as popular as ever with the townspeople. There was never a dull moment.

True to an old-timer's prediction to Ben on his first trip north, he found time in 1926 to look over some placer gold claims located on the Chena River, about 75 miles from town. The claims looked very promising to Ben, but he wanted the opinion of others who knew more about mining. He contacted the Fairbanks attorney, R. F. Roth (one of his first passengers in 1923), and through his office made contact with Frank Manley, who had carried on very successful placer mining in interior Alaska for 23 years and had earned about $7 million.

Manley wrote Ben that the option he had taken on 22 of the 160-acre association claims on the Chena River in the Fairbanks Recording District was on some of the most promising claims in the interior. Manley listed the advantages of the location of the claims, stating that there was an abundance of water in the Chena River at all times during open season to carry on hydraulic mining on a large scale. He said that the grade of the Chena River was about 50 feet to the mile, sufficient to handle successfully and cheaply the tailings from hydraulic mining operations. He estimated that the cost of mining the ground, including the investment, depreciation, and all other items proper to be considered, would not exceed 10 cents per cubic yard.

Shortly after Manley's letter arrived, Ben received a letter from Hatton telling about an offer for a well-paying flying job in Florida, and almost reluctantly, he decided to leave Fairbanks. He explained to his friends that the more flying he did, the better chance he had of getting a regular mail contract for Alaska. He found it much harder to tell his girlfriend goodbye, but she had long ago learned that his first love was flying. "Maybe someday," Ben said quietly, "things will be different. When I get the mail contract and have several pilots, then I won't be gone so much."

Wilkins remained in Fairbanks a little longer and assured the young lady, "Yes, Ben will be back. We both will. We intend to finish the work we didn't complete this year."

When Ben arrived in Seattle on June 28 aboard the steamer *Northwestern,* he found that his flights with Wilkins had given him a certain degree of fame. He was hardly off the boat when reporters surrounded him, begging for interviews. In the press he was hailed as "the only man who ever piloted an airplane north of Point Barrow to 73:30 North, 156 degrees West, sighting land never before seen by man on the momentous flight made on March 31."

But Ben was not the only celebrity in town. Roald Amundsen, Umberto Nobile, and Lincoln Ellsworth (the only American on the *Norge* in its flight over the top of the world) were also in Seattle. They were heading for Washington, D.C., to present President Coolidge with the only American flag carried across the North Pole.

Reporters questioned Ben closely about rumors of the fight between Lanphier and Wilkins and quoted Ben as saying, "Major Lanphier knew flying and not much about the Arctic. Captain Wilkins knows the Arctic and not much about aviation. That was the basis of their disagreements. . . . But there is much to be said for both sides. Their first quarrel was in Fairbanks, the second in Barrow, and the third will be in Detroit."

The reporters also interviewed the members of the *Norge* expedition and wrote: "Too many bosses on the *Norge* resulted in arguments between Amundsen and Nobile. The two haven't spoken to each other for six weeks."

A later report headlined, "Amundsen and Nobile bury the hatchet," and stated, "At a banquet on June 28, Amundsen and Nobile shook hands and indicated peace has been restored. . . . Apparently, they decided there was honor enough for all."

When Wilkins reached Seattle on July 12, he also was interviewed by reporters. He stated, "When I return to Alaska next year, Major Thomas Lanphier will not be included in the party. Lieutenant Carl B. Eielson will be the only member of this year's party to return." Then, as if for emphasis, Wilkins added, "With the exception of Eielson, there will be an entirely new crew next year."

After a brief stay in Seattle, Ben left for Hatton. His father was waiting to hear of his future plans. Ben explained that he wanted to take the job in Florida—at least until it was time to return to Alaska to continue work with Wilkins. It was no surprise to Ole that Ben had signed on with Wilkins again, for the story was carried in all the papers.

Ben's job was with Florida Airways, as the company's first pilot transporting both passengers and mail. He flew a fine tri-motor plane. Mechanics kept it in perfect condition for him and even rolled it out onto the field. All Ben had to do was fly it. The airfields in Florida were good and well maintained.

Ben flew the first load of mail from Jacksonville, Florida, to Atlanta, Georgia. He also blazed the trail from Tampa to Miami, flying over the Everglades. On his first trip over the Everglades, Ben recalled that his father had said, "Perhaps flying in Florida wouldn't be as dangerous as in Alaska." But Ben considered the Everglades the most dangerous terrain he'd ever seen. He figured it would be difficult to make a forced landing anywhere without striking a tree. The water was not clear enough to swim in, the morass not firm enough to walk on, and alligators were lurking and mosquitoes swarming.

After only a few weeks in Florida, Ben became homesick for Alaska. He remembered how he'd dived over the Yukon hills to surprise September herds of caribou; how he'd started his little Jenny alone, rushing back and forth; how he'd dropped copies of the *News-Miner* with little colored parachutes to the eager miners; and how he and Wilkins had skimmed above the Barrow ice pack and sighted polar bears hunting seals.

After his Florida flying became routine, Ben startled Miami residents one day by putting on an aerial stunt show in the tri-motored ship, doing loops, barrel rolls, and Immelmanns over the city. He told his boss that he thought a little advertising might pep up business.

As February neared, Ben reminded his employer that he had to leave for Alaska. The company hated to lose him and said that any time he wanted a steady job flying in Florida he should come back. But Ben told the manager that he planned to have his own company in Fairbanks someday.

Wilkins had kept in touch with Ben and informed him that he had secured the aid of the *Detroit News* and other backers to finance a second attempt at the blind spot. On the 1927 expedition, Wilkins planned to use the tri-motored Fokker, after some adjustments, and two new Stinson biplanes with Wright engines.

In the expedition party, which sailed from Seattle on February 11, were Wilkins; Ben; Alger Graham, a pilot with long experience with Stinson aircraft; Orval Porter, a mechanic; A. M. Smith, a representative of the *Detroit News*; and Howard A. Mason and A. Heinrich, two radio men. Wilkins told Ben that extra pilots could be selected from the growing number of commercial pilots in Alaska.

Wilkins decided to take the large Liberty engine from the *Alaskan* and build it into the longer-winged *Detroiter*. When this task was finished, the plane was equipped with skis. It proved airworthy on its first flight, but on the second attempt to take off, the Fokker smashed a ski. There was no replacement in town.

The accident to the *Detroiter* left Wilkins with the two Stinsons, which had a range of about 1,600 miles. Joe Crosson was signed on as a relief pilot, and Wilkins chartered the *Swallow*, which Crosson flew for the Alaska Aerial Transportation Company, because neither Ben nor Graham had enough room aboard for Smith, the reporter for the *Detroit News*.

On only three hours' notice, Crosson rolled out his open-cockpit Hisso-powered *Swallow* and prepared for the trip to Barrow. Crosson's trip was the first commercial flight between Fairbanks and Barrow. Several people in Fairbanks doubted Crosson's sanity, attempting the flight to Barrow in an open-cockpit plane.

Ben and Crosson got together several times, and Ben drew a detailed map of the route for him. They decided the best thing for Crosson to do was fly to Wiseman, 200 miles from Fairbanks, where he would land and refuel. Since Crosson didn't know the route to Barrow except for Ben's instructions, he was to wait at Wiseman until Ben flew over and then take off and follow him to Barrow.

Crosson, with his passenger Smith, arrived in Wiseman on

schedule, but he'd had his share of problems on the way. In the cold weather, the water-cooled engine had frozen just as he'd reached Wiseman. When Ben flew over the field at Wiseman and circled, Crosson was busily working on his plane at the snow-covered strip. Not wishing to delay the expedition, Crosson waved Ben on. Ben circled again and reluctantly flew on, trusting Crosson's ability to repair the *Swallow* and find Barrow on his own. Ben could not have landed the heavily loaded Stinson on the short strip at Wiseman.

Crosson took the radiator to the roadhouse, where he spent most of the day soldering it. When Smith came to check on his progress, Crosson told him he'd be ready to take off the next morning.

He was, but the trip from Wiseman to Barrow was a real challenge for Crosson. North of Wiseman the mountains rose steeply, and for 150 miles Crosson followed a maze of canyons and savage peaks. Crossing the Endicotts was just like Ben had described. With only an old ship's compass, Ben's directions, and a penciled route on the map to guide him, Crosson made it safely through. Smith was impressed by the skill of the Alaskan relief pilot.

When Crosson crossed the Arctic divide, it was just as Ben had told him. The timberline of the continent seemed to sink behind him. He headed north across the tundra, with hundreds of miles remaining between him and Barrow. He still faced the challenge of finding Barrow at the top of the continent. In clouds or fog it wouldn't be easy.

Crosson followed the Anaktuvuk River to its confluence with the Colville and then struck out for the coast. He was now navigating by the light of the dim sun, judging his position by the shadow of the struts on the *Swallow's* wing. He reached the shoreline 50 miles south of Barrow on schedule. As expected, he ran into snow flurries but followed the jagged coastline to Barrow. It was nearly dark when he landed on the lagoon with only a few gallons of gas in the tank. Ben and the others had waited patiently, confident that he'd make it.

That evening Ben commented to Crosson, "After I fly Wilkins to the blind spot and then to Spitzbergen, I know I can get financing to organize a new airline. Then I'll live in Alaska permanently, and I hope you will be one of the pilots when I get organized."

Crosson assured Ben that there was nothing he'd rather do. The two also discussed Crosson's return trip. Ben suggested that he follow the coastline south so that he'd be closer to settlements in the event he had any further engine trouble. He could refuel at Kotzebue. Crosson was anxious to explore that country and agreed to try the new route.

Two days later Crosson left Barrow with a rag doll for a mascot and headed south, where no aircraft except the *Norge* had flown. The first three hours out, the engine roared steadily along as the *Swallow* flew over drifted snowbanks and high-pressure ridges. Then, the thing that Crosson had been expecting happened. The Hisso engine began to boil. Fortunately, he was near a good landing place, so he put the plane down on the smooth ice of a lagoon.

He jumped out of the plane, leaving the engine running, and filled a can with chipped ice, which he poured into the leader tank. He was afraid to turn the engine off because he didn't know if he could start it alone. After the water tank was filled, he climbed aboard and took off.

Next, he flew into snow flurries, skirting the edge of a blizzard. Fortunately, he arrived at the Eskimo village of Kotzebue before the storm got too bad and landed safely. Almost immediately his plane was surrounded by laughing Eskimos. The Kotzebue natives had never seen a plane before, and they stood around and laughed and laughed.

In the midst of the hilarity, Crosson put a tent over the engine and drained the oil. He found a place to stay and remained in Kotzebue for four days until the weather cleared.

Taking off from Kotzebue, Crosson followed the Kobuk River to Noorvik, where he landed to check his engine. He broke the right landing gear strut and had to stay over for repairs.

Several days later Crosson headed toward Fairbanks, dodging storms all along the route. As he neared Fairbanks, he flew into a thick, raging blizzard but managed to land safely at his home field. He wired the news of his delayed, but safe, arrival to Ben in Barrow, where the expedition waited for the weather to clear. Fred Hopson was in charge there while Brower was in California.

Finally, on March 29, the weather was fair. Wilkins and Ben were all set to resume where they had left off in 1926. Wilkins hoped to discover an island north of the continent for a weather station.

Although they were helpful, the Eskimos at Barrow knew little about the fine points of flying and didn't realize what a beautiful takeoff Ben made at 6 o'clock on that bitter cold morning with his heavily loaded Stinson biplane. Their expressions turned to startled amazement as they noticed Ben and Wilkins heading due north from Barrow. To the north there was nothing, just the frozen wastes of the Arctic Ocean. The puzzled Eskimos turned and walked back to the village, thinking their friends had lost their minds. They were heading straight into the "land of never come back."

When Ben and Wilkins took off in the *Detroit News Number 1*, the temperature stood at 42 degrees below zero. When Ben reached an altitude of 1,000 feet, the strut thermometer registered 32 degrees below zero, and the cabin thermometer 18 degrees above—a far cry from flying in shirt sleeves in Florida.

Wilkins first planned to fly into the Arctic blind spot at a point about 78 degrees north latitude and 180 degrees longitude. There he and Ben would land on Arctic sea ice (something that had never been done before) and take soundings. If they found the ocean shallow there, they would continue, if possible, toward any land area indicated. Should the ocean soundings indicate deep water, showing their position to be well beyond the continental shelf, then they would fly about 200 miles and make a second sounding before they returned to Barrow.

The Stinson flew out over broken ice, across leads of open water, which looked for all the world like giant blue snakes. An hour out over the Arctic Ocean, the two men saw large pans of ice, large enough to land on. The farther they flew, the more ice they found. Huge expanses of rough ice were straddled by pressure ridges. Off to the southwest, Wilkins pointed out to Ben the vicinity in which the *Karluk* was crushed in the ice 13 years earlier when part of its crew perished. Wilkins was on the *Karluk*, but he was in the party of six led by Vilhjalmur Stefansson that dog teamed back to land for help.

Ben continued flying into the blind-spot region. The ice became more ridged, more checkered with cracks.[1] The smooth ice became sparse, and landing places few and far between. At 10:20 A.M. the engine began to miss. "What a spot to have engine trouble," Ben thought as he glanced at the tumbled ice pack. He revved the engine, then skillfully worked the mixture control to cause a backfire and clear the carburetor of any ice that might have formed in it. After spitting for two minutes, the engine settled to a steady roar.

Every half hour Wilkins struggled with the primitive shortwave transmitter, trying to send a code signal back to Barrow. It was wasted effort. The meter showed practically no current leaving the antenna.

The engine sputtered again. They had been in the air almost six hours and were about 450 miles from the mainland. Below was nothing but tortured pack ice. The engine began to kick harder. As Ben looked for a safe place to land, Wilkins handed him a note reading, "Think we better land and fix that engine."

Ben paused for only a moment. Could he do what no man had ever done before—land on the moving ice pack? Flying in widening circles in his search for a smooth place to land, Ben wiped tears of strain from his peering and squinting eyes. Finally, he took a deep breath and forced himself to think calmly. He studied the ice pack below and saw a patch of dull gray ice that looked flat enough to land on.

The plane plunged down into a cloud bank. With coolness and skill, Ben idled the engine, leveled the plane, and made a steady downward glide. Near sea level, the air was rough, but he calmly corrected each unsteady move. The altimeter registered 100 feet, then 50, then 25. The Duralumin skis touched and glided through snow, which was as crisp as ground glass.

The landing was a little rough, but the plane was safe. Ben thought, "The biggest test is yet to come. If I get the engine fixed, is there room enough to take off again?" Then the tension left. They had made a safe landing on the ice pack. Wilkins was elated. Against the arguments of many other explorers, he had prophesied a landing on the ice pack could be made. Ben had done what others considered the impossible. Wilkins actually seemed happy when they were forced to land. This gave him an opportunity to take a sounding.

While Ben worked on the carburetor, Wilkins hacked a hole through the thick ice. He called to Ben and asked if he would help detonate a sounding charge. Ben stopped work on the engine and obliged. He'd been careful to let the engine run, because it might not start again. Wilkins made a successful sounding, but Ben could tell that he wondered if it was accurate. "With the ship's engine roaring," Wilkins said, "maybe we didn't hear the detonation echo correctly. If you'll shut off the engine, we'll set off another charge."

Ben hesitated. A thought whirled through his mind. "If we stop the engine, it might never start again, and nobody but God and you and me will ever know what that sounding was."

He delayed a moment longer and then switched it off. They set another charge and found the depth of the ocean was three miles. This was the greatest depth ever recorded in the polar waters, proving that there was no land in that area.

Ben hurried to restart the engine. It didn't function properly, and after it warmed up, he shut it off again. In the bitter cold, he worked on the engine for two hours. He restarted it again. It still wasn't functioning properly, but perhaps they could get back to Barrow. By now it was getting dark. The sun was covered by great storm clouds, and a stiff wind was blowing.

On the fifth attempt, Ben got the Stinson into the air. He headed back to Barrow in growing darkness, the plane pitching this way and that way in the gale. The wind had shifted to the northeast and held the plane back like a giant brake. "She should be doing 1,600 rpm," Ben explained, "but I can only get 1,400."

Then the engine sputtered again and threatened to stall. At this point Ben was concerned about his fuel supply. The repeated attempts at takeoff had used much of the precious gas supply. Tensely, Wilkins watched.

In the growing darkness, ice ridges were hard to see. Twice Ben swooped low, then yanked the struggling plane up again. He finally found a level pan and connected with it. Wilkins said, "Ben, back in Fairbanks I heard bragging that you could land a plane on a blanket and never touch the hem. Now, I believe it. That was a fantastic landing!"

The strut thermometer registered 40 degrees below zero, but Ben had to remove his mittens and shut the engine off to work on it. He knew what would happen as soon as he touched the metal, but, he reasoned, being stuck on the Arctic ice pack without any hope of rescue was worse than frozen fingers.

Ben worked on the engine as fast as possible, but soon his exposed fingers were white and three fingers on his left hand were numb. To add to the difficulties, falling snow made the ice pan sticky.

Ben knew that he would have trouble getting the plane into the air. He started the engine. The first attempt at takeoff failed. But by keeping in the tracks of the first attempt, Ben finally got the plane into the air only a few feet from the cold waves of ocean water lapping against the edges of the ice-pan landing strip.

Guiding the plane with his numb hands on which the finger tips were likely frozen, Ben pulled the plane up to 4,000 feet. Above the blizzard, visibility was still almost nil. He estimated that they had enough gas left for about eight hours. They had taken off from the ice pan at about 2:00 P.M. If they were lucky, they might make it back to land. Suddenly, Wilkins and Ben realized that they were hungry. They ate heartily of biscuits and pemmican and nearly emptied the thermos of coffee.

It grew darker, and at 7:00 P.M. Ben was bucking the storm with wide-open throttle. By 9:00 P.M. they were flying through dull blackness. Holding a torchlight in his hand, Wilkins helped Ben read the turn and bank indicator. They figured that another hour's flight, *if* the gas held out, would bring them to the mainland.

Suddenly, at 9:02 P.M., the steady purr of the engine stopped. The silence was like a deafening blow. The only sound was that of the wind screaming against the wing struts. The engine was completely dead. Almost in disbelief, Ben snapped the switch from right to left. There was no response, just a metallic click. For the first time Ben could sense Wilkins' fear. He gave no orders, for he realized everything was up to Ben.

Calmly, Ben guided the plane as it pitched and plunged earthward in the blackness. Steadying the ship, he brought it into a glide. A few hundred feet above the surface of the ice pack, Ben thought he could make out a smooth place between jagged saw-toothed pressure ridges. The air was rough near the surface, but Ben steadied the Stinson and braced himself against the empty gas tank, ready for the final plunge, either against the jagged ice or into the water. The plane struck, bounded, then settled upon a solid icy surface. The ski stanchions were twisted. Ben had nicked an ice ridge.

After the almost endless minutes of anxiety, the fact that they were safe seemed like an impossible dream, but they were. Ben broke into a wild laugh and so did Wilkins. The sound of their laughter was almost hysterical, but it released their nervous tension. They were alive and had shelter from the storm.

Ben looked out the door of the plane into the gusty blizzard. Beneath them was the tremor of ice jarring against ice, the horrible growling and grinding of the ice pack. They were at the mercy of the storm. There was nothing to do. Ben felt almost guilty. They didn't have to drain the oil because they had no gas. They didn't have to cover the engine because it would never roar to life again. But they struggled out into the blizzard and darkness. After seeing Ben had barely squeaked onto a smooth patch of ice, they decided to drain the oil anyway and cover the engine. Ben knew he wouldn't feel right otherwise. Then they retreated back into what comfort the plane provided. Exhausted, they crawled into sleeping bags. In spite of themselves, they soon were fast asleep.

When they awoke the next morning, they were able to see exactly how lucky they were. The *Detroit News Number 1* was perched on a stretch of smooth ice about 90 feet long and 45 feet wide. Jagged pressure ridges rose on three sides.

Wilkins looked at Ben and said, "It's a miracle we're safe, Ben."

Silent for a moment, Ben finally said, "Yes, it's a miracle. I surely had a good co-pilot last night."

Wilkins was anxious to see which way they were drifting. Digging a hole through the ice, he dropped a short line and learned that they were drifting north of east at five or six miles an hour.

Later in the day, Wilkins determined by sun observation that they were marooned at 72 degrees north latitude and 155 degrees west longitude approximately 65 miles north and west of Barrow. Their location constantly shifted because the ice pan was drifting with a 30-mile wind.

They planned their return hike during the five days that they were held prisoners by the storm in the Stinson's cabin. Each new day, with desperate hope, both took turns cranking the wireless, although the current meter scarcely registered. Alger Graham in Barrow just might hear their message. He was their only hope of rescue.

By draining the five fuel tanks, they collected a half gallon of gasoline. Wilkins contrived a stove from a tin can and used lubricating oil for fuel and two slats of wood for wicks.

The two were quite comfortable in their sleeping bags. Any time either was hungry, he helped himself to food from his own bag of supplies. Their emergency rations—pemmican, biscuits, chocolate, nuts, raisins, and malted milk tablets could all be eaten cold. When they emptied their thermos bottles, they filled them with snow and melted it in the warmth of their sleeping bags to give them water to drink.

Each day that passed the two realized the helplessness of their situation. They were being driven farther and farther from land by the storm. They knew that the only way to save their lives would be to walk back to the mainland over the treacherous pack ice.

Each day Ben's fingers throbbed with increasing pain. Although hard to bear, the pain rather pleased Ben, for he knew the hurting fingers would recover. One finger had no pain, no feeling, and began to turn black. Gangrene was a possibility, so the trek across the ice back to Barrow couldn't start too soon.

They recorded the story of their flight on the ceiling of the cabin. Wilkins recorded the figures of his soundings. Even if they never got back, the Stinson might. Stranger things had happened in the Arctic.

They kept busy with preparations for their walk. They built two sleds from parts of the plane and loaded them with provisions and the equipment needed for survival. On the morning of April 3, 1927, Ben hopefully cranked their last wireless message: "140 miles northeast of Barrow; walking home."

ENDNOTE

1. The Arctic Ocean, some 6 million square miles in area, has a perpetual ice sheet 6 to 12 feet thick over more than half its surface. Though melting of the ice pack is rapid during the summer, new ice forms constantly from September to April. Slush develops as the water surface cools, and the cooling continues until the slush welds itself into pancakes, or small slabs, with jagged rims built by sloshing water. The ice pack doesn't freeze flat and firm. Currents from the world's oceans and rivers enter the polar sea, agitating the waters under the ice. They heave and surge, cracking the ice and forcing it up into pressure ridges as big as a car, a house, or a hill. New ice again forms on the surfaces thus exposed.

25

The Long Trek Back

IT WAS CLEAR and 60 degrees below zero when Ben and Wilkins abandoned the Stinson. They headed south towards Beechey Point, the coastal trading post, which now was closer than Barrow. Beechey Point, named for Captain Frederick W. Beechey, who did exploration work in the area in 1826, was east of Harrison Bay and served as a branch of the Barrow station. Tony Edwardson was running the Beechey Point station at the time. Wilkins figured it might be as little as 80 miles away. They started on skis but soon took them off. The surface was rough and hard in places. Snowdrifts were waist high in others. To drag their sleds over ridges, they sometimes had to claw their way up with ice picks. Five hours was all they could struggle their first day.

They picked out a sheltered camping spot for the night between ice ridges. Wilkins used a double-edged saw to cut large blocks of snow. He showed Ben how to stack them to make an Eskimo igloo. Wilkins noticed that Ben could scarcely carry the snow blocks.

"Ben, let's see your hands," Wilkins said abruptly, but Ben kept working. Wilkins approached and pulled off Ben's right glove. Only then did he realize that Ben was struggling with five frozen fingers. He pulled off the left glove. Deadpan, Ben said, "The fingers on my left hand are throbbing, but there's no threatening discoloration. It's the right hand I'm worried about." The right hand showed blisters, and the little finger was blackened and insensible.

Wilkins looked closely and said, "The discoloration is spreading to the next finger." He shook his head and said, "Ben, if it's necessary, . . . well, I have the instruments." He turned abruptly and went back to cutting snow blocks.

"I can finish up here," Wilkins said. "You rest."

But Ben wouldn't stop. He tried for an optimistic grin and replied, "They'll be all right until we reach land. That is, unless the going gets rougher than it was today and we have to walk on our hands."

When it was finally finished, the snow house turned out to be a welcome shelter. After a hasty supper, cooked on a tiny Primus stove, both men bedded down in their reindeer sleeping bags. Wilkins went to sleep immediately, but the pain in Ben's hands kept him awake for hours. Still, he rested.

As he lay sleepless, Ben thought about the real hazards ahead— the open leads of water, the stretches of forever-shifting broken ice, the danger that two cakes would tilt together and throw Wilkins and him into the icy water. He knew that the drifting pack ice was never still. "With luck," Ben thought, "we might make it to Beechey Point in two weeks. We can stand anything for two weeks."

Finally, toward morning, Ben slept fitfully. His last waking thoughts were what Wilkins had said the first time they'd landed on the ice pack. "We've made history. Ours is the first airplane to land on Arctic ice."

After their miraculous third landing, when the plane ran out of gas, Wilkins commented, "This is the third time we've landed safely on the Arctic ice."

Ben had laughed and added, "But this time we've set a new record. We're the first men ever to land a plane on the Arctic ice pack and then have to walk home. I'm glad you've had some experience along that line."

The second day of traveling didn't seem as bad as the first. Plodding through drifted snow, pulling their loaded sleds behind, the two trudged on hour after hour. The pain was so intense that Ben couldn't pull his sled with his hands. He finally looped the rope over his shoulders and gripped it against his sides with his arms. But the slow pace was disheartening. Once they had to detour for several miles around an open lead.

That night, Wilkins hurried to cut snow blocks for their shelter. Ben hauled most of the blocks under his arms, and Wilkins helped set them in place. Once inside the shelter they discussed the difficulty of pulling the sleds, which continually capsized or got stuck between hummocks of ice. They decided to eliminate more gear, dispose of one sled, and then spell each other, with one man breaking trail and the other pulling the sled.

They kept only the scientific equipment, Wilkins' camera, one sleeping bag, rifles and ammunition, and 30 pounds of food. As he watched the pile of discarded equipment—once thought absolutely necessary—growing, Ben thought briefly about the Stinson. The morning they left the plane and each day since, the weather had been clear and perfect for flying. "If we hadn't run out of gas," Ben thought, "we could have been back to Barrow in an hour."

After the forced landing, the Stinson was undamaged except for the skis, which Ben was certain he and Wilkins could have repaired. Ben shook himself. There was no point in looking back. He remembered what an old-timer in Fairbanks had told him when he had problems starting the Jenny. The sourdough had advised, "Sell it and get a dog team. That's the only reliable transportation in the North."

"Yes," Ben admitted to himself, "even a dog team would be a big improvement for us now."

By afternoon, they reached the first large expanse of open water. Wilkins glanced at the area ahead. He saw what appeared to be a ridge of ice cakes spanning the water. Ben hurried forward toward the natural bridge, but Wilkins called him back. As calmly as if they'd just stepped out of the Stinson and had plenty of gas, Wilkins said that he wanted to test the drift. He dropped his lines and found that they were now drifting east about two miles an hour.

More experienced in knowing which ice cakes would hold his weight, Wilkins crossed the bridge first, hopping from one to the other. While Ben followed him across, he suddenly burst into laughter. He'd just remembered the play he'd written about Alaska and how his sister Elma had played the part of Mrs. Hegge. When her boat capsized in Alaskan waters, she jumped from one ice cake pillow to another until she reached shore safely.

Startled by Ben's laughter at such a crucial crossing, Wilkins turned back. Ben waved him on. After they both reached solid ice, Ben caught up with Wilkins and told him he'd explain things that night after they made camp. Still puzzled, Wilkins plodded on ahead, catching the sound of laughter once more.

That evening in the comfort of their snow house, Ben entertained Wilkins by telling him of the play he'd written about Alaska so long ago. Wilkins had a good laugh, too. Both men took care of their parkas, boots, and socks as soon as they finished their meal. The first night out, Wilkins had taught Ben to turn the skin boots inside out, beat them against the snowshoes, and scrape the frost from them. They gave their outer garments and mukluks similar treatment. They took special care of their socks, laying them against their chests at night to dry out while they slept. Many evenings they didn't bother to cook a hot meal. They ate from their store of concentrated food, not stinting, but not overeating.

In the open water the next day, they saw seals for the first time. Leads of open water became more frequent as the days passed. Once, while Wilkins was crossing a lead by stepping from one ice block to another, the ice gave way beneath him. He stumbled forward and fell into the icy water. He thrashed around and eventually got his head above water, but the sinking ice cake flipped up and hit him, pushing him under again. It was not until he lodged his ice pick into solid ice that he was able to pull himself to safety. Ben watched helplessly from the opposite side.

Once on solid ice, Wilkins hurried to a sheltered place sur-rounded by towering ice ridges and stripped. He rubbed his outer clothing in the soft snow to blot out the water, all the time dancing around to keep up circulation.

By this time Ben was on the solid ice beside him. He'd run down the opposite side, then lowered himself to the ice, spread-eagled, and wriggled across. Despite the situation, both men laughed. With Ben's help, Wilkins lost no time unpacking dry socks and mukluks and putting them on.

Wilkins dressed hurriedly, confident that his clothing would dry on his body if he walked fast enough. He'd already wrung and blotted out most of the water. The two men were too tired to talk but walked as fast as they could. Ben knew that Wilkins was using every trick he'd learned from Stefansson to keep them both alive.

That evening, the men decided to abandon the remaining sled and pack the supplies on their backs. They promptly divided the items they carried into two piles. Each item had to balance its weight in usefulness. When they completed their work, each pack weighed about 80 pounds.

Ben's little finger was much worse that day. That night he couldn't sleep, but he didn't let himself think about what could happen if they didn't reach land soon. He did think how nice it would be to have Dr. Newhall, of Barrow, the only doctor in the Arctic, check his fingers. For the first time, Ben realized why some of the miners had appreciated his mercy flights so much. He wondered about the other plane.

The next day the ice ridges grew more jagged and were covered with snow. The men fell down so many times that they finally decided to crawl until they reached better ice. For Ben, each pain-filled day was a repetition of the day before.

Ten days went by. They had started with two sleeping bags; now they had only one. At night they slept in their parkas and put their feet into the same sleeping bag. Each night the pack ice creaked and groaned, struggling to the whim of the water beneath it. Even in the warmth of the shelter, the sounds chilled Ben.

After a day's journey, the feet of both men often were cut and swollen from the sharp ice. Sometimes, it seemed that Ben and Wilkins were so tired that they couldn't put one foot in front of the other. By now, their faces were covered with whiskers, and their breath froze white on their beards. Day after day, they trudged along—staggering, crawling, falling, getting up again, and hurrying on. Sometimes, they scaled high mounds of ice, crawling up one side and down the other.

When they came to leads of water too wide to jump across and there was no ice bridge, they boarded cakes of ice and used a snowshoe to paddle across to the next floe. At new "rubber ice," so thin they dared not walk across it, they lay flat on their stomachs, spread-eagle fashion, and wriggled across. Sometimes, they crawled on their bellies for two miles.

All the water they drank came from melted ice. They filled their extra pairs of mittens with ice and hung them inside their parkas. They became used to having a few loose hairs in their drinking water.

Toward evening one day, the ice suddenly splintered under Ben's weight, breaking the section he'd been walking on in two. He reached safety but did not soon forget the terrorizing sound of cracking ice beneath his feet. Wilkins called, "Steady. You'll make it."

That night, the snow-house shelter seemed like heaven. The next morning, nervous anxiety and the unending whiteness of the ice pack made the men's eyes smart, even with snow glasses. They often saw mirages ahead of them. Ben remembered dog mushers telling him stories about seeing roadhouses and dog teams when there were none. Ben, too, saw a roadhouse that day, far ahead on the ice, but he knew there was none there. Wilkins saw a mountain standing upside down on top of another.

That night, Wilkins tried to judge how many extra miles they had walked because of detours and the drifts. Each day he charted their course using a pocket compass.

Once, when an ice bridge that Wilkins had already used to cross an open lead began cracking under Ben, he went back to the other side. Wilkins threw him a rope. Ben attached it to his pack, which Wilkins pulled across. Ben then walked along the edge of the ice until he found a spot narrow enough to hop across. They finally reached ice solid enough to walk erect on, and then they made good time.

On April 16, 1927, 13 days and 125 miles away from where they had abandoned the Stinson, they came up over a high ice ridge formed by pressure of the outer floe against ice attached to the coast. Wilkins had described how things would be when they neared land. It was like that now. Ben almost cheered.

Looking through his field glasses, Wilkins sighted a pole, then a roof—the trader's post at Beechey Point. The two tired, bearded men began talking like a couple of school boys. "Your navigation on the moving ice is as good as your navigation in the air," Ben said happily. "Beechey Point, Alaska, here we come!"

Off in the distance, they saw two Eskimo mushers and their dog teams rushing to meet them. Ben thought he'd never seen anything so beautiful. Wilkins slapped him on the back and said, "Look at those beautiful dog teams, Ben."

That evening Wilkins and Ben sat down to their first full hot meal in 18 days. One of the Eskimos volunteered to drive his dog team 120 miles to Barrow with news that the men, who had been given up for dead, were very much alive after traveling for 13 days in "the land of never come back."

But rescue came sooner than would have been possible by dog

team. Following the instructions Wilkins had left with Alger Graham at Barrow, Graham had been flying the *Detroit News Number 2* up and down the coast, dropping messages to the Eskimos and to the trader at Beechey Point telling them to be on the lookout for Ben and Wilkins, who might be on foot. Graham also had made several attempts to fly out over the ice, but after the five-day blizzard, most of the Barrow residents had lost hope.

In the trader's home, Wilkins and Ben were exhausted. Their muscles had served them as long as they had to, and now the two men practically collapsed. They could hardly move. Ben's frozen fingers were in such bad condition that Wilkins finally decided to perform layman's surgery and got out his equipment. In place of an anesthetic, Ben decided to drink all the whiskey he could hold. Wilkins said, "When I perform this surgery, it might mean the end of you as a pilot for a while, but you can't stand to make the trip to Barrow by dog team for real medical help." Ben nodded and kept drinking.

Ben's operation was about to begin when he staggered to his feet and yelled, "Listen! That's an airplane I hear!" The room fell silent. Wilkins thought that perhaps Ben had had too much "anesthetic" and was hearing things.

"Come back here, Ben," Wilkins called. But out of the silence was heard the roar of an engine.

The men rushed outside. Alger Graham was just coming in for a landing on the lagoon in front of the trading post. Even before he got out of the plane, Ben and Wilkins were beside it. Graham was shocked to see them. "Let's go to Barrow," Wilkins said. "We've got a patient for the doctor."

The two happily climbed aboard the Stinson, and Graham flew them back to Barrow. Ben was immediately taken to the small hospital, where Dr. Newhall amputated the first two joints of the little finger on his right hand. Newhall said, "With luck, you can keep the rest of them." Under the doctor's expert care, all the other fingers were saved.

As soon as he could, Ben sent a wire to his family. Later, he wrote a letter and promised that as soon as possible he would send them a photo Wilkins had taken at Beechey Point when his face was still blackened from exposure and he hadn't shaved. When he sent the picture he wrote across the back, "After a walk on the Arctic Ocean."

Dr. Newhall told Ben that he'd better forget about flying for at least several weeks. "It isn't that you wouldn't be able to control the plane," he said, "but a forced landing and another 13-day walk could have dire consequences."

Wilkins was still eager to strike out again with the *Detroit News Number 2*. Ben volunteered to stay in Barrow and take care of things there while Wilkins and Graham flew over the ice.

During the next three weeks, Graham and Wilkins made several trips, but clouds were so thick that they couldn't see if there was any land or not. Ben would have been satisfied to have stayed in Barrow longer, but Wilkins finally decided it would be wiser to get him back to Fairbanks.

With Graham at the controls, the three left for Fairbanks, taking the coastal route so that they could stop at harbor towns if necessary. It was a good thing they did, for they got no farther than Wainwright when engine trouble forced them down. They remained at Wainwright while a dog team was dispatched to Barrow for parts from the supply depot there.

On May 14 they reached Fairbanks, where they received a royal welcome. Many people there had given Ben and Wilkins up for dead. One of Ben's friends said, "I'll never worry about your flying again. It's like a miracle you two survived."

Wilkins was determined to make more flights. He told Ben that he wanted to fly from Barrow across the Arctic to Greenland—a trip that would enable him to explore vast and unknown Arctic regions in a different direction. His plan was to land on the Greenland ice cap and walk out to some Eskimo encampment on Davis Strait between Greenland and Ellesmere or Baffin Island.

Because there was discussion about the Stinson not being stable enough for such a trip, Wilkins decided to fit the *Detroiter* with wheels. But after the Fokker was readied and tested, Graham didn't have enough confidence in it either. The load was transferred to the Stinson again, and Graham and Wilkins flew back to Barrow, leaving Ben to look after expedition matters in Fairbanks.

The two reached Barrow safely, but misfortune plagued *Detroit News Number 2* when they tried to fly over the ice. Wilkins and

Graham returned to Fairbanks. By this time the open season was at an end, and they could do no more work that year. Wilkins was greatly disappointed.

During Wilkins' absence, Ben was entertained by many of his friends in Fairbanks. His closest friends begged him to forget Arctic flying. They told him that he should have learned his lesson.

"But we haven't completed the work we started," Ben said firmly. "I'll admit the expeditions haven't been as successful as we hoped these last two years," he added, "but our time hasn't been wasted. We found out there wasn't land in places, and we tested the depth of the Arctic Ocean in several places. And think what our trips from Fairbanks to Barrow mean to the residents there. We proved it's possible to fly to Barrow regularly during the winter."

"What good did it do you to risk your life out on the Arctic ice pack?" one of his friends interjected.

"When you're flying you don't think about things like that," Ben said. "Besides, we proved that landings and forced landings on the ice pack are possible. We also proved that men forced down can walk to safety over the moving ice pack, even over distances of a hundred miles or more. But more important, Wilkins is doing pioneer work in meteorology. Some day it will be possible to predict far in advance when a certain part of the world will be subject to drought. Also, the world path of storms will be mapped out long before they make themselves felt in settled areas."

One night when Ben and Wilkins and the other members of the expedition were at a party in their honor, Wilkins suddenly asked, "If things work out, Ben, will you fly with me next year?"

Ben answered, "Sure! Where to?"

"Across the top of the world," Wilkins replied. "Maybe all the way to Spitzbergen."

Ben snickered and said, "That's what I expected you to say. You'll know where to find me."

To have refused Wilkins might have been smart, but it wouldn't have been Ben. He'd never turned down a flying challenge.

Ben was a little embarrassed when he found that his girlfriend had overheard the conversation. Ben hadn't told her that he'd be flying in the Arctic again. After she accidentally heard the news she'd been dreading to hear, Ben took her aside and explained why he had to go. She smiled and said quietly, "I wish you weren't going, but that's what I expected. I realize flying is still your true love." Ben didn't deny it.

While Ben was still in Fairbanks he received a letter from Hatton with another job offer. The Department of Commerce wanted him to work as an inspector-at-large for pilots, airplanes, and airfields. Of course, his father expressed the hope that after Ben's grueling experience walking back from the 1927 flight and the loss of a portion of his right little finger, he would give up flying for good.

The job offer with the Department of Commerce came about because of the Air Commerce Act that Congress passed in 1926, which provided for a Bureau of Aeronautics. The new bureau was authorized to license planes, approve airfields, set up and enforce air traffic, investigate accidents, and test new aircraft for safety.

Although Ben was excited about his new job, he also was very excited about reports of the dark-horse contestant in the New York to Paris nonstop flight—Charles Lindbergh. The flight, which offered $25,000 in prize money to the first pilot to complete it, had attracted much attention. The American public was less excited by the work Ben and Wilkins and other Arctic explorers had done during the past two years. Most Americans still thought of the Arctic as remote, dreary, and not really a part of their world.

When Ben got back to Fairbanks from Barrow on May 14, even Alaskans were talking about the New York to Paris nonstop flight. Ben found that every one of the pilots of the big multi-engined planes, built especially for the New York to Paris flight, had crashed.

On May 20–21, 1927, when the historic flight was made by Charles Lindbergh in a modified Standard Ryan M-2, the *Spirit of St. Louis*, many converts were won over to the monoplane design and air-cooled engines. The flight also won many converts to aviation. Americans took to the skies in increasing numbers, and passenger figures quadrupled in 1928. Financiers decided that aviation might become profitable. Securities of aircraft companies were marketed as infant airlines ordered big tri-motored ships and new airports were built to accommodate them. Struggling airplane makers got a new lease on life.

Through the summer and fall of 1927, Ben received brief letters from Wilkins telling of his continuing difficulty in raising money for the third expedition. Over and over Wilkins told prospective backers that the time spent in 1926 and 1927 on expedition work hadn't been wasted. When they asked about the forced landing in 1927 and the walk back over the ice, Wilkins said that even that wasn't a loss. The expedition had taken many deep sea soundings and proved that the islands other explorers had reported didn't exist.

Wilkins said that when the entire area had been scouted by air and it was determined that no land existed in the Arctic, it would be necessary to find out if ice would support a floating weather station. To do this, Wilkins said that the area had to be explored during midsummer with a submarine. The remark about using submarines in the Arctic caused eyebrows to raise, but Wilkins didn't bother to elaborate.

He said that there was still the vast area to the northeast in which Peary believed that land might be found. The object of the 1928 trip would be to fly over this section. He explained that if he and Ben didn't find land in this section, the second phase of the expedition would be to continue on to Spitzbergen. One prospective backer remarked, "Fly nonstop over the top of the world? A transpolar flight? Why, that would be one of the greatest adventures into the unknown since Columbus! I wouldn't tell too many people about your wild ideas, Captain Wilkins. They might think you're completely crazy."

"I don't care what people say about me," Wilkins said. "I'm going anyway, even if I have to go into debt and finance the expedition myself."

Fordson tractor, converted to snow disks for better traction, towing the first shipment for the Detroit Arctic Expedition, Fairbanks, December 1925. (SHSND)

Crashed Fokker, the *Alaskan*, with Eielson posing, Fairbanks, 1926. (SHSND)

Fokker tri-motor, the *Detroiter*, Fairbanks, 1926. (SHSND)

The *Detroiter* after
early test at Fairbanks,
1926. (SHSND)

The *Alaskan* over Barrow, 1926. (SHSND)

The *Alaskan* at Barrow, 1926. (HEM)

Eskimo at Barrow tending heater of *Alaskan*, 1926. (SHSND)

The *Alaskan*, heating stove and canopy removed, Barrow Lagoon, 1926. (SHSND)

The *Alaskan* at the Fairbanks airport on the return from Barrow, Spring 1926. (SHSND)

The *Alaskan*, Fairbanks, Spring 1926. (SHSND)

Refueling the *Alaskan* with the standard five-gallon cans of that era, Fairbanks, 1926. (SHSND)

George Hubert Wilkins and Eielson, Fairbanks, 1926. (SHSND)

Wilkins with camera, at Fairbanks. (National Archives)

H. Liebes Company Trading Post and home of Charles Brower family (manager), Barrow, 1926. (SHSND)

Trading post (structure with aerial, center) and teacher's home (right), at Barrow. (SHSND)

Wilkins and Fred Hopson, cook at Barrow Trading Post, 1926. (SHSND)

Eskimos clearing hard-packed snow from runway, with the *Alaskan* and the village in background, Barrow, 1926. (SHSND)

Dr. and Mrs. Newhall, Barrow, Eielson photo, 1926. (SHSND)

Polar ice, Point Barrow, Eielson photo, 1926. (SHSND)

Polar ice pressure ridge, Point Barrow, Eielson-Wilkins photo, 1926. (SHSND)

Dirigible *Norge*, commanded by Roald Amundsen, landing at Teller, Alaska, 1926. (HEM)

In the summer of 1926 Ben flew this plane for Florida Airways, delivering the first airmail between Jacksonville and Atlanta and other southern cities. (HEM)

26

Spitzbergen or Bust

Bᴇɴ ᴇɴᴊᴏʏᴇᴅ ʜɪs ɴᴇᴡ ᴊᴏʙ as inspector-at-large, flying from one end of the country to the other, but he always kept in touch with Wilkins. He found that many people were skeptical of Wilkins' proposed expedition for 1928. Wilkins discussed the expedition with Roald Amundsen, and he, too, was skeptical. Amundsen said, "What you propose to do is beyond the possibility of human endeavor."

Amundsen explained that because it was 2,200 miles from Point Barrow to Spitzbergen and because the route was over the Arctic Ocean, there wouldn't be any check points to verify navigation. Wilkins told Amundsen that he'd have to adjust the compass course perhaps 20 times during flight so that, in effect, his route, if drawn on a chart, would resemble 20 short lines bending in a great curve. He admitted that if he miscalculated by a degree or two, he'd never hit Spitzbergen but would end up lost somewhere on the Arctic ice. But Wilkins said that he had confidence in himself as a navigator and equal confidence in Ben as a pilot.

Amundsen didn't change his original assessment, and his skepticism carried a great deal of weight. Amundsen was well respected. He was the first to reach the South Pole, the first to make the Northwest Passage voyage around the top of North America, and the first to make a dirigible flight from Spitzbergen to Alaska. Amundsen also had tried using airplanes in the Arctic twice and had given up.

Amundsen's stand on Wilkins' 1928 expedition discouraged many prospective backers still interested in scientific work in the Arctic. Financiers told Wilkins that they objected to the high risk potential and possible loss of life, for they were certain he couldn't succeed. Of course, they also told Wilkins that they knew that the failure of his project would advertise the dangers and difficulties of polar exploration and make it harder for them to get financial backing for their personal projects.

Wilkins realized that he would have to finance the expedition himself. He took an inventory of the assets remaining from the 1926 and 1927 expeditions. He still had the two Fokkers in storage in Seattle. He knew that he couldn't afford to use the big Fokker because it would take five or six men to handle such a large plane and the expense for gas and oil transported to Alaska would be greater. He had only about 500 gallons of aviation gasoline left at Barrow—barely enough for one small plane.

One Stinson had been abandoned on the Arctic ice, but Wilkins still had the other one stored in Fairbanks, giving him three planes to sell. He decided to sell the big Fokker and the Stinson so that he could purchase a small plane.

The search for just the right plane proved to be a tedious job. As Wilkins sat dejectedly in the St. Francis Hotel, in San Francisco, one day he suddenly saw a trim, bullet-shaped monoplane fly over. He jumped up and rushed to the window. The plane was almost out of sight. He wondered if it had landed at one of the nearby airfields and rushed to call all the airfields in the vicinity. He was puzzled. He had never seen that model plane before. It was streamlined and just what he wanted for the Spitzbergen flight.

He phoned the airports, one after the other, but had little luck. When he asked about a streamlined plane with full cantilever wing, without struts, flying about 120 miles per hour, no one seemed to know what he was talking about. At each place Wilkins explained that he had seen the plane fly past and wanted to know the name of the plane and where it was built. Every airport manager reported that he had never seen such a plane and didn't believe one had ever been built.

Wilkins realized that he wasn't getting anywhere using the phone. He contacted his friend Ray Shrek, and together they drove from one Bay-area field to the other. Finally, they found the dream plane at the Oakland airport. Wilkins was elated. This plane had no external wires or exposed controls to offer wind resistance. The sleek bullet body tapered to a sharp point at the nose with the wing extended outward from the top of the fuselage. There was cabin space for two people. He told Shrek excitedly, "This is the plane Ben and I need to fly to Spitzbergen!"

Wilkins carefully checked the markings on the back of the plane and found Lockheed Aircraft Company, Los Angeles, with the model marking of a dark star and the word "Vega" next to it.

Wilkins was soon on his way to Los Angeles to find Lockheed. Once there, he met Allen Loughead and Jack Northrup, designers of the plane. Wilkins learned that the plane he had seen in San Francisco had just completed a trial flight from Los Angeles to San Francisco. It was the only one of its kind, and the owner planned to use it for the Dole prize flight to Hawaii. After looking at the blueprints and data of tests and of the trial flight, Wilkins decided that he must have a Vega for his flight to Spitzbergen. He told Loughead to build a plane for him. Two or three days after Wilkins had put in his order, the original Vega took off for Honolulu on the Dole prize flight and was never seen again.

Wilkins wrote Ben about the wonderful Lockheed Vega, but by the time Ben got the letter, there had been much unfavorable publicity about the Vega when it was lost over the Pacific. Yet, when Ben read Wilkins' letter filled with favorable comments on the plane, he replied at once that he trusted Wilkins' judgment. He added that if Wilkins purchased the Vega, he would fly it.

After work began on the Vega, Wilkins found a buyer for the big Fokker. Two Australian fliers, Charles Kingsford Smith and Charles Ulm, wanted to fly the Pacific from America to Australia.[1]

Wilkins still had the *Alaskan*, the plane that Ben had piloted on their first trip over the Arctic ice pack. It had strained under heavy loads, lifted them from the wretched field at Fairbanks, carried them safely between mountain peaks of the Endicotts, struggled with them through clouds, rain, snow, and sleet, and, in the end, when strained to its absolute breaking point, crashed on the Fairbanks field. Wilkins couldn't bring himself to sell that plane. It would be like dumping an old and trusted friend.

Wilkins next found that the aviation companies in Fairbanks were hard pressed for machines and were anxious to buy the Stinson he had stored there. After a short delay, he sold it. When both deals were closed, Wilkins paid for the Vega and rushed to wire Ben, saying that they were all set to leave for Fairbanks in February.

Lockheed built two Vegas, but the plane Wilkins ordered had many special features. It had a standard cabin and was powered with a Wright J5 Whirlwind engine with two gas tanks in the cabin in place of the usual seating. Two extra gas tanks were built into the wings. Two upper windows were left on each side and two were placed on the floor. The floor windows were aids in taking ground speed and drift observations without opening a trap door and suffering the cold rush of wind experienced on previous flights.

The machine was of wooden construction, which would eliminate many of the difficulties in navigation. Care was taken to keep all metal fittings likely to interfere with the compass away from the navigator's compartment. One window was hinged so that it could be opened for observing the sun.

The pilot's cockpit was entirely enclosed with windows of Triplex glass, giving excellent vision in all directions. A small window that could be opened to aid in cleaning the windshield during flight was installed on each side of the cabin.

Wilkins decided to name the plane *Detroit News* because of the paper's liberal support in 1927. The name and "Wilkins Arctic Expedition" were painted in letters as large as possible on the side of the plane. The rudder carried the registration number, "X3903." The plane was painted a bright orange so that it could be easily observed if forced down on the ice.

Hurricane lamps were installed for heating. A special aluminum tray was fitted beneath the cowling to hold blue-flame oil-burning stoves. Wilkins figured 45 minutes to 1 hour of warming would allow the engine to start. The design included a tight-fitting cowling.

When the plane was almost completed, Wilkins wrote to Ben asking if he could take leave from his job and be in California for testing. The two Vegas were to be tested on the same day. The test pilot who took up Wilkins' plane was pleased with its performance, but Wilkins wasn't at the field to hear the results. He had gone to meet Ben at the train, and they arrived just in time to see the test flight of the other Vega end in a crash. The test pilot, a friend of Ben from the Department of Commerce, found the Vega was fast in flight and apparently thought he should make a fast landing. He came racing down and smashed onto the runway. The landing gear broke, and the plane flopped on one wheel. When the wheel collapsed, the

Vega flipped on the other wheel and ground looped. The pilot got out and said, "Eielson, it flies fast and tricky; it's unreliable, hard to land."

Before Ben could respond, Wilkins asked him if he would like to take their plane up right away, and Ben couldn't resist. Watching from the ground, Wilkins could tell that Ben liked the Vega by the way he handled it. When Ben circled to land, he was blinded by the late afternoon sun and headed straight toward some high-tension wires. Wilkins thought everything was gone, but Ben zoomed up just in time and flew over the wires, missing them by a scant foot.

When he landed, Ben told Wilkins they'd better find a place to test the Vega where there was more room. The next day they located a good field farther out of town. Ben's confidence in the Vega grew each time he took it up. He wanted to put enough hours on the engine in normal temperatures to prepare it for the very low temperatures expected in the North.

Usually Wilkins accompanied Ben, but on the third flight one of Wilkins' friends wanted to fly with him. Ben had barely left the ground when the engine quit. He quickly made a turn from an altitude of a little over 50 feet and crashed in a plowed field. Even at 50 feet with no power, the plane had made a beautiful complete turn. It crashed but didn't flip; only the landing gear was wrecked.

Ben found the trouble was a vapor lock in the gas line. To guard against the same thing happening again, the complicated gas system was changed to a simpler arrangement, which Ben and Wilkins designed. At the same time, they installed heavier landing gear with special heavy axles. This gear worked so well it was added to later Lockheeds.

After all the modifications were made, Ben took the plane up 15 or 20 times a day until he knew it thoroughly. Once all the load tests were completed, the plane was prepared for shipment to Seattle on the *Emma Alexander* and then on to Fairbanks by railroad.

Adeline and Ole had traveled to Seattle to see Ben and Wilkins off. Ben's parting words to his father were "Don't worry about me, Dad. You know I've always wanted to visit Norway, and now's my chance."

Ole replied, "Son, let's hope and pray that you don't have any trouble."

During the boat trip to Seward, Wilkins worked on his calculations for the flight based on the expectation of clear weather over the Arctic sometime in early April. He and Ben would cover 171 degrees of longitude. The rapidity with which they would cross the lines of longitude would necessitate rapid changes in compass settings. Both men practiced Morse code.

The ship reached Seward on schedule, but Wilkins and Ben were delayed there several days because of snow slides on the Alaska Railroad. Shortly before they reached Fairbanks, Wilkins told Ben that while Ben test flew the plane in Fairbanks he would continue working on navigation problems. In their spare time they would continue practicing Morse code.

They finally arrived in Fairbanks on the evening of Sunday, February 26, 1928. The weather was warm, water dripped from the roofs, and the streets were ankle deep in slush. But within a few days the temperatures were back to 20 and 30 degrees below zero, so Ben and Wilkins prepared for test flights.

Because of previous experience, Ben and Wilkins needed only two men to help assemble the ship. In addition, many volunteers were available from among Ben's friends and from among a crew at the hangar who were busy assembling a machine for the Arctic Prospecting Company.

As Ben and Wilkins worked on the plane, they made several alterations, especially to the cowling. Each small hole in the cowling was, as far as possible, sealed. The carburetor was wrapped with asbestos, and all the exposed parts of the induction pipes were covered. The exhaust pipe leading to the carburetor heater was also lagged—a knuckle-skinning job.

After the initial work, Ben took the Vega up again. In spite of the closed cowling, enclosed exhaust pipe, and oil lines covered with asbestos, it still ran too cold with light loads. The engine spit and sputtered. Experience in previous years had shown Ben that it was advisable in cold weather to increase the size of the main metering jets. But this year, the main jets had been kept small to reduce gas consumption as much as possible.

Curves plotted after trials for engine speed and gas consumption showed that for the best air speed throughout the trip, the engine should run between 1,600 and 1,750 rpm. As long as the engine ran smoothly at 1,600 rpm, Ben preferred not to change jets. He didn't want to run out of gas this time and experience another walk over the ice pack.

Although Ben and Wilkins were happy with all the volunteer help, there was one big disappointment for them. When they first arrived, they found that much of the equipment they had left in Fairbanks was missing. When Ben made known his disappointment, some of the equipment mysteriously reappeared. However, they still were missing a special lightweight wooden block and tackle, which was made in New York in 1926 especially for Arctic use. Ben repeatedly dropped the word that they had hoped to take it along on the 1928 expedition so that if they were forced down it could move the heavily loaded plane on the sea ice. The block and tackle couldn't be replaced in Fairbanks, and there wasn't time to order another one from New York. Both men kept hoping it, too, would reappear, but it never did.

When they were almost ready to leave for Barrow, the officer in charge of the American Legion post in Fairbanks asked Wilkins if Ben could remain there long enough to attend the tombola (a type of lottery) to support the building fund for the post. Wilkins agreed, but he told Ben that they should leave for Barrow soon so he could get some rest before their flight to Spitzbergen. With Ben as guest of honor, the tombola was a success. The Legion members also asked Ben to carry an American flag on the top-of-the-world flight so that they could later display it at the post. Ben was surprised at their new-found faith in the flight and promised them a flag.

Finally, on the morning of March 19, 1928, Ben and Wilkins were ready to go. A teamster, using a heavy raft pulled back and forth by a team of horses, was hired to help level the field. The frozen surface was polished to perfection.

Ben's girlfriend found it difficult to say goodbye. She stood next to him by the Vega, listening to conversations of some of Ben's closest friends. She could tell that they, too, felt that the proposed flight had little chance of success.

Over and over they pointed out to Ben that there was no stopping place between Barrow and Norway. Ben didn't answer them but turned to his girlfriend and said, "Don't worry. I'll be back. I came back last year, didn't I?"

"Well, yes," she answered, "but not in the plane," and she left and disappeared into the crowd.

That morning it was 24 degrees below zero in Fairbanks, but even in the cold, well-wishers lined the field on both sides. Ben gave the Vega the gun. The ground crew swayed the tail of the machine. Gathering speed, the Vega slid along the polished surface. It climbed into the air, lifting from the improvised field as smoothly as from a concrete runway. Ben and Wilkins headed for Barrow.

Wilkins busied himself testing instruments and practiced sending a message on the wireless. The weather was clear, and Ben knew the course to Barrow by heart. They passed over Livengood at 115 miles per hour. The machine appeared eager to reach the Arctic Ocean.

When they came to the Endicotts, Ben climbed to 11,000 feet. Looking down at peaks between which he had precariously threaded his way in the Fokker in 1926 and the Stinson in 1927, Ben reveled in the loftier view.

After crossing the range, Ben swung the Vega to follow a river valley, which would afford a safe landing if necessary. The plane flew over a low bank of clouds, then ran into a strong wind. After a time, the wind stopped, and the rest of the course to Barrow was smooth.

This was the first trip over the Arctic Slope on which Ben and Wilkins could see every detail on the snow-covered tundra. Actually, details on the flat stretch of land between the Endicotts and Barrow were few and far between, but the two men spotted several herds of caribou. They passed over the Colville River and then followed the Ikpikpuk for a time.

As they neared Barrow, the wind rose again and they encountered drifting snow. It was hazy, but far ahead Ben spotted their regular landing place on the lagoon.

As they circled to land, the engine missed badly and stopped. Ben brought the plane down far short of the lagoon. Wilkins climbed out, and after one swing of the propeller, the engine started again. Ben took off, gained altitude, circled, and landed in the right place. The temperature at Barrow was 48 degrees below zero.

The bright orange Vega taxied to a stop near the trading post, where Ben and Wilkins received a warm welcome from their Barrow friends—Charlie Brower, Fred Hopson, and Harry Riley. Leon S.

Vincent, the new school teacher, and his wife were there, as well as the new nurse in charge of the hospital. Dr. and Mrs. Newhall were also part of the welcoming committee. Ben hurried to drain the oil and care for the engine. Then the Eskimos pitched in and helped carry gear to the station warehouse.

The two fliers almost felt that they were home again. During the past two years, Barrow had become their second home. Once inside the trading post, presents were passed out to everyone. When Fred Hopson was presented with a box of cigars, which in pre-aviation days had been a luxury in Barrow, he said, "Thanks, Cap. I haven't been without them all winter. Some you brought before, and there are still several boxes in the store."

Wilkins and Ben helped to lift the somber mood in Barrow. Brower told their aerial visitors the bad news. On January 18 the schoolhouse had burned and the teachers had lost everything they had. Brower thought that the probable cause of the fire was a defective chimney. The teachers had done all they could to fight the blaze. Even the school bell had cracked from the heat. School was held in a makeshift building.

Besides that, Brower added that it had been a bad year for furs. An unusual influx of red foxes had made the white ones scarce. In addition, Brower didn't know if he had made a mistake in ordering supplies on his own to keep the station going. Wilkins and Ben had brought Brower a letter from the company, but he merely stuffed it into his pocket. "If this is more bad news," Brower said, "it can wait."

Wilkins announced to the group that this year he and Ben were "going to Spitzbergen or bust!"

"But we'll need your help again," Ben added. "For one thing, we'll have to line up a crew to clear a 4,000-foot runway on the lagoon. As soon as the weather's right, we can get started." Ben paused and added thoughtfully, "Four thousand feet might not be long enough, but we can try it."

The snow would have to be cut into blocks and then carried far enough back to prevent the wings from hitting. Then the rest of the runway would have to be cleared with shovels. It would be backbreaking work.

The next day the natives who hadn't seen the plane the night before came down to look it over. Even the youngsters were attracted to the bright-colored machine. Although the weather was terrible for the first few days after Wilkins and Ben arrived, the plane became the center of the children's playground. Once or twice Ben told them to be careful and not get too close to the plane, but they were having so much fun he didn't get too rough. They chased each other round and round the plane, dodged beneath the tail, and hid by the landing gear.

Seated in the trading post one afternoon, the men were shocked when a breathless youngster rushed in and reported, "A crazy Eskimo boy shot into the wings of your plane."

Rushing out to see the damage, Ben found that a small boy, about eight or nine years old, was shooting at the wings with a small slingshot and pellets, but the missiles had scarcely dented the wood-work. Ben breathed a sigh of relief. Wilkins, standing behind Ben, couldn't help but think what a heyday the press would have had with such a story. He and Ben laughed when they thought about possible headlines.

But misleading headlines were nothing to joke about. Ben knew that Wilkins had every right to feel bitter about press coverage on their 1926 and 1927 flights. Newspaper readers didn't understand the scientific nature of the flights and did not consider them very sensational. Therefore, reporters had sometimes ridiculed Wilkins. Even after the forced landing on the Arctic ice pack and the courage and stamina it had taken for Wilkins and Ben to walk 13 days over the ice to civilization, one reporter had headlined an article, "IF AT FIRST YOU DON'T SUCCEED, WILKINS, FLY, FLY AGAIN!"

For the next three weeks the Lockheed Vega stood idle at Barrow, but much routine work had to be done. Wilkins was fully occupied studying his navigation project. Both fliers were fitted for fur garments. Under the direction of Mrs. Brower, the older women got busy sewing. Wilkins had also brought some pongee silk with him to use to make coverings for the fur garments. Snow didn't stick to the silk, so he thought that it would make the clothing a lot warmer in case of a forced landing. Memories of the biting cold on the 1927 trek were clear.

The younger women were busy, too, making sealskin boots, with the hair inside, suitable for the coldest weather. Also, two pairs of high waterproof boots were oiled, rubbed, and fitted. In their emergency supplies, both men had many extra insoles made of gunny-sacks cut into strips. Besides that, each man had four pairs of woolen socks, presented by the Detroit Woolen Mills. Each had one pair of fur trousers and one pair of sealskin trousers, plus a parka. They carried two one-man sleeping bags reaching to their hips. They also took skis and snowshoes.

The food supply was carefully checked. There were 20 pounds of malted milk tablets, 5 pounds each of chocolate, raisins, pemmican, and biscuits, and a few tins of army emergency rations. The explorers also carried a carton of cigarettes and some chewing tobacco. They had a Primus stove, a two-gallon aluminum pot, two spoons, two forks, and two enamel cups. In the previous year they had learned that it was better to have food that didn't require cooking. They took no coffee or tea because they didn't plan to boil water. It was better to drink cold water, as any steam in a tent or a snow house caused condensation.

They packed a can of alcohol for use in the plane in case of temporary delay. They also packed a can of ether in case of serious accident and the need for makeshift surgery. The ether could also be used for starting the engine in cold weather.

To supplement their food supply if necessary, they carried two Mannlicher rifles and 350 hand-selected hollow point cartridges. In addition, they had a long-handled spear suitable for killing seals through the ice. They had a tent ridge pole for use in taking soundings or recovering seals.

To demonstrate their confidence in reaching Spitzbergen, they took along toothbrushes, toothpaste, beard clippers, razors, and hairbrushes. These items were packed along with their sewing kit. After they checked everything, Wilkins commented that the razors, the beard clippers, and the hairbrushes were the only nonessentials.

One night Ben sat in the trading post at Barrow and wrote to his brother Oliver. He noted:

> We flew over here in 40 below weather making an average speed of 120 miles an hour. This plane certainly steps out when you give her the gas, makes 145 full out. In a few days, we are going to cross the unexplored territory to the northeast. We hope to land at Kings Bay, Spitzbergen, 2,200 miles away. We have to take off with 3,500 pounds of gasoline, etc. If we

smash up on takeoff, and there is always a good chance of it,
I will not be able to get home till September, the first boat.
The next mail does not leave here till August but I am sending
this letter with a fellow who leaves here tomorrow by dog team
for Nome. Best regards to all.

> Your brother,
> Ben

P.S. I expect to see you before you receive this letter.

Each day Wilkins practiced observing the sun with his Royal Air
Force bubble sextant and a small pocket sextant. Then he worked out
positions by astronomical methods, using a special stereographic
chart with curves and tables prepared and supplied by the American
Geographical Society. Still, he knew it was one thing to take observations of the sun in Barrow but quite another to take them accurately from an airplane under cramped conditions while speeding
along at 120 miles an hour.

Because of the difficulty Wilkins expected with magnetic decli-
nations on the course to be followed, he didn't bank on any help
from standard compasses. Instead, he decided to use an eight-inch
boat compass in the navigator's cabin and a prismatic surveyor's
compass, depending mostly on sextant observations.

Wilkins carefully marked every leg. He figured that the magnetic
variation would go from 30 degrees east to 180 degrees when the
north end of the compass would be pointing south, then on to 15
degrees west—in all, just 45 degrees less than a complete circle.

On plotting his course for the entire journey, Wilkins learned
that the greatest degree change would be between the tenth and
eleventh hours and would amount to 26 degrees. Since it would not
be possible to maintain an absolutely straight course, Wilkins would
have to keep a careful check on the variation and direction of flight
and, by constant observation and watchfulness during flight, compensate from time to time for the error.

During the entire stay at Barrow, Wilkins kept a careful eye on
meteorologic conditions. He predicted a three-day blow to begin
April 3. This would be followed by a clearing of the atmosphere and
a south wind on the sixth and seventh.

Everyone decided to go along with Wilkins' predictions. The big blow started April 3. No attempt was made to try to move the well-tied-down Vega, but Ben did postpone plans to complete the runway.

When the storm ended the afternoon of April 5, work on the runway began in earnest. Thirty Eskimos cut the snow into blocks, and others shoveled the runway. With the help of men and dog teams, the plane was moved to the part of the lagoon from which Wilkins hoped to take off. Wilkins paid each worker $5 a day plus overtime. It took 30 hours to clear a track 14 feet wide and 1 mile long.

Wilkins told Ben that the takeoff would be harder than any daredevil trick he'd ever tried. The Vega weighed 2,000 pounds, and they would be carrying a 3,500-pound load. Ben said briskly, "The runway might not be long enough. The only way I can possibly make it is to give her full throttle for the whole mile and then go up over the hill on the other end and hope she takes off before she goes down the other side."

Finally, on Saturday, April 7, all was ready for the takeoff. Everyone had worked late the night before. Once the engines warmed, Wilkins called, "All set?"

Ben answered, "All set," and gunned the Vega. The Eskimos wiggled the tail, the engine accelerated, and the plane rushed down the runway. It was obvious to Ben that he wouldn't get off before reaching the end of the runway and the hill. He pulled back on the stick to try to force the plane off, and the tail came down with such a bump that it shook loose the trigger they'd provided on the tail skid for an emergency brake.

Their brake worked so well that it scored a three-inch gutter in the tough sea ice. When the Vega bounced off the side of the runway, a side wind caught it and flung it to one side. It landed with most of the weight on one ski, which gave way. The plane plowed through the snow in a circle and stopped. One ski was badly wrecked, but the other was all right.

Fortunately, Ben and Wilkins had brought an extra pair of wooden skis to Barrow. They removed the metal skis and installed the wooden ones. They also drained the gasoline from the wing tanks.

With the aid of men and dogs, they soon had the Vega back on the runway and ready for flight. But by this time the wind had increased and the weather was not favorable for takeoff. The crew worked until 7:00 P.M. making the runway as long as possible, but only a few feet were added. At the end of the extended runway the bank of the lagoon rose about 15 feet.

Ben told Wilkins that even though it was late, he wanted to make a run by dog team five miles down to Elson Lagoon, which extended for many miles along the northern shore to the east of Barrow. When he returned, Ben said, "Well, if we can't get off the Barrow Lagoon, we'll use the Elson Lagoon, which means making a new runway."

Wilkins nodded and replied, "Let's hope for the best tomorrow."

For the next three days, however, fog and clouds engulfed Barrow. At 3:00 A.M. on Wednesday there was a light movement of air from the north. Wilkins said that if they left that day they would have clear weather but head winds for much of the way. They decided to chance another takeoff.

Once more the plane slipped smoothly down the ice runway, gathering speed. The wooden skis seemed to slide at least as well as the metal ones. But at the end of the runway the Vega struck the snow. It careened up the bank of the lagoon and over the snow-covered tundra at the top. It topped the hill, then went down the other side. When the plane first struck the snow, Ben gradually reduced the throttle and held it as steady as he could. The Vega came to a smooth stop, and no damage was done. A quick examination showed that everything was safe.

Ben and Wilkins were as happy as if they had taken off. This puzzled the Eskimos. Ben explained that now they were sure the machine could stand hard usage. He added that with a little stronger head wind the Vega would have been well away, but two failures on the short runway were enough for Ben.

"Well, we might as well haul the plane to Elson Lagoon," Ben said. "We need a longer runway." In a short time Ben rounded up two dog teams and a crew. The men drained the gas from the wing tanks again and lined the dog teams out for the trip to Elson.

By now, getting the two fliers into the air became a challenge to all Barrow residents. The first day Brower sent a crew of 23 men to Elson Lagoon. The next day he sent another 35 men down, plus a few late arrivals from farther up the point. Brower told Wilkins, "We'll get you into the air if we have to shovel a path clear to Tangent."

Everyone worked until late into the night. When the runway was a mile and a quarter long, Ben finally said, "That's long enough. Let's get some rest."

Before turning in for the night, Wilkins took the wireless receiving set out of the Vega and gave it to Mr. Vincent, the school teacher. Wilkins asked him to listen each hour from 10:00 A.M. on and try to catch any messages. He told Vincent that if he and Ben didn't take off early Saturday morning, they would take off on Sunday.

The next morning Ben and Wilkins were up early, but they were exhausted. Brower talked them into getting a day of rest before they left.

Finally, on April 15, almost everything was ready. Wilkins got up at 3:00 A.M. to check the weather and decided to warm the oil. He put it on the kitchen stove to heat. Then he got busy with something else. The oil boiled over on the stove and ran onto the kitchen floor. Fred Hopson, just coming to start breakfast, lectured Wilkins severely. Wilkins grabbed the mop and started mopping furiously. It took 45 minutes to clean up the mess.

Ben rushed in from Elson Lagoon to see what was causing the delay. He saw the red-faced Wilkins, on his knees, diligently mopping up the oil under Hopson's watchful gaze. Ben started to laugh, which relieved the tense air in the kitchen. In order to make up for his angry reaction, Hopson hurriedly prepared a good breakfast.

Ben was too excited to eat much. He finally jumped up and wrapped the warm oil in a sleeping bag and headed for Elson. Wilkins followed closely. Just before Wilkins and Ben left, Fred filled their thermos bottles with hot coffee.

Wilkins and Ben had planned to start at 6:00 A.M., but they were now several hours behind schedule. Because of the long delay, Ned, the Eskimo who was left to keep the stove going to warm the engine, feared the engine would become overheated, so he thoughtfully removed the oil stove. This caused another delay as it was necessary to reheat the engine, which meant the oil had to be reheated, too.

By this time the wind had increased. It was almost too dangerous to attempt a crosswind takeoff, but since everything was ready, they decided to go ahead anyway. Wilkins figured that if they did get into the air and conditions were too bad, they could dump the gasoline and return.

Finally, the engine was warm again. All the grease caps on the rocker arms of the engine were filled, and the stoves were removed. Once more they were ready to start.

Both men were concerned because the gas tanks weren't quite full. They had intended to pour in five more gallons that morning, but the fuel had leaked out of the can during the night. Still, they felt that they had sufficient gas.

The Eskimo ground crew yawed the tail of the plane, and the Vega skidded off the boards that were beneath the skis to keep them from sticking to the snow. Ben gave full throttle, and the ship got underway. As the speed increased, Ben had a difficult task keeping the plane within the width of the runway. From the cabin window, Wilkins could see the tail swaying and missing by no more than a foot first one bank and then the other. That's when he was glad that Ben was at the controls. An error of a few pounds' pressure on the rudder, a swing of a few inches one way or the other, and they would have hurtled into a snowbank, the skis buried beneath the blocks of snow the Eskimos had thrown from the runway on both sides. Ben kept his nerve, and Wilkins prayed.

Finally, the plane lifted, swung sickeningly, touched the ice once more, and then soared into the air. Wilkins later reported, "Never was there a more fervent prayer of thanksgiving than the one I uttered."

The greatest danger of the historic trip was now past. They had taken off from an inadequate runway in an overloaded plane. Wilkins noted later, "I thanked God for the understanding of the men who designed her, for the honest, conscientious men who had built her, and for the skill and wisdom of the man at the controls. I was conscious of the great privilege of guiding the Vega on her course."

All the exhaustion from hard work and the tension that had built up during the past weeks fell away. Wilkins passed a note to Ben: "Wonderful takeoff. How's everything?"

Ben shouted back through the speaking tube, "Everything's great. She handles fine. Engine turning at 1,725. Temperature 120." Today's jet pilots might smile at Ben's pride in the single-engine Vega soaring away on a 2,200-mile trip from Barrow, across the Arctic ice to Spitzbergen, Norway, but to Ben it was the best ship he'd ever flown.

Thirty miles out over the Arctic Ocean, Ben and Wilkins found the horizon to the north and east clear. The ice, after they had skimmed over the lagoon and crossed the round high-pressure ridge near shore, was badly broken with much open water. Those conditions prevailed for the first 50 miles. The loose ice was stationary or, if moving at all, was going against the wind. This indicated that the wind from the east would soon be over. Wilkins figured that it would swing to the southeast, south, and southwest. They were assured of fine weather for the first few hundred miles.

The first few hours Wilkins was busy settling everything in the cabin. He put out his charts and tested both sextants for index error and put them in order. Next, he tried the gas pump to see that it was clear and made sure the dump valves were free in case they had to use them. He tested the wireless aerial to get the best resonance. He checked the drift indicator to make sure it registered true. He found his stopwatch would not function if left in the cold cabin, so he had to keep it in his pocket.

Wilkins had little time to write notes or to examine the ice closely. Yet, he could see that a forced landing at this point of the trip would have been their last. There was no ice smooth enough or fields large enough for a plane to land. The ice pack was broken up too badly.

For the first 100 miles, Ben flew at an altitude of from 500 to 800 feet. Looking down, he noticed that the ice was becoming heavier and ridged. The heavy packs coming from the northeast and moving against the shore pressed the lighter ones moving west. The direction of the ice falls indicated the direction of greatest pressure. Ben was reminded of Wilkins' and his walk the previous year. They had stood on the ice while it squirmed and piled into jumbled masses. At night, they had listened to it groan. To stand in its midst, not knowing whether or not the ice would, in the next moment, rise and tilt to spew them into the mass, was unforgettable. Now, riding high above the pack in the plane, both men recalled the ordeal of walking to Beechey Point.

After 11 hours of flying, carefully watching the ice pack, both men felt certain that they had sighted no land. Except for about an 80-mile stretch of low-hanging clouds, visibility was good.

Ben finally passed Wilkins a note: "Engine been turning 1,650.

We are using approximately 18 gallons of gas an hour. Now about 40 gallons left in the wing tanks. Oil temperature 105."

Wilkins was comparatively sure of his observations but was soon cheered by the fact that they obviously were near shore ice (ice less than 100 miles from shore). Ahead, too, high clouds like those observed only near land rose to considerable heights. The plane plowed through several cloud banks and then headed due north to clear the clouds.

Looking out the windows, Ben and Wilkins glimpsed the tops of the rugged mountains of Grant Land. Ben flew parallel to the coast, where the clouds were more broken. At frequent intervals he could see towering steep-sided masses showing darkly through the gray mist. Beneath him, he caught occasional glimpses of broken sea ice.

In what they believed to be the neighborhood of Cape Columbia, Ben and Wilkins sighted a level ice flow, which they thought was the position where Peary had established his shore headquarters before striking out over the ice for the Pole. The place was named Crane City after Zenas Crane, president of the Peary Club and the father of one of Wilkins' friends and supporters in Los Angeles.

Wilkins felt the work of exploration was now essentially over. They both were thrilled that the plane had performed so well. The engine had been faithful for every minute of the trip. Contented, Wilkins settled back to pour a cup of coffee for himself and Ben. He also put out some pemmican and biscuits to munch on.

But the relaxed mood didn't last long. Soon they were flying over a local storm. Wilkins figured that they would run into a storm over Greenland also. He knew that if they kept on for an hour and then had engine trouble, they could hardly return to Grant Land. Neither could they fly crippled through the storm to land at Greenland. From Peary's writings, Wilkins knew that the ice at Greenland was treacherous.

Wilkins interrupted his snack to write Ben a note: "There are two courses open. We are above the storm now. Down there we can land and wait out the storm. Can we get off again? If we go on, we will meet the storm at Spitzbergen and might not find land. Do you wish to land now?"

Ben replied, "I'm willing to go on and chance it."

Biscuits and pemmican forgotten, Ben flew on. Soon they were approximately 200 miles northwest of Spitzbergen and slightly east of their course. The wind from a little west of north drifted them eastward. Ben knew that they had only about four hours of gas left.

For the next 1½ hours Ben flew through cloud lanes, occasionally seeing patches of almost ice-free water. Once in a while the two fliers saw the sun, but most of the time it was hidden behind high clouds.

Both men knew that they were nearing the mountains at the north end of Spitzbergen, but clouds covered the mountains and extended to the water. Flying below them was impossible. Even the air above the clouds was turbulent. The plane, now almost out of gas, tossed like a cork on a stormy sea. Loose items in the cabin tumbled and rattled. With nothing to get a firm grip on, Wilkins tumbled about, too.

The winds increased—a real blizzard. It was then that Ben's training and cool skill showed. With the plane nosed down and the engine full on, it bucked like a bronco. Never losing the upper hand, Ben held and guided the plane cautiously around the rugged mountain tops. The mountains came down to within a few feet of the ice-strewn water near the coast. The surface wind was furious, and salt spray whipped from the sea filled the air.

Over the land, the snow drifted high and thick. Ben searched for a place to land. A patch of smooth snow-covered land was passed in an instant's flash. Dead ahead loomed a mountain. With an adroit swerve, Ben narrowly avoided the peak. He knew that it would be dangerous to follow the coast too closely, so he swung broadside to the wind and headed out to sea. The plane was like an imprisoned bird beating against a windowpane. The storm worsened.

Ben knew that they were running short of gas. If they didn't land soon they'd be without enough gas to move again. He had no choice but to keep searching for a level landing spot. When it appeared that there were none ahead, Ben decided to turn back and relocate the one smooth patch of ice he had spotted. By now, the windshield was almost totally obscured with snow and frozen oil. Ben's vision was through the small open window on each side.

Wilkins passed notes, but Ben had little time to read them. Wilkins marveled that Ben even found time to grab them. When Ben thought that they were in the clear spot of level land, he swung out to sea in a narrow circle, heading into the wind. He came in low for a landing, then leveled the ship and lowered it gently until lost in the swirling snow. Ben braced himself for anything, but the Vega came smoothly to rest. Once on the ground, the men found the snow and the wind blinding. Ben jumped out of the plane and hurried to cover the engine and drain the oil before it froze. Ben steadied himself against the plane. The constant throb of the engine left him stone deaf.

Wilkins soon joined Ben. High drifts formed around the plane as the wind continued with hurricane force. The two men hurried to stamp the snow about the skis so that it would pack down and freeze, keeping the plane from turning over.

When they'd climbed back into the plane, Wilkins shouted, "Thank God the plane's safe." Ben nodded solemnly. Even if hearing each other had been easy, their minds and hearts were too full for conversation.

With each blast of wind the plane trembled, but it held its own. After a few minutes Wilkins reached for the remainder of their snack. Soon they both munched on dry biscuits and pemmican, as well as some chocolate. There was still coffee enough for both in the thermos bottles. Neither could sleep for a long time after the strain. Ben smoked a cigarette, and then both men settled down to compare statistics.

Their coast-to-coast nonstop flight had taken 20 hours 20 minutes in the air. Although it was less than 30 minutes since they'd sighted the twin mountain peaks, to them that part of the flight was the longest.

From dead reckoning, Wilkins figured that they were in the neighborhood of Kings Bay, but an island they had seen in flight was confusing. On their chart there was no island near Kings Bay. The snow-covered mountains gave no clue, for they were not indicated on the chart either. There would be nothing to help them until the sun shone, but Wilkins still figured they were on the west coast of Spitzbergen near Green Harbour.

Ben estimated that they had at least 20 gallons of gas left. "If we're where we think we are, then we've got enough gas to get to

Green Harbour, because it's less than 100 miles," Ben said optimistically.

"We have flown just about halfway around the world in one hop," Wilkins replied. "Think about that!"

Then they talked about Charlie Brower and Fred Hopson and all their Eskimo friends at Barrow. They pictured them eating breakfast while the inhabitants of Spitzbergen, if that's where they were, would be eating their evening meal. Ben wondered out loud if Mr. Vincent had received any of their messages. "It'll be a long time before we know," Wilkins said.

Finally, their strained nerves relaxed and they slept. When they woke up a few hours later, the snow was still drifting, but the wind didn't seem as bad as it had been. Ben said, "Maybe we're just getting used to it."

When they next opened their eyes, they found the sun clear in the east and above the mountains. They jumped from the plane to explore but discovered the snow was knee deep. They put on their snowshoes and climbed to a high point.

Using binoculars, both men scanned the mountains and the valleys nearby. Wilkins thought that he saw the houses of a town off in the distance. Ben looked and thought he saw houses, too. But both men were used to Arctic mirages; they had been fooled many times. Wilkins took another fix on the sun. It placed them on Spitzbergen. "Ben, we made it!" he shouted above the wind.

Then, the wind got worse. Reluctantly, they climbed back into the plane. The wind raged all day, piling new snow in drifts about the Vega. That night they slept through until morning. The storm continued during the next day, and the wind howled all that night, rocking the Vega.

The following day it was still storming, but they decided to hunt for driftwood to melt snow for water, but the driftwood they found was so sodden and salty that it refused to burn. Ben saturated it with old oil from the engine, but it still didn't make a hot blaze. An hour's effort produced only enough melted snow to almost fill the two thermos bottles with lukewarm water. For further liquid, they resorted to their small store of alcohol.

During a lull in the storm on Friday, Ben measured the gasoline, running it through the carburetor to make sure that all he measured would reach the engine. He drained only five gallons from the two starboard tanks, but he figured there was about that much in the wing tanks. Another five gallons were collected. The two men's spirits dropped. If they had trouble taking off, they wouldn't have enough gas to reach Green Harbour. Determined to drain every ounce, Ben took the seals from the cabin tanks. Warily, he set the can beneath one tank and opened the dump valve. To Wilkin's and his amazement, a stream of gasoline came forth. Soon, the five-gallon can was filled and there was more to come. Wilkins used his bare hand to stop the flow, and Ben hurried to empty the can so that they could refill it. The same procedure was followed on the other cabin tank. After all the gas was collected, they had 20 gallons left. "That's exactly what you figured before, Ben," Wilkins said. He laughed, for he knew that Ben kept track of the gasoline like a miser did money.

More relaxed now, the two climbed back into the plane and had a meal of pemmican, raisins, and chocolate. As they turned in for the night, Ben said, "Let's hope for clear weather tomorrow. I want to get going."

By afternoon of the next day there was a lull in the storm. They climbed out and tramped down the snow around the plane. Then they slid back and forth on snowshoes until they had a runway nearly 1,000 feet long, but they knew that they couldn't take off yet.

They had first sighted Spitzbergen at 6:15 P.M. on Monday, April 16. It was not until Saturday, April 21, at 3:00 A.M. that they felt the weather was fit for flying. Again, they cut and shoveled snowdrifts for six hours to clear the machine.

Takeoff would be tricky, for it was downhill at the head of the runway. Ben placed the stove beneath the engine and also heated the oil on the Primus stove in the cabin. When everything was ready, both men climbed aboard, but the plane wouldn't start without a push. Wilkins got out to push the tail but had a hard time climbing back in while the plane was moving. It was then that they really missed the block and tackle stolen in Fairbanks.

The engine died. Wilkins got out and pushed again. As he tried to get in, he fell off, but Ben didn't know it until he was in the air. Fortunately, he turned back and saw Wilkins. He circled and landed.

Wilkins next slung the rope ladder from the cabin door and then went back to push the plane. The Vega started again. Wilkins rushed to get into the cabin. His hands were numb with cold, so he grabbed the rope ladder with his teeth before he lost hold of it. When he hit the snow, he jarred his front teeth loose.

Again, Ben took off without Wilkins. Because the snow was anything but smooth and the wind still blew across the ridges, it was necessary to land at right angles to them. Both men feared the landing gear might snap. Wilkins was still winded from his last fall, so when Ben landed, the two men paused to think. "Let's block up the tail section," Wilkins said. "That ought to help."

"Now we've got to figure some way to keep you inside and still make you able to give us a push," Ben said. He looked around and spied a big chunk of driftwood. Wilkins rushed to pick it up.

"Pretend you're in a gondola in Venice," Ben said. "Get in the plane and start rowing!"

Wilkins fixed himself in position, gripped the driftwood, and pushed with all his might. The tail swayed an inch or so, as allowed by the play in the skis, but would move no further. Wilkins pushed again, and the ship lurched free. Dropping the driftwood, Wilkins steadied himself inside the plane.

Ben shouted, "Is everything all right?" Wilkins was unable to answer. Ben took off, hoping Wilkins was safe. Before Ben had time to circle, Wilkins let him know he was okay.

Wilkins wanted to get a general view of their position as soon as possible. Just as he stuck his head through the open cockpit window, he heard Ben shout, "Look over there in the bay to the left!"

From an altitude of nearly 3,000 feet, Wilkins looked to the left. His eyes filled with wind-born tears, but he was elated. He saw what Ben had seen—two tall radio masts in the distant group of houses. Ducking his head back into the cabin, he hurriedly wrote Ben a note: "Must be Green Harbour. Go over and land where you think best."

The Vega crossed over about five miles of open water, and then Ben swung across a mountain top. He circled as he lowered the plane down close to the ice. The snow surface on the harbor was smooth. Ben flew beyond the radio masts for a mile, passing the immense surface machinery of a coal mine. Circling again over the ice, he came in to land at the foot of the radio masts. The expedition's flight from Barrow over the top of the world to a town on Spitzbergen was ended!

Ben landed at 10:30 A.M. local time. Wilkins and he saw few signs of life. A small white dog frisked on a snowbank, while others, jet black, romped in a yard. But even before Wilkins had time to climb from the cockpit, he saw four men skiing down the slope toward them. Wilkins joined Ben, already busy taking care of the engine and the plane that had brought them 2,200 miles over Arctic ice and sheltered them during a five-day storm. Their faithful Vega now stood proudly in Norway, in weather as perfect as the day the plane had left its birthplace in California, U.S.A.

The approaching men might have thought it odd that the two strangers made no attempt to stop working and greet them. But both were too busy draining the oil and covering the engine.

A portly gentleman with an old-world grace and charm introduced himself as Bowitz Ihlen, manager of the Svalbard Government Radio Station. Wilkins and Ben smiled and shook hands with him. Many others quickly joined in, all speaking excellent English. They were pleased and astonished when Ben greeted them with an old Norse phrase, although his accent showed a decided American influence. Wilkins smiled. He'd been listening to Ben practice his greeting in Norwegian during their forced stay in the plane's cabin. Ben's Norwegian greeting brought a real brotherly acceptance. Wilkins told the Norwegians briefly about the 2,200-mile flight and the five-day storm. Then the group waited while Ben and Wilkins finished tying down the plane. When the work was finished, Ihlen said, "You must come with us to our quarters and make yourselves at home." As they turned to leave, Ihlen gave one last look at the plane and said, "It hardly seems possible that you came halfway around the world in that small plane."

Ben and Wilkins stopped to put on snowshoes to walk even the short distance to the station. Their new friends reported that the heavy snow was the result of the five-day storm that had forced the fliers to land. As they walked to the station, Ihlen said, "It's time to celebrate." Soon they were all seated in the living room of Ihlen's home holding drinks in their hands. "Skall!" Ihlen called, then added, "Skall to you, and the very best of health and future success!"

The Norwegians reported that in their 11 years of residence in Green Harbour, they had never seen such weather in April. Ihlen said that the government-operated radio station was their communications with Norway. At that time of the year the station operated from 8:00 A.M. to 9:00 P.M. He said, "The station here is available at your convenience." Ihlen rushed to get some paper and pens and, in his perfect English, said, "You must surely have many telegrams to send. Please feel at liberty to attend to your affairs and call upon us for any assistance you may need."

Wilkins explained that nobody really knew that he and Ben were safe. He said that he'd left his receiving set at Barrow with the school teacher, who had promised to monitor it during their flight. Wilkins explained that Vincent couldn't send messages from Barrow but promised that he'd send his information by mail in the summer to the nearest telegraph line.

Wilkins said that he'd sent messages to Barrow every 20 minutes to the hour. His last message had read: "Now within a hundred miles of Spitzbergen. We are in a bad situation. Heavy clouds about us. Have two hours' gas left but cannot see land. All open water below."

That message was repeated several times because at that point Wilkins was plainly worried. While he was repeating the message for the fourth time, he broke in to say, "Spitzbergen in sight! Spitzbergen in sight! We will make it!" But still he didn't know if Vincent had got the message.

Wilkins told Ihlen that Ben and he were thrilled to have the powerful government station at their disposal. Ben added, "It will be lots easier than using the small set in the plane."

Ben sent a short message to Hatton: "Arrived Spitzbergen safely. Home soon."

Wilkins sent a short message about the flight to Detroit and added the code words, "No foxes seen," which meant that no new land had been discovered.

Then Ihlen sent a message to the chief of the government radio station telling him that Ben and Wilkins were at Green Harbour. He also presented Wilkins with a wire from the *New York Times*. With confidence in the success of the flight, one of Wilkins' friends had first sent the telegram to Kings Bay but then tried the next closest station at Green Harbour. Wilkins sent a message to the *Detroit News*.

Returning to the living quarters used by the radio staff, Wilkins and Ben found that the steward had arranged a room for them. They had comfortable beds, a writing table, a typewriter, paper, and every accommodation they might expect in a first-class hotel.

Three hours after their arrival, wires began coming in from friends. The world had learned of their safety. With the two explorers having been out of touch for the period of their stay in Barrow and the entire length of the flight, plus the five days they were marooned during the storm, everyone was thrilled and relieved to hear reports of the successful flight.

Congratulations came pouring in from the King of Norway; the Secretaries of State and War, at Washington; the President; premiers; ambassadors; high commissioners; Dr. Isaiah Bowman, of the National Geographic Society; aero clubs; scientific bodies; and other explorers, including Nansen, Stefansson, and Amundsen, who of them all most realized the importance of the flight.

ENDNOTE

1. The three-engined Fokker, the *Detroiter*, was renamed the *Southern Cross*, and Smith and Ulm flew it from Oakland, California, to Australia in three long jumps, setting a new world record for long-distance flying—3,138 miles from Hawaii to Fiji nonstop. Later, they flew the *Southern Cross* around the world, including a hop across the Atlantic from Ireland to Newfoundland.

27

Arctic Heroes Tour Europe and America

BEN THOUGHT Wilkins would never finish sending telegrams. He sent one to everyone even remotely connected with the Spitzbergen flight. One went to the Pioneer Instrument Company for providing most of the essential instruments. Others went to Lockheed, the Wright Aeronautical Company, the Richfield Oil Company, and the Pennzoil Company, followed by still others to personal friends and backers and everyone in Barrow. Ben sent several personal telegrams, too.

The telegrams sent from Green Harbour about the Spitzbergen flight made headlines across the world. As news of the flight spread, telegrams kept pouring in. Aviation experts sent wires calling the flight the greatest aviation feat in history. Then the invitations started. Soon the two fliers received invitations to visit many of the capitals of Europe. Roald Amundsen sent a special invitation asking them to stop at his home in Norway for several days. Ben told Wilkins that he looked forward to that visit.

Wilkins told his hosts about the 1926 and 1927 flights. In contrast to the large number of people involved those two years, he said that he and Ben were the entire staff in 1928. In the middle of his storytelling, a telegram arrived from the *New York Times* with an offer to buy Wilkins' exclusive story of the flight. Wilkins laughed. "This offer comes none too soon." Ben grinned. They'd spent most of the balance of their cash in Barrow for building runways. "Lucky we made it," Wilkins added. "Now we have eating money."

Wilkins immediately wired acceptance. From then on, Wilkins

settled down to send out detailed reports. His first told how, on the morning of April 15, 1928, the Lockheed Vega, its engine wrapped in asbestos, nosed down the Elson Lagoon runway near Barrow and took off for its target—Spitzbergen—and aviation history. "We blazed a curved path around the polar region." To compensate for the magnetic deviation, it was necessary to change direction some 50 times to maintain course. On one part of the journey, direction changes were required every five minutes.

As Wilkins worked on his reports, telegrams kept pouring in to Green Harbour. Ben was drafted to help answer them. Wilkins said that he would take the telegrams dealing with the scientific aspects of the flight and the navigation problems, but he hoped that Ben would answer those connected with the pilot's part.

In 1928 most of the world had just settled down from the thrill of Charles Lindbergh's solo nonstop flight across the Atlantic; now attention swung to the top of the world.

Navigators wired that the Spitzbergen flight was the most wonderful feat of navigation ever known. Explorers and scientists alike knew that it had required courage and a little of the gambler instinct in both men. The sight of the sun on such a trip was necessary and could have meant the difference between life and death. Because there was no way of knowing what the weather would be like in the blind spot, the flight was a gamble, especially so because a compass was not reliable in the Arctic region of maximum declination.

The men at the station still marveled at the small size of the Vega, amazed that the tiny ship had traveled 2,200 miles without engine trouble. To point out the superiority of airplanes for Arctic exploration, Wilkins offered by way of comparison the fact that in their flight, Ben and he had covered three times as much territory in one day as Peary had covered in 23 years. He added, "The Aero Arctic Society, in Berlin, is planning to establish 35 meteorological stations in the Arctic. The sites of two were discovered by us in the last two years. Now we have much more valuable data to study."

Although they were safe at Green Harbour, the fliers actually were marooned again. There was no aviation fuel available for the Vega except what little was left in the tank. The plane was slightly damaged in landing and needed minor repairs, too. The Spitzbergen coast was ice-locked, and no boats would reach Green Harbour until the spring thaw.

At the end of two weeks, they learned that a small Norwegian whaler, the *Hobby*, would be coming to the edge of the ice pack, about 20 miles from Green Harbour. The *Hobby* was at Kings Bay, where it had delivered supplies for the Nobile expedition to be made in the dirigible *Italia*.

Wilkins and Ben set out on foot across the ice pack to meet the ship. The captain not only agreed to take them and the Vega to Tromso but offered them a dog team so they could return to the plane faster.

The Vega was buried in snow. They had a hard time digging it out and clearing a runway. After some repairs were made, Ben figured that they had enough gasoline to fly 20 miles, providing everything went just right.

On the evening of May 9, the night before their planned flight to the *Hobby*, the men at the wireless station threw a farewell party in their honor. Norwegians, Danes, Dutch, and Germans from the coal mining community nearby gathered at the station. The dress varied from regular outdoor Arctic wear to dinner jackets worn by several officials. The climax of the evening was a dance led by Wilkins and Ben attired in their fur flying clothes.

The morning after the farewell dance Wilkins and Ben were up bright and early. Ben had no trouble taking off from the ice and landed only a few yards from the whaler. He told Wilkins that he doubted there were even a few cupfuls of gas left. He was right; the tank was nearly bone dry.

The captain swung the boom over the side and lifted the Vega aboard easily. Then the *Hobby* started pushing through 100 miles of pack ice. Wilkins took pictures from the deck of the whaler that showed vividly the breaking up of the Arctic ice pack. Ben shivered. He realized again how lucky they'd been on their 13-day walk.

At 3:00 A.M. on May 15, the *Hobby* arrived in Tromso, Norway. As Ben and Wilkins stood on the deck in their parkas and mukluks, they were surprised to see throngs of milling people gathered to welcome them. Even at that early hour, children cheered and waved Norwegian, American, and Australian flags. The fliers stepped ashore to thundering applause from the crowd lining the wharves.

Tromso had been the base of operations for Nansen, Andree, Sverdrup, and Amundsen, so the local people understood what Arctic explorers were trying to do. They realized that over 1,400 miles of previously unknown Arctic needed no longer to be classified as "a blind spot" or "unknown."

The head of the Tromso official committee welcomed Ben and Wilkins to the city with an enthusiastic speech about the greatest aviation feat in history. Next, Wilkins spoke from the flag-draped speakers' stand, thanking Tromso for its warm welcome. Then Ben was ushered forward. He spoke a few phrases in Norwegian, and a hush descended on the crowd, which had grown to 2,000 by then. Ben smiled and said in Norwegian that he had expected Tromso residents to be in bed like proper Norwegians at that time of the morning. But he added that he was happy to receive a warm welcome in Tromso, the Paris of the North.

At the end of Ben's speech, the two heroes were carried down the street on the shoulders of young men to the Grand Hotel. At another reception there, Tromso officials hailed Ben as a daring Viking aviator and Wilkins as a great Arctic explorer and navigator.

Their fur parkas and mukluks were much too warm for indoor social life, so as soon as Wilkins and Ben had a break in the festivities, they rushed out to buy more appropriate clothes. Wilkins hinted to Ben that they would soon need formal evening clothing.

After purchasing a complete change of clothes, the fliers hurried to a lunch in their honor attended by city officials and dignitaries. Then there was another press conference. Again, Wilkins told the story of the Spitzbergen flight and introduced Ben. He said a few words about the Vega and the forced landing in a blizzard on what had turned out to be Dead Man's Island.

That evening an elaborate banquet was held for the two explorers at the Grand Hotel. Before the banquet, huge crowds gathered under the balcony of their room and called, "Speech! SPEECH!" Ben and Wilkins shook their heads, smiled, and appeared on the balcony.

Wilkins spoke first and praised Ben: "From nearly a hundred applicants for the place of chief pilot of our Arctic expedition, it was my great fortune to choose a man of Norse heritage, Carl Ben Eielson, a man in whom I have had complete confidence these past three years. He has never failed me." Then Wilkins continued with his regular speech.

When Ben stepped forward to speak, the crowd cheered loudly. It was easy to see that they claimed Ben as one of their own. Ben was deeply moved and, on impulse, quoted to them a verse from a Norse poem his mother had taught him years before:

> There lies a land near the eternal snow
> Where only the fissures have spring-like flow;
> But around her the sea sings of great deeds done
> And loved is this land as mother by son.

When he finished the verse, Ben paused for a few moments and then added a few remarks of his own in Norwegian.

The next day the *Tromso Dagbled* reported:

> Ah, yes, we had a great day of it. . . . The Norse people are not given to a lavish display of feelings, they believe that a heart can beat warmly under a calm exterior. But today we have been scarce able to control ourselves. Today, the heart of Tromso has beat so loudly for the two Pole fliers that our heart can both be seen and heard.

Ben and Wilkins were royally entertained for three more days in Tromso. Then they boarded the *St. Svithun* and started down the coast of Norway. Wherever the ship docked, crowds waited to cheer the two heroes. At Trondheim, the whole town turned out in inclement weather to meet them. Wilkins and Ben led the procession through pouring rain to the site for the official city welcome.

On May 23 they arrived in Bergen. Again, they were escorted down flag-draped streets. At the Hotel Norge, they spoke from the balcony. After learning they were to be dinner guests of his Majesty, King Haakon VII, at his country place outside the city, they hurried to buy formal attire. (The tuxedo and the shirt that Ben wore at the royal reception are now at the Hatton Museum.)

Ben was nervous at the prospect of meeting royalty, but when he and Wilkins were presented to the tall, dignified monarch and Ben saw the kindly twinkle in his eyes, he relaxed. Later in the evening, when King Haakon presented him with the Leif Erickson

Memorial Award, Ben was able to speak with ease. His cordial response brought a warm smile to King Haakon's face.

During his stay at King Haakon's country home, Ben couldn't help but wish his mother and his father could have been there with him. He grinned when he thought about the fact that flying was the reason for his invitation to meet the King of Norway. "Perhaps," Ben said to himself, "when Dad finds out the warmth the Norwegians have towards Arctic fliers, he might change his mind about flying."

At Oslo, Ben and Wilkins were met by a large group of dignitaries. The little daughter of Hjalmar Riisen Larsen, Amundsen's navigator on the *Norge*, presented them with a huge bouquet of flowers. Royal carriages waited to take them to the official welcoming stand. As they were driven down the street, the crowds cheered wildly. Six hydroplanes circled overhead and dropped flowers. Later, they were driven to the country home of Roald Amundsen.

Ben was almost as thrilled at the prospect of meeting Amundsen as he had been at the opportunity of meeting King Haakon. Although Amundsen had early criticized Wilkins' proposed flight to Spitzbergen both privately and publicly and said that it was "beyond the possibility of human endeavor," the grand old veteran of the Arctic now welcomed the two fliers with sincere congratulations.

Amundsen proclaimed their Spitzbergen flight as the most important ever made over unexplored territory. He presented each of them with a Norwegian Aero Club Medal of Honor. He also gave Ben a personal gift of a tie pin set with a small stone that he had brought back from a South Pole expedition.

Not content with the formal official ceremony, Amundsen brought out an enormous cake decorated with a map on which the route traveled by the Vega was outlined in red frosting. The cake was served at a grand tea following the formal reception and awards presentation.

After their four-day visit at Amundsen's country home, the heroes were ensconced in the royal suite at Oslo's Grand Hotel. At an elaborate banquet at the hotel, they dined with a host of dignitaries, including six members of the *Norge* crew. After the introductions, Wilkins told how he'd viewed the *Norge* from Barrow in 1926. Following the banquet, the two were made members of the Norwegian Air Navigation Society.

On Sunday, Amundsen took them to the Arctic Museum, near Holmenkollen. Ben and Wilkins presented the museum with a small bundle of their Arctic flight souvenirs.

While Ben and Wilkins were visiting Amundsen, they learned that Umberto Nobile, Amundsen's dirigible pilot on the *Norge*, had gone down in the Arctic. His dirigible, the *Italia,* had collapsed on a return flight over the North Pole. Amundsen took off the next day to join in the search for Nobile and the crew of the *Italia*.

After a successful nonstop flight in the *Italia*, which had lasted 69 hours and covered much unexplored territory, Nobile had taken off for the North Pole. He set a course in an arc toward Greenland to cover territory where others had not been. After eight hours he reached the Pole. On the flight back to Spitzbergen, the airship dived onto the ice 250 miles northwest of Kings Bay. The shock tore off the pilot's gondola and the rearmost of the engine gondolas, while the rest of the airship, considerably lightened by this, rose once more and disappeared with six men aboard. Eight men lost their lives in the *Italia* disaster. Nobile survived, but his career was ruined because of the accident and adverse public opinion.

Ben and Wilkins offered their services for the extensive Arctic search being organized, but they received word that Premier Mussolini felt that there were enough searchers already. Italian, Russian, French, Swedish, and Norwegian aviators joined in the search. Amundsen led a French-sponsored rescue expedition into the Arctic mists, from which he never returned.

Next, Ben and Wilkins flew to Copenhagen, where Crown Prince Frederick presided at a magnificent banquet in their honor. The Danes paid elaborate tribute to the American and the Australian and presented them with gold medals from the Royal Aeronautical Society. At that reception they met Lange Koch and Knud Rasmussen, famous Danish explorers. The Danish airmen also presented Wilkins and Ben with porcelain polar bears to add to their growing collection of trophies, medals, and mementos. The government gave them vases of Imperial pottery.

The next day, in a Junkers monoplane, the largest plane Germany had, Ben and Wilkins were flown to Tempelhof Airport, in Berlin, escorted by two squadrons of 16 German fighter planes. At Tempelhof they were welcomed by 10,000 people, including the British ambassador, the American ambassador, and a representative of Field Marshal von Hindenberg.

For the next few days, they were kept busy as guests of the Germans. Again, the two collected more medals and honorary memberships in aeronautical and scientific organizations. One evening during their stay, they were guests of the Komische Opera Theatre, where singer Hans Alber performed a song composed in their honor.

On June 4, they arrived at Schipol Airport, at Amsterdam. The Netherlanders had several receptions for them, showering them with gifts and honors. At a formal reception, Queen Wilhelmina presented them with official awards.

On June 6, they flew to London. Wilkins was hailed as a "second Balboa." L. S. Amery, Secretary of State for the Colonies, said, "Never before in the history of man has so much of the world's map been cleared up in one day."

When the King of England's official birthday honors were made public on June 4, Wilkins' name was on the list of Knights, but he and Ben were in the Netherlands. Wilkins was informed that he and Ben would be honored in a special ceremony on June 14.

In the meantime, the two heroes flew to Paris. Reporters called Ben "an internationally famous Arctic pilot." He couldn't help but smile as he considered how different his reception would have been in 1918, when he was first assigned to go to France.

In France, they had a military escort. Both were becoming a little weary of the official protocol and the endless speeches they were called upon to make. Ben told Wilkins, "Well, we've been having a grand time but not getting much sleep!" Ben added that he longed to get into the Vega and fly someplace—anyplace. He consoled himself with the thought that when they got back to New York, the plane would be there, too.

Wilkins said, "We can tour the states in the Vega. That should make you happy. I can see that you'd rather be flying instead of being entertained and honored."

The following evening, during a formal banquet in their honor, a count approached Ben and asked, "You are Monsieur Eielson?" Ben grinned and said that he was, not knowing what was coming next. The French count said, "Permit me to present my wife. She wishes to kiss you." With that introduction, the bejeweled countess kissed Ben resoundingly on the cheek.

After their Paris visit, both men felt sated with acclaim. Yet, they had to return to London on June 14, where Wilkins was given his greatest honor of all.

On the day of the special ceremony, Wilkins and Ben were ushered into the grandeur of Buckingham Palace. The Australian knelt before His Majesty, King George V, to receive the accolade of knighthood. With the symbolic touch of the King's sword on his shoulders, Ben's friend became Sir George Hubert Wilkins.

Standing in the midst of the glittering ceremony, Ben suddenly remembered the last time he'd seen Wilkins kneel—the morning in Barrow when he was mopping up the spilled oil under the wrathful gaze of Hopson, the cook.

Ben was proud that his skipper had finally received the honor after 15 years of work in both science and in exploration. Wilkins had first gone north with Stefansson in 1913. Within a week of the ceremony at Buckingham Palace, the highest awards from the American Geographical Society, the Royal Geographical Society, and 15 additional scientific associations in many countries were presented to both men.

None too soon, their European tour ended. They had been welcomed and honored by Norway, Denmark, Sweden, Germany, the Netherlands, Belgium, France, and England.

Wilkins and Ben found the trip across the Atlantic in the liner *Stavangerfjord* a welcome change from their recent crowded schedule of public appearances in Europe, which once included three banquets in one day. Even aboard the ship, there were special parties to honor Ben and the new British knight, but there also was time to catch up on sleep.

While the fliers were on their way to a reception one night, Ben said, "Captain, I'm beginning to feel like this is part of our work. The parties people are giving us aboard ship make newspaper headlines. Now it appears people all over the world want to know what we've done and what we're going to do next. With all the publicity we've had, you should have no trouble lining up a sponsor for your trip to the Antarctic. It might even help me get an airmail contract."

Wilkins replied, "You're right, Ben. I don't think we'll have financial problems next year."

The *Stavangerfjord* was scheduled to dock on July 3 at New York, where Ben and Wilkins expected another series of receptions and parties and probably a noisy welcome. They were right. As soon as the great liner entered the harbor, New York City's official welcoming boat, the tug *Macon*, came out to take Ben and Wilkins aboard.

On the *Macon*, the band played and a host of officials and dignitaries met them. The official welcoming committee included 10 reporters; city officials; Vilhjalmur Stefansson; Dr. Isaiah Bowman, of the National Geographic Society; and I. S. Sikorsky, an airplane builder. President Coolidge sent his congratulations and a representative to greet them.

However, the first people to greet Ben when he stepped aboard the *Macon* were his father and his brother Arthur, who was very proud of his hero brother. Although Ben was delighted to see them, he was looking for Stefansson, and his eyes grew round as he spotted the famous explorer coming toward them.

Stefansson, who had already greeted Wilkins, gripped Ben's hand in cordial welcome. He told Ben that he was more pleased than ever that he'd been the one to bring Ben to Wilkins' attention by recommending him as an Arctic pilot.

Then all conversation stopped. With a loud blast of its siren, the flag-decked *Macon* started back for the Battery. Soon other ships and boats set their whistles blowing to give the heroes a clangorous American reception. A Junkers monoplane circled above the *Macon*. A white handkerchief fluttered down and dropped at Ben's feet on the deck. Ben looked up and recognized his friend, George King, from Alaska, who had made the long trip to greet him on his triumphal return to the United States.

While Wilkins told reporters about the Antarctic expedition he was planning, Ben informed the press that he wanted to get back to Alaska to an airline he'd started to organize with George King. Wilkins told reporters he'd already asked Ben to be the chief pilot for the Antarctic expedition. After whispering to his father that he had intended to tell him about the new expedition, Ben finally replied, "As I started to tell the other reporters, what I want more than anything else is an airmail contract for Alaska so that we can start operating our airline company there. But if that doesn't materialize, then I'll be going with . . . Sir Hubert Wilkins to the Antarctic."

During a lull in the conversation, someone suggested that Wilkins meet a fellow Australian, actress Suzanne Bennett, then appearing in a New York play. After some picture taking, Wilkins arranged to meet the actress again. Ben could see that Wilkins appeared more interested in Suzanne than he had ever been in any other woman. Mayor Jimmy Walker was late for the official reception, so the *Macon* cruised around the harbor. This gave Wilkins and the actress more time to become acquainted.

When the *Macon* finally docked, the heroes were rushed to an open car decorated with American and Australian flags. They were sped to City Hall for the official reception, while noon-day crowds cheered lustily and showered them with ticker tape. Ben was especially glad that his father was seeing the importance attributed to Arctic flying.

There were dinners, luncheons, theater parties, and visits backstage with celebrated actresses and actors. Ben shared the entertainment whirl with Wilkins, his father, and Arthur. Sometimes Suzanne Bennett accompanied Wilkins. One day the Quiet Birdmen, a select group of aviators listing less than 30 on its rolls at that time, made Ben a member, honored him at a banquet, and presented him with a memento.

On July 7, Ben and Wilkins attended a special luncheon given by Commander Richard E. Byrd in honor of Amelia Earhart. She had just flown the Atlantic—the first woman to do so.

Ole told Ben that the folks back in Hatton were planning a welcome for their "hero son." Ole reminded Ben that he should be in Hatton on July 20, his thirty-first birthday.

After New York, the fliers were scheduled for appearances in Buffalo, Philadelphia, Atlantic City, Detroit, Cleveland, Milwaukee, and Des Moines. On July 15, they were special guests at the Chautauqua program in Chautauqua, New York.

Ben flew the Vega from Buffalo to Chautauqua. After circling over the golf-course field several times, Ben swooped down gracefully and sped up the fairway toward hole 14, coming to a stop at the foot of a hill. A crowd of more than 3,000 was on hand. Security police had a difficult time holding back the autograph seekers, photographers, and reporters. Only a hastily erected picket fence prevented damage to the Vega.

A crowd of well over 6,000 people gathered in the amphitheater to accord an unprecedented ovation to Wilkins and Ben. Wilkins began his speech by saying, "In 1926 the world thought that Commander Byrd, Amundsen, and myself were in a three-way race to see who would be the first to carry the flag across the North Pole, but my plan was never anything other than to fly from Alaska to Spitzbergen."

Australia, England, Scotland, Ireland, and Canada were all represented among the guests who gathered that evening for the dinner put on by the Chautauqua Chapter of the English Speaking Union to honor the two fliers. Wilkins used the Chautauqua gathering to outline the scientific purpose of his projected Antarctic expedition. He said that he planned to fly to the Antarctic in another Lockheed Vega, this time a seaplane with a Wasp engine that had a top speed of 155 miles per hour. The Vega used in the Arctic would also be along.

He explained that there would be only three or four men in the expedition and that they would leave New York in late September or early October. The expedition would headquarter at Deception Island, where they would live aboard the Norwegian whaler *Hectoria* and make flights from the sea ice. The venture was an independent expedition, but the American Geographical Society would give support. He said that the purpose of the trip was to choose sites for one of the 12 meteorological stations he hoped to establish in the Antarctic.

Wilkins added that if Ben joined the Antarctic expedition, he would be the first ever to fly a plane in the Antarctic and he would use the same Vega he'd flown in the Arctic. Ben smiled. He knew that Wilkins wanted him to commit himself right then, but Ben decided that he'd have to check on his proposed airline in Alaska first. An editorial in the *Chautauqua Daily*, July 19, 1928, stated:

> Chautauquans yesterday had the privilege of seeing and hearing two great men and received direct impressions of what two of the foremost fliers have done and what they will do.

. . . We found them as simple as their great accomplishments would lead one to expect, as direct and frank as real men who have done great things are, as gracious gentlemen . . . and as appreciative of courtesy as the truly noble are.

Ben and Wilkins continued their tour of American cities, celebrating the success of their Arctic expedition. At 10:30 A.M. on July 20, they took off in the Vega from the Milwaukee airport for Fargo, North Dakota.

28

Homecoming at Hatton and Ben's Thirty-first Birthday

A̲ᴛ 4:00 ᴘ.ᴍ. ᴏɴ Jᴜʟʏ 20, Ben roared the Vega over Fargo, circled three times in traditional salute, then landed at Hector Airport. He and Wilkins were met by a vanguard of North Dakota friends, old and new, and were in for another heroes' welcome.

That night the two were guests of honor at a birthday party and testimonial dinner. Wilkins' birthday wasn't until October 31, but the MC told him that the town had decided to celebrate his birthday along with Ben's because both men probably would be on their way to the Antarctic by the end of October.

Early the next morning a wire was received from Hatton reading: "Land at Staven's field." Both men looked forward to the quiet of Hatton, but if they had seen the columns of the *Hatton Free Press* they'd have known that the Hatton Homecoming Committee had other ideas. The reports read:

> One of the greatest homecoming celebrations ever to be put on in the entire Northwest . . . awaits Lieutenant Carl B. Eielson, Hatton's own favorite son, and Sir George H. Wilkins . . . when they arrive here on Saturday morning. . . . Immediately following the parade, a program will be held at the ballpark with Congressman O. B. Burtness as the principal speaker. Other speakers will be President Kane, of the University, and Governor A. G. Sorlie, as well as other prominent men throughout the state and nation. . . . There will be over 20 eating places. . . . Truckloads of eats, candies, cigars, and drinks are being ordered here and are being delivered daily and one firm has ordered two carloads of pop and malt for

the two days. It is estimated that at least three tons of pork, wieners, and hamburgers will be disposed of easily. . . . Eight hundred people, including 300 children, will take part in the big parade. . . . [L]anding space must be provided for at least thirty planes. Lyle Thro and W. P. McFail, pilots for the Mid-plane Transit Company, which operates an airline between Fargo and Minneapolis, will put on a program of stunt flying following the ball game in the afternoon, and there will be an aerial race. . . .

Early Saturday morning, an unsuspecting Ben brought the Vega in for a perfect landing. When Ben shut off the noisy engine, he heard the roar from the tremendous crowd at Staven's field. Everyone rushed to meet the guests of honor. The warmth, affection, and idolization stunned Ben. He shook his head and turned to Wilkins. "I never expected a hero's welcome in Hatton. How can these people I've known all my life think of me as a hero?"

He pointed out an older woman in the crowd who stood smiling and waving her handkerchief at him and said, "Look. Even Mrs. John-son thinks so. Why, she used to complain about me to Dad all the time. She said I always mixed up her grocery orders. She told Dad I was the worst clerk he ever had. If Edwin and I were alone in the store, she'd make Edwin wait on her. Now she thinks I'm a hero!"

Ben caught sight of two men standing on top of an automobile, waving happily at him. "There are Harvey Wambheim and Dr. E. N. Hegge. We used to eat cheese and crackers together in the store."

Wilkins smiled broadly and said, "Relax, Ben. You might as well enjoy the hero worship from your old home town."

Ben pointed out another familiar figure in the crowd. "Look over there," Ben said laughingly. "That's the farmer who read me the riot act when I had to land the Jenny in his field one day. He said I'd never amount to much flying an airplane. He told me I'd do myself and my father a big favor if I'd settle down and do some useful work in Hatton."

After Ben and Wilkins took their seats on the bandstand, for the first time they could view the crowd, estimated at 5,000. Governor Sorlie stepped to the speaker's stand and asked that Ben come forward. He presented Ben with a beautiful gold medal from the home folks in Hatton. Ben stood silently for a minute or two, looking at the three-dimensional replica of the globe with the Lockheed Vega flying above the top of the world. Deeply moved, Ben glanced out at the wash of faces looking up at him expectantly. It was hard for him to speak. Then he noticed his high school debate teacher sitting in the front row. He knew he'd better do a good job. He faltered, but then he gained his usual composure. He thanked the people of Hatton for their generous gift and for the time, the thought, and the hard work that had gone into the homecoming celebration. "It's always good," Ben added, "to come back home to Hatton."

After a tremendous round of applause and calls of "Speech, SPEECH," Ben briefly told of the flight from Barrow to Spitzbergen. He spoke of the series of tumultuous receptions that had begun in Norway and continued across Europe and the United States to Fargo and Hatton. "They're in North Dakota," Ben jokingly added. Ben repeated that he didn't feel that "20½ hours of flying and two cold meals in the air" qualified him for raves. He spoke about Roald Amundsen, saying that his fate was not yet known. Although an extensive aerial search was still in progress, there was not much hope. "Amundsen," Ben added, "is a real hero in the Arctic and Antarctic." Then Ben introduced his friend, "Sir Hubert Wilkins, my skipper on the Arctic expeditions."

During his speech, Wilkins praised Ben's ability as a pilot and said that he could not have asked for a better companion in the Arctic. When he finished, Wilkins received a tremendous ovation.

Ben was glad when the aerial circus began so he could stop shaking hands. As he watched the performance, he remembered the day he'd put on Hatton's first aerial show. He glanced at his father and noticed that he was much more relaxed watching the aerial circus today. "I do believe," Ben thought, "Dad's getting used to the idea of flying. He's just as interested in the stunt show as I am."

When the aerial circus was over, Ben and Wilkins went to the Eielson home, but they found no privacy because an open house was being held. Ben whisked Wilkins upstairs to a guest room so he could have a few minutes alone. Downstairs, Elma, Adeline, Helen, and Hannah were busy serving guests. People overflowed the big house, the porch, and the lawn. The fliers were frequently called outside to have their pictures snapped.

That evening the streets were still jammed. Hatton residents allowed visitors to pitch tents on their lawns. Elma called and told Ben and Wilkins to get dressed for the banquet. "The menu is a surprise for you," she said. "We're having lots of fancy foods."

Dr. E. N. Hegge was toastmaster; Congressman Burtness was the first speaker, followed by Dr. Thomas F. Kane and W. P. McCracken, Assistant Secretary of Commerce for Aviation. McCracken spoke briefly about Ben's contributions to aviation while he worked for his department in the summer of 1927. He congratulated both men for their dedication that led to the Spitzbergen flight. Marvin A. Northrup, of the Marvin A. Northrup Company, spoke about the future role of aviation for the business world. The last speaker of the evening was L. A. Ward, of the Fargo Aeronautical Club. He credited Ben with stirring up early interest in flying in North Dakota.

Ben grinned as he read the dinner menu. Each item was named after a plane or an airplane company: Travelair Cocktail, Celery Curtiss, Olives Fokker, Fried Spring Chicken Eagle Rock, New Potatoes in Cream Ryan, Pickled Beets Waco, Sweet Potatoes Fairchild, Cream Gravy Lockheed, Salad Stinson, Rolls Buhl, Brick Ice Cream Bellanca, Angel Food Cake Monocoupe, Fattigman Ford, and Coffee Swallow.

As Ben sat in St. John's Lutheran Church the next morning, he thought about how good it was to be back in his regular seat with the family. After the hectic month filled with accolades and entertainment, he felt at home. He looked around; the church was packed. He hoped that the simple sermon would give the people an opportunity to put the hero worship into proper perspective.

Sunday afternoon brought another round of festivities. There were ball games and another aerial circus. In the evening, there was another special dinner and more speeches.

Late Sunday, just before Wilkins went to his room for a much-needed rest, Ben told him of plans for the next day. They would return to Fargo as guests of honor at the state fair and at the National Reliability Air Tour.

On Monday morning they learned that they were booked solid from Monday noon through late Tuesday night. On the morning of July 24, they left Fargo for Omaha and another public reception and testimonial banquet. By now, whenever they were called upon, either one would launch into a vivid description of Arctic flying and then talk about the proposed Antarctic expedition. As Ben talked about the Antarctic, he pictured himself flying the Vega there. Wilkins looked pleased. He was almost sure Ben had decided to go with him.

On July 25, after the Vega was stored in St. Paul, Wilkins went east to complete arrangements for the Antarctic expedition. Ben promised an answer about accompanying him by August 10. "First," he said, "I want to find out what's happening in Alaska."

After returning to Hatton, Ben had his first real rest in eight months. He slept as long as he wished. Once they were alone, Ole asked Ben what his plans were. Ole seemed resigned that his son would be taking off for the Antarctic in about two months, but Ben said that he had until August 10 to make up his mind.

Ben heard that there had been a great celebration in Barrow when the residents had finally learned that the Spitzbergen flight had been successful. He also found that Leon S. Vincent had received most of the messages sent by Wilkins from the Vega. Vincent had gone to church on Sunday morning after Ben and Wilkins had taken off, but from 4:00 P.M. until 3:50 the next morning, he had carefully recorded each wireless message Wilkins had sent. The final message heard in Barrow noted: "Silent trip to here, 17½ hours."

When a plane had appeared in Barrow on May 14, residents at first had thought that it was Wilkins and Ben returning. But the plane was piloted by Noel Wien and carried Mr. Hart [no first name available], who was part of a group wishing to take motion pictures of the Eskimos' spring whaling in Barrow.

Wien handed Charlie Brower a bundle of mail, which contained a wire from Wilkins announcing Ben's and his safe arrival in Spitzbergen. When Brower read the wire, every Barrow resident cheered. The hilarity of the occasion was hardly lessened when Hart innocently informed Brower that none of the messages sent by Wilkins during the flight had gotten through. However, Vincent had recorded them as follows: At 10:00 P.M., "Clear, but clouds ahead." At 11:00 P.M., "Stormy here, but we are not far from the coast." At 12:00 midnight, there was no message. At 1:20 A.M., "K.Z.D. Wilkins Arctic Expedition. Greenland storm. 100 miles from Grant Land." At 2:00 A.M., the message was too weak to be taken, but Vincent got two words, "out tanks." At 3:30 A.M., the signal was too faint to be understood. At 3:50 A.M., "Silent trip to here, 17½ hours." As the weeks had passed and nothing further was heard, the phrases "Greenland storm" and "out tanks" took on ominous significance. That's why everyone was in a mood to celebrate when Wien had delivered the long-delayed telegram from Wilkins.

Ben received a letter from Washington, stating that the dog-team mail contract had not expired and new bids wouldn't be called for until next year. He'd already met with George King, in New York, to go over the formation of an airline. Finally, Ben wrote to King saying that he'd decided to go to the Antarctic with Wilkins. He said that as soon as he returned, he'd be visiting New York again to try to arrange financing.

There was another letter Ben dreaded to write. He had to tell his girlfriend that he would be gone about six months on the Antarctic expedition.

On August 8, Ben sent a wire of acceptance to Wilkins, who responded immediately that he'd found no trouble lining up backers. William Randolph Hearst, the publisher, paid him a $25,000 advance for exclusive reports from the 1928 Antarctic expedition.

By September 21, Ben was back in New York and faced a steady barrage of reporters. The photographer from the *Nordiske Tidende* asked Ben to stand on his head as a publicity shot of the famous Arctic flier at the bottom of the world. Ben laughed but obliged. "This pose should attract attention if nothing else," he said. "But tell your readers that it won't be long until I'll be flying around at the bottom of the world."

29

First to Fly in the Antarctic

ON SEPTEMBER 22, 1928, the Wilkins-Hearst Antarctic Expedition party boarded the Munson liner *Southern Cross* to sail from New York to Montevideo, Uruguay. Joe Crosson came as second pilot, and Orval Porter as mechanic. William Gaston was hired to operate the wireless, sparing Wilkins the task. Before leaving New York, Wilkins had deposited the wages of expedition members in a bank. He paid Ben and Crosson $500 a month, plus all expenses; the mechanic, $400; and the wireless operator, $100. A second Lockheed Vega was secured, and both planes were lashed to the deck. The initial flight in either plane would be a historic first in the Antarctic. The Vega that had flown to Spitzbergen was named *Los Angeles*, and the new one *San Francisco*.

Until the *Southern Cross* docked at Montevideo on October 10, there had been plenty of time for resting, reading, and long leisurely talks. Two days before he'd left New York, Wilkins had asked Suzanne Bennett, the Australian actress, to marry him. She had said yes!

On October 23, 1928, Ben wrote a letter to his sister Adeline, a school teacher in Wenatchee, Washington. Written on stationery from the Hotel La Alhambra, it read: "We are leaving tomorrow on the whaleboat *Hectoria*. Have had an interesting trip through South America. . . . The planes got here in fine shape. . . ."

At Montevideo the men waited 13 days for the Norwegian whaling ship that would be their headquarters for the expedition. The expedition party boarded the 16,000-ton *Hectoria*, the mother ship for six smaller whale catchers of the N. Bugge Whaling Company, on schedule. The *Hectoria* had started life as a White Star liner. Many of the first-class cabins and salons were left intact, which provided luxurious living conditions during the expedition, quite a contrast to some of the accommodations in the Arctic.

The planes were secured aboard the *Hectoria*, and the whaleboats headed southwest, past the Falkland Islands. The worst part of the journey was through the kelp and rough waters of the Burdwood Bank. Everyone was relieved when the shallow, seaweed-choked area was behind and the *Hectoria* was once more in deep, blue water. Pack ice was encountered about 300 miles north of Deception Island. This bothered Wilkins, because in his 1920–21 expedition the sea was open all the way. Perhaps this spelled trouble, for it meant that the weather was unusually warm and the pack ice broke up early. The unseasonable weather would knock out the harbor ice for a landing field.

At first, the *Hectoria* experienced no difficulty breaking through, followed by the small whale catchers. But the farther south it went, the more difficult the struggle became. Finally, on November 7 the peaks of Deception Island were sighted. It took a full day for the *Hectoria* to force its way through the pack ice and steam into the harbor.

A tiny cluster of buildings on shore was overshadowed by the blue-black peaks. The buildings made up the whale carcass reducing plant, which a whaling company had maintained for 14 years in the landlocked bay.

Wilkins said that in 1920–21 there was little snow on the lower slopes and the harbor ice was thicker. Then, the ice had been 6 feet thick and could have served as a runway for the planes. Now, the ice was less than 3 feet thick.

The island, which was deserted all winter, gradually came to life. The whaling crew reopened the factories, unloaded their supplies, and fired the boilers. The expedition also made camp. When they had time for a break, Ben and Crosson explored the beach of black sand. In places it was steaming hot. The sailors told them that at low tide the sand sometimes was too hot to touch. It appeared that they would be unable to use the harbor ice for a landing field. Warmer weather set in and a steady rain fell, covering the ice with water.

The whale catchers were already out for whales, and the plants were ready to go. Four days after the *Hectoria* reached Deception Island, the *Los Angeles* was slung from the end of a long boom and lowered to the water on pontoons. Ben attempted to take off from the water, but it was too dangerous. There were hundreds of small albatross-like water birds in the way. They lived on the island year-round and flocked to the water as soon as the ice was broken. They were not afraid of the plane. When Ben got up speed, they flew with the plane, dashing into the propeller and making it impossible to take off.

Because Wilkins had served in Antarctica with the Sir Ernest Shackleton expedition, he often was called upon to identify the various species of birds. There were skua gulls, shags, cormorants, and the different petrels, but everyone was most amused by the fearless penguins. Ben, Crosson, and Porter had their pictures taken with penguins sitting on their knees.

After the unsuccessful attempt to take off, the *Los Angeles* was towed ashore on the beaching wheels, making it the first plane to rest on the Antarctic continent. Soon, the *San Francisco* also was beached.

Ben and Crosson scouted for possible landing fields. They finally spotted a hillside with very limited possibilities for wheeled takeoffs. It consisted of volcanic tuff, a hardened coke-like substance that would cut into the rubber tires if the snow melted. They consoled themselves with the thought that if they could take off, they might be able to locate a better spot for landing and for future use.

After the planes were readied for flight, a thick, pea-soup fog set in. Ben and Wilkins boarded one of the whaling vessels and viewed the coasts of other islands in the vicinity, hoping for a better base. When they returned, they put skis on the *Los Angeles* and waited for the weather to clear. The boredom of waiting was lessened by accordion music provided by one of the sailors and by other music from two phonographs aboard the *Hectoria*. There also were books to read.

On November 22, after 11 days of waiting, the weather cleared enough for a trial flight. Ben and Wilkins took off in the *Los Angeles*. That evening, Wilkins wired a message to Ole in Hatton: "Ben made first Antarctic flight today. Regards, Wilkins."

The following day it was Crosson's turn to test fly the *San Francisco*. Things looked great, but in one day the snow melted, stripping the runway to bare cinders. The search for a new runway began.

Ben and Crosson located another landing spot across the peninsula and began the hard work of making a new runway. When completed, it would be the strangest of any from which Ben or Crosson had ever flown. They would first have to run the plane up a sloping hill, then turn about 20 degrees in a "dog leg" to the other side of the hill, go down an incline, climb another hill to a crest 100 feet higher than the original starting point, turn again, and take off, if they were lucky.

From such a short, hazardous spot, Ben knew that it was almost impossible to take off with a full load of fuel for the long exploration flight. Ben hoped that cold weather would return and freeze the harbor ice so that Crosson and he could use it.

Armed with picks and shovels and with wheelbarrows to cart away the stones, the expedition crew worked to smooth the lava surface. It was backbreaking work. The men wore out many pairs of gloves and often cut their hands on the sharp rocks.

One cloudy day they all decided to visit the penguin rookery, which was located on a hill 5,000 feet high. The tedious trip was worthwhile. They found about four square miles covered with penguins, living so close together that they barely had room to move. For more than a century, whalers had robbed their bare stone nests of eggs, but the birds made no objection when the expedition men gathered eggs. The temperature had risen to 50 degrees, a heat wave almost unheard of in that latitude. It was so hot the penguins panted.

With the advent of a cold snap later in the week, Wilkins thought that the harbor ice might have thickened enough to hold a plane. He hurried out to test it, found a spot he thought solid enough, and marked the area.

Ben and Crosson both attempted takeoffs and landings. They managed to take off from the strange runway and came flying through the gap in the mountains at the harbor's mouth. Ben came down first. He found the ice so slippery that he couldn't stop the plane within the limits of the marked area. He shot past the safe area and, with a sickening thud, the wheels went through the thin ice. The plane turned up on its nose. Within seconds, the ice gave way beneath it and the engine went under.

The bystanders froze. No one dared to start forward. They watched in horror as the plane slipped through the ice. It stopped when the wings held, preventing the rest of the plane from slipping through the hole. All stood motionless, holding their breath. As they wondered if Ben would get out alive, he climbed cautiously out of the plane and treaded water. Holding onto the plane, he reached carefully over the edge of the broken ice. As if in a slow-motion movie, he moved along the rim, testing the ice carefully. Slowly, he swung himself onto the ice, where he lay flat on his stomach, spread-eagled on the safe, firm surface. The adventure reminded him of his experience during the 13-day Arctic walk in 1927.

"We've got to get that plane out before she drops any more!" Ben yelled.

"Are you all right, Ben?" Wilkins asked. "We're more worried about you than the plane!"

"I'm fine now. But we need some planks and heavy rope," Ben said.

"What you need are some dry clothes," Wilkins added. Then the men started slowly toward the plane.

Crosson was horrified when he saw the accident from the air. He circled and went back to the runway, where he came down safely. He reported the trouble to the whalers, who immediately left their work and hurried to the rescue with ropes and planks. They even brought dry clothing for Ben, plus extra, just in case.

Carefully, the men laid the planks in place. The work was tedious because the ice around the plane continued to sink. Several of the whalers broke through the ice, but the others always managed to get them out safely. The icy water was a rude shock, and the supply of extra dry clothing was quickly exhausted.

Ben expected the plane to slip from its perch any minute and go to the bottom. Finally, ropes were fastened to the tail and the wings were lifted with levers. Slowly, the plane came out of its icy dungeon. The men cautiously slipped the planks under the skis, then dragged the plane back to solid ice.

Altogether, it took 18 hours of nonstop labor to recover the plane. Wilkins thanked the whalers. His men would never have been able to save the plane without their help.

After the plane was hauled to shore, the mechanic immediately cleaned the engine. It was all right except that salt water had gotten into the cylinders, which were replaced.

On December 8, news came to the wireless operator that Ben had been awarded the Distinguished Flying Cross in recognition of his part in the flight over the top of the world. The entire camp cheered, but there was no time to celebrate.

Wilkins decided to try again for a better runway. He again arranged for the use of one of the whaleboats, and Ben and he searched the neighboring islands for a suitable site. Instead of a field, they found pack ice that was thin and broken. Whenever they approached land, they were confronted with sheer walls of ice. On the islands themselves, the ice was seamed with deep crevasses.

When Wilkins and Ben returned to Deception Island, Wilkins decided to experiment with the seaplane and assigned Crosson to pilot it. With a motorboat preceding it to clear the way of swarming birds, the pontooned plane started out, but it took to the air slowly. Crosson circled a few times and started to return. As he began gliding down, the birds, in close formation, glided down with him, winging close above the waters. Ben watched nervously as a large bird flew into the propeller. He saw the plane hesitate as the bird crashed into the hub.

When the plane came to a stop, Ben hurried out in the motorboat to help Crosson. Both men examined the propeller. Aside from being smeared with the remains of the bird, it seemed to be okay.

Another attempt to get a plane into the air with a load of equipment and supplies ended in failure. The overloaded Vega couldn't lift out of the water. Wilkins decided that the only way left to get airborne with a full load was to put wheels on the *Los Angeles* and use the unfinished runway.

Armed with shovels, rakes, buckets, wheelbarrows, and more work gloves, the crew was more determined than ever to hack a decent runway. Ben figured that the Vega needed a run of 900 yards to be really safe, but he knew that the greatest length that could possibly be obtained from the unfinished runway was just over 800 yards. The runway included two 20-degree bends, two small hills, and three ditches. As the men tossed stones out of the way on either side of the runway, the walls of stone grew higher. For 16 hours the expedition members slaved—chopping, digging, and raking the coke-like volcanic debris.

The Antarctic summer generally lasted from November to the

end of February, but in Graham Land, the good weather usually ended about the first of the year, so time was getting short to make the exploration. Even though everyone had worked late, Wilkins woke Ben at 4:00 A.M. and asked that he take him up on a trial flight to test the instruments. Ben jumped up and prepared for the flight. In the early morning mist he carefully guided the *Los Angeles* along the treacherous runway. Ben was happy when it roared into the air. "This must be our lucky day!" he shouted to Wilkins.

For the next half hour Ben circled while Wilkins tested the instruments. Everything seemed in good order, so Wilkins signaled for Ben to land. He made a perfect landing.

Porter and Crosson met the plane. They immediately began to fill the tanks with an additional 200 gallons of fuel, which they had carried up to the gravelly runway. In the meantime, Ben and Wilkins tramped the length of the runway. Ben finally said, "It needs another day's work to make it really safe, but I know we're running out of time. The weather's good, so if you want to take off, I'm ready."

Wilkins nodded. Plans went full speed ahead for the long-delayed exploration flight. Providing the weather was clear, as Wilkins predicted, they'd leave about 8:30 A.M.

Ben and Wilkins knew that, using wheels, it would be almost impossible to land anyplace away from the base. The chances of finding another fairly level spot were remote. In case of emergency, both carried a two-months' supply of rations, as they had in the Arctic—biscuits, pemmican, chocolate, nuts, raisins, and malted milk tablets. Their packs were separate. If one man was lost on the ice, the other could go on. Each man also carried a block and tackle for pulling himself out of crevasses. During the flight both wore light-weight camel's-hair wool outfits, but they carried the same fur clothing they'd used in the Arctic. It was now or never, they thought, as they boarded the plane.

Jolting over the rough ground, the *Los Angeles* gained speed and went up the first hill, over it, around the dog leg, and over the ditches. The plane ran up the last slope, made a sharp turn, then ran downhill to the harbor. Ben thought surely the landing gear would smash when the Vega hit the bottom of the last incline, but it held. At the edge of the water, Ben managed to pull the plane up to skim over the harbor and climb to safety. Once in the air, he relaxed.

Without circling in the traditional pattern, Ben headed through the narrow gap between the mountains and turned south. There was enough gasoline aboard for 1,400 miles of exploration. Ben thought how strange it was to be in the Antarctic and wondered if their flight would be successful.

Wilkins mentioned Byrd, who was also coming to the Antarctic that year. At that time Commander Byrd was establishing his head-quarters 2,000 miles away, hoping to make the first flight over the South Pole. When Byrd had first heard that Wilkins planned to use a plane in the Antarctic, he attempted to get Wilkins to sign a document stating that he would not try to fly over the South Pole before Byrd had a chance. Wilkins didn't sign, but he assured Byrd that his main interest was in survey work.

Byrd arrived in the Antarctic in December 1928, with three ski-equipped planes—a Ford tri-motor, a Fokker, and a Fairchild. As Wilkins and Ben were starting their flight, Byrd and his men were just getting established at Little America.[1]

Ben was happy with the performance of the *Los Angeles*. During the first part of the flight, things went well. The plane cruised at 125 miles per hour. Wilkins was thrilled at the thought of exploring territory never before seen by man from the air. He scarcely had time to sketch the principal terrain and shoreline before the scene changed. For the first part of the trip they flew over the iceberg-studded waters of Bransfield Strait. Ahead was Trinity Island, with peaks rising to 6,000 feet. They flew around it, heading for Graham Land, the big peninsula jutting out from the Antarctic continent. Eight years before, Wilkins had tried to map the area on foot. It had taken three months to map 40 miles. Now they covered 40 miles in 20 minutes.

They continued southward, over ice-filled fjords and sparkling snow. The blue-black peaks, outlined with glittering snow-covered slopes lapped by dark blue-green waters specked with icebergs, appeared wild, unearthly. In spite of its expansive beauty, the Antarctic struck Ben as being more desolate than the Arctic. The Antarctic had an eeriness of its own. Unlike the Arctic, this land had never been inhabited to anyone's knowledge.

Suddenly Wilkins shouted, "Hey, Ben! Graham Land is supposed to be part of the Antarctic continent, but it looks to me as if we're flying over several islands. Look! They're separated by ice-filled channels and straits.[2]

Shortly after, they crossed a frigid strait, which Wilkins photographed. He named it Stefansson Strait. He later named the mainland to the south Hearstland, in honor of the newspaper magnate who helped support the expedition.

No one had ever climbed the Graham Land plateau summit. Now, for the first time, human eyes saw it. Ben and Wilkins discovered that peaks thought to be 6,000 feet towered more than 9,000 feet. Ben was reminded of their first trip over the Endicotts in Alaska. The explorers followed along the coast, climbing until they reached an altitude of more than 9,000 feet before they could turn southward. As they sailed in over the continent, Wilkins shouted, "You know, for the first time in history, new land has been discovered from the air!"[3]

Wilkins plotted their course by dead reckoning and by the sun. The area before them was uncharted, and as landmarks emerged, Wilkins hurriedly sketched them on his map.

A broad bay opened before them, so broad that they had to turn westward to follow the coast. They swerved far out and found that it was not a bay but a channel running into the sea on the other side of the land mass and cutting Graham Land in two. The long, thin body of land to the north was, therefore, not part of the Antarctic continent, and the peninsula they had been mapping turned out to be an island.

By now they were 600 miles from Deception Island and had used half their gas. A dark storm was developing ahead of them. Wilkins shouted, "Ben, we'd better turn back!" The actual turning point was estimated at 71 degrees 20 minutes south and 64 degrees 15 minutes west.

The violence of the storm increased and prevented them from flying over new territory on the way back. Their gasoline supply would barely take them back to Deception Island, even by the shortest route.

A little less than 11 hours after they'd left Deception Island, they came in over the anchored *Hectoria*. Keeping inside the tunnel of storm clouds, Ben held the plane steady and circled down. Dense fog shrouded their weird runway, but Ben found a hole and took the plane in. After they landed, Ben sat motionless until he was able to hear again. Wilkins shouted, "It's been a great flight, Ben."

They had left Deception Island that morning at 8:30 A.M., flown 1,200 miles—much of it over unknown territory—, set the plane down, drained the oil, covered the engine with a storm hood, went to the *Hectoria*, bathed, dressed, and sat down to their regular 8:00 P.M. dinner.

At dinner, Ben commented, "Lady Luck was with us today. The weather is getting worse. We made it back just in time."

The storm grew more severe and kept up for days. In the meantime, news of the flight was wired to the world beyond the Antarctic. Ben sent a telegram reading: "Just returned from 1,200-mile flight over previously unexplored territory. Discovered six new islands. Merry Christmas."

Commander Byrd, at his base at Little America, wired a message: "Heartiest congratulations on a great flight. Don't forget, you will find a warm welcome at our base."

The two Antarctic bases were only about 2,000 miles apart, but the news had to travel from Little America to New York, then to San Francisco, and back to Deception Island, a distance of over 20,000 miles.

The weather was unfit for flying, but no one minded. It provided a chance to get ready for Christmas. Captain Hansen, of the *Hectoria*, happily cooperated. Since all meals were eaten on board ship, the men didn't have to worry about Christmas dinner, which was special. Even without the traditional presents, everyone appeared to have the Christmas spirit. The expedition party celebrated as only a group of lonely men away from home on Christmas can.

As 1928 came to an end, the men sat around the supper table early on New Year's Eve and talked about what the past year had brought to them. For Ben, it had brought international fame but continued frustration in his attempts to get a mail contract for Alaska. For Wilkins, it had brought a new romance, added fame, and a British title. The frustrations Wilkins experienced in 1926 and 1927 were overshadowed by the accomplishments of 1928. For Joe Crosson, it had brought the thrill of participating in the Antarctic expedition and cementing his friendship with Ben.

The expedition men and the whalers celebrated the advent of

1929. New Year's Day was the only break in the grueling work of the whaling season. The whalers made the most of it, singing, playing games, eating, and drinking. Ben, Crosson, and Porter boomed the harpooning guns on the *Hectoria*, sending multitudes of birds whirring into the air amid shouts of "HAPPY NEW YEAR! HAPPY 1929!"

After New Year's Day, there was not much the expedition men could do except sit back and wait for the weather to clear. On January 10 it cleared enough for flying. Crosson and Wilkins took off in the *Los Angeles* to attempt to locate a more southerly base for use in the next season of exploration. They found nothing except sheer walls of ice fronting on the sea and deep crevasses on the few stretches of level land they did see. After a 250-mile flight, they returned to Deception Island without sighting a suitable new landing field.

The weather turned bad again, and Wilkins determined that the members of the expedition had done as much as they could during the Antarctic summer and decided to store the planes until next season. He radioed for a boat in the Falklands to take them back to civilization.

While they waited, the men removed the larger wheels from the planes, installed small iron wheels, and buried them and the tail skids in gravel. After the engines were swamped with oil in every cylinder and a thick coat of grease was put on all exposed parts, the planes were covered with tight-fitting canvas. The wings were stored in the warehouse.

Ben felt a little sad when saying goodbye to Captain Hansen and his crew. The accommodations had been excellent, and they'd had a good time together. Ben's Norse also had improved after his close association with the Norwegian crew members.

When the chartered steamer arrived, the Wilkins crew said their final goodbyes and boarded. It took them a week to reach the Falklands.

As guests of the Royal Mail Steampacket Company, the expedition members came back through the Straits of Magellan, up the west coast of South America, and through the Panama Canal to New York. They reached New York City on March 13, 1929.

The expedition party was met by Mayor Jimmy Walker's Committee for Distinguished Guests. The party was then escorted to city hall for an official welcome.

Things weren't quite as hectic as they had been after the homecoming from Europe, but Wilkins and the others had to make several public appearances.

Ben went to visit with Dan Sutherland in Washington, where they discussed the progress Ben had made in obtaining financial backing for his Alaska airline. Ben told Sutherland that he hoped to organize the airline soon even though he did not have an airmail contract.

Ben was presented with the Distinguished Flying Cross when he was in Washington. Everyone in Hatton read about it in the papers. The citation read, in part: "The severity of the weather, the storm area passed through with no hope of outside aid in case of a forced landing, and the complete success of the enterprise, distinguishes this as one of the most extraordinary aerial accomplishments in history." Ben also was awarded the First Flier of 1928 trophy by the International League of Aviators, at Paris, France.

Ole had gone to New York to meet Ben, and when they later arrived at the Hatton station, a huge crowd gathered to welcome them. After all the well-wishers had left and the big Eielson home was finally quiet, Ben said, "I just want to relax for a while."

The family members were still concerned about Ben's flying career and openly expressed their sentiments. "From what I've been able to discover," Ole said, "you almost lost your life when your plane fell through the ice. I understand that on your exploration flight you passed over crevasses so deep that the airplane could have dropped down in one of them and nobody would ever have seen you and Wilkins again." His father was depressed but was resigned to his son's future, almost as though he had a premonition.

To challenge Ben, Ole said, "I was telling Elma the other day that I can't remember the last time you were home for Christmas. I don't suppose you'll ever spend another Christmas in Hatton. You said Sir Hubert Wilkins got engaged just before you left for the Antarctic, Ben. Now, if he can make plans to settle down, I don't see why you can't do the same."

"Well, he's not really going to settle down for a while. He's already planning another expedition to the Antarctic in about six months. He hasn't set a wedding date yet. He has a chance to make a trip around the world in the Graf Zeppelin, too," Ben said.

Then Ole asked, "Did he ask you to go to the Antarctic with him again?"

"Well, yes," Ben replied, "but I haven't decided what I'm going to do yet. It depends on what happens when I go back to New York."

ENDNOTES

1. It was not until November 28, 1929, that Bernt Balchen, famed Norwegian polar flier, flew Byrd over the South Pole in a tri-motored Ford monoplane, the *Floyd Bennett*.

2. While Wilkins believed that Graham Land was split into a series of islands, a later Australian expedition working on the ground found that what appeared to Wilkins from the air as islands were mighty glaciers extending from one end of the peninsula to the other.

3. Among the mountains Wilkins and Ben passed on this historic flight were lofty peaks mapped and named in 1947 by an American expedition led by Captain Finne Ronne, of the U.S. Navy. At that time, a group was named for Wilkins and a cape was named for Ben.

The Hotel Alaska

T. H. FOSTER, Proprietor   FAIRBANKS, ALASKA *March 16, 1927*

Last Will and Testament of Carl B. Eielson

I hereby give and bequeath all my property to my father, O. Eielson, Hatton, North Dakota. This includes money deposited in Farmers & Merchants National Bank of Hatton North Dakota, life insurance government $10,000.00. adjusted compensation money, stock in Alaska Consolidated Airways of Fairbanks, Alaska (1/3 of promotion stock) and all other property. I would leave part to my brothers and sisters except that I know that it amounts to the same thing when latter has it. We know we are beginning a hard while

Ben's Last Will and Testament, dated March 16, 1927. (HEM)

Lockheed Vega in California, 1927, prior to going to Alaska. First plane to fly over the Arctic and the Antarctic, 1928–29. (HEM)

Wilkins and Eielson prior to Spitzbergen flight, in Barrow Trading Post, 1928. (SHSND)

Ben and Wilkins take off from Barrow to fly over the Arctic to Spitzbergen, April 15, 1928. (HEM)

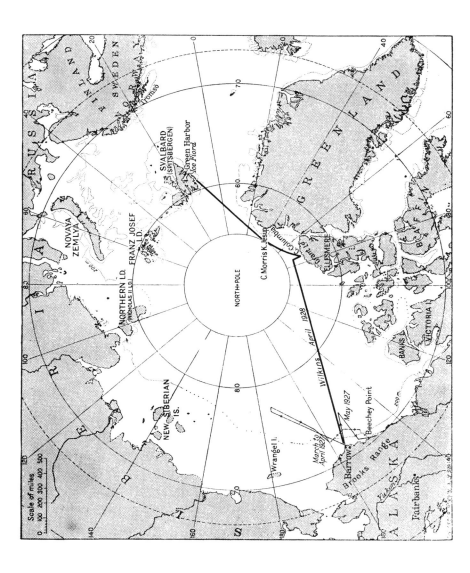

Map of Wilkins-Eielson Arctic flights, 1927 and 1928, including the route of the 13-day trek in 1927 to Beechey Point. (Smithsonian Institution)

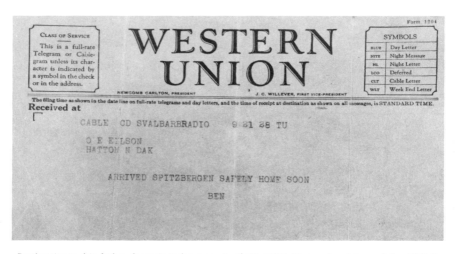

Ben's wire to his father from Spitzbergen, April 21, 1928. Note misprint on date. (HEM)

Pennzoil supported the Wilkins Arctic expedition. (George "Ed" Young Collection, U. of Alaska)

Ben and Wilkins on the balcony of the Grand Hotel, Tromso, Norway, May 1928. (HEM)

Roald Amundsen pinning Norwegian Aero Club medal on Ben, Wilkins at left, May 25, 1928. (HEM)

Wilkins, Roald Amundsen, and Ben aboard ship, Norway, 1928. (HEM)

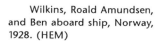

Ben, Joe Crosson, and Wilkins discussing their planned Antarctic expedition, December 1928. (HEM)

Wilkins, Eielson, Crosson, and Porter prior to departure for Antarctica, 1928. (Smithsonian Institution)

Advertisement by Mobiloil regarding the Antarctic expedition, 1928–29. (HEM)

Joe Crosson, Orval Porter, and Ben with penguins in the Antarctic, February 1929. (HEM)

Lockheed Vega, on pontoons, being loaded with five-gallon containers of fuel, Antarctic, 1929. (HEM)

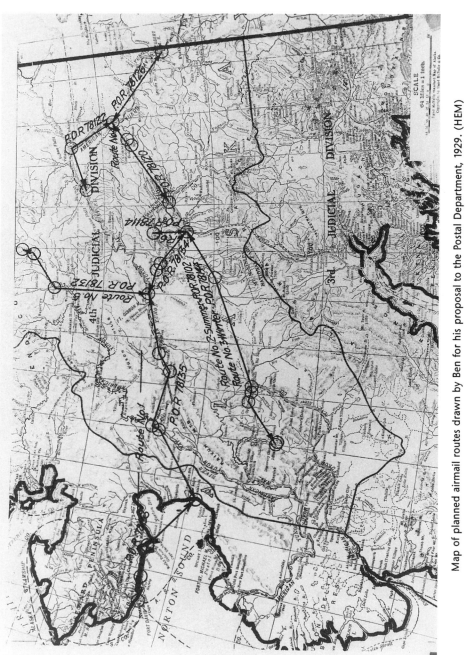

Map of planned airmail routes drawn by Ben for his proposal to the Postal Department, 1929. (HEM)

President Herbert Hoover presenting the Harmon Trophy for 1928 to Ben on the White House lawn, April 9, 1929. (HEM)

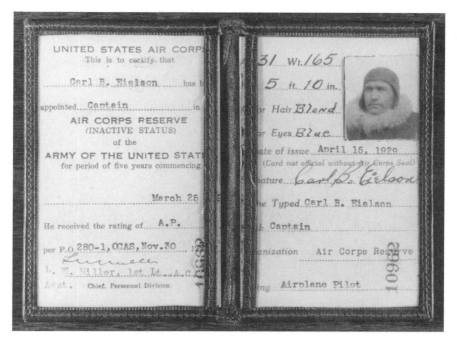

Ben's appointment to captain inactive status in the U.S. Army Air Corps Reserve, April 15, 1929. (HEM)

Ben receiving a gold watch as a token of appreciation from the people of Fairbanks, August 7, 1929. (HEM)

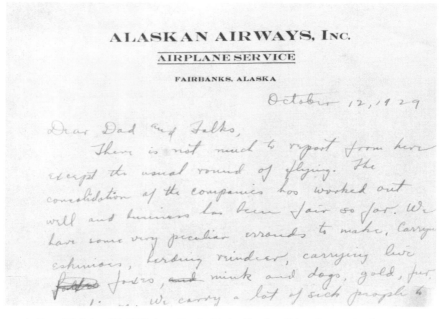

Letter of October 12, 1929, from Ben to his family, describing the new business venture. (HEM)

30

Alaskan Airways, Inc.

To HELP PASS THE TIME, Ben worked around the house, but he was frequently interrupted by callers. He also was honored in several more North Dakota cities. On April 3, he attended a testimonial dinner at Fargo. After a banquet at Grand Forks, Governor George Shafer commissioned Ben a colonel in the National Guard.

While in Grand Forks, Ben was asked to turn the first spade of dirt for the new Wesley College building, at the University of North Dakota, which was donated by John Hancock, another distinguished alumnus. The school also elected Ben to the "Who's Who" of the university alumni. Wisconsin paid him a similar honor, although he had been a student there less than a semester. When Ben returned to Hatton, he received word that he had been commissioned a captain in the Air Corps Reserve.

More honors came. In a special ceremony on April 9, President Herbert Hoover, whom Ben had first met in Fairbanks in 1923, awarded him the Harmon Trophy for the most outstanding feat in aviation for 1928. Charles A. Lindbergh had received the trophy in 1927.

Then came the normal barrage of interviews. One reporter referred to Ben as the Lindbergh of the North. Another pointed out that in flying the Atlantic, Lindbergh had crossed about 1,950 miles of open water plied by at least one steamer or other craft every 100 miles, while Ben and Wilkins had crossed over 2,200 miles of uninhabited Arctic ice, most of which had never before been seen by man. The story continued that Ben and Wilkins had looked at more moving ice during their trip than anyone else and had, in fact, erased three islands from the maps—Keenan Land, Crocker Land, and Harris Land.

Another reporter said that it wasn't an easy job for Ben to keep the engine warm in 50-degree-below-zero temperatures. At least 50 times from Barrow to Spitzbergen, Ben had had to clear the fuel lines of moisture accumulation while in flight.

Ben hoped that the postal officials would read the publicity he was getting. He and Dan Sutherland agreed that it would take an act of Congress to enable Ben to carry first-class mail by plane to and throughout Alaska, but such negotiations were underway in Washington.

Next, Ben went to New York for another conference with officials of The Aviation Corporation of America. Each time he'd talked with them about establishing a subsidiary in Alaska, they became more favorable to the idea. The memorandum of agreement dated June 11, 1929, established that The Aviation Corporation was interested in securing three existing commercial aviation companies in Alaska and their nine planes, three hangars, and other equipment. The Aviation Corporation authorized Ben to pay up to $150,000 for the companies and their rights. Ben was employed for three years, commencing June 1, 1929, and was paid $10,000 for work he had done up to that date. His salary was $100 a month.

The Aviation Corporation would put capital into Alaskan Airways, Inc., in exchange for stock at $20 per share for the purchase of the existing airlines. Then The Aviation Corporation would purchase another 12,500 shares, to provide funds for working capital and hangars.

The Aviation Corporation agreed to put 5 percent of Alaskan Airways shares aside as additional compensation for Ben, to be paid out over his three-year contract. In addition to being executive vice president of Alaskan Airways, Ben also would serve as one of its five directors.

As soon as arrangements were completed, Ben rushed to wire his friends in Fairbanks that he would see them soon. He also sent a wire to his father and told him that he would be leaving for Alaska. Before he left New York, Ben completed arrangements for the purchase of three new planes he had been authorized to buy for the company.

On the steamer to Alaska, Ben met Florence Barrett Willoughby, an attractive young author of many books on Alaska. She was on her way to Ketchikan to gather material for a new novel. Willoughby first came to Alaska from Wisconsin in 1896 with her parents and was raised at Kattala. She included much of the spirit of Alaska in her historical novels.[1]

Ben and Willoughby took an instant liking to each other and found that they had many things in common, including a great love for Alaska. Ben told her all about the new air transportation company that had just been formed. He added that his dream would be fulfilled when the merger was completed and air service was extended to all points in the interior.

Off St. Mary's Island, near Ketchikan, Ben and the other passengers aboard the *S.S. Aleutian* watched and speculated about a Lockheed Vega that kept circling the ship. The pontoon-equipped Vega, the *Juneau*, piloted by Anscel C. Eckmann, landed near the ship. Eckmann stated that he had instructions to pick up Ben.

Just two weeks prior, Eckmann and copilot Robert E. Ellis had made the first nonstop flight from Seattle to Juneau. The 940-mile trip was made in 7 hours 48 minutes. They launched a new service for the Alaska Washington Line, owned by Joseph L. Carman, Jr. The sea lift of Ben from the *Aleutian* was one of the new operation's first charters. It was a momentous occasion, for it marked the establishment of air commerce to and within Alaska.

Eckmann stopped in Ketchikan, where Ben was guest of honor at a luncheon hosted by the American Legion. Next he was taken to Juneau for another hero's welcome. Juneau officials and residents, as well as Alaskans from all parts of the Territory, were in the welcoming group. The parade from the governor's dock to the capitol was led by the American Legion, with music furnished by the Juneau city band.

The following day Ben was honored in formal ceremonies at the capitol, where a joint resolution honoring him was read. Ben was a modest man and undoubtedly was embarrassed by some of the statements made in the resolution.

He continued his journey by train from Seward. A few miles out of Fairbanks he heard the roar of planes. Three planes from Wien Alaska Airlines swooped down over the railway and dipped their wings in salute. Ben guessed that it was Noel and Ralph Wien in the two front planes and was later delighted when he learned that Freddie Moller had been flying the third one. It seemed so long ago that he'd first met Freddie in Nenana, where they discussed prospecting by plane. Although Freddie enjoyed flying, he never became a famous pilot.

Hundreds of residents were at the depot to meet Ben. Festivities began with a huge banquet in his honor, followed by a public reception. He was presented with a beautiful watch fob in the shape of the Golden Heart of Alaska. Ben then presented the Dorham H. Baker American Legion Post with the banner he'd carried over the top of the world.

In his prepared remarks Ben explained that his work in the Arctic and the Antarctic had not been an end in itself. He said that those flights only served to make it possible for him to arrange financing for the planned system of air service for Alaska. His dream was nearly fulfilled.

One of his friends interjected, "We know you could have gone almost anyplace to fly. You're very much in demand. But we're proud you wanted to come back to Fairbanks."

"After I purchase the three airlines here," Ben replied, "we'll merge them into a strong, stable organization in Alaska. But our ultimate aim is to launch a route to the Orient. At last the money is available to develop northern flight on an international scale."

Ben found that there were many changes from 1926 to 1929. Alaska already had 54 municipal and territorial landing fields, including Weeks Field and Wilkins Field, in Fairbanks.

Rodebaugh and pilot A. A. Bennett had formed the Bennett-Rodebaugh Company and purchased three new open-cockpit Waco 9s. They were speedy and fuel efficient, but within six weeks they were wrecked. After two of the Wacos were back into operation, the company hired a new pilot, Ed Young.

In the fall of 1926, the 200 Iditarod miners all had wanted transportation to the outside. Bennett-Rodebaugh had competed with the Fairbanks Airplane Company for the $75,000 in fares. But accidents happened in rapid succession, and four planes were smashed. Both companies were hard pressed to pay their bills.

Then, in early 1927, came the trial of the "Black Bear," from Iditarod. A well-known frontierswoman was charged with stealing

$30,000 from the dog-team mail carrier. Her trial was set in Fairbanks, and everybody wanted to be in court to watch the controversy. Both airlines were back in business.

In the meantime, Noel and Ralph Wien had founded an airline flying between Fairbanks and Nome. Business was good from the very beginning. Because of the memories of the 1925 diphtheria epidemic, possibly no Alaskan community appreciated air service as much as Nome.

On August 8, 1929, the Fairbanks *News-Miner* announced that Wien Alaska Airways, pioneer operating line of the interior and Seward Peninsula, had been purchased by Ben for his company. It was merged with the Bennett-Rodebaugh Company, also bought by Ben. Soon after, Ben purchased the Anchorage Air Transport Company. He was elated; his dream had finally come true.

Alaskan Airways, Inc., was opened for business—the largest air service in Alaska, with 12 planes, 3 hangars, and assorted miscellaneous equipment. Pilots included Ben, Joe Crosson, Ed Young, Matt Niemenen, Frank Dorbandt, Russ Merrill, and Harvey Barnhill. Mechanics were Freddie Moller, Earl Borland, Orval Porter, Gordon Springbett, Alonzo Cope, and Jim Hutchison. Harold Gillam and S. E. Robbins joined the company later.

Ben was itching to earn money for the new company. The officials in New York were pleased with the results of the negotiations, and the Alaskans greeted the news with joy.

Ben commanded a fleet of 12 planes, and his payroll was second only to that of the gold mining company whose mammoth dredges operated on all streams in central Alaska. The first charter flights were to Takotna and Tanana.

Although Ben was supposed to run the company, he couldn't resist making a few flights. But to his family in Hatton, he wrote that his flying days were over. "Maybe a little trip now and then," he wrote, "but you can quit worrying. You can rest assured that I'll stick to my desk and put Fairbanks on the map and prove to the New York financiers that their trust in Alaska aviation has not been misplaced."

When Ole read Ben's letter, he smiled. "We all know Ben isn't going to quit flying," he told Elma. "I'm sure he's just trying to keep me from worrying." Ole paused and added, "How many times did I plead with Ben to find a safer job? But, Ben was right. Aviation is coming into its own."

Elma replied, "Dad, you always said you thought young men should get out and see the world, and Ben has certainly done that. Now Oliver is going to South America, and Arthur says he's going to New York."

Ole was right. Ben flew every time he could find an excuse. As new planes were added to Alaskan Airways, Inc., Ben took them on test flights. The latest plane had been in Fairbanks a few days, but Ben waited for Barrett Willoughby to arrive so she could go along when he put the plane through its paces. She arrived on schedule, and Ben arranged to take her on her first flight.

Ben noted how times had changed since 1923, when his fragile Jenny was the lone plane flying regularly in the skies over Fairbanks. From different directions, three cabined planes were also winging through the late sunset. One carried a wealthy eastern sportsman, along with trophies of his hunt in the Koyukuk region, 200 miles away. Another was ending a 700-mile flight from Nome carrying $115,000 in gold dust. The third was rushing an expectant mother to St. Joseph's Hospital and the nearest doctor within 300 miles of her wilderness home.

Fairbanks citizens were so accustomed to the commercial planes that they paid them no more attention than they did winter dog teams. But on that day there was a crowd at the airport because many were anxious to see what Barrett Willoughby thought about her first ride in an airplane. They also wanted to get Ben's reaction to the high-powered open-cockpit biplane, the latest addition to the air fleet of Alaskan Airways, Inc. Willoughby saw first hand that the renowned polar flier was one of the best-loved and most distinguished people in Alaska.

She wasn't surprised. As soon as Barrett Willoughby had arrived in Fairbanks by train, she'd heard tales of Ben's superb courage in the air, his daring skill, and his dedication to Alaska. But by listening to proud Fairbanks residents talk, she learned that it wasn't Ben's spectacular flights with Sir Hubert Wilkins that pleased them so much as the fact that Ben had come home to Fairbanks at the age of 32 much the same as he had been before he received the 14 decorations for his service to aviation.

It was not international honors that gave Ben the affection and gratitude of all Alaskans. It was that he had come to them after World War I when aviation was in its infancy and offered them a dream. He was a youthful ex-military aviator turned school teacher with no plane, not much money of his own—nothing, in fact, but a dream of Alaska air transportation, at which many Alaskans, long accustomed to hardships in transportation, were inclined to laugh. But within seven years, Ben had made his dream come true.

Now, standing on the Fairbanks field, Willoughby said that she thought one of the most extraordinary things about the hazardous interlude, which won Wilkins a British title and Ben world fame, was Ben's superb courage and piloting skill. Ben replied, "I went with Wilkins to get more Arctic flying time and the prestige it would bring to enable me to finance an Alaskan air transport company."

Fairbanks people reminded Willoughby that fame hadn't turned Ben's head. She saw for herself that it hadn't.

That day, when people asked what she thought about her first flight in the fastest plane in the Territory, she replied, "Ben was like a boy with a new toy. . . . The flight was the most glorious experience of my life so far."

During her stay in Fairbanks, Ben took Willoughby on other flights that surpassed the first one. On one of the trips, a storm overtook them, and they had to set the ship down in a remote little native village, where they waited for good weather.

On another occasion, Willoughby talked Ben into trying some fog flying. It turned out to be more than she'd expected. After crossing the Endicott Range, they flew into dense fog. For four hours she watched Ben flying blind through a blowing Bering Sea fog so thick that they could scarcely see the wings.

Ben placed ads in many newspapers. One ad read: "WE REACH ANY POINT IN ALASKA ANY TIME OF THE YEAR. OUR PILOTS, MECHANICS, AND PLANES ARE ALL LICENSED UNDER THE DE-PARTMENT OF COMMERCE REGULATIONS. For rates apply by Wire or Letter."

Another ad read: "FISH A VIRGIN LAKE. WE FLY YOU IN, SET YOU DOWN WITH YOUR GEAR AND SUPPLIES, AND PICK YOU UP AFTER YOU'VE CAUGHT YOUR LIMIT."

Business was brisk. But on September 16, 1929, the sad news

reached Fairbanks that Russ Merrill was lost on a flight to the Nyac Mine. Merrill had left Anchorage in his heavily loaded pontoon-equipped Travelair, taking off from Cook Inlet, heading for the Nyac Mine, near Bethel in the Kuskokwim area. He never reached the mine. For the second time in two years a search was launched for Merrill. He had previously been forced down on a trip to Barrow, and Noel Wien had headed that search operation.

During the next two weeks, Ben, Crosson, Ed Young, Frank Dorbandt, and Harvey Barnhill flew more than 10,000 miles searching for Merrill or some trace of his plane. They found nothing. Finally, on October 3, Frank Smith, a fisherman, found a piece of airplane fabric on the beach at Cook Inlet. Mechanics Alonzo Cope and Charley Bisel identified the fabric as coming from the tail section of Merrill's plane. The mystery of Merrill's disappearance was never solved. Merrill Field, in Anchorage, is named for the pioneer pilot. It and Merrill Pass, which cuts between towering peaks of the Alaska Range due west of Anchorage, are reminders of Russell ("Russ") Hyde Merrill.

After the search, Crosson, Ben's chief pilot, asked for a leave to go to California to get married. When his colleagues heard that Crosson was getting married, they threw a huge party. As Crosson left for California, the last words that he told Ben were "If you need me for anything, I'll drop everything and come right back. I'm just as anxious for this company to be a big success as you are."

In early October 1929, a unique opportunity presented itself to the new company. Ben received a wire from Olaf Swenson, who was aboard the American fur-trading ship *Nanuk*, frozen in the ice at North Cape, Siberia. The Swenson Fur Trading Company, with headquarters in Seattle, needed airplanes to rescue 15 passengers and a $1 million cargo of Arctic furs. Swenson offered Ben $50,000 to bring the passengers and the cargo to Alaska. He feared a market collapse in the unsettled conditions of 1929 and wanted the furs removed immediately for shipment to New York and London.

Ben could not have hoped for a bigger contract. He was jubilant, but he realized that the flights to North Cape in October would be no pleasure hops. They would be long and hazardous over a little-known region of brewing storms.

Noel Wien was the only pilot who had ever flown from Alaska

to Asia, and he had done it in clear March weather. Now, the long, dark cold of the Arctic winter would soon shroud land and sea, and Wien had also married and was away on his honeymoon.

As Ben went about making arrangements for the flights, he decided to write to his family and to his girlfriend, who was taking postgraduate courses at a university outside. "As soon as I have enough money saved," Ben thought, "I'll follow Joe's example and get married."

To his family Ben wrote that he would now make an exception to his promise of not flying much. He said that there must be no delay in reaching the *Nanuk* and that he would be making some of the flights. "Don't worry," he said. "You'll be hearing from me soon."

To his girlfriend he wrote that he could not sit at a desk in Fairbanks while other pilots, particularly men with families, made the flights. Then he told her not to worry.

Soon many wires were being sent back and forth between those involved in the transaction—the Swenson Fur Trading Company, the only American company having a concession to trade furs in the Soviet Union, a country not recognized by the United States; the Soviet authorities; and Ben, in Alaska. There was much red tape to wade through before the contract was completed. Finally, Ben wired New York and informed company officials that negotiations had been finalized. "It will take four or five trips to complete the job," he added. "I plan to make some of the flights."

ENDNOTE

1. Florence Barrett Willoughby's book *Pioneer of Alaska Skies*, a children's biography of Ben, was written in collaboration with Edna Walker Chandler. She also included Ben in a book on famous Alaskans, entitled *Alaskans All.*

31

The Fatal Flight to the Nanuk

BEN KNEW that the dangers in flying the 2,250-mile round trip in late October or early November were great. But he kept thinking about the 15 people stranded in Siberia with limited food supplies. Furthermore, the lucrative contract was hard to beat. He learned that life insurance was available in limited amounts at very high rates. He learned, too, that hull insurance for airplanes, in case of a crash, was not available under any conditions. The insurance situation clearly indicated the high degree of risk involved.

Reliable weather reports were difficult to obtain because the Russian weather stations would not supply weather reports to the United States. Ben had to depend on reports from the *Nanuk*, which were good only for a restricted area. In the fall, the weather was subject to abrupt changes and rolling fog.

His biggest problem was choosing the pilot to go with him. Had Crosson been in Alaska, Ben would have picked him. The two thought alike and worked well together. Frank Dorbandt, one of the pilots from the Anchorage company Ben had acquired, was stationed in Nome with a Stinson. Dorbandt was a very capable pilot but was reckless and impulsive. He was hot tempered and loud talking and often took unnecessary risks. Ben had tangled with Dorbandt on several occasions. Their last harsh words came over a charter trip Ben had postponed because of inclement weather.

Dorbandt often had trouble with his fellow pilots and worked better alone. It was bush-pilot practice for each pilot to decide for himself, based on his own knowledge and capabilities, about flying conditions. Dorbandt, for one, had a contempt for the elements.

Ben had no trouble picking the mechanic to accompany him in

the Hamilton he planned to fly. Earl Borland had worked for Noel Wien and was the most familiar with the Hamilton of any of the mechanics. Besides, Borland was enthusiastic about aviation.

Borland and his wife had a small celebration when Ben told him he would go along as mechanic on the flight to North Cape, Siberia. Borland had come to Alaska in 1921 to work as a mechanic for the Alaska Road Commission. He had married an Alaskan girl in 1922, and they had two young sons. In 1927, at age 28, Borland had started work as an airplane mechanic and had saved money to go outside for flying lessons. He told his wife, Irene, that the extra money he'd earn on the long flights to Siberia would give him enough to get his wings. Ben promised Borland a job as pilot as soon as he had completed training.

Ben decided to leave Ed Young in charge at Fairbanks until Crosson returned, with Matt Niemenen in Anchorage and Harvey Barnhill and S. E. Robbins as extra pilots. Because Dorbandt was already in Nome and using the Stinson, the other plane Ben had picked to use, Ben felt that it would be easier to have Dorbandt go along on the flights to North Cape. It proved to be the biggest mistake Ben ever made.

Ben was too busy attending to the details of the flight to worry about Dorbandt. He worked hard to complete clearance papers to a foreign port for the two planes. The planes had to be checked through customs in Nome. On the first flight this included aviation gasoline, groceries, and other supplies for the *Nanuk*.

Ben wired Dorbandt in Nome and told him to carry enough gasoline for the return flight, emergency rations, and some supplies for the stranded passengers. He also told Dorbandt to pick up his clearance papers at the Nome port and then meet him in Teller.

By then, the *Nanuk* had been icebound off North Cape for two months. The crew had signed on for 19 months, if necessary, before they left Seattle, but only the winter crew had really expected that they might possibly stay that long. They knew Olaf Swenson was trying to make arrangements for Ben to remove the furs and the passengers. One day Swenson's daughter Marion told the cabin boy, Clark Crichton, "Well, we're going to have company. Daddy just had word from Moscow that everything is set for Ben Eielson from Alaskan Airways to come."

The village of North Cape consisted of two wooden houses and many native skin houses. There were only two Russian families there but almost 100 natives. The natives often came to the ship to visit, drink tea, eat bread, and sometimes obtain medicine.

The *Nanuk* was caught fast in the ice, with little hope of rescue. Swenson had given the order to fit the ship for winter. The engines were started, and the ship was rammed close to shore, where it could be tied down and prepared for the long enforced stay.

Swenson had already lost the *Elisif* that year when it was rammed by an iceberg and was abandoned on the beach. The crew salvaged some of the furs and also managed to land a small boat on the rocky shore of Little Diomede Island. They were then rescued by a Coast Guard cutter from Nome. Noel Wien had hauled one load of furs from the *Elisif.*

The *Nanuk's* hold was full of fox, ermine, squirrel, reindeer, and wolf pelts, all packed in big cases. White fox skins were the most valuable.

When Marion broke the news that Ben was coming, there was speculation as to which passengers would be lucky enough to go home. Then a storm hit and lasted for five days. When the storm was over, speculation increased. Many became more eager than ever to leave. Their work was done for the season, and they did not look forward to staying for the winter.

Everyone marked time, waiting for the planes to arrive. At night they played cards and guessed who would leave first. They took the dog teams out for hunting, but even this diversion was restricted because of the shortage of dog food.

Each day they checked with Bob "Sparks" Gleason, the wireless operator, to get the latest news. Finally, Gleason received a wire from Dorbandt saying that he was in Teller and was waiting for Ben.

Ben was first delayed in Fairbanks filling the order for supplies for the stranded passengers. Inclement weather further prevented his departure. When the weather finally cleared, Ben and Borland left Fairbanks for Nome. They had a rough flight and had to stay in Nome for repairs. On October 25 Ben wired Dorbandt in Teller and gave him permission to take off with his mechanic, Bassett, for the *Nanuk.*

All during the period of waiting on the *Nanuk*, Gleason sent weather reports to Teller and received messages so that the *Nanuk* passengers knew as soon as Dorbandt was in the air. It wasn't much longer before everyone in the village, including the stranded Americans, the Russians, and the natives, knew that the plane was on the way, bringing some of the food supplies requested.

Gleason sent a message to the wireless operator on the Russian trading ship *Stavropol*, which was frozen in about a mile from the *Nanuk*. The two operators were in the habit of sitting at the keys for hours at a time, talking back and forth in Morse code. When the Russian operator came over to the *Nanuk* to wait for the plane to arrive, he and Gleason couldn't understand each other. It was only on the telegraph keys that they spoke the same language.

Dorbandt took off from Teller at 8:30 A.M. on October 26. The people on the *Nanuk* figured the flight would take about five or six hours. The weather there was the best it had been in weeks.

At 1:30 P.M. one of the Chukchi men saw the plane, a tiny speck in the sky over a point of land east of the Cape. He hollered and ran to the *Nanuk*. Soon, a huge group gathered at the ship. It wasn't long before they heard the drone of the engine and the speck grew larger. The natives, and even the dogs, all started over the ice from the village. The Russians from the village and the crew of the *Stavropol* joined them.

Dorbandt and Bassett, in the Stinson, swooped down. Just as the people thought Dorbandt was going to land on the smooth ice in front of the *Nanuk*, he gave the Stinson the gun and zoomed up in an Immelmann, his idea of saying hello. Then Dorbandt circled, landed with a jolt, and taxied right up to the *Nanuk*. Some of the people were disappointed when they found that Ben was not the pilot. They had heard so much about the famous Arctic flier that they were anxious to meet him. Dorbandt told them that Ben would be over as soon as the Hamilton was repaired. Then Dorbandt received a boisterous welcome. "Even Lindbergh didn't get a better reception in Paris," Swenson told Ben later.

Two days later, Ben and Borland arrived in the fast Hamilton, making the trip from Teller in less than five hours. But Ben had wheels on his plane instead of skis. He circled several times, looking for snow hard enough for a landing. He checked the wind carefully, for he was heavily loaded with gasoline, canned milk, coffee, and groceries. The aviation gas for the return trip was packed in cases.

Ben landed near the east end of the bay and taxied up to the

Nanuk without any trouble. He and Borland received a warm welcome. With both planes there and ready for loading, there was a lot of rejoicing aboard the *Nanuk*. Following dinner that evening, Swenson came into the mess room, called the crew together, and paid them. He said that six men could accompany the pilots on the return trip. Each man was restricted to 20 pounds of baggage. Then Swenson read the list of the men who could leave. Marion Swenson remained with her father, Gleason, and the other men.

The crew of the *Nanuk* had been busy at two portable sewing machines, operated by hand cranks, making burlap sacks to pack the furs into bales to fit into the planes. By the time Ben arrived, they had 200 bales of white fox furs ready.

Ben, Borland, Dorbandt, and Bassett were soon busy preparing the planes for the return flight. They had covered the engines with heavy canvas hoods, and a Primus stove was left burning under each cowling cover to keep the frost off the engines and to warm the oil. All the baggage was loaded aboard Ben's plane, plus all the furs it would hold. Seats were removed to make more space for the fur bales. Ben said that they could carry about 1,500 pounds of fur on the first trip. Four passengers got into the plane with Dorbandt, and the other two got in with Ben and Borland.

Dorbandt took off at 9:30 A.M., leaving first in case he had any trouble. Ben took off 15 minutes later. After he was airborne, Ben experienced trouble with the heaters in the Hamilton. A small fire started, which at first threatened to damage the plane and the furs. After the fire was put out, Ben returned to the *Nanuk* to leave the heaters.

Near Cape Serdze, Dorbandt ran into heavy fog and rough weather. His plane bounced around like a kite on a nervous boy's string. The passengers clung tight to their fur-bale seats. An hour after hitting the storm, Dorbandt decided to land. He came in through a hole in the fog, and the skis hit with such a jolt that the plane bounced as high as a house. Then it settled down. "Well, here we are!" Dorbandt yelled. No one said a word. None of them knew exactly where they were.

The men were dressed in furs, but it was cold in the cabin. Dorbandt decided that three men should go to look for the coast and maybe a native settlement. One of the *Nanuk* passengers said that they were not too far from shore because the ice was smooth. But even before they got started, they heard the roar of the Hamilton above them. They all shouted and waved for Ben to come down.

As soon as Ben landed, natives approached by dog team. George, a *Nanuk* passenger, could speak Chukchi and asked if the men could accompany the natives to their village to sit out the storm. The natives obligingly showed them the shortest way to the village only half a mile away. Before leaving, Ben, Dorbandt, and the mechanics carefully covered the planes. Each man took a portion of the emergency rations along in case the group became stranded for several days.

The Russian native house in which the men stayed was built of driftwood and was rectangular in shape, with an opening covered by a heavy reindeer skin. The native woman who lived there with her 10-year-old son had seal oil lamps for heat. All were thankful for the shelter.

"Hello, Mamma," Dorbandt yelled. "You've got company for dinner!" He slapped the youngster on the back and called him Charlie. When the people from the other homes came to visit, he called the older man Chief, called his son Prince, and gave the other natives American names. The natives were puzzled by his behavior.

The visitors sat out the storm for five days. The Chukchi native told George that the weather had been very erratic, very changeable—the worst winter in many years.

The 10 men from the planes slept on the floor on one side of the room, and the native woman and her son slept on the other side. There wasn't much variety in their meals. The regular fare consisted of reindeer stew, seal stew, and Russian tea. For a treat one night the woman made sourdough donuts fried in seal oil. They were a welcome change.

The men usually talked until late at night. Dorbandt was always kidding someone and had many stories to tell, but the men from the *Nanuk* often interrupted him to ask Ben about his experiences in the Arctic and the Antarctic.

The trader at Cape Serdze had heard that there were two planes down and sent a native driver with a 16-dog team to bring a letter to Ben asking him to pick up special supplies for him on his second trip to the *Nanuk*. He also sent a bundle of mail and asked if the Americans would mail it in Nome.

The native musher had made the trip from Cape Serdze in a little over half a day. He and the dogs were exhausted, but they rested only a short time and started back the same day. Only dog teams could travel in the stormy weather.

Each day Ben and the others checked the planes. The wind blew in gale force, making clean sweeps across the frozen Arctic. Even after the winds died down, visibility was too restricted for takeoff.

Ben and Dorbandt were reported lost on October 29 when they failed to check in at Teller. The news that they were down hit all the newspapers in Alaska and in Seattle. Oddly enough, when Ole heard that Ben was lost in Siberia, he wasn't worried. Ben had been reported lost before and then turned up safe. Alaskan Airways officials also said that they were confident the fliers were safe. In the meantime, Ben hoped none of the other pilots would set out on a search mission.

Ben lamented the lack of exchange of weather reports between countries, especially in the Arctic. The Russians had weather stations at Wrangel Island, at Cape Serdze, and aboard the *Stavropol*. Had information from any of the three been available, Ben and Dorbandt wouldn't have taken off from the *Nanuk* into the blizzard an hour's flight away.

Ben appointed Paddy, an old seaman from the *Nanuk*, as "weather prophet." Each day the men checked with Paddy. One night there was a low sunset, and Paddy announced that the weather would clear up the next day.

Everyone got busy digging the planes out, warming them, and breaking them loose from the ice. The men packed their gear aboard. Just before they left, Ben took another supply of rations back to the natives where they had stayed. He told the natives, through George, who had written down the native words he'd learned each day, that on his next trip he would bring food supplies to replace those used by the 10 visitors. He also decided to bring presents to repay them for sharing their small food stocks.

Again, Dorbandt left first. Ben told him that after the planes crossed the Bering Strait he would head for Nome with the biggest load of furs. He told Dorbandt to land at Teller and change from skis to wheels for landing at Nome.

Just after passing East Cape, which was high like North Cape, the *Nanuk* passengers were very excited, as they knew that Alaska was only about 50 miles away. In a short time Ben passed beneath Dorbandt and waggled his wings in farewell.

As the Hamilton approached Nome, Ben noticed that the water was still open most of the way. One of the *Nanuk* men noted that if they had been able to break loose from the ice at North Cape and then worked their way beyond the floating ice pack, they could have sailed the *Nanuk* all the way to Nome without much trouble. He said that getting lost in the ice was a freak combination of circumstances.

Ben landed safely at the Nome airfield and arranged to have the furs hauled to the *Sierra*, the last boat of the season, scheduled to leave Nome in about seven days.

After Dorbandt circled to land at Teller, and the men thought that they could rest in civilization at last, Dorbandt zoomed up again in a fancy turn to show off. One passenger reported, "I almost lost my reindeer stew breakfast."

They were all glad when Dorbandt landed in front of the Teller Roadhouse. The dozen or so buildings at Teller looked like palaces to the men who had been icebound on the *Nanuk*, then stranded in the tiny native village. The trip from the Russian village to Teller lasted four hours. They ached from being cramped in the small plane. The first thing they did was walk to the roadhouse and order dinner. It was six days since they'd left the *Nanuk*, and they were hungry for a good meal and wanted to take a bath.

After dinner, Dorbandt switched to wheels, as Ben had told him there was not enough snow at Nome for a ski landing. It was only 100 miles from Teller to Nome, and the men arrived there within an hour. But before landing, Dorbandt couldn't resist showing off once again, although he knew that Ben would surely have something to say about stunting in a company plane with passengers aboard.

After he did a loop or two, Dorbandt saw a man standing along the runway, looking upward. He turned the ship and dived straight down at him. The man ducked involuntarily and dashed away from the field. Dorbandt followed him and dived again, this time very low.

The passengers were sure he would crash, but Dorbandt pulled on the controls and zoomed high to circle the field. Finally, he landed.

Ben and Borland were at the field with Dorbandt's wife, who lived in Nome. "After you get the plane taken care of," Ben said curtly, "I want to talk to you in the office." Borland, Bassett, and the *Nanuk* passengers knew what Ben was going to say.

Soon everyone was settled in the Golden Gate Hotel, with bathrooms, soft beds, clean sheets, and easy chairs. The *Nanuk* passengers said that they felt like kings.

After checking with officials, Ben informed the *Nanuk* passengers that they would have to wait in Nome a week before they could board the *Sierra* and leave for Seattle. He'd already arranged passage for the six, and the furs were loaded into the *Sierra's* hold. Slush ice was beginning to form, and soon Nome would be icebound for eight months.

Early in November, the *Nanuk* passengers sailed from Nome. Ben and Borland had already left for Teller after picking up supplies for the *Nanuk*, the Russian trader at Cape Serdze, and the villagers. Ben also bought Christmas presents for the natives where they had stayed, as he'd promised.

When Ben and Borland had first reached Nome, Borland sent a telegram to his wife at Fairbanks: "Arrived at Nome from Russia yesterday, November 5. Stormbound on the ice five days. Leaving today for the second trip. Easy flying conditions. Don't worry. Love, Earl."

For the next week, flying conditions were terrible. Bad weather at Teller made a second trip to the *Nanuk* impossible. Ben kept in touch with the ship every day. He kept telling Borland how much easier things would be if they could get regular weather reports from the Russian stations.

Ben had been advised on his first trip that Captain Milozorov, from the *Stavropol*, wanted to be taken to an American hospital for much-needed medical attention. Ben hoped to pick up the captain as well as rescue the remaining passengers on the *Nanuk*.

Ben was anxious to complete his contract but didn't want to take unnecessary chances. The many obligations, especially toward those waiting on the *Nanuk*, weighed heavily on his mind.

During the enforced stay at the Teller Roadhouse waiting for good weather, Ben made plans for expanded operation of the airlines in Fairbanks, Anchorage, and Nome. He relaxed by reading magazines and resting, but Dorbandt was plainly irritated.

On November 8, as Ben lay on the bed in his upstairs room reading a magazine, he could hear Dorbandt's loud voice from downstairs. "I'm fed up waiting for good weather reports," Dorbandt said. "Anybody with guts at all can cross the Bering Strait. It's not so difficult. Tomorrow morning I'm going to leave, and just let anybody"—he jerked his thumb upwards toward Ben's room—"try to stop me."

Ben smiled and continued reading. Dorbandt had made the same threat once or twice before. He knew Dorbandt well enough to know that the boastful words were meant for his ears. Dorbandt had actually left the roadhouse on several occasions, telling all who'd listen that he was leaving for Siberia and they could sit there if they wanted. But he always changed his mind and came back to the safety of the roadhouse, muttering about fog and dirty weather.

The other men in the roadhouse ignored Dorbandt's threat that day. They knew that he was a braggart. Bassett, Dorbandt's mechanic, finally said, "It's better to be inside here than to be caught in a fog or a blizzard."

Dorbandt swore under his breath and said, "You just wait until tomorrow. I'm crossing the Bering Strait—alone, if necessary. You hear me?"

Nobody bothered to answer. The men turned and left the lobby, leaving Dorbandt pacing the floor and muttering to himself.

November 9 dawned gloomy and cold. A fog blanket still shrouded the sea. After breakfast, Ben, Dorbandt, Borland, and Bassett went into the lobby. Jack Warren, the owner, was there also. All the men except Dorbandt sat down and started reading. Dorbandt paced the floor, looking out the windows.

"Well," Dorbandt finally demanded, "are we going to leave today or not?"

Ben looked up from his magazine and replied, "No. We're going to wait until we get a good weather report from the *Nanuk*. There's no point in taking unnecessary chances. Relax, Frank."

But Dorbandt kept pacing the room. Suddenly he stopped. "All we have to do is cross the Bering Strait and hit for the *Nanuk*," he said loudly. "There's nothing to it."

"Look, Frank, we know it's foggy over the Bering Strait," Ben said, "but we have no idea of what the weather is like in Siberia. If we get a good weather report from the *Nanuk*, at least we'll have some idea of what to expect."

Dorbandt resumed pacing. Ben looked toward the mechanics and said, "Guess it's time for the routine checks on the planes." Bassett and Borland nodded.

"Well," Dorbandt said loudly, "I'm leaving."

Borland and Bassett went down to the planes. In a few minutes, Dorbandt followed them. Borland returned to the roadhouse first. "It doesn't look very good out there," he said to Ben.

"How's Frank doing?" Ben asked. "Has he cooled off yet?"

Borland shrugged. "He said he was leaving," Borland replied, "but he's still down there."

The men had almost forgotten Dorbandt's threat, but at 10:45 A.M. they heard the roar of the Stinson's engine. "If there wasn't such a shortage of trained pilots in Alaska," Ben thought, "I wouldn't keep Dorbandt on the payroll another minute." Then he brightened. "There's Harold Gillam coming up and Earl," he thought. "Things will soon be different."

Suddenly Ben looked out the window and saw the Stinson hurdling across the ice. Dorbandt was taking off!

Ben shook his head and sighed. He turned from the window, faced Borland, and said calmly, "Earl, we had better go, too."

With Borland following him, Ben went upstairs. The two men returned shortly, dressed for flight. The roadhouse manager was plainly uneasy as he said goodbye. Dorbandt's abrupt departure without waiting for the weather report from the *Nanuk* upset him. He knew that Ben would have to follow, if for no other reason than to assist Dorbandt should he experience any trouble. An injury in the Arctic, no matter how small, could tie a man down to one location. With no assistance, exposed to the elements, and unable to get help, a person with even a minor injury could die.

Ben and Borland got the Hamilton ready to take off. Ben waved to Warren, who stood in the doorway of the roadhouse, watching as the two men climbed into the plane. Warren waved back.

At 11:15 A.M., Ben and Borland took off. The Hamilton bumped over the rough sea ice and slowly disappeared into the shifting mist.

It was gone from sight, swallowed up in the fog boiling up from the open waters. Warren shivered, went inside the roadhouse, and closed the door. For some reason, he felt strangely depressed.

Ben and Borland weren't gone more than a few minutes when Warren heard the roar of a plane's engine. He was surprised to see the Stinson glide back to settle down on the ice. Dorbandt and Bassett returned to the safety and comfort of the roadhouse.

"There's not a pilot living who can get across the Bering Strait today," Dorbandt said shortly. "Never saw such damn weather!"

In the main room of the roadhouse, everyone turned away from Dorbandt. Jack Warren looked over at his wife helplessly. He turned toward Dorbandt, then checked himself. He turned to his wife instead and said, "If only Ben gets through. . . ." Dorbandt and Bassett went upstairs to take off their flying clothes.

Several times during the day, Warren put on his parka and went outside to stand peering into the darkness. He strained his ears to catch the drone of the Hamilton returning. But the only sound was the terrible wailing of the wind as it lashed the coast.

Six hours passed, but Ben and Borland didn't return. They didn't reach the *Nanuk* either. Tension in the roadhouse grew. Soon after Ben and Borland disappeared, the sun dropped below the horizon, not to rise again until the upcoming new year was a month old. Only a few dim hours around noon each day gave light enough for flying. But the weather was impossible, exceptionally stormy. Then the temperature dropped to 40 degrees below zero, and 70-mile-an-hour winds swept between the two continents.

Jack Warren, who had managed the roadhouse a long time, told Bassett that in all his years in Teller, he'd never seen such terrible weather for that time of the year. Every day the wind blew and the snow swirled around the roadhouse in furious blasts.

Each day the same message came from the *Nanuk*: "No word from Ben. Ceiling and visibility nil. Still storming."

"Maybe," Warren told Bassett, "Ben is down someplace, sitting the storm out. He's done that before. Maybe he's in a native village and can't contact anybody."

Two weeks passed. By now, Dorbandt was bitter with remorse as he realized how tragic might be the consequences of his impulsive flight. The other people turned away from him, as though they couldn't stand the sight of him sitting comfortably in the roadhouse, safe from the storm.

The day after Thanksgiving, Warren heard the muffled roar of a plane. His heart surged with joyful relief. He expected to see the Hamilton flying in out of the mist. The dim shadow of a plane circled. He peered into the gloom. It was too small for the Hamilton, but he grabbed his parka and rushed out to the ice.

Joe Crosson crawled swiftly from an open-cockpit plane. "Hi, Jack," Crosson said. "I've come to start searching for Ben."

Crosson had heard the news that Ben was missing while he was outside. Without hesitation, he'd returned to Alaska with his new bride. He'd contacted the officials of Alaskan Airways outside and told them his plans. Then Crosson left his bride in Fairbanks and flew 600 bitterly cold miles to Teller to try to find Ben and Borland "before it was too late." "Harold Gillam," Crosson added, "will be here soon to help."

32

The Search for Ben and Borland

When Joe Crosson had returned to Fairbanks, Harold Gillam, who had previously made only one cross-country flight, had met him at the office of Alaskan Airways, Inc. "Give me a plane," Gillam had pleaded. "I want to help look for Ben."

When it seemed as if he was about to get turned down because he didn't have a pilot's license, Gillam said feelingly, "You know if it were any of us lost out there, Ben would fly the wings off his plane trying to find us."

Crosson and the others at the office didn't say anything for a minute. "Give me a ship," Gillam begged again.

Crosson hesitated, but in the end Gillam had his way. He was given an open-cockpit Stearman.

Though Gillam had come to Alaska in 1923, he had been flying only since 1927. When Joe Crosson's sister, Marvel, came to Fairbanks for a visit in 1927, she had dated Gillam.[1] Gillam was one of the first to solo from the Fairbanks field. At the time of Ben's search, he had had only 40 hours of solo flying.

When they left for the search area, Gillam took off after Crosson. In Teller, just as Crosson finished saying that he expected the inexperienced but determined Gillam, Gillam flew over. He circled the strip on the ice to come in for a good landing in front of the Teller Roadhouse.

The two were soon ready to take off again, but the weather turned bad. The planes were anchored to the ice. Crosson, Gillam, and Dorbandt waited in the lobby of the roadhouse for the weather to improve. Messages from the *Nanuk* advised that winds were high and visibility was zero.

The trio grew more edgy each day. Crosson and Gillam felt a driving sense of urgency and an almost brooding sense of hopelessness at being tied down. Both knew that as each day passed, the chances for the survival of Ben and Borland decreased. They did all they could to avoid Dorbandt.

Each morning, in almost total darkness, the men went down to the ice airfield in front of the roadhouse. They warmed the planes with fire pots and kept the runway clear, just in case the *Nanuk* should report good weather. These jobs usually took three hours, and generally they were an effort in futility. Time after time, Crosson, bundled in furs, took off, only to return with the news that the Bering Strait was impassable.

Dorbandt also took off several times. He broke the axle on the Stinson on the first try, a ski on the second, and finally the landing gear. The Stinson was the only cabin plane at Teller. Laid up for repairs, it represented a real loss. Crossing the Bering Strait in an open-cockpit plane was not a task many looked forward to. As time dragged and the weather worsened, Dorbandt verged on a nervous breakdown.

It seemed impossible that the weather could continue so bad for so long. The extreme fury of storms off the Seward Peninsula is largely due to geographic formation. The Bering Strait, connecting the Bering Sea to the south and the Chukchi Sea to the north, is a bottleneck only about 60 miles across at the narrows. One hundred miles south of the Bering Strait, St. Lawrence Island squats fairly in the path of winds from the south. This giant breakwater—actually the peak of a mountain range jutting 2,000 feet from the ocean—diverts the fury of the storms toward Norton Bay and the south side of the Seward Peninsula, where the violence of the sea is incredible. Storms are so plentiful that Nome is called the City of Storms.

It took the disappearance of Ben and Borland to make some Americans aware of the ocean-bridging location of Alaska. At the Bering Strait, the Pacific is less than 60 miles across. The Little (American) and the Big (Russian) Diomede Islands are only about two miles apart.

On November 19, an unconfirmed report came from North Cape that the wreckage of Ben's plane had been sighted 60 miles from the *Nanuk*. This dashed everyone's hopes. Later, the report was changed, claiming that natives had reported instead that they had heard the engine of Ben's plane on November 9 about 50 miles from the *Nanuk*. But they said that they hadn't actually seen the plane in the fog. The amended report revived hope that Ben and Borland had been forced down and were still alive.

In the meantime, Graham Grosvenor, president of The Aviation Corporation of America, parent of Alaskan Airways, Inc., named Alfred Lomen, of Nome, director of the search for Ben and Borland. Lomen was manager of the Lomen Reindeer Corporation and also a member of the board of directors of Alaskan Airways. He reported that Alaskan Airways was sponsoring a relief expedition, with Major Howard C. Deckard, production and factory manager for the Fairchild Aviation Corporation, in Seattle, in charge of shipping three Fairchild 71s to Fairbanks. Lomen said that the planes were being crated at the Boeing Airplane Company's hangar at Boeing Field. Lomen also reported that Canadian fliers were being sent to Alaska to fly the Fairchilds because the U.S. Army and Navy felt that they were unprepared to attempt the search. They had no pilots—except for Ben—experienced in Arctic flying.

The answer to the appeal for help from the U.S. Army and Navy surprised some people, even in Alaska, where they were used to official ignorance of conditions. Alaskan pilots were gloomy because they feared large-scale rescue operations would not come soon enough.

In the meantime, Crosson doggedly arranged to have additional aviation gasoline flown to Teller. He wired Lomen that he and Gillam planned to take off from Teller as soon as the job was completed and the weather permitted. The Stinson was the only plane with enough range to make the flight without refueling, but it still was not flyable. The Waco and the Stearman that Crosson and Gillam flew had open cockpits and only the crudest of instruments and would require refueling on the Siberian side. Jack Warren shook his head in amazement as Crosson went about his work, but he agreed with Crosson when he said that if the Alaskan pilots were looking for comfort and security, they wouldn't have been there in the first place. Their aim was to try to find Ben and Borland before it was too late.

On November 26, it was reported from the *Nanuk* that a smoke signal believed to be from an icebound camp of Ben and Borland had been sighted by Russian dog-team searchers. The news was sent by Dorbandt to Grosvenor, who gave reporters the following message:

> Another dog team arrived from Kolyuchin Bay and re-ported seeing smoke in the foothills 36 miles from North Cape. No natives in that district. Probably Eielson. Unfavor-able weather and shortage of fuel make immediate search impossible. Returning to the search as soon as possible. Rus-sian plane leaving from Providence Bay to seek Eielson.

The dog-team searchers, both Russian and those from the *Nanuk*, intensified their search as a result of the report but found nothing.

In New York, Stefansson suggested that help be sought from the Soviet Union. He said that Russians had done considerable work in the field of Arctic flying and could be a big help in the search efforts, but State Department officials declined to act. Stefansson persisted and succeeded in enlisting the help of the former Assistant Attorney General Mable Walker Willebrandt, who was then serving as counsel for The Aviation Corporation. Together, the two sought help from the Russians on an individual and an unofficial basis.

Finally, two cables were sent to Moscow, one by Senator William E. Borah, of Idaho, chairman of the Foreign Relations Committee, and one by Secretary of the Interior Ray Lymen Wilbur. The Russians acted promptly to assist in the search for Ben. They had great respect for him as a pioneer in Arctic flying. Yet, they couldn't resist a dig against the United States. In the Soviet newspaper *Chudak*, a cartoon appeared with the caption: "The fact that we Americans do not recognize the Soviet Union, that is nothing. But if they do not recognize our planes on account of the fog, that will be bad."

The Russians offered help in several ways. They immediately sent additional dog teams from the *Stavropol* and from Wrangel Island and mainland points across the ice pack and overland to begin the search. In addition, Moscow officials offered a sum of 2,000 rubles—about $1,000—as a reward for news of Ben. Notice of the reward was sent to all villages in Siberia and to remote reindeer camps. At the same time Soviet planes proceeded from Moscow to North Cape.

When Stefansson learned that Alaskan Airways officials were sending the Wasp-powered, ski-equipped Fairchild 71s ordered from a Canadian corporation to aid in the search, he tried to get them to fly the planes to Alaska, following the Mackenzie River. But the officials decided to have the planes crated and shipped to Alaska.

Forty days had passed since Ben and Borland had disappeared. Although Crosson knew that they carried emergency rations for only 30 days, he wasn't concerned about them going hungry, for they also carried a case each of eggs, bacon, and ham. They also had the extra supplies for the native trader and the supplies Ben had planned to leave at the native village to replace those used by the men when they were stormbound. They also carried a small gasoline stove and other emergency equipment. Both men were experienced Alaskans, and Crosson figured they could exist for months unless they were injured. He also knew that they carried 18 cases of aviation gasoline as well as 160 gallons in the wings.

On December 16, Crosson, Gillam, Ed Young, and Harvey Barnhill hopped off from Teller. After a futile two-hour battle with snowstorms and fog, they were forced to return to their base. In the meantime, Matt Niemenen flew in from Fairbanks to bring repair parts for the Stinson.

On the stormy morning of December 19, Crosson and Gillam loaded the Waco and the Stearman with extra gasoline and provisions to last several weeks. Dressed in fur parkas and mukluks, Crosson and Gillam waved goodbye to the group of men at Teller. Because they did not have radio contact between planes, Crosson ordered Gillam to stay beside him.

Heavy fog rolled up from the Bering Strait, and the winds seemed to blow in 20 directions at once. But, by following dark streaks of open water, the two fliers made it to Siberia. The fog was thinner there, but it was almost dark. They followed the winding banks, searching for a place to land. Finally, Crosson sighted a native village and landed the Waco safely on the ice. Gillam followed, landing in Crosson's ski tracks.

As soon as they landed, a group of Soviet Eskimos, dressed in skin clothing and wearing strange-looking separate hoods, like helmets, came to meet them. Without saying a word, they matter-of-factly helped Crosson and Gillam drain the oil from the planes and cover them. Then the natives led the pilots to their oval-shaped hut, where the village chief greeted them.

Far into the night, Crosson and Gillam conversed with the natives by using sketches and gestures. The chief told them that they were near the south end of Kolyuchin Bay, about half way to the *Nanuk*. He described how he had heard about the lost plane and had seen it fly overhead. His sketch showed that it was flying toward North Cape and the *Nanuk*. Crosson was elated. This was the searchers first real clue. They now knew that Ben and Borland had made it to the Siberian side.

Early the next morning, Crosson and Gillam warmed the engines, refueled their ships, and took off toward North Cape. Shortly after they were airborne, they ran into heavy fog and a howling blizzard. It was so bad that Crosson decided to turn back. He expected Gillam to follow and rocked his wings to signal him. Then Crosson lost sight of Gillam. Visibility was so bad that Crosson couldn't see the ground. He flew blind until he caught a glimpse of a pressure ridge and followed it back to the native village. As he circled to land, his goggles clouded over with frost. He pushed them back so he could see to land. In just a short time he frosted his eyes, adding to the discomfort and danger in the weeks ahead.

The natives gathered quickly when he landed. They helped drain the oil and cover the ship. Again, they motioned Crosson inside the native hut for shelter. Crosson expected Gillam to land at any time, but Gillam did not return.

Now, besides worrying about Ben and Borland, Crosson had no idea where Gillam was. After a restless night, Crosson got up early and prepared the Waco. Once airborne, he searched both sides of the bleak shores for Ben's Hamilton or Gillam's Stearman.

At the end of three hours, he approached the small trading village of North Cape and saw the icebound *Nanuk* and *Stavropol*. There was another dark speck on the ice, too. Crosson was excited. Was it Ben or Gillam? As he drew nearer, he realized that the black speck was too small to be the Hamilton and saw that it was Gillam's plane. At least his search for one of the two planes was over.

Gillam, the novice pilot without a license, had made his way to the *Nanuk*, flying blind part of the distance. He'd used only a compass until the fog lifted enough so that he could get his bearings from the hand-drawn map he carried. Crosson learned that he, too, was reported missing and that Swenson and Gillam had planned a search for him.

The previous day Gillam and Swenson had made a short flight to search for Ben but were hampered by a shortage of fuel. Swenson tried to make arrangements for the American pilots to use 500 gallons of aviation gasoline stored aboard the *Stavropol*. The day after Crosson landed at the *Nanuk*, word came from Moscow granting permission for them to use the gasoline, providing it would be replaced by the time the Russian planes, then on their way to North Cape, arrived to join the search.

An even worse storm struck, and from aboard the *Nanuk* Crosson and Gillam wired: "The weather is bad, visibility poor, and search missions impossible. We have received weather reports from Wrangel Island but we do not understand them and have sent them a message requesting that the reports be sent in English type."

In the Arctic, on the Siberian side, U.S. citizens cooperated with Soviet weather station reporters to get weather reports, but it wasn't until nearly Christmas when U.S. officials cut the red tape and received word from Moscow that Russia would provide the official weather reports that were so desperately needed.

Crosson reported to Lomen that he and Gillam and a group of native workers were building a temporary hangar out of snow blocks near the *Nanuk* to shelter the planes from the storm. The pilots ran the noses of their planes inside the snow house, protecting the engines from wind and cold weather. At that time they had no idea that the bad weather would continue for a month.

Olaf Swenson's daughter, Marion, sent a message to Teller saying that there would be no turkey carving aboard the *Nanuk* on Christmas. Instead, she and the men would dine on borscht, ducks, roast reindeer, and Russian tea with lemon. She added that the Christmas present that would please the passengers and Crosson and Gillam the most would be finding Ben and Borland alive and well.

Since the two days of passable flying weather that had permitted Crosson and Gillam to make their way to the *Nanuk* but had not brought Ben and Borland to the ship, fear for the safety of the lost fliers had increased. Crosson knew that if Ben had been at all able to get his machine back into the air, he would have taken advantage of the short break in the impossible storms that had battered the Arctic. Even Ben's friends in Fairbanks, who had refused to believe that Ben would not be found alive and safe, now admitted that he and Borland must surely be injured and perhaps suffering from exposure.

Back in Seattle, the search expedition experienced some difficulties in getting underway. Government officials offered the use of the Coast Guard cutter *Chelan* to transport the planes to Seward, which would save seven or eight days.

George Montigo was the first pilot to arrive from California at Seattle's Boeing Field in one of the six-passenger Fairchild 71s. Another Fairchild came from Los Angeles, and the third from Montreal, Canada. Slowly but surely, the pilots and the mechanics gathered in Seattle. Finally, all that the expedition was waiting for was spare plane parts from Los Angeles and plane skis from Winnipeg. The Canadian pilots told reporters that they were determined at all hazards to rescue the two lost Americans.

The expedition personnel included several famous Canadian Royal Air Force wartime fliers with thousands of hours of Arctic flying to their credit since the war. There were many other Canadians, all highly qualified to cope with Arctic flying.

The spare engine parts finally arrived from the Pratt and Whitney plant in California, and the skis from Winnipeg. The rest of the Canadians had arrived from Vancouver, but there were two more unbelievable delays.

Eight bottles of Jamaica rum being brought to Seattle in bond from Vancouver when the last two pilots arrived caused one problem. When the fliers received their baggage, six of the bottles of rum were held by custom's officials. Major Deckard was elected to dislodge the rum from customs. He told officials that the rum was intended for consumption in Siberia and for first aid to the missing American fliers should they be found alive. "And that," he added, "is the truth." His efforts to pick up the rum proved successful.

A second delay occurred when a 10-year-old stowaway was discovered asleep in one of the *Chelan's* lifeboats at 3 o'clock on the morning the ship was to leave. It took hours to locate his parents and put him ashore.

Just before sailing, Captain R. W. Dempwolf, of the *Chelan*, received a report that a typical southeaster was brewing in the ship's path. He assured passengers that they would be landed in Seward by Christmas Eve or, by the very latest, Christmas morning. Major

Deckard reported: "We shall have the first plane in the air 24 hours after its arrival in Fairbanks. We have what I believe is the pick of northern fliers, and they will be equipped with planes that can go anywhere."

The first time Ben had been reported lost in Siberia on his return flight from the *Nanuk*, Ole hadn't been worried. However, when word that Ben was lost on the second trip to the *Nanuk* reached Ole, he seemed apprehensive. He told Elma, "Well, I suppose we will have to send for Oliver this time."

Many people were upset that Canadian instead of American pilots and planes were used. Several editorials along that line were printed. One editorial from a Seattle paper concerning the search was entitled "Misdirected Energy." It read in part:

> More than five weeks have passed since Carl Ben Eielson, famous Arctic flier, and his mechanic, Earl Borland, disappeared while on a flight from Teller, Alaska, to the fur ship, *Nanuk*, imprisoned in the ice near North Cape, Siberia. The lack of official concern for the safety of the lost fliers has shocked the public. Only recently has the United States government displayed any interest whatever in the duty of rescuing the men. And now, after much delay, six Canadian fliers have been engaged to undertake the search.

In late December, a cable from Carl Theile, acting governor, to Lomen, at Nome, read: "In accordance with a request from Secretary Wilbur, Department of the Interior, we are authorized to ask for aid from the Russian ice breaker *Litke* and the trading ship *Stavropol* in the search for Eielson and Borland."

Wilbur had also wired: "Am advised Soviet ice breaker *Litke* and perhaps the *Stavropol* are equipped with planes, dog teams, etc. Suggest you radio directly to both vessels asking immediate assistance in Eielson search, particularly by use of dog teams which Stefansson strongly recommends in preference to planes. State Department has no objections."

Crosson sent a report from the *Nanuk* to Lomen, saying that a native musher reported that natives in a reindeer camp had heard Ben's plane circling overhead on November 9 for a long time, looking for a place to land. The natives lived in the vicinity of the *Nanuk*, near the Amguema River.

As news of the reward spread, natives inland and along the coast all became involved in the search. Many reports had gone to officials concerning the plane, but the Soviets considered a report from a native woman at a reindeer camp in the area where the plane was thought to be down the most important clue so far. The woman had first written to her husband and told him that a plane had been heard twice in one day. This tied in with the report that the plane was in the Amguema River area.

On December 23, Lomen received a message from Crosson on the *Nanuk*:

> It is probable that pilots Ed Young and Frank Dorbandt will . . . land someplace between Cape Serdze and Kolyuchin Bay. It is important to get from the natives one or more pokes of seal or walrus oil for mixing with rice for dog food. On our first search we located three reindeer camps about 25 miles into the interior in a mountainous region. It was inland from where Eielson's plane was last heard, but there was no place we could land.

Later that day Lomen wired Seattle:

> If Ben Eielson and Earl Borland aren't found, it won't be because our boys didn't try. Today (December 23) sees the greatest activity since the search began. Our men are determined to find their buddies before the arrival of the expedition from Seattle. They are risking their lives in open cockpit planes in an effort to accomplish the undertaking.

Dorbandt sent Lomen a report from Teller saying that he and Ed Young would both take off for the *Nanuk* with full loads of gasoline, plus food supplies and dog food.

Crosson wired from the *Nanuk* that there were only about 5 hours of daylight each 24 hours. He added that the temperatures at North Cape hovered around 50 degrees below zero.

Crosson and Gillam reported a food shortage aboard the *Nanuk* when they first landed. The ship was completely out of eggs, bacon, and ham and also was short of coffee. Supplies of these items were in the load that Ben carried. Crosson asked that the provisions Ben had aboard be duplicated and sent on the first plane.

From Seattle, R. S. Pollister, resident manager of the Swenson Fur Trading Company, commented that any report of a food shortage was not strictly correct. He told reporters: "Maybe they are out of ham, eggs, bacon, and coffee, but those are delicacies. They still have flour and basic food supplies, and they are always able to get seal and reindeer meat and other game foods."

After that, Crosson said no more about the food shortage but relayed that the Russian ice breaker *Litke* was at Petropolovak on December 15 and that the Junkers planes it had brought had left Providence Bay and would fly to North Cape as soon as the sun came back, about January 10 to 15. He also said that the *Litke* was erecting a short-wave receiving and sending set.

From New York, Stefansson was pleased about the response from Russia. Partly because of his efforts, assurances from Russia were transmitted to the Interior Department through Boris E. Skavorsky, Washington representative of the Soviet Union Information Bureau and also the Soviet newspaper *Tass*.

Senator Borah received a cable saying that the Russian expedition was commanded by Semion Shestikof, the famous Soviet pilot who had recently completed a flight from Moscow to New York. This news was gladly received. Stefansson knew that Shestikof was familiar with the area where Ben and Borland were believed to be down. The two Russian airplanes, located at Providence Bay, were also participating in the search, but there was little hope that they would arrive in North Cape for at least a week.

Newspapers and magazines were filled with articles speculating whether or not the two men were still alive. One of the most down to earth came from Fargo, North Dakota, where William Morris, who had sailed aboard the *Nanuk* in 1926 as a cook, wrote:

> Eielson's chance is a gamble like everything else in that land of snow. I've seen the Arctic at its worst. . . . It's one of the toughest things a man can run up against, this fighting nature herself. Of course, it all comes down to one thing, the condition Eielson was in when his plane came down. If he was able to get to a village of Eskimos, he's as well as if he were at

home. They treat a white man like a king. If that is the case,
we may not hear from him until spring.

On Christmas Day, Dorbandt and Alonzo Cope reached Siberia
but found no traces. Crosson and Gillam made short flights from the
Nanuk then, too, but found no sign of the Hamilton and their
buddies.

When Dorbandt and Cope returned to Teller, they found communications with Nome cut off. Impatient, Dorbandt flew to Nome
to see what caused the disruption. He learned that fire had destroyed
the radio station in Nome on Christmas Day. Lomen instructed
Dorbandt to stand by and wait for the Canadians to arrive in Nome.
Young was instructed to stand by in Teller.

Dorbandt found much activity in Nome preparing for the Canadian planes. Two runways were being made, using three tractors to
level off the snow. It was 40 degrees below zero at the field, with a
stiff wind. When communications were re-established with Teller,
Young suggested to Lomen that the Canadian pilots first search in
the area on the west side of Wrangel Island on the northern coast of
Siberia. He said:

> My theory is that Eielson was trapped above fog along
> the Siberian coast with a north wind blowing, and that he flew
> to sea a short distance. If he did that, the lee or south side of
> Wrangel Island would be plainly visible. Conditions on the
> coast or at Roger's Harbor should be found clear and permit
> a landing. A mishap to the landing gear of Eielson's plane
> would prevent the possibility of taking off, holding them
> until relief finds them.

Completing the fastest, though roughest, trip in years, the
Chelan delivered the three Fairchilds, the crews, and their equipment
to Seward on Christmas Day as predicted. Actual sailing time on the
trip north was 3 days 22 hours. The cutter entered Seward harbor in
a blinding snowstorm, receiving bearings from the Signal Corps on
shore.

The Canadian pilots and mechanics left for Fairbanks at
5:00 P.M., six hours after the *Chelan* arrived in Seward. Gondola cars
were moved to the dock spur near the *Chelan,* and huge cranes lifted

the planes from the snow-covered deck and placed them aboard the train bearing the fliers and the rest of their equipment.

In Fairbanks the pilots and the mechanics received a warm welcome, but new problems arose. Pilot William Broatch quit the expedition several days after the group arrived in Fairbanks. Exactly why he decided to leave was not clear, but the consensus was that he felt that the rescue efforts were too late to do any good.

At Fairbanks, work commenced as soon as the planes arrived. On January 2, Gifford Swartzman and Pat Reid took off from the Fairbanks field, but Swartzman was too heavily loaded and couldn't clear the treetops a short distance beyond the end of the field. He made a forced landing, plowing into the underbrush. The plane was completely demolished; only the engine was salvaged. Swartzman quit the search team.

Everyone was heartsick. Major Deckard wired Lomen, at Nome: "One ship washed out; two leaving in the morning. Will order another six-passenger Fairchild to replace the one Swartzman cracked up."

Lomen wired Deckard requesting an acetylene welding outfit be added to the equipment to be taken to the *Nanuk* by the first plane that made it over.

From the *Nanuk*, Crosson reported that he and Gillam were unable to fly because of poor visibility. On January 4, Lomen said that the search remained at a standstill due to continued unfavorable weather from Fairbanks to North Cape. The Arctic was experiencing the most extreme ice conditions in years. Reid and Niemenen were unable to take off because of heavy snow and poor visibility. With one of the Fairchilds demolished, pilot Swartzman had planned to return to Seattle, but while he was still in Fairbanks another accident happened, and he took a job with Alaskan Airways, Inc.

When the weather finally cleared in Fairbanks, Niemenen and Reid took off for Nome, expecting clear weather all the way. After passing Nulato, they ran into a blizzard just after they had flown about five miles over Norton Bay. It was snowing so hard that Niemenen lost sight of Reid. He spent a half hour in an effort to rejoin Reid, but failed. Then, realizing the storm was such that he couldn't go any farther, Niemenen turned around and went back to Nulato, but Reid didn't follow. Neither did he reach Unalakleet.

Niemenen wired Lomen that Reid was lost. Lomen promptly arranged a search for Reid and his mechanics, Bill Hughes and Jim Hutchison.

The weather at Unalakleet was impossible for flying, as the ceiling was too low for safe flight over the mountains.

When Dorbandt, who had experienced a near nervous breakdown and had requested leave to rest, heard that Reid was missing, he took to the air to search for him, but all efforts to find Reid's plane were in vain. Dorbandt flew for four hours searching for the big Fairchild but was forced down by darkness at Solomen. He called Lomen and reported that there was perfect visibility on his side of the mountain range. He could see all the landmarks as far as Unalakleet. During his search, he'd covered the area around Norton Bay but found no trace of the missing plane.

In Fairbanks, H. S. Oakes and Swartzman tested an Alaskan Airways plane, preparing to take off to look for Reid if the plane was capable. The search for Ben on the Nome and Teller end was stalled until the pilots could discover what had happened to Reid, Hutchison, and Hughes. From Nome, Lomen radioed: "Crosson and Gillam have an almost impossible task in carrying out the Eielson search in the Siberian country without cabin planes."

Another day passed without any word from Reid and his two companions. Lomen wired: "Frankly, we are mystified. If it weren't for Reid's experience as an Arctic flier, his long absence would be alarming. At this point, there is only one plane left of the three sent to Alaska, the one Niemenen has in Nulato."

A report from North Cape sent to Lomen stated that five dog teams from the *Stavropol* had joined the search for Ben. Captain Milozorov went to the *Nanuk* saying that he had received word from Moscow to send out the teams. He also said that Moscow was making elaborate plans to search along the northeastern coast of Siberia. The Russians were certain that Ben and Borland would be found in that area, as natives had heard the plane between Cape Vankarem and Kolyuchin Bay.

Milozorov reported that the five dog teams would have native drivers but that three members of the *Stavropol's* crew would accompany them. There was a shortage of dog food on the *Stavropol*, so the Russians fed their dogs rice mixed with lard. They used lard because they had little seal or whale oil due to the fact that the ice was so thick that year that hunting was too difficult.

Milozorov added that the Russians aboard the *Stavropol* hoped to replenish their dwindling food supplies from stores landed on Providence Bay by the *Litke*, which had provisions for 30 men for seven months. It was a long mush to Providence Bay, but he said that distances in the Arctic were nothing. The question was entirely one of weather conditions. Unfortunately, the dog-team trails weren't very good. The natives reported that it took three days to cover a trail that normally took one.

On January 9, Marion Swenson reported from the *Nanuk* that Tazret Berdieff, driving the ship's dog team, had returned after being held up for several days in a blizzard. He brought what might be the first real clue, or at least brought news that would narrow down the search area from the air. Berdieff said that Ben's plane had flown low over the reindeer camps in the foothills east of the *Nanuk*. The natives told him that one man had heard a plane. The man said that he had not been afraid but that the old women and the children had become frightened and had run into the huts to hide, believing they had heard an evil spirit. Berdieff estimated that the area was about 25 air miles from the *Nanuk*. He said that a second reindeer camp in the foothills confirmed the story. Natives there had also heard the plane.

In Nulato, Niemenen, Major Deckard, and Sam McCauley were waiting for weather to let them continue their search for Reid. Visibility was zero, but the barometer was rising rapidly, indicating that the weather was not settled. Dog teams joined the search for Reid in the vicinity of St. Michaels.

There was much speculation about what had happened to Reid. One thing everyone agreed upon was that Reid had two top mechanics with him. If the Fairchild was damaged in a forced landing, they could repair almost anything and get it back into the air. This faith in the two mechanics and Reid was not misplaced.

Back in the Alaskan wilderness near Unalakleet, where Reid had crashed, he, Hutchison, and Hughes were indeed busy repairing the Fairchild. Landing in a blinding fog that hung close to the ground, Reid had hit a snow-covered stump and crashed, cracking 4 feet of the end of one of the wings. Hutchison and Hughes repaired the broken ribs with baling wire and a wooden frame from a Christmas box. It took more than a week to make the temporary repairs. When the makeshift work was finally completed, Reid flew to Unalakleet and reported in to Lomen. He refueled and waited for favorable weather. When the weather cleared, he took off again for Nome, landing there on January 15. On January 21 a message came that Young and Reid were ready to leave for Teller to join Crosson and Gillam in the search.

In the meantime, the Russians dropped a bombshell on January 17 with an unconfirmed report that Ben and Borland were alive 120 miles southeast of North Cape in the Amguema River district. This caused the north country to erupt in feverish excitement. But a few of Ben's friends, although they desperately wanted to believe the report, had no faith in the Moscow dispatches. Many other people wanted to believe the unconfirmed report, reasoning that if Ben and Borland had shown up at a trapper's cabin, the radio station operator at Tinkignen would have promptly notified Moscow instead of the *Nanuk*.

Lomen advised Crosson of the Moscow report. He added that if the men had been found in the locality reported, they probably would have come out by way of a trapper's cabin at Teagit, at the smaller mouth of the Amguema, 53 miles southeast of the *Nanuk*. He directed Crosson to fly there at the earliest opportunity.

Lomen also reported that pilots Young and Reid were standing by at Nome. Both carried a large amount of gasoline and other supplies for the *Nanuk*, including food to relieve the reported shortage. Lomen also said that Dorbandt had been reassigned to Fairbanks in the Stinson to do commercial flying out of there for Alaskan Airways.

On the *Nanuk*, life went on. Marion Swenson flew with Crosson to see the sun and to search for Ben. The sun had been absent since November 15 and was a happy sight. Below them, on the high bluff of North Cape, a throng of natives gathered, hoping for a glimpse of the sun, too. To them, as to the others, the sight of the sun brought new hope. The natives shouted, jumped, and waved their arms in delight as the horizon lightened.

The January days were now longer and the nights lighter. For the past two days, *Nanuk* passengers had gone for two hours without lighting their lamps. After two months of darkness and lamplight during all their waking hours, everyone was delighted.

Since their first optimistic report, the Russians intensified the search. Additional dog teams and airplanes were ordered from Providence Bay to the position given in the report from Tinkignen. In Seattle, R. S. Pollister told newsmen that the unconfirmed report was plausible. "This," he quoted, "is the locality those of us who have studied the situation had in mind as a likely place where they would be found. There are one or two permanent houses in an area of several hundred miles. That would explain their long absence."

News of the unconfirmed Russian report that Ben and Borland were alive had reached Ole in Hatton, too. Several times during those days, Ole mentioned the possibility that he might make a trip to Alaska and find out about the search firsthand. He said that he might even try to get across the Bering Strait to the *Nanuk* so he could help. "I've always wanted to see Alaska, and this may be my time. I believe I'll make arrangements right away."

ENDNOTE

1. Marvel was the first woman pilot to fly from the Fairbanks field and attracted much attention. Marvel left Alaska and continued flying. She was killed in an air crash at the Women's Air Derby, in Arizona, in August 1929.

33

The Search Ends

SIR HUBERT WILKINS was at Deception Island on November 9, when he heard that Ben and Borland were missing. He received daily radio messages from San Francisco and immediately ordered that every bulletin on the search be sent to him at his Antarctic base. When Ben had changed his mind about going to the Antarctic with Wilkins for the second expedition, he had sent Parker Kramer to Wilkins. Joe Crosson, who stayed with Ben to work for Alaskan Airways, Inc., had recommended Al Chessman. Wilkins had hired both men and had no complaints. Still, Wilkins had grown so used to working with Ben that he missed him and often wished he'd signed on again. Wilkins, who had always been so excited at the prospect of exploration flights over new territory, could scarcely keep his mind on the flights scheduled over the west side of Graham Land. He would not rest until the Russian report was either confirmed or branded false.

From the *Nanuk*, Marion Swenson wired that the Russian report was still not confirmed but that every possible clue was being investigated. On January 10, she sent word that Berdieff, the dog-team driver spending his first winter in the North and assisting in the massive search, became lost from the native driver accompanying him, which almost caused another tragedy. Berdieff was fortunate to find an empty trapper's cabin, but the native spent an agonizing night bedded down in his sleeping bag near his dogs.

The next day, both men broke camp early and headed toward the *Nanuk*. When they arrived, they were hungry and had frostbitten faces. After a cup of hot tea, Berdieff reported that he had some good news. The natives at the reindeer camp had heard and seen Ben's plane on November 9. It flew low over the camp, but they didn't know which direction it was flying. Upon hearing this, Crosson and Gillam planned an immediate search of that area. But 10 more days of bad weather prevented any flying.

On January 20 Reid and Young made the last preparations to take off from Nome for Teller. On January 21, a month to the day after the *Chelan* left Seattle, Reid and Young took off from Nome at 9:30 A.M. Both men carried heavy loads of gasoline, food, and other supplies for the *Nanuk*. They planned to stop only briefly at Teller and then take off again and fly directly to the *Nanuk*.

When the people at Teller first heard the roaring engines of the two big Fairchilds, everyone gathered at the improvised air strip in front of the roadhouse. After Reid and Young landed, they were given a heartwarming reception.

Jack Warren, who had had many trying days since Ben and Borland disappeared on November 9, reported: "Everyone in Teller experienced a feeling of vast relief when those beautiful planes circled the village and the steady roar of their powerful Pratt and Whitney Wasps was heard. For such a hazardous expedition, no better equipment could have been mustered."

Spirits on both sides of the Bering Strait were lifted even higher when a report came from the *Nanuk* that two Russian planes were approaching North Cape. The two Arctic pilots, Mavriki Slepnev and V. L. Galyshev, who were attached to the Soviet ice breaker *Litke*, were flying Junkers planes and were almost at the *Nanuk*. In addition, six other planes, piloted by some of the foremost Arctic airmen of the Soviet Union, were also heading northeast toward the *Nanuk*. Following closely on the waves of that report, the Soviet Air Force announced a second expedition of three planes was being sent to North Cape to assist in the search.

From Nome, the Associated Press reported: "A big aerial drive for Eielson is under way. . . . Airplanes manned by American, Russian, and Canadian aviators are today either moving toward North Cape, Siberia, or poised at various places in Alaska—Nome, Teller, and Fairbanks—awaiting favorable weather to solve the mystery of Eielson's fate." Persistent storms on both sides of the Bering Strait kept all planes grounded.

Stefansson had written earlier: "It's the tradition of exploration not to give up the rescue work so long as there is a reasonable chance."

Based at the *Nanuk* since before Christmas, Crosson and Gillam took off whenever possible in their open-cockpit planes to search. They dug out their drifted planes, warmed the engines in the snow-block hangar, and took to the air in the gloom of the Arctic days. One flew north and the other south, first searching the coastline and then penetrating far inland. The line between hazy sky and snow-covered earth was almost impossible to distinguish. Crosson still suffered from having frosted his eyes.

From the beginning of the search, Crosson and Gillam were drawn toward the region near the mouth of the Amguema River, though this site was more than 60 miles from the *Nanuk*. The site was in the area where a trapper named Brokhanov insisted he'd heard and seen a strange plane. He reported that the plane circled his hut three times, apparently looking for a place to land, and then, judging from the sound of the engine, headed inland.

Both pilots had carefully searched this area many times but found nothing. After they returned from one of their trips there, Crosson told Gillam, "I just have a strange hunch that we'll find them in that area."

On January 22 an editorial about the search reflected the feelings of many:

> Whether his comrades of the air succeed . . . or not, the efforts in that direction again serve to emphasize the courage and faithfulness of that little group of airmen who have written and are now writing some of the most brilliant chapters of American aviation. . . . There are no refuges along the Siberian coast and in the interior of bleak Siberia, save those created by the daring pilot, no landing fields and short distances to succor in the event of a mishap. Such flights entail every hazard encountered in the conquest of poles. Every challenge of nature is accepted and the price of failure is death.

On the morning of January 25, the sun rose low and red on the horizon beyond the *Nanuk*—a welcome, brightening sight. The weather was beautifully clear. Crosson and Gillam took off to check another rumor from a native woman near the region on the Amguema that had haunted them both.

After flying for an hour, Crosson suddenly sighted a suspicious-looking shadow, a minute fleeting signal in the white expanse. Crosson signaled Gillam, then circled. The furtive shadow looked like it might be the underside of a snow-covered wing, standing at about a 45-degree angle. Crosson landed.' Gillam came down beside him.

Seventy-seven days of suspense ended when they recognized their find as the wing of the Hamilton monoplane Ben was flying on November 9. Stunned, the two men stood staring at the strange shadow and then at each other. To them, it looked as if the plane had been traveling at full speed when it hit a small hummock in a lagoon. It appeared that the right wing had hit first and was torn off, causing the plane to cartwheel, breaking the fuselage in two just behind the baggage compartment.

The emotions that gripped the men as they dug in the drifts can only be imagined. They found all the longerons were broken just ahead of the forward cabin bulkhead, which had let the engine shoot ahead 100 feet, ripping out the pilot's cockpit and controls. The main cabin of the plane was intact; the door opened freely. As Crosson pulled it open, a slab of bacon fell at his feet.

The glass on the clock on the instrument board was broken. The clock had stopped at 3:40 P.M., when darkness was already falling. The altimeter hands showed 1,000 feet. The throttle was bent over in a wide-open position. The wreckage was near a small village halfway between Takakokogen and Cape Vankarem, about 90 miles from the *Nanuk*, about 100 miles inland from the coast, and 30 miles west of Cape Vankarem.

There seemed to be no hope that Ben and Borland might still be alive. As far as Crosson and Gillam could tell, the food supply was untouched, which meant that the two were either buried by the cased gasoline or were thrown clear of the plane.

Crosson thought that the accident might have been caused by a faulty altimeter. He advanced the theory that Ben, trusting to the height indicator, believed he was 1,000 feet above the earth when suddenly he saw the hummock ahead and pushed the throttle to full power in a vain attempt to clear it. Normally, the throttle would be partially retarded.

Snow, which had drifted and packed about the wreckage, prevented Crosson and Gillam from finding the bodies. Crosson found that some of the gas cans had broken on impact but that, strangely enough, the case of eggs was intact, not one egg broken.

"I guess Ben overshot the *Nanuk* in the fog and then circled those reindeer camps 25 miles south of the *Nanuk* trying to find a place to land," Crosson said. Gillam, surprised to hear the long-silent Crosson breaking the eerie stillness, merely nodded in agreement. Slowly and methodically, they retrieved the much needed food supplies from the plane. Then they packed several cases of gasoline in their planes and headed for the *Nanuk*.

When those aboard the ship heard the drone of the engines, they ran to meet the planes. Marion Swenson reached Crosson's plane just as he stepped out of the cockpit. He pushed his goggles back wearily and said, "Well, the search is over."

Marion didn't understand the look on Crosson's face. He seemed drained of all feeling. "What's the matter?" she asked.

Crosson didn't answer. Instead, he pointed to the forward cockpit of his plane. Marion peered inside and saw a bundle of crushed metal. Puzzled, she turned and asked, "What is it?," not daring to think they'd found the Hamilton.

"Metal from Ben's plane," Crosson spelled out slowly.

The others came dashing up. Crosson explained that he and Gillam had located the wrecked plane and had landed near it. Then he went back to the Waco and pulled out bacon, ham, a case of eggs, and some coffee. He said abruptly, "From Ben's plane."

Crosson's news spread quickly. Soon the *Nanuk* was filled with people from the *Stavropol* and from the village. Gillam joined in the telling of their discovery. He knew Crosson found it hard to talk. Soon Crosson was busy, making plans to return to the wreck. Swenson arranged for dog teams from the *Nanuk* and the *Stavropol* to go to the wreckage. The trip would take the teams two days if they left early in the morning.

At dinner that evening hardly a word was spoken, and no one had much of an appetite. Later, no one wanted to visit or play cards. All were exhausted by the tremendous nervous strain they had been under, living in the hope that somehow Ben and Borland were safe. Now that hope was gone. After 2½ months of planning, checking rumors, and searching endlessly, the hope had died. The problem now was to call off the widespread search and recover the wreckage and the bodies.

In their written report, requested by the Russians from the village and from the *Stavropol*, Crosson and Gillam specified that the demolished all-metal monoplane was the Hamilton. They added that the engine was of a well-known American make. Crosson noted, "A faulty altimeter upon which Eielson was forced to rely because of poor visibility was the probable cause of the crash."

Crosson wired Lomen, in Nome, and then Ole: "Sorry to inform you found Ben's plane badly wrecked about ninety miles east here. Plane buried in deep snow. Did not locate bodies. Very evident killed instantly. Pilot's cockpit torn away from engine which lies about hundred feet from cabin. Dispatching dog teams to excavate snow around plane. Joe Crosson."

Ole was visiting his daughter Helen in Grand Forks when he heard the tragic news. At first, he was dazed. He asked to have Crosson's telegram read several times. He turned to Helen and said, "I knew it was going to be like that. . . . But I think I'll feel better now; the suspense has been terrible."

When a reporter came to interview him, Ole said, "It is sad to think of Ben being taken in the prime of his career like this. But I think if a man has been able to pack as much into a brief career as Ben did, that is compensation for his not having lived longer."

Ole departed for Fairbanks immediately. In Seattle, he was met by Borland's father, William, and was invited to the Borland home. The two fathers found solace in mutual grief. "We've got to bear up," Ole said sternly. "It's not over yet."

Under Crosson's direction, the searchers established a camp at the site of the wreck. In the hectic days that followed the discovery of the plane, men from three nations congregated at the *Nanuk* and flew supplies to the crew digging through hard-packed snow in search of the bodies.

At Teller, as soon as Reid got news of the wreck, he tuned up his Fairchild and prepared to take off for the *Nanuk*. Young, in the other

Fairchild, accompanied him. Mechanics Hughes and McCauley completed the party.

Crosson's and Gillam's close examination of the wrecked plane and their explanation about the altimeter helped to clear up the lingering mystery in the minds of some as to how an expert pilot such as Ben, with over 60,000 miles of Arctic and Antarctic flying, could have met with a fatal accident in the element he knew so well. "The first warning he had that his altimeter registered incorrectly must have been just before . . . impact as he struck the side of a little hummock with the ship's throttle wide open because he was attempting to lift up over it," Crosson said.

After further discussion, Reid speculated that Ben may have experienced a whiteout, making it impossible to see outside the cabin. "Perhaps no instrument, faulty or otherwise, could have prevented the accident. The weather was responsible for the crash," Reid said.

In Minnesota, Stefansson was lecturing at the university and met with reporters. His plain-spoken interview, as reported to the Associated Press on January 27, 1930, shocked many people:

> Probable death of Carl Ben Eielson was viewed tonight by Vilhjalmur Stefansson as signalling the need of divorcing science from international politics. . . . Lack of weather reports available in Russia and Siberia but NOT available to Eielson because of broken relations between the United States government and the Soviet government forced Eielson and other Alaskan pilots to fly blind. . . . Weather reports from Russia have been made available during the Eielson rescue hunt by special order of the Russian government and some way should be found to continue this scientific data, because aviation is the life blood of Alaska.
>
> The death of Eielson is, in one way of looking at it, the tragic results of political differences. He had to fly without benefit of weather reports which could have been reported to him from Wrangel Island, the Kolma Delta, the ship *Stavropol*, and various other stations which the Russians have located just right for broadcasting the weather of western Alaska and Bering Strait.
>
> Eielson had nothing so much at heart as the progress of northern aviation. Nothing could have gratified him more than to know that part of the result of Secretary Wilbur's and

Senator Borah's appeal to the Soviet government for aid in the search for him has been that, about TWO MONTHS AFTER HE NEEDED THEM, the Russian weather station at Wrangel Island began to send weather reports to Nome. Surely they do not have to cease now!

On January 29, under a gray sky with a chill wind blowing, Ole Eielson started for Seward on the steamer *Northwestern*. Just before the ship pulled out, Ole told Borland's father, "I'll keep in touch. . . . The only thing left is to find the bodies."

The day before, Seattle reporters had headlined Ole's trip north: "TWO NORTH DAKOTANS TO SAIL NORTH ON WIDELY DIFFERENT MISSIONS." The article continued:

> Arthur Johnson, of Jamestown, North Dakota, who will be succeeding Carl Ben Eielson as resident manager of Alaskan Airways, Inc., a subsidiary of The Aviation Corporation, will be responsible for the completion of the contract in the performance of which Eielson is believed to have lost his life. . . . Ole Eielson, . . . is sailing on the same ship in hopes that his son's body will be found. . . . To the offer to provide a military funeral and burial at Arlington Cemetery in Washington, D.C., for his famous son, Ole Eielson said, "There are many persons buried at Arlington. Ben knew everybody at home, and I'd like to have the boy rest with his mother and brother at the little cemetery in Hatton. I think he'd rather be there, and after all, what is fame?"

34

Ben's Last Flight

ON JANUARY 30, Marion Swenson, on the *Nanuk*, wrote:

> Where are the bodies of Eielson and Borland? The North
> Country refuses to tell. . . . Five days ago, the wreck of the
> plane was found. . . . Since that time, a crew of four men has
> worked ceaselessly in an effort to find the bodies . . . in the
> hard packed snow covering the wreckage.

While the crews hunted with picks and shovels, newspapers
everywhere paid tribute to Ben. The sorrow and suspense were wearing on everyone.[1] But still the work of finding the bodies, which
would mean the final acceptance of the loss of Ben and Borland,
dragged on. Then, news came from the ship that Borland's helmet
had been found, together with his broken goggles and his mittens.
This followed the finding of tools and seat cushions from the plane,
all widely scattered.

Fifteen men from the *Stavropol* went to assist with the digging.
It was a slow job. Extra housing was needed; the first men had made
headquarters at the cabin of Brokhanov, the trapper who lived about
six miles from the wreckage.

Next, Crosson wired Lomen about his concern over the shortage
of gasoline. He said that he didn't know how many more flights
could be made to supply the workers at the site. Six planes, flying
almost constantly, had eaten rapidly into the gas stockpile. Crosson,
Gillam, Reid, Young, and the two Russian pilots all had been flying
missions whenever the weather permitted. In a report to Nome,
Marion Swenson noted that Brokhanov was helping the men in any

way he could. She commented that it seemed ironic that help had been so near when Ben and Borland crashed.

Seattle used that report to make headlines: "HELP NEAR WHEN EIELSON'S PLANE CRASHED." The article continued:

> The wreckage is reported to be within a stone's throw, as distances go in the north, of a trapper's cabin, indicating that Eielson and Borland could not have escaped alive. . . . Sunless days, plus the fact that the trapper was engaged in attending to his trap lines along the coast and near the ice pressure ridges, accounted for the fact he'd seen nothing suspicious, although he did report hearing the plane circle three times on November 9. . . . [T]he presence of the nearby cabin seems to dissipate the theory . . . that the men may have escaped uninjured and left the plane to seek refuge.

Crosson reported to Lomen from the site of the wreckage that when Ben and Borland left Teller, they had been carrying 18 cases of gasoline. Only seven were so far accounted for. The rest had been completely lost when the force of the impact squashed the cans or shot them out of the rear cabin when the cockpit and the tail of the plane had broken off. The diggers had found more tools, parts of the engine, the batteries, provisions—everything, in fact, except the missing gasoline and the bodies of the two men.

Digging trenches through 4 feet of hard-packed snow, the men searched the area where the right wing and the engine were found. But Brokhanov encouraged them to dig in a different direction because of the location of wolf tracks. He said that the airplane lay on a sloping mound, deep in drifts.

The Soviet crew doing the digging was under the direction of pilot Commander Slepnev, who instructed Kalinen, one of the Soviet workers, to keep a daily log. On February 5, the Hamilton's engine base, stained with blood, was located about 50 feet from the plane. The tired men felt that their efforts that day had been worthwhile.

Like motorists lending one another a hand on a lonely country road, the Russians assisting with the prolonged search maintained relationships that were friendly and informal with the Americans and with Reid, the Canadian pilot.

The Russians from the *Stavropol* had the hardest work of all. The crew had labored steadily for over a week in below-zero weather, hacking trenches through deep snowdrifts packed as hard as concrete.

On February 12, Crosson flew to the wreckage with supplies. When he departed, he took two natives back with him. His wire that day read:

> I made a trip to the wreckage today. The Russians are still working hard and expect to find the bodies soon. They will have all wreckage dug out within three days. It is believed they will find the bodies near where the ship hit, which must have been several hundred feet from where the cabin is now. They have cleared all the snow from the cabin and the engine and are going in the direction the plane first struck. They are now about 300 feet. Today, they found Eielson's helmet and part of the cockpit.

Lomen wired back: "Pat Reid and mechanic Bill Hughes took off in a Fairchild for Cape Serdze this morning with 18 cases of gasoline for the Russians. Reid will attempt to make the trip to Cape Serdze and back to Teller today, weather permitting."

Most of the men in the digging crew had traveled by dog team each day from Brokhanov's crowded cabin to the site of the wreck. When the weather moderated, they spent the night in tents at the wreck.

On February 12, Kalinen recorded in his log book: "Last night was the first time we slept in the snow on the open tundra under the light of the moon, by the wreck of the plane. Joe Crosson arrived this morning with provisions. He departed this afternoon, taking two natives back with him. Brokhanov found another pair of mittens, probably Eielson's."

On the morning of February 13, the diggers were up at 7:30. They went to work as soon as they had had tea. After several hours of digging, they found Borland's body lying face down, head toward the wreck, clothed in parka and mukluks. The parka had been turned over his head by the wind. Darkness fell before the workers were able to get the body completely free. That night, Kalinen recorded: "The natives did their work today. It was T. Jakobson who was the first to find the body."

On the morning of February 14, an all-day blizzard hit. Visibility was about 15 feet, almost impossible for the crew, so they gave up and went to the tents. After some discussion, four men left for Brokhanov's cabin for provisions and dog food. There was a shortage of both at the wreckage site. When the men returned, Slepnev and his mechanic, Fabrio Fahrig, ordered the provisions brought back from the cabin carried into the tents. The rest of the crew was put to work cutting snow blocks for a better windbreak for the Junkers 177, located about 350 feet from the tents. Snow was already drifted to the top of the plane on one side. The temperature had dropped to 20 degrees below zero, making it miserable for the block cutters.

The two tents housing part of the crew were pitched close together. One was 10 × 12 feet, and the other 8 × 10 feet. Most of the workers returned to Brokhanov's cabin for the night when they could; only four remained at the tents. Even though the cabin was crowded, it was much warmer than the tents.

When the men awoke on February 15, they found their tent flaps frozen shut, the canvas sagging from the weight of heavy snow that had fallen during the night. They had to dig their way out, which took until 9:00 A.M. Outside, the storm appeared to be at its height. By afternoon, the temperature was a little warmer—10 degrees below zero. Visibility was zero. It was so cold in the tents that when the men stopped for a break, they chilled their fingers on the tin cups while getting hot tea. The tents were warmed with both a wood stove and a Primus stove. The wood was hauled from Brokhanov's cabin.

During the afternoon, the tents collapsed under the new snow and had to be braced up in several sections. When the men finished, they ate and then went for more wood, which was stored by the Junkers plane. Stakes were driven into the ground to mark the 350 feet between their tents and the plane, but still the men lost their way. It took them quite some time to return to the tents to warm up. They succeeded in getting the wood on their second try.

The weather was still below zero and looked as if it would stay that way. Kroskov was sent by dog team to get another load of wood from Brokhanov, but the workers knew that he would be unable to get back until the next morning.

On February 16, when the men awoke at daybreak, the storm still raged. New snow piled in large drifts around the tents, and once again the men had to dig their way out. When the wind died down a little, Kroskov arrived from Brokhanov's cabin with a load of much-needed firewood. Later, one of the other men in the crew arrived by dog team for work. By then, Slepnev decided that there would be no digging that day, so some of the men returned to the trapper's cabin. Before they left, Slepnev told them that if the weather was favorable, they should return to work early the next morning.

On February 17, the men in the tents got up at 7:00 A.M., but a sharp wind with ground drifts made it useless to start work. While they were still eating breakfast, they heard the screeching of sled runners and the barking of dogs as five Russian sailors from the *Stavropol* and a Chukchi native arrived from Brokhanov's cabin.

When the wind stopped blowing, the men went back to digging around the left wing of the wrecked Hamilton. The recent blizzard had made the drifts twice as high as when they'd first found Borland's body. Now, it would take much more time and effort to recover it.

Around noon, Dazrov, a Russian, arrived at the *Nanuk* with a dog team loaded with provisions, gasoline, and a sail from the *Stavropol*. At 12:30 P.M., Gillam and Brednevya landed near the wrecked plane with more provisions. As he stepped away from the plane, Gillam saw the men lifting Borland's body out of the snow. Gillam looked quickly, then turned and walked swiftly back to his plane, where he leaned against the cabin door, trying to compose himself. Then he opened the door and began unloading the provisions, working so fast that he broke into a sweat in the chilly air.

The Russians carried Borland's body to the Junkers plane. Fahrig, Brokhanov, Jakobson, and Kosteakov carefully wrapped it in a tent, and Slepnev helped place the body in the Junkers. Slepnev locked the cabin of the plane and walked over to Gillam. Gillam, still shaken from the shock of seeing Borland's body, said, "Well, I should have been prepared, . . . but . . . well, anyway, . . . we appreciate all the work you're doing." Gillam turned. He didn't think Slepnev really knew how much he appreciated the work the men were doing under such trying conditions, but he just couldn't say any more.

About 3:00 P.M., Gillam and Brednevya returned to the *Nanuk* to relay the news. At 7:00 P.M. the sled crews departed for Brokhanov's cabin. Slepnev, Fahrig, Dubrovin, Platov, and Kostenko remained in the tents. They didn't envy Gillam his job of reporting the latest news.

As soon as Gillam circled the *Nanuk*, Crosson rushed out to the ice. He could tell by Gillam's expression as the flyer climbed out of the plane that one or both of the bodies had been found. Gillam said, "It's Earl. The team found his body several days ago, . . . but with the storm . . . well, they just recovered the body today. . . . No sign of Ben's body yet. But they are expecting to locate it any time. If they don't find Ben's body soon, I'm going to try to get permission to join them."

"Yes," Crosson said. "I feel the same way, but there are certain procedures we must follow." He looked away, then added, "First, we've got to send some telegrams."

On February 18, after a difficult night in the tents, the workers got up at 8:00 A.M. Shortly after they finished breakfast, the other workers arrived by dog team. They started digging in the front trench to the left of the plane. It was hard going.

About 2:00 P.M., Jakobson suddenly stopped. He had discovered Ben's body, lying in his parka, his head pointed away from the plane, his face downward. His left hand and arm were beneath his heart and his right arm stretched forward. His face was the same as that of Borland, a frozen mass of blood.

When Jakobson stopped, the other men stopped, too, and rushed over. The men worked late that day. Finally, the body was wrapped and stored, joining Borland's in the Junkers.

Ben's body was found 120 feet from the wreck, a little farther away and to the left of where Borland's body was found. Long after darkness settled, the workers ate supper. Finding Ben's body was a relief to everyone. It meant that the wearisome, nerve-straining search was over. That night, Kalinen wrote in his diary: "It was decided that most of us will leave tomorrow. Some by dog team and some by plane. Those to remain with the last sleds are Dubrovin, Scheakov, and Jakobson."

On February 19, the temperature was minus 30 degrees, with a brisk northwest wind. The men in the tents had early tea and breakfast. They loaded the dog sleds, preparing for departure. Fahrig, the mechanic, worked on the Junkers. After much tedious work, he found that water had frozen in the fuel lines. In the meantime, another severe snowstorm had started. Snow was already drifting in piles around the sleds and the plane. It was decided to abandon further efforts until the storm abated.

The men drained the water from the plane's radiator and ran for shelter. Toward evening, the weather improved and three dog teams left for Brokhanov's cabin. While sitting in one of the tents warming water on the Primus stove for the plane, Dubrovin talked about plans for the next day.

On February 20, Dubrovin fired up the stove in the tent and went back to bed for a short time. Later, he got up and prepared water for tea. The men were instructed by Fahrig to have the plane warmed in two hours. They started work on the plane by pouring hot water into the lines.

Fahrig was still warming the Junkers when Gillam landed. Gillam announced that if Ben's body hadn't been found yet, he wanted permission to help the diggers. When he was informed that the body was in the plane, Gillam asked if he could look at the remains of his friend.

The men led him to the Junkers, explaining that Ben's body was wrapped in a tent and stored inside the cabin along with Borland's. Gillam climbed into the cabin and stood silently looking at Ben's remains. None of the Russians said a word. They knew what a tremendous loss the deaths of Ben and Borland were for their American friends.

Gillam slowly left the plane and walked to where the men were working. Fahrig and Dubrovin were giving the Junkers its final check. They'd just discovered the flow line to the carburetor was not sufficient, so they were working to thaw the lines again. But the Junkers wouldn't start. Gillam got out his blowtorch. He showed Fahrig how to operate it and left it with him.

About 2:00 P.M., after many fruitless attempts to start the plane, Slepnev decided to leave with Gillam so he could officially report the finding of Ben's body. Fahrig was still working on the Junkers but about to give up for the day. When Fahrig finally quit, Kostenko was left in charge of the men who remained in the tents. He was instructed to cover the engine and keep the fire pot going.

A short time later, Fahrig, with a disgusted look on his face, was just leaving his tent after a cup of tea. He glanced toward the plane

The *Nanuk* frozen in at North Cape, Siberia, 1929–30. (Upper photo: Joe Crosson Collection, U. of Alaska. Lower photo: HEM)

The Hamilton used by Eielson and Borland on the fatal flight, November 1929. (George "Ed" Young Collection, U. of Alaska)

Earl Borland, mechanic/copilot for Eielson on the fatal flight. (George King Photo Collection, U. of Alaska)

Joe Crosson by one of the planes used in the 1929–30 search. (HEM)

Commander Mavriki Slepnev, leader of the Russian search party, January 1930. (HEM)

Crosson under the wing of the Hamilton on the day the plane was located, January 25, 1930. (HEM)

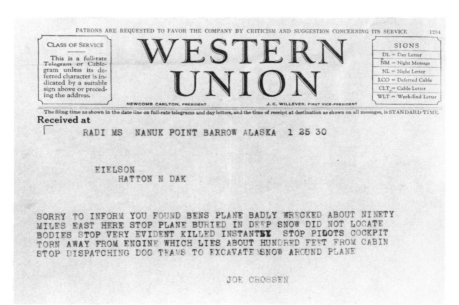

Received at

RADI MS NANUK POINT BARROW ALASKA 1 25 30

EIELSON
   HATTON N DAK

SORRY TO INFORM YOU FOUND BENS PLANE BADLY WRECKED ABOUT NINETY
MILES EAST HERE STOP PLANE BURIED IN DEEP SNOW DID NOT LOCATE
BODIES STOP VERY EVIDENT KILLED INSTANTLY STOP PILOTS COCKPIT
TORN AWAY FROM ENGINE WHICH LIES ABOUT HUNDRED FEET FROM CABIN
STOP DISPATCHING DOG TEAMS TO EXCAVATE SNOW AROUND PLANE

JOE CROSSEN

Wire from Joe Crosson on the *Nanuk* to Ole Eielson upon discovery of the wrecked plane, January 25, 1930. (HEM)

Russians digging around the wrecked plane in 4-foot-deep snow in search of bodies. (HEM)

Russians digging in snow, searching for bodies and plane parts. The Xs mark approximate spots where the bodies were. (HEM)

Russian and American planes at North Cape, Siberia, February 1930. Photo taken by Russians. (HEM)

Shelter made by search crew under the wing of a Junkers plane. (HEM)

Members of Russian search party from the *Stavropol* resting in a tent at the wreck site. (HEM)

WESTERN UNION

CLASS OF SERVICE

This is a full-rate Telegram or Cablegram unless its deferred character is indicated by a suitable sign above or preceding the address.

NEWCOMB CARLTON, PRESIDENT   J. C. WILLEVER, FIRST VICE-PRESIDENT

SIGNS

DL = Day Letter
NM = Night Message
NL = Night Letter
LCO = Deferred Cable
NLT = Cable Night Letter
WLT = Week-End Letter

The filing time as shown in the date line on full-rate telegrams and day letters, and the time of receipt at destination as shown on all messages, is STANDARD TIME.

Received at 113 Cherry St., Seattle, Wash. ALWAYS OPEN

1930 JAN 31 AM 6 59

MB31 182 NL 6 EXTRA 1/142 =

MS NANUK PORTBARROW ALASKA 30 VIA FARGO NDAK=

OLE EIELSON=FRYE HOTEL SEATTLE WASH=

VERY DIFFICULT UNCOVER WRECK STOP HAVE SEVEN MEN AT WORK STOP
OWING DISTANCE FROM HERE LACK DOG TEAMS AND SHORTAGE GAS HERE
IMPOSSIBLE WORK FASTER STOP PLANE VERY SCATTERED SNOW ABOUT
FOUR FEET DEEP AND HARD SLOW WORK STOP BELIEVE IT IMPOSSIBLE
THEY COULD HAVE ESCAPED ALIVE PERSONAL EFFECTS AND CARGO IN
PLANE UNTOUCHED SINCE CRASH STOP FOUND PILOTS SEAT CONSIDERAB
DISTANCE FROM CABIN BADLY CRUSHED STOP ALSO FOUND BORLAND

Wire from Joe Crosson on the *Nanuk* to Ole Eielson describing the wreck of Ben's plane, January 31, 1930. (HEM)

THE WHITE HOUSE
WASHINGTON

February 6, 1930.

Mr. Ole Eielson,
Hatton, North Dakota.

My dear Mr. Eielson:

My profound sympathy goes out to you and your family in the loss of your son. The memory of his fine character and high courage should be a continuing consolation to you.

Yours faithfully,

Herbert Hoover

Letter from President Hoover to Ole Eielson, February 6, 1930. (HEM)

SIGNAL CORPS, UNITED STATES ARMY
WASHINGTON-ALASKA MILITARY CABLE AND TELEGRAPH SYSTEM
TELEGRAM

RECEIVED AT

FB
2 ** R   31 RADIO   VIA PTBARROW

MS NANUK FEB 19 1930 5 PM

OLE EIELSON

FAIRBANKS

BENS BODY FOUND EIGHTEENTH UNABLE GET INFORMATION

SOONER STOP WAS KILLED INSTANTLY STOP BODIES WILL BE BROUGHT

NORTHCAPE TOMORROW AND TAKEN THROUGH FAIRBANKS SOON AS POSSIBLE

JOE CROSSON

917PM

Military cable from Joe Crosson to Ole Eielson, telling him Ben's body had been found, February 19, 1930. (HEM)

Bodies of Ben and Earl Borland draped in flags made by Russian women at North Cape prior to the release of the corpses by the Russians. (HEM)

Marion and Olaf Swenson,
North Cape, March 1930. (HEM)

On the steps of Old Main at the University of Alaska, Fairbanks, at the memorial service for Ben and Borland, March 12, 1930. L–R, front: Peter W. Nicholoff, Joe Crosson, Matt Niemenen, Mavriki Slepnev, Pat Reid, Bill Hughes, Fabrio Fahrig, Sam McCauley. L–R, back: Harold Gillam; Dr. Frank de la Vargne, mayor of Fairbanks; Charles Bunnell, president the University of Alaska; Otto Wm. Geist. (HEM)

Marie Banks, who, according to Mrs. Joe Crosson, was the school teacher Ben courted, and Ole Eielson, at Fairbanks, March 1930, during memorial services there. (HEM)

Estimated crowd of 5,000 at Ben's funeral, St. John's Lutheran Church, Hatton, North Dakota, March 27, 1930. (HEM)

and yelled, "FIRE!" Dubrovin ran to help. Hearing the alarm, the rest of the men came stumbling out of the tents. All hands helped put out the blaze. Then the oil was drained, a new tent put in place, and the Primus stove put under the hood. The radiator was drained, and the entire crew went back to the tents. They were thankful Slepnev had left with Gillam and hadn't seen the blaze.

By the time the men finished their evening meal, the temperature was 35 degrees below zero. A sharp northerly wind was blowing, and they decided to remove the Primus stove from under the tent hood. The exhausted men planned to get up early the next morning and have the plane heated by the time Slepnev returned in Gillam's plane.

When Gillam landed near the *Nanuk*, Crosson ran out to meet him. When Crosson saw Slepnev in the plane, he knew something was up. He looked at Gillam closely; Gillam looked ill.

"What happened?" Crosson asked.

"They found Ben's body . . . five days after they found Earl's body," Gillam said. "The last thing Ben heard was the roar of the engine, a sound he . . . I don't think he suffered. He must have been killed instantly. Earl, too."

"Well," Crosson said, "let's get this plane taken care of. Then we'll have to make our report. After I wire Lomen, I must send a telegram to Ben's father in Fairbanks. It's a good thing some of Ben's friends have taken him under their wing."

Slepnev had been standing by, silent. Crosson turned to him and said, "Looks like the dog team from the *Stavropol* is coming this way. Do you want to hitch a ride back with them?"

Slepnev looked in the direction Crosson pointed. At times, even though the Russians and the Americans couldn't completely understand each other, they talked just the same. "Let's have some tea first," Crosson added.

One of the *Nanuk* passengers who could speak Russian told Crosson that Slepnev would return to the *Stavropol* with the dog team so that he could make his official reports. "If the weather's better," Crosson said, "Gillam will be leaving first thing in the morning." The Russian-speaking *Nanuk* passenger relayed the message to Slepnev. The Russian pilot nodded and shook hands with Crosson and with Gillam.

"I'd better take another blowtorch with me," Gillam said shortly. "The men were having trouble getting the Junkers started. I left mine there."

When Ole had arrived in Fairbanks on February 14, he had been met at the depot by a large group of Ben's friends. After the greetings were over, Ole had said, "I'm beginning to find out why my son loved Alaska so much. Everyone has been most kind to me. But now, I'd like to check into the hotel and then take care of my son's personal belongings." Ben's friends realized that everything would be just as Ben had left it early in November when he'd left for Teller, so excited about the trip to the *Nanuk*.

Several telegrams from Hatton and one from the White House were at the hotel when Ole arrived. The one from the President read: "My dear Mr. Eielson: My profound sympathy goes out to you and your family in the loss of your son. The memory of his fine character and high courage should be a continuing consolation to you. Yours faithfully, Herbert Hoover."

At 5:00 P.M. on February 19, 1930, Ole received a telegram from the *Nanuk*. It read: "Ben's body found eighteenth. Unable to get information sooner. Was killed instantly. Bodies will be brought North Cape tomorrow and taken through Fairbanks soon as possible." It was signed simply, "Joe Crosson."

But still more and more delays were in store. The weather at North Cape had turned bad again. The crew at the site of the wreck had been having the worst of it. When they got up on February 21 they found the tent flaps frozen shut again. Much new snow had fallen, and they had to dig their way out. After more shoveling, they reached the Junkers and began warming the engine. With the help of the blowtorch left by Gillam, Fahrig finally started the engine about 12:30 P.M. But snow was still falling, and the weather was miserable. Fahrig shut the engine down and waited for Slepnev and Gillam. When Gillam hadn't arrived by 3:00 P.M. the workers drained the oil and the radiator and put the tent over the engine again.

On February 22, the men at the tents repeated the activity of the day before. Still Gillam and Slepnev didn't arrive. The weather turned bitterly cold, with the temperature dipping to 50 degrees below zero that night.

On February 23, the men repeated the procedure with the Junkers and waited. The weather moderated some, but visibility was still bad. About 10:00 A.M., Jakobson and three Chukchi natives arrived from Brokhanov's cabin. At noon, Gillam landed. Then, with Slepnev at the controls, Fahrig made the final check to get the Junkers airborne.

When the other workers saw that Slepnev was about to take off, they returned to the tents for hot tea prior to dismantling their tents and preparing the dog team to leave for Brokhanov's cabin and then for the *Stavropol*. Jerdyn and Kostenko planned to fly back with Gillam. Fahrig was going with Slepnev.

Before Slepnev could take off and while the others were still in the tents, the men heard the roar of another plane. It was Pat Reid in a Fairchild. Because of poor visibility, he landed among the snowdrifts and damaged one ski. He swerved sharply and broke out the window on the left side of the cabin.

Reid jumped out, uninjured, and called, "Let's drain the oil and barricade the plane against the wind."

The men ran to assist him in repairing the window, and Reid packed his belongings into Gillam's plane. Slepnev told Jerdyn and Kostenko to watch Reid's plane. When all was secure, Reid, Slepnev, and Gillam headed for the tents.

Once inside, Reid handed Slepnev a telegram from the U.S. government requesting Reid to bring the bodies of Ben and Borland back to Alaska, accompanied by the Russian plane. Slepnev thanked him, adding that he had to first deliver the bodies to the *Stavropol* so that they could be examined by the doctor to complete the official reports.

While repairs were being made on the Fairchild, the other planes were again made ready. When all was set, Slepnev, Gillam, and Reid prepared to take off. Slepnev gave the Junkers full throttle, but only with great difficulty was he able to get airborne with his heavy load. Gillam followed in his tracks. Reid went behind Gillam.

When the Junkers 177 landed near the *Nanuk*, which had its flags flying at half-mast, there was a large group of people from the village and from the *Stavropol* standing in a solemn circle to meet the plane. Off in the distance, the flag of the *Stavropol* was also at half-mast. Three dog teams from the *Stavropol* were pulled to the landing site. Everyone gathered around the Junkers.

Slepnev directed the men who began unloading the bodies and placing them on the dog sleds so that they could be taken to the *Stavropol*, where Dr. M. V. Kreszanev could examine them. When the procession reached the ship, the captain and Dr. Kreszanev stood at attention and saluted as the bodies were carried aboard. The *Nanuk* passengers and the people from the village either left by dog team or walked back to the *Nanuk* in silence.

By February 24, the bodies had thawed sufficiently so that they could be thoroughly examined by the doctor. It was already manifest that the shock of the crash had brought instantaneous death to both men. After the examinations, the bodies were sewed in white drill cloth. Siberian women from the village had painstakingly made American flags, improvised by sewing strips of red, white, and blue muslin to squares of white ship's canvas.

On February 28, the weather cleared slightly. A final salute was paid to Ben and Borland while their bodies were placed on the sleds for the trip to the *Nanuk*. The men from the *Stavropol* followed the procession in solemn double file.

After the procession came alongside the Fairchild plane, Captain Komorovsky and Slepnev, on behalf of the Russian Relief Expedition, presented the bodies to Crosson, Gillam, and Young. The chairman of the Cuckolsk district, who had traveled more than 400 miles by dog team to be present at the ceremony, expressed his sorrow that the tragic loss had occurred on Soviet soil. On behalf of the U.S. government, Crosson, Young, and Gillam expressed thanks for Soviet aid.

With the Russians and the Americans standing at attention, the bodies were placed in the Fairchild, the windows shrouded in black. "Well," Gillam said, "Ben's finally ready for his last flight." He turned and walked away. Crosson followed.

When Crosson boarded the *Nanuk*, Marion Swenson handed him a message from Lomen in Nome. Lomen advised that plans to receive the international aerial funeral procession, which would bring the bodies of Alaska's air hero and his mechanic to Nome following the 500-mile flight from North Cape, Siberia, were underway.

Lomen asked the American pilots to accompany the Canadian pilot, Pat Reid. He said that the Russian pilots, Slepnev and Galyshev, and mechanic Fahrig, had been granted permission by the U.S. government to land in Alaska. But while the pilots made final preparations, another storm hit North Cape and caused over a week's delay before the funeral plane and the American and the Soviet escort planes could leave North Cape.

The first stop for the funeral squadron was at Teller, where the residents had played such an important part during the lengthy search. The minister from the Lutheran mission, a good friend of Ben, led the touching tribute to Ben and Borland.

The aerial funeral squadron then proceeded to Nome. Lomen had instructed that the plane carrying the bodies circle the courthouse, which would be a signal for the fire siren to blow, notifying the townspeople of the arrival of the funeral squadron. There, the tribute was under the direction of Thomas Alfred Ross Post No. 9 of the American Legion. Nome residents had not forgotten that Ben had blazed many air trails in Alaska and that his mechanic, Earl Borland, had hoped to follow in his footsteps.

The next stop was Ruby, where nearly everyone in town gathered. Ruby residents had been very air-minded ever since Noel Wien had landed the big Fokker there on an inadequate field. For Ruby residents, their days of relative isolation were over as Ruby became a scheduled stop on the Alaskan Airways route to Nome.

Finally, on March 7, 1930, the last flight of Ben and Borland ended when the planes escorting their bodies circled over Fairbanks. The black-shrouded Fairchild cabin plane, piloted by Young, accompanied by Crosson and the Canadian mechanic Sam McCauley, was the first to touch the ground. The Russian plane, carrying Slepnev and Fahrig, touched down seconds later. Gillam landed next, followed by Reid in the other Fairchild, accompanied by mechanic William Hughes.

Johnson, the new manager of Alaskan Airways, Ben's replacement, started out to greet the flyers but halted so that Ole could precede him. Ole embraced Crosson and then Gillam, the two bush pilots who had found his son. Ole stepped back, and Irene Borland paid her respects. Ole shook hands with Young, Reid, the Canadian mechanics, and then the Russians.

Fairbanks paid its last tribute to Carl Ben Eielson and Earl Borland on March 12, 1930. Short, but impressive, memorial services in the Moose Auditorium were conducted jointly by Dorman H. Baker

Post No. 11 of the American Legion and the Pioneers of Alaska. After the services, Legionnaires escorted the bodies to the Legion Hall, where they remained until the train was ready to depart the next morning. A guard of Legionnaires was on duty throughout the night.

Ole was surprised at the number of memorial services scheduled throughout Alaska. Even in Barrow, a memorial service was held. The people there remembered that Ben had made trail-blazing flights and that he and Wilkins had established their first wireless connection with the world outside.

Even in death, Ben was a pioneer. To the men who participated in his search, Soviet-American friendship created by the expedition was an unusual experience. The exchange of messages between Moscow and Washington at the time of the search was probably the first official communication involving friendly cooperation between the two nations.

As the expedition proceeded to disband, the following message was sent to Moscow: "On behalf of our government we express our sincerest thanks and appreciation for sympathy and cooperation of your government. Our loss is mutual. Our lost friends were world characters. They climbed fame's ladder and mounted to the skies."

Slepnev and Fahrig were excited and proud when permission was granted for them to travel to the United States representing the Soviet Union. One of the ironies of the memorial service at Fairbanks was that Mayor Frank de la Vergne, as a practicing physician in Petrograd, had visited the Fahrig home and had met their small son. Now, before him in Fairbanks was Fabrio Fahrig, the mechanic on the Russian Junkers, which had played such a leading role in the search for the missing fliers.

During the search, Alaskans learned a new meaning of international relations. Before Ole left Fairbanks, a notable group of aviators from the search crew, representing Canada, Russia, and the United States, gathered at the University of Alaska for a special ceremony. During the informal reception following the speeches, one Fairbanks resident remarked that one reason the Canadians and the Russians thought so highly of Ben was that pilots from those countries had greater assistance from their governments and their planes were superior to American aircraft. In Alaska, Ben was almost alone in pioneering Arctic flying.

Ben was 32 years 4 months of age at the time of his death. Earl Borland was almost 30.

A letter in the *News-Miner* from the Fairbanks City Council addressed to Ole Eielson, read:

> With profound sorrow, the members of the Fairbanks City Council individually, and for the people of Fairbanks, offer to you and your family heartfelt condolence with the grief which is yours. The passing of Colonel Ben Eielson comes as a distinct loss to our community and leaves therein a vacancy which we deplore. . . .
>
> Even though taken from our midst, he must remain the teacher, for can we not, inspired by the memory of his life, and the glory of his accomplishments, still learn wonderful lessons of modesty, of moral and physical courage, of clean living, manliness, and of devotion to duty with a loyalty to friends and co-workers, which is not surpassed in the histories of the world's greatest men.

ENDNOTE

1. In Seward, Editor Jessen vented his sorrow in an editorial headlined "A VIKING SPIRIT RELEASED":

> Without wresting one leaf from the laurels won by his compeers of the air lanes, Colonel Eielson may be said to have contributed more to utilitarian air travel than any man since the pioneer days of aviation. He was indeed a pioneer of a distinctive field, that of proving that the airplane was suitable to the work of penetrating trackless reaches, including the Arctic with its low temperatures and multiple hazards. . . . Colonel Eielson and his courageous aides have emblazoned their names imperishable upon the history of Alaska. . . . They occupy a position that time cannot eradicate.

35

Final Tributes

THE FUNERAL CORTEGE planned for Ben in Seattle was the most impress-ive yet mustered to honor the valorous dead. The procession included units of the Seattle Police Department, followed by military and Legion units, North Dakota Guard units, the Russian and the Cana-dian pilots, Olaf Swenson and daughter Marion, the Alaska-Yukon Pioneers, and the Sons of Norway, with heads of various other groups bringing up the rear.

The funeral committee asked that all Seattle be notified of the arrival of the funeral ship Saturday night by the blowing of the *Seattle Times* whistle. Immediately following, the city observed a minute of silence in honor of the two men. Because the ship arrived after sunset, a planned 21-gun salute was canceled.

Ole had been touched and somewhat amazed by the outpouring of grief in all parts of Alaska. After the funeral ship reached Seattle, he was stunned by the tremendous crowds paying homage to Ben and his mechanic.

Following last rites for Ben and Borland at Butterworth's Mortu-ary chapel, Borland was laid to rest in the Acacia Mausoleum, with the Alaska-Yukon Pioneers conducting the service. Then an honor guard of fliers placed Ben's flag-draped coffin on an artillery caisson. Crowds lined the streets and stood in silence as the caisson trans-ported Ben's body to the railroad station.

While the Eielsons and the Borlands said their goodbyes, Ben's body was placed aboard the private Pullman, "Fort Yukon," which Amundsen had used to return east after his polar flight. Accompa-nying Ben's body back to Hatton were Ole and Adeline Eielson; the North Dakota Honor Guard; Pat Reid; the two Canadian mechanics,

William Hughes and Sam McCauley; and Olaf Swenson. The Russian pilot, Slepnev, and his mechanic, Fahrig, rode the funeral train for 30 miles to Everett, where they departed to return to Moscow. "Commander Slepnev almost wept because he had to go back," Pat Reid said. "He knew no English, but he was a fine gentleman and well liked by everyone in the search party."

Ole had received a telegram in Seattle from Sir Hubert Wilkins saying that he and Orval Porter would fly to Hatton. Crosson and other Alaskan Airways pilots were unable to attend the funeral service because they were committed to returning the aviation gas borrowed from the Russians.

When the funeral train crossed the border into North Dakota, skies were overcast and gloomy, but Williston, the first stop in the state, was teeming with activity by 6:00 A.M., nearly an hour before the train arrived. The color guard from Watford City had come to Williston the night before, and representatives of many Legion posts in the area were on hand. As the train drew to a halt, the residents were allowed aboard. The casket, heaped high with floral tributes, lay in plain view at the rear of the private coach. Several hundred people walked through the coach before the train departed.

It was a silent tribute that Williston paid to the state's distinguished son. There were no bands, no drum corps, only color guards of uniformed men standing at stiff attention on either side of the platform.

As the train moved away, post and national colors were dipped in farewell salute. A monoplane piloted by Ed Canfield, of Williston, zoomed in salute, almost touching the top of the car with its wheels.

Crowds at each tiny community met the train, and a huge crowd was on hand at Minot. There, a Lockheed Vega, piloted by Cecil Shupe, circled over the train in salute. At the station platform, the Minot band and drum corps performed. An official delegation boarded the train to greet Ole.

Twelve miles west of Devils Lake, an airplane met the train and followed it into the city. That community and its adjacent territory paid homage to Ben as the train stopped there for half an hour. The band played as the train slowly pulled out of the station. A colonel's salute was given by the Howitzer Company, of the 164th Infantry, and taps were sounded.

Interest in the funeral train had not been confined to North Dakota. All along the way from Seattle, scores of people had waited at stations and at crossroads to catch a glimpse of the funeral train and the coffin. But there was something distinctly personal about North Dakota's tribute. Hardened Norsemen, roughly clad farm workers, school children, derby-hatted salesmen, members of the military and various lodges all were there, and on their faces was written their high esteem for the dead pioneer flier.

Frequent stops were made from Devils Lake on. When the train reached Larimore, the funeral car and the passenger coach were attached to another local train. The freshly painted locomotive had a large funeral wreath placed on its front, and Ben's picture was pasted over the headlight.

Small bouquets, huge wreaths, and great masses of roses were heaped about the casket in the funeral car. The bouquets were mostly from North Dakota towns, but Alaska towns were also represented in the florals. The casket was draped with two flags—one, the home-made banner fashioned by the Siberian women at North Cape, and the other, the American flag.

When interviewed by reporters at one stop, Pat Reid said that he'd never realized the vast interest people had taken in Ben's work. He reported that the crowds in Seattle had been so huge that streets were blocked in many directions.

Adeline and Ole were relieved when the train arrived at Hatton. Hotel facilities were inadequate to care for outsiders who came for the funeral, so townsfolk opened their homes. Others were cared for in the Legion Hall, which was equipped as a temporary barracks.

A reporter aboard the funeral train predicted that the funeral ceremony in Hatton would be very impressive, with speeches by great men, leaders in civic and state affairs, and the military. "But," he added, "no more sincere tribute could be paid than that already made by the hundreds of people and school children gathered in the villages and at the crossroads, bareheaded in the cold air, waiting for just a glimpse of the funeral car."

The battleship-gray casket was taken from the railroad coach at 6:00 P.M. on March 25 and placed on the depot platform where, as a youngster, Ben had watched the trains arrive and depart.

Pat Reid had hardly stepped from the funeral coach before he was surrounded by reporters. He told them a little about the search and then told of the impressive memorial services that were held at Teller, Nome, Ruby, Fairbanks, Anchorage, Seward, and Seattle. "All along the route of the funeral train, it was the same," Reid said. "But no tribute can match this in Hatton. The sight of hundreds of Ben's friends, standing silently, with tears in their eyes, their heads bared to the biting wind, as the funeral train pulled slowly in and stopped by the black-draped platform . . ." Reid paused and then added slowly, "This is something I'll never forget." Then he fell silent.

Out of the silence, a church bell tolled. A company of National Guard came to attention. Legionnaire pallbearers lifted the casket to a waiting hearse, which proceeded through the streets lined with flags at half-mast. The throng at the station slowly started to leave, but many stayed to greet members of the Eielson family.

A letter from Minnesota Governor Theodore Christianson, presented to Ole by Lt. Col. Joseph E. Nelson, Assistant Adjutant General of Minnesota, who would lead the five planes representing Minnesota at the funeral, read: "Minnesota is honored to join her sister state in paying public tribute to the gallant memory of your son, the late Colonel Carl Ben Eielson."

Once at home, Ole recounted the events of his trip. He commented about the throngs of people at every stop. "No matter what the hour," he added, "the station platforms were lined with representatives of organizations who came aboard the train to lay wreaths at the casket. A big crowd was at Havre, Montana, at 10 o'clock last night, and at 2 o'clock this morning, when the train halted briefly at Glasgow, Montana, a small, shivering delegation handed up a wreath to members of the train crew, who placed it on the bier."

Oliver added that banks, city and county offices, and schools would be closed for the afternoon and all business suspended for a brief memorial. More than 200 other Legion organizations throughout the state would simultaneously hold services when the Hatton post held its. The University of North Dakota announced that it would hold special memorial services.

Local planes were scheduled to run an hourly taxi service between Grand Forks and Hatton starting at 8:00 A.M. When Elma learned that, she said excitedly, "Oh, Ben would love to see that. Wouldn't he be pleased if he knew about it? He always said someday there would be direct flights between all major towns in North Dakota."

The day of Ben's funeral came, cold and bleak, with a north wind blowing snow flurries over the throngs of people. But the forbidding atmosphere failed to make any noticeable impression on the crowd, which began thronging in Hatton at daylight and continued until after the ceremony ended in the afternoon.

Other towns had activity connected with the funeral, too. In Fargo, led by the American Legion drum and bugle corps, a procession moved up Broadway to the Great Northern station at 9:45 A.M., its participants bound for Hatton.

As services were held in the little St. John's Lutheran Church, where Ben had worshipped when he was a boy, nearly 4,000 persons who were unable to gain admittance to the church packed the churchyard. Loudspeakers carried the messages by Rev. Olaf Jenson, of St. John's; Rev. David Stove, of Fargo, president of the North Dakota District of the Norwegian Lutheran Church of America; Rev. H. E. Baalson, of Sunborg, Minnesota, Ben's uncle; and friends.

Governor George Shafer told of Ben's fine work. "Years alone," he said, "can bring us to a full realization of the loss we have suffered." He added that Ben would be remembered through eternity as the man whose daring and genius opened the way to the successful establishment of aerial transportation across both the top and the bottom of the world. He continued:

> His fame will endure the ages. . . . Every generation in the history of our country has produced its heroes, not many in number but high in quality. . . . To this small group of American heroes belongs Carl Ben Eielson. By every test of character and achievement his name is entitled to be enrolled among America's immortal and heroic dead. . . . Where adventure beckoned, he went.

Following the service, more than 1,000 people walked the two miles to the cemetery to witness the graveside service. Thousands more made the journey by car, and the remainder of the throng heard the service over the churchyard speakers. As the procession to the cemetery was about to begin, a squadron of five planes from St. Paul slowly circled the city. They traveled in formation, engines throttled back to reduce the noise.

At the cemetery, after a prayer by Rev. Olaf Jenson, Rev. A. C. Hill, state chaplain of the American Legion, took charge of the rites. A firing squad composed of men who had known Ben throughout his life stepped to the edge of the grave, raised their rifles, and fired three volleys. As the squad moved away from the grave, Rev. Hill passed to Ole the flag that had draped the casket on its long journey from the Far North. For one of the few times since he had been exposed to public gaze, Ole displayed emotion. With tears in his eyes, he tenderly held the country's colors. As taps faded away in an echo, the casket was lowered into the grave, and Colonel Carl Ben Eielson, who flew to glory in the far regions of the earth, rested at last in the graveyard at Hatton.

Ben was not forgotten in Washington, for on the day of his funeral, the Hon. Olger B. Burtness and the Hon. Dan A. Sutherland made speeches asking that Congress award Ben the Congressional Medal of Honor. Burtness said in part: "I deem it entirely appropriate that the House cease labors for a few minutes this afternoon to do honor to a fine, upstanding American, who but a few short months ago gave up his life while engaged in an errand of mercy on behalf of his fellow men and whose name is known throughout the civilized world." Burtness told of Ben's contributions. About the 1928 flight to Spitzbergen, Burtness said: "This is the flight which another world famous and intrepid aviator, Roald Amundsen, declared to be the greatest in history. It is the only flight so far made from America to Europe across the Arctic."

After Congressman Burtness announced that he had introduced a bill on April 15, 1929, to award Ben the Congressional Medal of Honor, he yielded to Dan Sutherland, who closed his appeal as follows:

> That bill has been in the committee for two sessions of Congress. It would be a splendid thing if this tribute could be paid posthumously at this time, in order that his father, his friends in his home, as well as the people of Alaska may know that Congress felt so kindly toward Ben Eielson as to honor him in this way after his death.

The medal was never awarded, however, because Ben's actions were not connected with military activity.

The Sioux Indians also honored Ben. Two Shields Hall, in historic Fort Yates, North Dakota, was the scene of old ceremonial rites on March 26, 1939, for Colonel Carl Ben Eielson. "Chase Flying" was the name selected to honor Ben, the hero of the Arctic and the Antarctic. The aged warrior, Two Shields, said, "Kinyan Wakuwa, the Sioux, did not die in war, but passed to the Happy Hunting Grounds after he had worked for the advancement of his people. He was as valuable a man in peace as in war. Thus lived and died the white flier. He, too, survived the dangers of war and went to his death fearlessly serving the cause of his people."

Epilogue

Joe Crosson did more than any other pilot to take over Ben's work in Alaska. Pan American eventually merged Alaskan Airways, Inc., with other local flying firms into a subsidiary called Pacific Alaska Airways (PAA). In the years that followed, PAA spent millions of dollars and gave Alaska its first fleet of radio-equipped multi-engined transports and a flight communication system. It also brought a new look to bush-pilot attire, for PAA pilots wore trim Pan American uniforms.

Crosson was made chief pilot but was soon promoted to a managerial position. By 1937, he headed PAA but did not enjoy his new non-flying role, although he was good at it. With the help of other bush pilots, Crosson selected the best fields and station sites for Pan American's northern routes.

Service between Alaska and the Lower 48 was launched in 1929 on a charter basis. In the 1930s, PAA, initially with clippers, then with land planes, inaugurated the first regularly scheduled airline service.

Crosson found that PAA was something of a stepchild for Pan American. He had many policy conflicts with the New York managers, and in 1944 he left PAA and moved to Seattle, where he managed an aircraft and parts supply business at Boeing Field and maintained contact with Alaskan aviation.

Harold Gillam earned a reputation as one of the ablest pilots in the North. His contempt for fog, snow, rain, and wind became legend. While other pilots were grounded by weather, Gillam kept flying. He pioneered air service to the copper mining region, near Cordova on the southern coast of Alaska. Within six months in 1931, he had six wrecks and went broke. He returned to Fairbanks and secured financing for three planes, which were used on the run from Fairbanks to Cordova.

In 1938 Gillam carried mail on the Kuskokwim routes mapped out by Ben in 1924-25. His star route contract called for stops at 20 river towns on the 525-mile route between Fairbanks and Bethel, in the southwest. Although his contract didn't require it, Gillam was determined to haul the mail on schedule. No matter what the weather, people in the villages could set their clocks by his arrival. He sometimes made an entire round trip while other pilots remained stormbound.

The Civil Aeronautics Authority (CAA) began its Alaska construction program in 1939, but it wasn't until 1942 that Gillam completed his training and secured an official instrument rating. However, instruments did not save him from a fatal crash in southeastern Alaska in 1943.

Ben's dream of airmail service between Juneau, the capital, and Fairbanks came true in 1938. Fred Milligan, manager of the PAA airport in Fairbanks and a former dog-team mail carrier, told a gathering at Juneau on the evening of May 2 that about four hours would be required to transport the mail from Juneau to Fairbanks. He pointed out that in the 1890s the first mail carried from Juneau to Circle had required 60 days.

On May 3, a PAA Lockheed Electra took off from Juneau shortly before 1:00 P.M. Piloted by S. E. Robbins and Walt Hall, it carried 306 pounds of "First Flight" mail. It touched down after four hours five minutes of flying time from Juneau.

Following Ben's death, Frank Dorbandt continued to make a name for himself as the "bad boy" in Alaska aviation. The burly extrovert flew out of Anchorage. Although almost everyone in Alaska recognized his flying ability, he never had many close friends.

One of Dorbandt's best-known flights came in 1930, when he accepted a challenge turned down by several other bush pilots to fly a Fairchild monoplane taking Father Hubbard, head of the Geology Department at Santa Clara University, inside the crater of the Aniakchak Volcano. Herb Larson went along as mechanic. The venture was a success, but the party reached a nearby cannery with empty fuel tanks. Dorbandt landed in the bay in front of the cannery, and his passengers paddled the last 100 feet to shore.

Dorbandt flew the tri-motored plane with the same abandon he'd used with smaller planes. Possibly because of his constant need for attention, he often performed acrobatic maneuvers just before landing at his destination, as he'd done in Nome in 1929. He lost his license for 30 days after one such incident.

The end came for Dorbandt after he injured his hand trying to start his plane at a village on the Yukon. He slipped on the ice while pulling the propeller through, and the whirling blade hit his hand, nearly severing it at the wrist. He waited three days for another plane, but none arrived. Eventually, he headed for Fairbanks in his own plane, carrying one passenger. At Fairbanks he was treated at St. Joseph's Hospital, where he remained for several days. He gave the sisters and the nurses such a bad time with his ribald humor and crude jokes that they were glad when he was discharged. He died shortly after of pneumonia.

The account of Dorbandt's death in the *News-Miner* was marked by pointed tact and accuracy. At the end of the news item, which usually would have contained a brief eulogy of the deceased, was this simple statement: "After arriving in Alaska, Frank Dorbandt carved a unique career for himself."

Ole Eielson was not long in following his son. He died in December 1931 of pneumonia. Messages of condolence, including one from Sir Hubert Wilkins, came from Moscow, from Alaska, and from throughout the United States. Wilkins had visited Hatton after Ben's funeral, accompanied by balloonist Arthur Schlosser. At that time Wilkins told the Eielsons that he would present the *Alaskan*, the plane Ben had used to deliver supplies to Barrow, either to the state of North Dakota or to the Eielson Memorial Committee. [That plane was given to the North Dakota State Historical Society but was later returned to Hatton.] He also planned to recover the Lockheed Vega in which he and Ben had flown to Spitzbergen. It had been sold to the government of Argentina.

Wilkins made four additional expeditions to the Antarctic with Lincoln Ellsworth, during which they mapped more of that continent. Sir Hubert and Mrs. Wilkins crossed the Atlantic in the dirigible *Hindenberg* on its maiden voyage in May 1936.

In 1937 the Russian pilot Sigismund Levanevsky disappeared on an attempted flight from Moscow across the North Pole to the United States. As if in payment for Russian help during the 1929–30 Eielson search, Joe Crosson, Harold Gillam, and other Alaskans joined the search for Levanevsky. Gillam did much of the crucial freighting of gasoline and supplies between Fairbanks and Barrow.

Wilkins joined the search for Levanevsky, sometimes called the Soviet Lindbergh. Along with S. H. Chessman and Herbert Hollick-Kenyon, Wilkins flew over the pack ice 1,000 miles a day for a month. During the search they covered about 170,000 square miles of the Arctic Ocean, much of which had never before been seen in winter. They navigated by moonlight, something new in the world of aeronautics.

Later, Wilkins said that that was his last great adventure in the Arctic, for he realized how many of his hopes and dreams of early years had been fulfilled. He'd flown thousands of miles, not in a rickety crate, but in a sturdy, powerful plane, in perfect safety. With shortwave radio, he was never out of touch with the rest of the world. Pilots no longer flew by guess, because meteorological resources of several governments were at their disposal, enabling them to avoid needless risks.

In 1941 Wilkins became an advisor for the Military Planning Division and served as a liaison officer and consultant on Arctic survival. He died in 1958 at age 70. On March 17, 1959, Navy Commander James

Calvert, of the nuclear submarine *Skate*, took Wilkins' ashes to the North Pole, surfaced, and scattered them there.

Wilkins, General Billy Mitchell, and General H. H. "Hap" Arnold all warned that Alaska could be invaded in a future war. The developments in the North Pacific were no surprise to them or to Alaskans when World War II commenced. As early as 1925 Ben had made the rounds, telling of the strategic importance of Alaska and asking that planes be stationed there.

In 1941 the CAA received funds for the construction of military airports in Alaska. Men worked at a feverish pace, selecting the sites and collecting engineering data so construction could begin in the summer. The first project was Ladd Field, the air corps' cold-weather experiment station, near Fairbanks. The U.S. Army received valuable assistance from the experiences of Alaskan bush pilots, especially Noel Wien and Bob Reeves.

After 1941, Ladd Field grew into a defense bulwark north of the rugged Alaska Range. With the rapid growth of Ladd and its importance in ferrying lend-lease aircraft to Russia, expansion was urgent. Construction soon began on an auxiliary field at a point 26 miles south of Ladd, which first became known as Mile 26 Post.

At a chamber of commerce meeting in Fairbanks, when a name for the satellite field was being considered, businessman Paul Greimann said, "I propose that Mile 26 be named Eielson Air Force Base.'" Though it had been 18 years since Ben had crashed in Siberia in 1929, everyone remembered and agreed. At that time Greimann recalled: "I arrived in Fairbanks in September of 1923. The day after I arrived, I was startled to hear an airplane. . . . Airplanes were uncommon in that day, even in Chicago. . . . Naming Mile 26 Eielson Air Force Base will assure that the name of Alaska's first citizen of the air will live forever."

On July 20, 1956, the anniversary of Ben's birth, a monument depicting his life, his contributions to aviation, and scenes of Alaska was dedicated at the base. Ben's siblings were brought to Alaska by the U.S. Air Force to partake in the ceremony.

In 1938 the Ben Eielson Memorial Arch, commanding the main entrance of St. John's Cemetery, one mile north of Hatton, was dedicated. It came about through the efforts of the Eielson Memorial Committee, formed shortly after Ben's death. "Carl Ben Eielson" is carved across the upper part of the arch. At the left on the bronze plaque is engraved a likeness of the famous aviator-explorer; at the right, an inscription containing a condensed story of his life.

In Hatton, the ornate frame house in which Ole and Olava Eielson raised their nine children is preserved as a museum. It contains a library, trophies, souvenirs, and photographs—a tribute to Ben. Several schools in North Dakota are named after Carl Ben Eielson.

The University of Alaska, near Fairbanks, has an Eielson Memorial Building and an Eielson display at its museum. Ironically, off campus, stored in a shed under lock and key, is Ben's Jenny, shorn of its wings, its trail-blazing days over.

Editors' comment: Soviet aviation historians salvaged the remnants of the plane from the 1929 crash site in the late 1980s. After negotiating with members of the Interior and Arctic Alaska Aeronautical Foundation and with the cooperation of then Governor Steve Cowper, the Soviets flew the remnants in a cargo aircraft to Fairbanks. The plane arrived in Fairbanks on March 5, 1991. It was stored in Richard Wien's hangar at the Fairbanks International Airport until it was transferred to its final destination at the Alaskaland Pioneer Aviation Museum.

Bibliography

Books

Adams, Samuel H. *Incredible Era: The Life and Times of Warren G. Harding*. Boston: Houghton Mifflin Co., 1939.

Andrew, C. L. *The Story of Alaska*. Caldwell, Ida.: Caxton Printers, 1938.

Brower, Charles D. *Fifty Years Below Zero*. New York: Dodd, Mead & Co., 1942.

Chandler, Edna Walker, and Florence Barrett Willoughby. *Pioneer of Alaska Skies*. Boston: Ginn & Co., 1959.

Colby, M. *A Guide to Alaska*. New York: The Macmillan Co., 1939.

Crichton, Clark. *Frozen In*. New York: G. P. Putnam's Sons, 1930.

Davis, M. L. *Uncle Sam's Attic*. Boston: W. A. Wilde Co., 1930.

———. *We Are Alaskans*. Boston: W. A. Wilde Co., 1931.

Driscoll, J. *War Discovers Alaska*. New York: J. B. Lippincott Co., 1943.

Franck, H. A. *The Lure of Alaska*. New York: Fredrick A. Stokes Co., 1939.

Gauvereau, E. H., and L. Cohen. *Billy Mitchell: Founder of Our Air Force and Prophet Without Honor*. New York: E. P. Dutton & Co., 1942.

Greeley, A. W. *Handbook of Alaska*. New York: Charles Scribner's Sons, 1909.

Gruening, E. *The State of Alaska*. New York: Random House, 1954.

Gurney, Gene. *A Chronology of World Aviation*. New York: F. Watts, 1965.

Herron, E. A. *Wings over Alaska*. New York: Washington Square Press, 1967.

Hilscher, H. H. *Alaska Now*. New York: Little, Brown & Co., 1950.

Hurley, A. F. *Billy Mitchell: Crusader for Air Power*. New York: F. Watts, 1964.

Marshall, R. *Arctic Village*. New York: The Literary Guild, 1933.

Means, G. B. *The Strange Death of President Harding*. New York: Guild Publishing Corp., 1930.

Moore, S. T. *U.S. Air Power*. New York: Greenberg Co., 1958.

Morison, S. E. *The Oxford History of the United States*. London: Oxford University Press, 1927.

Potter, J. *Alaska Under Arms*. New York: The Macmillan Co., 1942.

———. *Flying Frontiersmen*. New York: The Macmillan Co., 1956.

———. *The Flying North*. New York: The Macmillan Co., 1947.

Rolfsrud, E. N. *Brother to the Eagle*. Alexandria, Minn.: Lantern Books, 1952.

Russell, F. *The Shadow of Blooming Grove: Warren G. Harding and His Times*. New York: McGraw-Hill, 1968.

Seidenfaden, Gunnar. *Modern Arctic Exploration*. London: J. Cape Co., 1939.

Sinclair, A. *The Available Man*. New York: The Macmillan Co., 1965.

Smith, F. C. *The World of the Arctic*. Philadelphia: J. B. Lippincott Co., 1960.

Stefansson, V. *Great Adventures and Explorations*. New York: Dial Press, 1947.

———. *Unsolved Mysteries of the Arctic*. New York: The Macmillan Co., 1939.

Thomas, Lowell. *Sir Hubert Wilkins*. New York: McGraw-Hill, 1961.

Tompkins, S. R. *Alaska: Promyshlennik and Sourdough*. Norman: University of Oklahoma Press, 1945.

Ungermann, K. A. *The Race to Nome*. New York: Harper & Row, 1963.

Wickersham, J. *Old Yukon: Tales—Trails—Trials*. Washington, D.C.: Washington Law Book Co., 1938.

Wilkins, George H. *Flying the Arctic*. New York: G. P. Putnam's Sons, 1928.

Willoughby, Florence Barrett. *Alaskans All*. Freeport, N.Y.: Books for Libraries Press, 1961.

Newspapers, Magazines, and Miscellaneous Material

Alaska Sportsman, now *Alaska Magazine*, Edmons, Wash.:

Barr, F. "Story of Frank Dorbandt."

Carpenter, F. "I Followed the Lure of Gold."

De Armond, B. "April in Alaska's History, Round-the-World-Flight," April 1965.

———. "July in Alaska's History, Aviation Meeting in Fairbanks," July 1965.

Jones, R. F. "Blazing Alaska's Early Air Trails," February 1961.

Pearson, G. "The Seventy Mile Kid," June 1950.

Seppala, L., and R. Thompson. "When Nome Needed Serum," January 1962.

Thompson, R. "Sled Dog Trails," March 1965.

Vincent, L. S. "King of the Arctic," October 1949.

Watchel, P. "The Flying Cowboy," December 1965.

Alaska Weekly:

"Ben Eielson," October 10, 1924.

"Ben Eielson," March 21, 1930.

"All Alaska Review—Aviation," *Cordova Times,* 1928.

Anchorage Centennial Aviation Committee. "100 Alaska Bush Pilots," 1967.

Anchorage Daily Times:

Clippings from Eielson Collection, 1924–1930.

"Eielson Nicknamed 'Moose Ptarmigan' by Indians in Interior," October 10, 1924.

Baalson, H. "Carl Benjamin Eielson," *Lutheran Church Herald,* Christmas Issue, 1930.

Burtness, O., U.S. Congressman from North Dakota. "Ben Eielson," Speech, *Congressional Record,* 1930.

"Carl Ben Eielson," *Sioux County Pioneer Arrow,* Fort Yates, N.D., July 28, 1930.

Deckard, H. S. "Plane Operation in Alaskan Area," *Airways Magazine,* 1930.

Eielson, Adeline. Clippings on Eielson in scrapbook, 1928–1930.

Eielson, Arthur. "Arctic Flyer Has Western Kin," *Western Electric News,* July 1930.

Eielson, Ben. Aviation clippings collected by Ben's clipping service, 1923–1929.

———. Personal correspondence and contacts, 1924–1929.

Eielson, Elma. Taped personal interviews by Vi Bjerke, 1968–1972.

Eielson, Oliver. Personal letters from Ben, 1924–1929.

Eielson Friendly Times, Eielson Air Force Base:

Eielson Memorial Edition, July 16, 1957.

Fairbanks Daily News-Miner. Clippings, Eielson collection—Ben, Adeline, and Oliver, 1923–1929.

Fargo Forum:

Yokum, E. "Life Story of Ben Eielson," 1930.

————. "North Dakota's Hero Son," January 12, 1930.

————. "Ole Eielson Might Hunt Son," 1930.

————. "Thousands Attend Eielson Rites," March 27, 1930.

Grand Forks Herald:

"Carl Ben Eielson," March 27, 1930.

"Eielson Cortege," March 27, 1930.

Harris, Jess, State Senator, Alaska. Excerpts from laws of Alaska, 1929.

Hatton Free Press:

Eielson Memorial Dedication Edition, 1938.

"Millions Mourn Eielson's Death," March 27, 1930.

Henderson, L. D. *Alaska*, 1929.

"In Memory of Our Friend, Carl Ben Eielson," November 11, 1955.

Jemtrud, Oscar. Scrapbook of clippings on Eielson search, purchased by Vi Bjerke, 1929–1930.

Kalinen, ———. Russian search log obtained from Oliver Eielson, 1929–1930.

McLain, C., Nome, Alaska. Letters on early-day Nome and Teller and personal interviews, 1926–1930.

Nome Nugget. Clippings on Eielson search, 1929–1930.

Pollock, H., U.S. Congressman from Alaska. Material from Library of Congress, 1928–1930.

Seward Daily Gateway. Jessen, clippings on Eielson, 1924–1930.

Sheehy, Helen. "Story of Ben," *Brown and Bigelow Intercom* Publication, July 1930.

Stanton, P. *Ben Eielson*, Seattle (no date).

Stevens, T., U.S. Senator from Alaska. Copies of Ben Eielson's reports to the Post Office Department on flights to McGrath, 1924.

Thompson, W. F. Articles on aviation and Ben Eielson, *Fairbanks Daily News-Miner*, 1923–1925.

"Wilkins and Eielson," *Chautauqua Daily*, July 18, 1928.
Wilkins-Eielson Expedition Reports, *Detroit News*, 1926–1928.

Note: Space prohibits listing all articles, letters, and personal interviews with Alaskans.

Highlights in the Life of

Carl Ben Eielson

407

ABOUT THE AUTHOR

DOROTHY GUZZI PAGE, *1921-1989, was born in Minneapolis and after high school moved to Arizona, where she worked as a medical secretary and then operated a trading post and cafe. In 1959 she married Vondolee Page, and the following year the couple took a vacation to Alaska, where they became permanent residents.*

Vondolee Page was named superintendent of schools, first at Dillingham and in 1962 at Wasilla. In 1965 Dorothy Page became chairperson of Wasilla's Alaska Centennial Committee. Through that involvement she "initiated the idea of reopening the historic Iditarod Trail" for a sled-dog race, which has become world renown. She is referred to as the "Mother of the Iditarod."

In 1966 she began writing a weekly column in the local newspaper and extended that to writing feature articles and articles of historical interest for several papers and magazines. Starting in 1973 she commenced writing Iditarod Trail Annuals, for which she won state and national awards. At the same time she was active in the local history preservation group, the Republican party, the library, the city council, and other civic functions.

Much of the last eight years of her life was spent in producing this biography of Carl Ben Eielson. May this posthumous publication of the book to which she and Vi Bjerke, who started research on Ben in 1965, serve as a fitting tribute to her memory.

ABOUT THE EDITORS

DR. HIRAM M. DRACHE *was a professor of history at Concordia College, Moorhead, Minnesota, 1952–53, 1955–91. In September 1991 he was named Historian-in-Residence at Concordia. In addition to his writing and teaching, he has spoken in 36 states, 6 provinces of Canada, Australia, and Germany. He has written:*

- **The Day of the Bonanza:** A History of Bonanza Farming in the Red River Valley of the North
- **The Challenge of the Prairie:** Life and Times of the Red River Pioneers
- **Beyond the Furrow:** Some Keys to Successful Farming in the 20th Century
- **Tomorrow's Harvest:** Thoughts and Opinions of Successful Farmers
- **Koochiching:** Pioneering Along the Rainy River Frontier
- **Plowshares to Printouts:** Farm Management as Viewed Through 75 Years of the Northwest Farm Managers Association
- **Taming the Wilderness:** A History of the Northern Border Country, 1910–1939

Drache has been a contributing author to seven books and has written over 50 articles on contemporary agriculture and/or agricultural history.

ADA M. DRACHE *has served as grammarian, word-processor operator, and editor for her husband.*